The British in the Adriatic, 1800-1825

The British in the Adriatic, 1800-1825

Malcolm Scott Hardy

ARCHAEOPRESS ARCHAEOLOGY

ARCHAEOPRESS PUBLISHING LTD
Summertown Pavilion
18-24 Middle Way
Summertown
Oxford OX2 7LG
www.archaeopress.com

ISBN 978-1-80327-725-7
ISBN 978-1-80327-726-4 (e-Pdf)

This book is available direct from Archaeopress or from our website www.archaeopress.com

Contents

Foreword...ix

Part 1: The British Navy, Rijeka and A.L. Adamić: War and Trade in the Adriatic 1800-25

The Arrival of John Leard in Rijeka, 1802...3

Nelson, convoys and naval supplies, 1803-04..6

The Oak Timber Project...11

The War of the Third Coalition...16

Trade War 1806-9..19

The War of 1809..30

Travels 1810-12..36

The Timber Contract of 1812...43

Adamić's Return to Rijeka, 1812...47

The Aborted Insurrection, February-April 1813...50

The British Attack on Rijeka, July 1813..52

Nugent liberates Rijeka, August 1813..58

Adamić's return to Rijeka, autumn 1813...62

The End of the War...65

Leard's return to Rijeka, July 1814...67

The Last Timber Contract 1818-20...70

Epilogue..73

Part 2: The British and Vis: War in the Adriatic 1805-15

Introduction: The British and the Adriatic...81

The defence of Lissa: A safe harbour..91

The defence of Lissa: Delays and surveys.. 106

The defence of Lissa: Occupation and fortification... 144

Life on Lissa.. 168

The British leave Lissa.. 184

Appendix 1: Sources... 196

    1 Primary Sources... 196

    2 Published Sources: Select Bibliography 197

Appendix 2: Names... 199

    Place-names.. 199

    Peoples 199

    Individuals 200

    Naval and military designations 201

    Maps and charts 202

    Glossary of place-names 203

Appendix 3: Biographical notes... 209

    British 209

    French... 212

    Austrian (and Croatian).. 213

Appendix 4: Ships and soldiers..215
    Warships...215
    Boats 218
    Gunboats 219
    Supplies 220
    Visibility at Sea 221
    Sources 221
    Soldiers 221
Appendix 5: Remains..226
    Vis (Lissa) 226
    Korčula 228

Part 3: A Diversionary Attack in the Adriatic 1812

The British, Montenegro and Russia 1812 231
Admiral Fremantle goes to Lissa 235
News of Chichagov...244
Admiral Grieg arrives in Sicily...248
Fremantle and Montenegro: Second Phase 252
After Chichagov..257

List of Figures

Part 1: The British Navy, Rijeka and A.L. Adamić: War and Trade in the Adriatic 1800-25

Figure 1A. Andrija Ljudevit Adamić (1766–1828) (unknown artist, Museum of Rijeka). 3

Figure 1B. John Leard, master mariner. 3

Figure 2A. The Admiralty in 1818, built 1722–6, and the screen added 1759–61 (by Joseph Constantine Stadler, London Metropolitan Archives). 4

Figure 2B. Board Room of the Admiralty (Thomas Rowlandson, Metropolitan Museum of New York). 4

Figure 3. Somerset House, begun in 1775, the seat of the Navy Board. 5

Figure 4A. Gilbert Eliot, Lord Minto (1751–1814) (by James Atkinson, National Portrait Gallery). 5

Figure 4B. The victualling yard at Deptford. 5

Figure 5. The PREVOYANT at Porto Re (Kraljevica), 1802. 6

Figure 6. The Adriatic. 7

Figure 7. Horatio Nelson by George Baxter, after Lemuel Francis Abbott. 8

Figure 8. View of the Siege of Valetta. Malta was besieged captured by the British in1800. Print after Major James Weir. 9

Figure 9. HMS ARROW, sunk in battle, 1805, detail of oil painting by Francis Sartorius. 11

Figure 10. The fortress town of Karlovac. 14

Figure 11. Deptford Dockyard, detail of oil painting by Joseph Farington (Royal Museums Greenwich). 15

Figure 12. Trieste, drawing by William Innes Pocock, 1813. 18

Figure 13. Admiral Cuthbert Collingwood (1748–1810). Book illustration based on an original portrait. 20

Figure 14. Types of vessel, drawing by William Innes Pocock. 21

Figure 15. Sir Robert Ardair (1763–1855), oil painting by Thomas Gainsborough (Baltimore Museum of Art). 28

Figure 16. The harbour of Mali Lošinj. 29

Figure 17. Sir William Hoste, c. 1833 by William Greatbach. 30

Figure 18A. Eugène de Beauharnais, c.1802–1804, oil painting by François Gérard. 31

Figure 18B. Auguste de Marmont (1774–1852), oil painting by Jean-Baptiste Paulin Guérin.. 31

Figure 19. Admiral William Hargood (1726–1839), oil painting by Frederick Richard Say. 33

Figure 20A. Benjamin Bathurst, British diplomat (1784–1809) (unknown artist). 34

Figure 20B. Archduke Charles of Austria (1771–1847) (by Jean-Baptiste Isabey, Louvre). 34

Figure 21. Croatia 1809–13. 37

Figure 22. General Henri Bertrand (1773–1844) (unknown artist). 38

Figure 23A. Laval Nugent (1777–1862) (unknown artist, Trsat Castle, Rijeka). 39

Figure 23B. William Bentinck (1774–1839), by C.H. Gifford. 39

Figure 25. Malta, the entrance to Valletta (Museum of the Order of St John). 42

Figure 24. The fortifications of Valletta, Malta, illustration from *L'Illustration*, 575 (XXIII), March 4, 1854. 42

Figure 26A & B. Somerset House; the Navy Board occupied the south wing. A. aquatint by Samuel Ireland, 1791. B. engraving for Dugdale's *England and Wales Delineated* (1845). 44

Figure 27. The courtyard of Somerset House, by Thomas Rowlandson and Auguste Charles Pugin.. 44

Figure 28A. Somerset House: stairs leading to the Navy Boardroom. 45

Figure 28B. West India Dock for sugar & colonial crops, by Thomas Rowlandson and Auguste Charles Pugin (Metropolitan Museum). 45

Figure 29. The Rhinebeck Panorama, showing London between 1806 and 1811 (Museum of London). 46

Figure 30. View of London from Greenwich, showing the Deptford Dock Yards, 1809 (Royal Museums, Greenwich). 46

Figure 31. Admiral Thomas Fremantle (1765–1819). 49

Figure 32. British brig off Pula, February 1813, drawing by William Innes Pocock (National Maritime Museum)... 51

Figure 33A. Karolina Belinić, popularly believed to have saved Rijeka by petitioning the British commander... 53

Figure 33B. Poster for the film Karolina Riječka, 1961. 53

Figure 34. Scene from the opera Karolina Riječka. 54

Figure 35. The British bombardment of Rijeka (the Adamić sugar refinery can be seen on the left).. 55

Figure 36. The British bombardment Rijeka with Učka mountain and the sugar refinery. The batteries at the mouth of the Riečina are unprotected and unmanned. 55

Figure 37. HMS BACCHANTE at Deptford 1811, commanded by Hoste in the bombardment of Rijeka (National Maritime Museum).. 56

Figure 38. A caricature of Napoleon, published Berlin 1813 and sent by Adamić to Fremantle. 59

Figure 39A. William Cathcart, by Henry Meyer, after John Hoppner (National Portrait Gallery). 60

Figure 39B. Klemens von Metternich, oil painting by Thomas Lawrence (Royal Collection).. 60

Figure 40. The Louisa Road into Rijeka.. 62

Figure 41. The Pool of London in the 1820s (the Customs House is on the right) (by Robert Havell). 72

Figure 42A. Andrija Ljudevit Adamić, identified here as 'Deputy from Fiume' (Rijeka)........... 73

Figure 42B. Laval Nugent, who was buried in his residence of Trsat Castle, Rijeka. 73

Figure 43A & B. John Leard and his wife. 74

Figure 44A & B. Paintings of Rijeka: A. from the sea and B. of the waterfront showing the Adamić Sugar Refinery. 74

Figure 45A & B. Adamić Sugar Refinery, by A.C. von Mayr. 75

Figure 46. The Sugar Refinery Palace, today the Town Museum. 76

Figure 47. Trsat Castle before Nugent's restoration.. 76

Figure 48. Trsat Castle in 1837 with Doric Temple. 77

Figure 49. Trsat Castle today. 77

Part 2: The British and Vis: War in the Adriatic 1805-15

Figure 1.Map of the Adriatic including the Ionian Islands... 82

Figure 2. Valletta, Malta, during the British siege of 1800, drawn by Major Weir. 83

Figure 3. Types of vessels in use in the northern Adriatic, watercolour by William Innes Pocock (National Maritime Museum). 87

Figure 4A. the trabaccolo, a small cargo vessel, suited to cabotage (drawing by Aldo Cherini) 88

Figure 4B. A model of a chebec, a swift merchant vessel, typical of the northern Adriatic. ... 88

Figure 5. The Adriatic in 1806 91

Figure 6. The Adriatic in 1809, showing French territorial gains.. 92

Figure 7. British frigate of 38 guns. 93

Figure 8. Istria and Kvarner (Umago lies between Pirano and Cittanova, Lussin is bottom right)... 94

Figure 9. Piccolo Lussin/Mali Lošinj, engraving by Jacob Emil Schindler.............................. 94

Figure 10. Auguste de Marmont (1774–1852), oil painting by Andrea Appiani. 95

Figure 11. Lesina/Hvar harbour, photographed in 1908... 97

Figure 12. Admiral Lord Collingwood. Succeeded Nelson as commander-in-chief of the British fleet in the Mediterranean. Oil painting by Henry Howard, after a painting by Giuseppe Politi (National Portrait Gallery).. 99

Figure 13. Captain William Hoste. Most famous of the British naval officers serving in the Adriatic but never an Admiral. Drawing by William Greatbach (National Maritime Museum)... 102

Figure 14A. Eugene de Beauharnais, portrait by Jean Duplessi-Bertaux. 103

Figure 14B. Bernard Dubourdieu (1773–1881), led the French raid on Lissa in 1810 and was killed at the Battle of Lissa, 1811... 103

Figure 15A & B. Battle Lissa 1811. A. Map, created by Ruhrfisch; B. watercolour by Nicholas Pocock (Tate). 105

Figure 16A. Admiral Sir Charles Rowley (1770–1845), portrait by George Sanders. 107

Figure 16B. Admiral Edward Pellew (1757–1833), portrait by Samuel Drummond (Royal Albert Memorial Museum and Art Gallery)... 107

Figure 17A. Sir Murray Maxwell (1775–1831), etching by Richard Dighton (National Portrait Gallery)... 110

Figure 17B. Captain James Alexander Gordon (1782–1869), engraving by an unknown artist. ... 110

Figure 18. Admiral Sir Charles Cotton (1753–1812), by Henry Meyer (National Portrait Gallery)... 111

Figure 19. Lord William Bentinck. Commander-in-chief of the British army forces in the Mediterranean and British Minister to the Court of Sicily. Portrait by Thomas Lawrence... 113

Figure 20. Hudson Lowe (1769–1844), British commander on the island of Santa Maura, portrait by R.C. Seaton.. 114

Figure 21. Admiral Thomas Fremantle, commander of the British naval squadron in the Adriatic, 1812–13. 118

Figure 22. Captain Bennett's sketch map of the port of St. George, October 1811 (University of Nottingham Portland (Welbeck) Collection). 121

Figure 23. Captain Smith's map of Lissa, October 1811. He may not have surveyed the whole island in person as Comissa (Komiža) is misplaced. (Nottingham University Portland (Welbeck) Collection). 132

Figure 24. A traversing cannon in the battery on Hoste Island. From Austrian drawings in 1854. Although from 40 years after the British had built the batteries, little has changed... 134

Figure 25. Comisa (Komiža) in a nineteenth century view with the Venetian Tower. The important spring that served as a watering place for the British warships is inside the harbour to the left. (Fisković Collection). 134

Figure 26A & B. Captain Smith's map of Port St. George, October 1811 with the hills numbered and named according to English conventions, e.g. Hornby Hill, Cove Hill etc. The note at the bottom (B.) is initialed F.M. (Frederick Maitland). (University of Nottingham Portland (Welbeck) Collection). 137

Figure 27B. HMS WEAZLE, 18 gun brig. Watercolour by Nicholas Cammillieri (National Maritime Museum)... 142

Figure 27A. Captain John Talbot (1769–1851), commanded the British ships in the action against the RIVOLI. Portrait by Catterson Smith (National Maritime Museum). . 142

Figure 28. The battle between the new French ship-of-the-line RIVOLI and HMS VICTORIOUS with their escorts near Pola. Oil painting by Thomas Luny (National Maritime Museum). 143

Figure 29. HMS WEAZLE in action against French gunboats in Bassoglina Bay (Zaljev Marina west of Trogir) in April 1812. (National Maritime Museum). 143

Figure 30. Chart of Port St. George with soundings made by the sailing master of HMS EAGLE in March 1812 and copied into his sketchbook by William Innes Pocock. (National Maritime Museum). 145

Figure 31A. Lt. Colonel George Duncan Robertson, appointed commander at Lissa in February 1812.. 146

Figure 31B. Captain of the 35th Regiment of Foot which provided the main body of soldiers sent to Lissa in April 1812. Caption reads 'from Colonel Luard's "Dress of the British Soldier"'. 146

Figure 32. Uniform of the De Rolls Regiment, a company of which served at Lissa. 147

Figure 33. Captain Henryson's sketch map of the entrance to Port St. George, April 1812, showing the sites he chose for the fortifications. (University of Nottingham Portland (Welbeck) Collection). 151

Figure 34. Admiral Thomas Fremantle, print from a portrait by Edmund Bristow................. 153

Figure 35. HMS BACCHANTE, the newly built 38 gun frigate in which Captain William Hoste returned to the Adriatic and Lissa in August 1812. (National Maritime Museum). 156

Figure 36. Curzola/Korčula showing the British tower to the left of the town. Detail from a Panorama of Dalmatia by Giuseppe Rieger (Fisković Collection). 161

Figure 37. Plan of Curzola/Korčula showing the fortifications of San Biaggio (Sveti Vlaho), including the British tower on the hill above the walled town. From the 1835 Austrian survey of fortifications (Kriegsarchiv, Vienna). 162

Figure 38A. The original design of Curzola Tower by Captain Taylor of the navy and Lieutenant Cole of the army, neither of whom were trained engineers. (Buckinghamshire Record Office). 163

Figure 38B. Korčula Tower today. 163

Figure 39A. Jean Andoche Junot, Governor of the Illyrian Provinces, May–July 1813............ 165

Figure 39B. Joseph Fouché, who succeeded Junot in July 1813, portrait by Claude-Marie Dubufe, after an original by René Théodore Berthon (Palace of Versailles). 165

Figure 40. Port St. George Harbour. Martello Towers are seen on the hills to the left and right of the harbour (Fisković Collection). 166

Figure 41. Port St George/Vis Harbour today showing the sites of the British fortifications...... 166

Figure 42. Plan and elevation of Fort George. Modern drawing based on originals. Changes were made in the Austrian period although projects that would have resulted in its complete replacement by a new and larger fortress were never realised........ 166

Figure 43A. Fort George from the approach to the harbour, 2012 (author's photo). 167

Figure 43B. Fort George entrance, 2013 (author's photo)... 167

Figure 44. Port St George with the Franciscan Church on the other side of which Fremantle established his dockyard. 169

Figure 45. The Franciscan church today. 170

Figure 46A. Admiral George Anson (1697–1762), who circumnavigated the globe and served as First Lord of the Admiralty during the Seven Years War. Midshipman Charles Anson was his grandson. Portrait in pastels by Francis Coates (Shugborough Hall). 170

Figure 46B. The Anson family seat of Shugborough Hall. 170

Figure 47. The tombstone of Midshipman Anson on Vis (author's photo). 171

Figure 48. View of Hoste Island looking towards Lessina (Hvar) and the mainland beyond. By William Innes Pocock (National Maritime Museum). 175

Figure 49. Port St George with the 74 gun ship-of-the-line HMS EAGLE, on which the artist, William Pocock served as Lieutenant. (National Maritime Museum)..................... 178

Figure 50. Royal Marines private, 1815, aquatint by J.C. Stadler. 181

Figure 51A. Graf Laval Nugent in 1837, watercolour by Moritz Michael Daffinger. 183

Figure 51B. Francis Archduke of Austria-Este (1779–1846) visited Lissa in September 1813. Portrait by Adeodato Malatesta (Palazzo Ducale, Modena)................................... 183

Figure 52. Grenzer Uniforms. By late 1813, Italian and Grenzer troops made up the majority of Napoleon's forces in Illyria.. 184

Figure 53A. Baron Franjo Tomassich (1761–1831), Governor of Dalmatia from 1814. 186

Figure 53B. Sir John Gore (1772–1836) (Unknown artist, National Maritime Museum)......... 186

Figure 54. Lord Aberdeen (1784–1860), British ambassador to the Emperor of Austria in 1814. Portrait by Thomas Lawrence. 188

Figure 55A. François-Xavier Donzelot (1762–1843), commander of the French forces in Corfu. Portrait by Charles Mullié. 190

Figure 55B. Lord Castlereagh (1769–1822). Portrait by Thomas Lawrence (National Portrait Gallery)... 190

Figure 56. Henry Bathurst (1762–1834). Engraving by Henry Meyer after Thomas Phillips (National Portrait Gallery). 193

Figure 57A & B. Fort George Gate and Inscription to George III 195.......................... 195

Figure 58. Plan of HMS MILFORD, designed by Jean-Louis Barrallier and built by Jacobs of Milford Haven, 74-gun 3rd rate ship-of-the-line (National Maritime Museum). ... 216

Figure 59. Frigate of 38 guns, built 1805 (National Maritime Museum)................................. 218

Figure 60. HMS REINDEER, 18-gun Cruiser-class brig, built 1804. 219

Figure 61. British Army Gunboat, 1800.. 220

Part 3: A Diversionary Attack in the Adriatic 1812

Figure 1. Peter Petrovich Njegos (1748–1830), Serbian Orthodox Prince-Bishop of Montenegro. 231

Figure 2. French power in the Adriatic before Napoleon's attack on Russia in 1812. 232

Figure 3A. Stratford Canning, 1st Viscount Stratford de Redcliffe (1786–1880), British Ambassador to Constantinople. Portrait, aged 29, from biography by Stanley Lane-Poole, 1888. 233

Figure 3B. General Mikhail Kutuzov (1745–1813), supreme commander of the Russian forces, 1812, portrait by R.M. Volkov, 1850. 233

Figure 4A. Tsar Alexander I (1771–1825), oil painting by Stepan Shchukin, 1809 (Regional Art Museum, Tver). 234

Figure 5. Admiral Pavel Vasilyevich Chichagov (1767–1849), portrait by James Saxon, 1824 (State Hermitage Museum copy from Saxon portrait). 234

Figure 4B. Prince Michael Andreas Barclay de Tolly (1761–1818), detail of portrait by George Dawe, 1829 (Military Gallery of the Winter Palace, Saint Petersburg). 234

Figure 6. Colonel George Duncan Robertson of Strown (d. 1842), commander of the garrison of Lissa (Vis) 1812 (artist unknown). 235

Figure 7A. General Lord William Bentinck (1774–1839), commander-in-chief of the British armies in the Mediterranean, lithograph based on a painting by Sir Thomas Lawrence. 236

Figure 7B. Admiral Thomas Fremantle (1765–1819), in command of the British navy in the eastern Mediterranean, artist unknown. 236

Figure 8. Admiral Edward Pellew, 1st Viscount Exmouth (1757–1833), commander of the British fleet in the Mediterranean, portrait by James Northcote, 1804 (National Portrait Gallery). 237

Figure 9A & B. Field Marshal Laval Nugent von Westmeath (1777–1862), commander of Austrian actions against the French in the Adriatic area. A: original lithograph1848; B: oil painting by Friedrich Ritter von Amerling (undated). 238

Figure 10. Bishop Maksimiljan Vrhovac of Zagreb (1752–1827), portrait by unknown artist. 239

Figure 11A & B. Admiral Aleksey Greig (1775–1845), admiral of Scottish extraction in the Russian navy. A: portrait by Georg von Bothmann, 1877 (Hermitage Museum); B: lithograph by unknown artist. 245

Figure 12A. Andrey Yakovlevich Italinsky, Russian ambassador to Constantinople, portrait by Orest Kiprensky. 246

Figure 12B. Sir Robert Liston (1742–1836), ambassador to Constantinople, oil painting by David Wilkie, 1811 (National Galleries of Scotland). 246

Figure 13. Sir Robert Wilson (1777–1849), engraving by Roberts from an original picture for C. H. Gifford's History of the Wars Occasioned by the French Revolution, 1827. 247

Figure 14. General Jean-Joseph Gauthier (1765–1815), général de brigade in the French Illyrian provinces (Jura Musées). 254

Figure 15. The battles of Napolean's Russian campaign 1812 and Russian occupied lands to the west of the Black Sea. 256

Figure 16A. Henry Bathurst, 3rd Earl Bathurst (1762–1834), engraving by Henry Meyer after Thomas Phillips' stipple engraving, 1810 (National Portrait Gallery). 259

Figure 16B. Christoph von Lieven (1774–1839), copy of original portrait by Sir Thomas Lawrence c. 1826 (Hermitage Museum). 259

Foreword

In the early 1970s when I first lived and worked in Zagreb I was intrigued by references in guide-books to British activity in the Adriatic during the Napoleonic wars and the existence of British fortifications on the island of Vis. However, given its strategic importance, it was not until the 1990s that foreigners were able to visit it.

In 1994 my friend Goran Nikšić, responsible for the conservation of historic monuments in Split, made enquiries concerning the possibility of British funding for the restoration of the forts on Vis. In the following year 1995 our friend Professor Toni Lešaja drew my attention to the British tower above the town of Korčula. After this I made my first visit to Vis.

On my return to London I began to search in British archives for documents related to British activity in the Adriatic in the larger context of Napoleon's schemes to invade and partition with Russia the Ottoman empire in the Balkans and to attack the British in India. By 2000 I had amassed a lot of material and written a number of chapters with little prospect of publication without giving my research a narrower focus on the British and Vis.

With the help of academic friends Igor Fisković and Joško Belamarić 'The British and Vis' was published in Croatian and English (but without English appendices and notes) by Književni Krug (the literary association) of Split in 2006.

In the meantime in 2003 Flora Turner, then cultural attache at the Croatian Embasy in London, put me in touch with Ervin Dubrović of the town museum in Rijeka who needed research undertaken on the British links of the merchant Adamic. This resulted in a lengthy illustrated chapter translated into Croatian within the book 'Adamovićevo doba' published in 2005. Later in the same year Archaeopress published this in English but without illustrations.

Archaeopress again came to the rescue in 2009 by publishing the full English edition of 'The British and Vis' with illustrations and appendices.

In 2011 my wife and I were invited to Vis to talk in an international symposium on aspects of the history and architecture of the island organised by architect Boško Budisavljević. In 2012 for the subsequent symposium I wrote the third part of the present edition exploring the links between the British on Vis and Napoleon's 1812 invasion of Russia. In 2013 Fort George on Vis was partially restored and reopened as a venue for wedding receptions etc. by a Swedish entrepreneur. I advised on the contents of a museum but this was not realised.

After recently being given the BBC's most recent version of 'War and Peace' I illustrated the third section and gave it to David Davison. To my surprise and delight he then proposed the present fully-illustrated omnibus edition.

My thanks go to all the friends who have encouraged and helped me over 30 years and particularly to my wife Vesna who translated my work into Croatian.

Malcolm Scott Hardy
London January 2024

Part 1:
The British Navy, Rijeka and A.L. Adamić:
War and Trade in the Adriatic 1800-25

The Arrival of John Leard in Rijeka, 1802

Research in British archives yields a wealth of detailed documentation on British activity in the Adriatic during the Napoleonic wars and their aftermath. Although some link documents are lost or difficult to trace, it is possible to re-establish long sequences of correspondence. As far as Rijeka is concerned, what emerges is the long (from about 1800-1825) but not always happy or fortunate relationship between the merchant, A. L. Adamić, John Leard, and the British Navy Board, within the context of the ebb and flow of the wars, and the commercial, diplomatic and military activity of the British in the Adriatic.

To maintain the naval supremacy that guaranteed its survival, Great Britain needed timber and other products, such as hemp, canvas and tar, to build new warships in its dockyards at home, or to keep them seaworthy and in good repair when in service. Such naval stores usually came from the Baltic, but changing circumstances (especially when Russia was strictly neutral or an ally of France) could endanger this supply. In the Mediterranean, far away from the Baltic, the main British arsenal or dockyard at Malta needed constantly to look for closer sources of essential supplies to repair the fleet in the Mediterranean, which was almost constantly at sea, whether blockading enemy ports or guarding against further French expansion against Sicily or the Ottoman empire.

The British navy was governed by a committee of Lord Commissioners of the Admiralty, but its everyday administration, including the building, repair and supplying of its warships, was the responsibility of the Navy Board, which came under the Admiralty. The Navy Board

Figure 1A. Andrija Ljudevit Adamić (1766–1828) (unknown artist, Museum of Rijeka).

Figure 1B. John Leard, master mariner.

maintained a network overseas of agents to negotiate the purchase or control the quality of its naval supplies. These were usually master mariners or shipwrights, with the necessary expertise.

John Leard was one such master mariner. Born about 1757 he received his warrant as master with the rank of junior lieutenant in the Royal Navy in 1780. In 1793-99 he was given command

VIEW OF THE ADMIRALTY.

Figure 2A. The Admiralty in 1818, built 1722–6, and the screen added 1759–61 (by Joseph Constantine Stadler, London Metropolitan Archives).

Figure 2B. Board Room of the Admiralty (Thomas Rowlandson, Metropolitan Museum of New York).

Figure 3. Somerset House, begun in 1775, the seat of the Navy Board.

of an experimental 'ambi navigator' vessel, KENT, which was possibly the first sailing ship to try to use steam power. He then commanded the navy storeship EMPRESS MARY, taking supplies to the Mediterranean and the West Indies. But in 1802, on the death of its agent in Rijeka, a Mr Ulny, Leard was sent to Rijeka to sort out the Navy Board's affairs. This was during the only short interval of peace from March 1802 to May 1803 in the long war from 1793-1814 between Britain and France. Austria had also been at peace with France from February 1801. Under these more promising circumstances, Leard must have liked the look of Rijeka, because in 1802 he bought a house there (without the knowledge or approval of the Navy Board, although it was so satisfied with Leard's handling of the late Mr Ulny's business that they decided to leave him there as their agent).

On his arrival in Rijeka, Leard must have immediately met Adamić, who at least from 1800 was supplying the Navy Board. The first appearance of Adamić in British archives is in a letter from the Foreign Office to the British ambassador in Vienna, Lord Minto, dated 5 December 1800. Adamić was described as a respectable merchant of Vienna who had offered to contract with the Victualling Board to send 6000 bags of biscuit from Rijeka, or other Austrian ports in the Adriatic, to Malta. Lord Minto was asked to secure the permission of the Austrian authorities.[1]

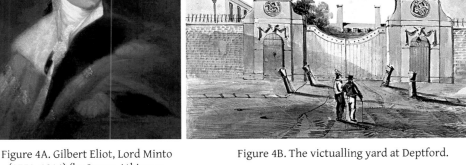

Figure 4A. Gilbert Eliot, Lord Minto (1751–1814) (by James Atkinson, National Portrait Gallery).

Figure 4B. The victualling yard at Deptford.

---

[1] National Archives (NA), FO 7/61

Figure 5. The PREVOYANT at Porto Re (Kraljevica), 1802.

In April 1802, Leard, describing himself as acting agent for the Navy Board, wrote from Rijeka to the Navy Board to say that only 340 of a large consignment of 466 large bales of hemp, to be transported to a British dockyard by order of the commander-in-chief of the British navy in the Mediterranean (Nelson), could be loaded on the navy store ship DILIGENT at Trieste. The remainder would be brought to Rijeka and loaded on ABUNDANCE. Two other transports, WESTMORELAND and SUCCESS would be loaded at Kraljevica with other unspecified supplies. It would take about £10,000 sterling to settle the balance of the account (a very large sum at that time).[2] But the Navy Board seems to have changed its mind about the need or desirability of taking all of the hemp, which Leard had procured on its behalf. A delayed letter dated 5 June reached Leard on 14 November 1802 to inform him that the PREVOYANT was being sent out via Malta to Kraljevica to load hemp; but another letter of 15 June instructed him to resell hemp that he had obtained. In his reply of 15 November 1802, Leard informed the Navy Board that for reselling the hemp, he would seek the assistance of Mr Adamić. It is possible that Leard had bought the hemp from Adamić in the first place.[3] This is the first reference to Adamić in Leard's letters from Rijeka.

Nelson, convoys and naval supplies, 1803-04

On 13 May 1803, war again broken out with France. In 1803 the French only held a stretch of the north-western coast of the Adriatic from the mouth of the Adige in the north to the border of the Papal States between Rimini and Pesaro in the south. From 1797, Bonaparte had allowed Austria to take possession of Venice and its possessions down the eastern seaboard of the Adriatic. British merchants, whether from Britain or Malta, were sending ships up the Adriatic to the Austrian ports of Venice, Trieste and Rijeka. When war broke out again in May 1803 between Britain and France, Admiral Nelson was sent out to take command of the British fleet in Mediterranean. His main preoccupation was with the renewed blockade of the French fleet within its ports (particularly Toulon) and fears that the French might launch an invasion of the Morea in the Ottoman empire from the ports of Apulia on the Adriatic coast of southern Italy which they seized in June 1803. But another of Nelson's more troublesome tasks was to provide frigates or brigs of war to escort the vessels of British merchants up and down the Adriatic, and to protect them from the privateers which the French were sending out of Ancona and Rimini on the Italian coast. Complaints from merchants, British consuls in overseas ports, or from the insurers at Lloyds coffee-house in London, that the protection was inadequate and requiring Nelson to explain and justify his arrangements, were forwarded

[2]   NA, ADM 106/1559, 23 April 1802
[3]   Igor Žic in his article on Adamić in Riječka Luka, Muzej Grada Rijeke, 2001, says that by 1802 Adamić had become rich from selling hemp to the British navy.

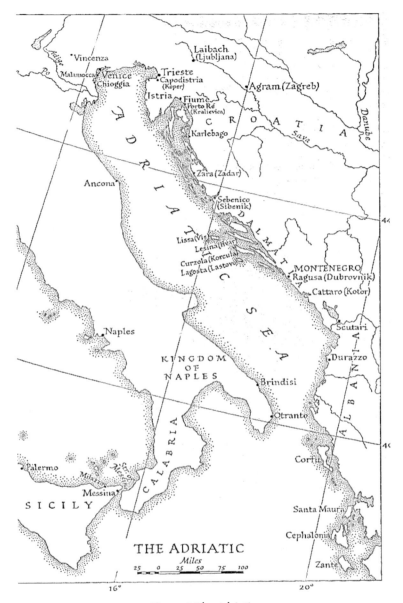

Figure 6. The Adriatic.

to him by the Admiralty. On the other hand there was a stream of complaints that British warships had infringed the neutrality of friendly states, such as Austria, by chasing the predatory French privateers who sought refuge in its harbours, such as Trieste or Umag. In Nelson's correspondence these issues loomed almost as large as the strategic considerations and demanded considerable time and attention.[4]

---

[4]   Sir Nicholas Harris Nicolas, Dispatches and Letters of Nelson

Figure 7. Horatio Nelson by George Baxter, after
Lemuel Francis Abbott.

As well as negotiating purchase of essential naval supplies, Leard was also keeping the Navy Board informed of enemy activity on the other side of the Adriatic. As early as August 1803 he had reported that French troops were constantly moving downwards towards Brindisi and Otranto and that small craft were being collected as privateers on the Italian coast of the Adriatic. In November he again reported that the French were increasing their forces and building gun vessels. He ventured the opinion that the French were preparing to cross the Adriatic to take possession of the Morea and Albania for the sake of the timber of that region.[5]

The dangers for unescorted British merchant ships trying to reach Rijeka are exemplified in the case of the BETSEY. It was reported to Nelson in February 1804 that MORGIANA commanded by Captain Raynsford had been ordered up the Adriatic with the Fish Ships (these were probably carrying fish exports from the North Sea harbours of England). The master of the BETSEY bound for Rijeka became impatient with the delay involved in staying with the convoy, especially as he would have had to go as far as Trieste before being escorted back to Rijeka. Raynsford gave him permission to leave the convoy off the island of Susak, just south of Istria. Because of a lack of wind, the following morning BETSEY was still in sight but flying an enemy in sight signal and firing warning shots. Raynsford ordered the convoy to gather in, and signaled BETSEY to rejoin it. As BETSEY did not return but sailed away out of sight, it was assumed that it had been a false alarm. But BETSEY was taken by a French privateer off the island of Cres. Representations by Lloyds and a gentleman in Trieste (possibly the British consul there) that BETSEY had been incautiously left by the convoy led to the Admiralty instructing Nelson to enquire into it, and the repercussions of the incident were to go on for some time.[6]

---

[5]   NA, ADM 106/1559, Leard-Navy Board dated Fiume 24 Nov 1803, copied to Admiralty 11 Jan 1804
[6]   NA. ADM 1/408 various dates

Figure 8. View of the Siege of Valetta. Malta was besieged captured by the British in1800. Print after Major James Weir.

Almost incredibly, given all his other concerns, Nelson also took a close and direct interest in the details of the procurement of naval supplies for the repair of his fleet. It is partly in Nelson's orders to the captains of the frigates escorting the convoys, his reports to the Admiralty, and in his letters to the storekeeper in the dockyard at Malta, that we can build up a picture of Leard's activity in Rijeka and the development of his relationship with Adamić.

The problem of escorting merchant ships up the Adriatic was clearly linked with that of bringing back down to Malta the naval supplies which Leard and Adamić were supplying. Almost immediately after his arrival in the Mediterranean in June 1803, Nelson sent CYCLOPS to escort ships from Malta up the Adriatic and to bring back whatever British ships it found there. (It called at Rijeka in August and Leard sent a letter with it to Nelson with information on the build up of French troops on the western side of the Adriatic). Leard had already sent down to Malta 5-6 inch rope made at Trieste or Rijeka in June 1803.

Nelson made further arrangements in August 1803 for a small squadron to patrol the lower Adriatic to detect and check any French movements there, and for the sloop ARROW to convoy any merchant ships arriving at Malta from England up the Adriatic. A first voyage with a convoy in September-October took in Trieste, Venice and Rijeka (25-28 October). On a second voyage, ARROW arrived at Rijeka on 23 November, when because of bad weather, the vessels that it was to escort took several days to load. Naval supplies must have been involved as, in reporting this, Leard said he would send an account of the cargoes and cost to the Navy Board.[7] ARROW left Rijeka on 1 December with three vessels under convoy, arriving Malta on 19 December. In a reply dated 24 January 1804 to the report on his mission from the captain of ARROW, Nelson wrote that he was much pleased with his attention to government concerns up the Adriatic under the direction of Leard, who had informed Nelson of the purpose of his being in Rijeka and had sent him bills of lading of stores sent to the dockyard in Malta in

---

[7]   NA, ADM 106/1559, Leard-Navy Board 24 Nov. 1803

MENTOR, GIURO (presumably the two ships escorted by ARROW) and the Imperial (Austrian) schooner HUNGARIA. Nelson hoped that the HUNGARIA would soon arrive at Malta, as the stores she had on board were urgently required.

However, Nelson was also beginning to have doubts about the need to obtain expensive supplies from the Adriatic if they could be obtained more cheaply elsewhere. Nelson told the Admiralty in a letter of 10 February 1804 that, although he had ordered the naval officer at Malta to use every means for making rope with the hemp lately purchased up the Adriatic, he suspected that, from the storekeeper's reports on the transaction, purchases and supplies from that quarter would be very limited. On the same day, Nelson replied to a letter to the storekeeper Malta of 23 January 1804 enclosing papers and documents from Leard. Nelson hoped that, with the summer season approaching, supplies from the Adriatic would not be needed. He sent the storekeeper a list of prices in Smyrna (Izmir in Turkey), which he should compare with the Adriatic prices. He nevertheless hoped that the HUNGARIA schooner would soon arrive with rope and tar. And in another letter of the same date to Malta he said that he was glad to have heard that the 5 and 6 inch rope supplied to the fleet had not been manufactured in Malta but at Trieste and sent from there the previous June by Leard. (As is made clear from later correspondence, it was made in Rijeka. It seems that Nelson frequently confused Trieste with Rijeka). From further correspondence between Nelson and the storekeeper at Malta, it appears that the HUNGARIA did not arrive at Malta until late February 1804.[8]

Nelson had written to the naval agent or storekeeper at Malta on 5 November 1803 in reply to his letter of 29 October to thank him for preparing a transport to go up the Adriatic. This may have been the THOMAS AND MARY transport, which the storekeeper reported to Nelson on 5 December to have gone to Trieste for hemp under the protection of the brig/sloop JALOUSE. As this hemp was to be taken from the person in charge of government hemp and other stores i.e. Leard, it is more likely that the transport was to go to Rijeka. The storekeeper had drawn bills on the Navy Board for £10, 500. These were to be sent with the transport and negotiated at the best terms.[9] JALOUSE had left Malta on its first convoy up to Trieste on 22 November with as many as 14 vessels, one of which parted company off Cape Kamenjak at the south end of Istria to sail on its own to Rijeka. JALOUSE was at Trieste from 8 December 1803 until 6 January 1804 when it sailed with 14 vessels in convoy to Malta. It was soon back at Trieste at the end of February 1804, picked up merchantmen for convoy off Malamocco (the entrance to the Venice lagoon), and met THOMAS AND MARY, which had come out of Rijeka, off Cape Kamenjak on 9 March. If THOMAS AND MARY had gone up to Rijeka with JALOUSE as early as November, there must have been considerable delay in loading the naval supplies and waiting for the escort to return to Malta. JALOUSE and its convoy reached Malta on 29 March 1804.

However useful these naval supplies from the Adriatic, by the end of July 1804 Nelson was reprimanding the storekeeper at Malta for ordering canvas and timber from Rijeka because it was more expensive than that readily available from Naples. He should only procure naval stores from such sources in the face of emergency. There were also complaints about the

---

[8]   In 1806 the Navy Board was asked by Admiralty to summarise the supplies sent to Malta from the beginning of 1804. They listed bills of lading received from Leard dated 2 March 1804, 26 March 1805, 19 June 1805, 3 Oct 1805 and 27 April 1806. The first and last give the name of the ship as HUNGARIA imperial schooner, master S. Zugolic or Saverio Zuzulick. The first bill of lading lists ropes and 119 barrels of tar, the others include planks and spars, canvas, hemp and tar. NA, ADM 106/2240 Navy Board –Admiralty 30 Dec.1806

[9]   Nelson Correspondence, Vol. 5, Nelson-Nathaniel Taylor, storekeeper Malta, 22 Dec. 1803

Figure 9. HMS ARROW, sunk in battle, 1805, detail of oil painting by
Francis Sartorius.

quality of the rope that Leard had sent from Rijeka to Malta. These reached Leard either soon
before or while he was in England from June-September 1804.[10] He wrote to the Navy Board
to protest that the rope had been made in Rijeka under his personal supervision, in a public
rope-ground by the best rope-makers in Rijeka, from rope yarn which his predecessor as
agent, Mr Ulny, had bought in Venice. Even ARROW had been supplied with some of the rope
before she left Rijeka the previous November. Some had been used to load the TRURO (GIURO)
and MENTOR with spars and found to be strong. But by this stage the Navy Board had become
much more interested in obtaining heavy timber from the Adriatic.

The Oak Timber Project

The project which was to dominate the relationship of Adamić, Leard and the Navy Board
for the best part of 20 years was for the supply of very large quantities of oak timber of the
right quality and large dimensions to be used in the construction of the large ships-of-the-
line and the smaller frigates of the British navy. The details of the agreements between them
concerning the quantities and the amount of money involved are complicated. Given that
some of the key documents cannot be traced, the story has to be reconstructed from later
summaries of the project and the claims and counter-claims after it had run into difficulties
and delays, and from the subsequent renegotiations of the contract. It is particularly difficult
to resolve what constituted the 'loads' of the different kinds of timber on which payments
were based, and there are wide differences between the exchange rates of the forint to the
pound sterling in the various calculations.

---

[10] Nelson also received a letter dated 17 May from the storekeeper Malta enclosing a letter from Leard with an
account of the cordage sent from Rijeka. Nelson Correspondence, Nelson-Nathaniel Taylor, 28 July 1804.

The story of the project was marked by frequent delays, caused not only because of the slowness of communication and of that of the Admiralty and the Navy Board coming to decisions, but also because of the tremendous difficulties in moving the huge quantities of large trees overland to wherever they could be more easily transported by water. In addition to these problems, there were the complications caused by outbreaks of war, French pressure on Austria, while it was neutral, to close its ports to British ships and trade, and ultimately the French occupation of the lands where the trees had been felled.

On 23 March 1803 the Navy Board reported to the Admiralty that, because of the scarcity of timber, it had appointed John Leard, 'a very intelligent officer who has been some time resident in that country', to be their agent to look for oak timber in the neighbourhood of Trieste, Rijeka and other navigable ports on the east side of the Adriatic. A master shipwright from Gibraltar called Churchill had been appointed to assist him, and Leard had been given authority to buy and send back to England up to 100 loads of timber as samples. Leard had reported that oak timber from Istria was of excellent quality and of a size suitable for line-of-battle ships. He had sent in estimates of the costs of purchase and transport, and recommendations on the ports to be used. Further correspondence from Leard and another agent, Mr Danelon in Trieste, regarding the availability of timber, was sent on 28 March by the Naval Board to the Admiralty, which then copied the correspondence to Hammond, the under secretary at the Foreign Office. A sample of the timber from Istria had been received, sent by Leard (almost certainly supplied by Adamić) on PREVOYANT (on its return voyage from Rijeka with hemp). On May 26 the Navy Board forwarded to the Admiralty reports by Leard and Churchill on forests and woodlands in Croatia, then considered distinct from Istria, copies of which were also sent to Hammond. They had visited the imperial military forests of the Sluiner (Slunj) Grenzer (Border) regiment, consisting of about 200,000 acres south of Karlovac, as well as several private forests of the nobility between Karlovac and Zagreb.[11] The renewal of the war between Britain and France in May 1803 made the procurement of timber even more urgent, but also more difficult.

There were now some of the first delays. On 25 March 1804 the Admiralty asked the Navy Board if they had received any more letters from Leard since the previous March, whether the sample timber had arrived and if it had been found suitable. It was only on 14 May 1804 that the Navy Board sent a long and detailed report to the Admiralty,[12] summarising all the communications it had received from Leard. Although Leard's original letters to the Navy Board cannot be traced, this report (supplemented with details from later correspondence) gives a good idea of the development of the project.

In June 1803 Leard had informed the Navy Board that he intended to go to Vienna to find out whether the Austrian government would approve the export of Croatian timber. He went to Vienna with Adamić and wrote again in August 1803 to report that Adamić had been informed from Vienna that all the government departments involved had unanimously and officially agreed to his proposal to export 3000 oak trees annually for five years (i.e. 15,000 trees). This was to begin as soon as the new road was finished in the spring of 1805. (This was the Louisa road from Karlovac to the ports of Rijeka, Kraljevica and Bakar, begun in 1801 and privately financed by a Hungarian company, in which various members of the Hungarian aristocracy,

---

[11] NA, FO 7/137 Leard-Gordon, 29 Nov. 1817 enclosed Leard-Foreign Office.
[12] NA, ADM 106/2234

the Bishop of Zagreb and Adamić himself had invested).[13] If even greater quantities of timber were required, it was anticipated the Emperor would soon give his approval. Leard added that a merchant in Trieste. Mr Tomasine would also be making proposals.

In September 1803 Leard had written two further letters to the Navy Board to say that Adamić had received permission to export timber from Croatia and Slavonia, extending to 'as many trees as can be spared'. (When Leard and Adamić had gone back the Karlovac, the officers of the imperial forests had told them that the figure of 1570 trees per annum had been deliberately conservative and that twice or three times that number could be spared).[14] Timber from Istria, more conveniently near the coast, could not be spared, as it only met local needs. Timber might also be procured from Turkey via the Danube and the Black Sea, but this would be more expensive, so the only practicable sources would be Croatia and Slavonia. Leard argued that the Croatia and Slavonia option would open up trade advantages for exporting British manufactured goods into Hungary (the Louisa road was indeed being constructed to facilitate Hungarian imports and exports).

Leard enclosed a letter from Adamić himself, in which he stated that he had committed himself so much to the project (presumably by persuading the Austrian authorities) that his honour was at stake, and he urged the Navy Board to given urgent approval for the project to go ahead.

Adamić gave a range of estimated prices for different kinds of timber, which he admitted were high, but that this was because of high initial costs and that he hoped to be able to bring the prices down as the project progressed. He estimated the cost of timber when delivered to the place of shipment to be £5.15.0 to £10.15.0 per load according to size for the bigger timber for line-of-battle ships, 5% less for timber for frigates and knee timber (curved timber) from £7.15.0 to £11.15.0.

Leard himself submitted an estimate of the cost of procuring 507 trees or 1014 loads (i.e. two loads per tree) from the forests of Szlewing (?) and Karlovac in Croatia, to be delivered at Rijeka or Kraljevica within one year, to be £5.3.0., including Adamić's commission. This was considerably lower than the costs quoted by Adamić (and also considerably higher than those later quoted as having been eventually agreed by the Navy Board). The estimates from Mr Tomasine in Trieste had been even higher than those of Adamić and Leard had abandoned any further discussion with him (although one suspects that Leard might have involved him only to make Adamić's prices seem more reasonable). Leard proposed that instead of making a contact with Adamić, he should be paid a commission of 5%.

On the basis of the above-quoted prices, and assuming 3000 trees per annum or about 6000 loads, the total annual cost could have ranged from about £30,000 to 65,000, with a commission to Adamić of £1500 to £3250. Using one of the exchange rates used by Leard of 12.5 forints/£ sterling, this was about 375,000 to 815,000 forints and 19,000 to 40,000. But, as we will see things worked out very differently and there was to be considerable disagreement over what was and what should have been paid to Adamić.

---

[13] Žic, op cit, also Melitta Pivec-Stele, La vie economiques des provinces illyriennes, Paris, 1930
[14] NA, FO 7/137 Leard-Gordon, 29 Nov. 1817 enclosed Leard-Foreign Office.

Figure 10. The fortress town of Karlovac.

However, in 1803, the Louisa road was far from ready. Leard had already argued in September that the trees in Croatia should be felled before the completion of the road and laid up at Karlovac to season. Both Leard and Adamić were in a hurry to start supplying timber, so, even though Leard had argued for Croatia and Slavonia, they looked at other interim possibilities. In November 1803 Leard wrote to the Navy Board to argue that it would be advisable to obtain supplies of timber as soon as possible. Adamić had told him that it would be possible to procure between 1000 to 2000 loads of timber in the next year, mainly for frigates but with some for line-of-battle ships, but secrecy was required as it would come from the Cisalpine Republic (French-controlled north Italy, which since the renewal of war in May 1803 was enemy territory).

The other possibility (of interest because of Leard's and Adamić's future activity and movements) was that of obtaining oak timber from Turkish Albania. From October 1803 until March 1805 Leard wrote a number of letters to the Navy Board. He first had received a letter from Mr Stuart at the British embassy in Vienna to say that he had received proposals from Dubrovnik for the supply of timber, through the shipbuilders of Dubrovnik, from the neighbourhood of Durazzo (now Durres). Leard asked Stuart for more information and proposed to go to Dubrovnik and Durazzo to explore the possibility. Stuart provided him with a letter of introduction to Count Caboga, a senator of the still independent Dubrovnik republic, but Leard decided it would be impolitic to go himself. He accepted the offer of a Mr Henry, an Austrian subject in Rijeka to go in his place. Mr Henry's mission resulted in a promise from a count Triporick (?), farmer-general of the pasha of Scutari (now Shkoder), that he would be in Trieste at the end of March 1804 when he would give information on the quantity and price of the timber that might be obtained from Turkish Albania.

Figure 11. Deptford Dockyard, detail of oil painting by Joseph Farington (Royal Museums Greenwich).

In the meantime, another letter from Leard to the Navy Board in November 1803 enclosed a copy of a decree to Adamić and another letter from Adamić to Leard concerning the quantity of timber that could be spared from Croatia. The decree of 10 November 1803 authorised Adamić to cut 1570 trees per year for five years from 1805 in the imperial military forests of the grenzer regiments, mainly from those of the Slunj regiment, but some also from those of the Varazdin and Gradiska regiments east of Zagreb and along the river Sava. The remainder of the 3000 trees per annum agreed was to be made up from trees in private forests.[15] Rather ominously, it seemed that some of the districts from which they could be taken were more distant from water transport or the New Road than Leard had reckoned in making his earlier estimates of costs. Adamić repeated that he considered his reputation to be at stake. (The Navy Board commented that. in the whole of the correspondence with Adamić, he had stressed the difficulty in procuring supplies because of the intrigues, influence and power of the French).

The Navy Board concluded its report of 14 May 1804, summarising all of the above developments, by informing the Admiralty that a report had been received from its officials at the royal shipyards at Deptford confirming that the timber sent home on PREVOYANT from Rijeka was of a strong tough quality fit for shipbuilding. Despite its high price, the Board recommended that a quantity of it should be imported during the present scarcity. The Lords Commissioners of the Admiralty agreed and formally requested Lord Harrowby, the Foreign Secretary, to make representations at the court of Vienna and instruct HM ministers and the consuls at the different Adriatic ports to facilitate the exportation of the timber.

In a report to the Admiralty of 15 June 1804 concerning all possible sources of timber, the Navy Board repeated its understanding that Adamić, 'a merchant well known at Fiume', had permission from the Austrian government to export annually for a certain number of years 1570 trees,[16] which he had offered either to deliver on contract or to send to England on a commission. If, however, it were judged expedient to push up this quantity, it would be

---

[15] NA, FO 7/137, Leard-Gordon, 29 Nov. 1817.
[16] This was only the number of trees that could be cut in the military forests.

advisable to have an agent on the spot to regulate all particulars. So an increased supply was not ruled out and, although nor stated, it was clear that the agent would continue to be Leard.

What happened next appears quite extraordinary, given the Navy Board's cautious approach and the differing predictions of the number of trees that might be available, and was to be the cause of future difficulties for Leard and Adamić, and considerable disagreement and dispute.

Leard was now in England (from at least early June until autumn 1804). On 26 July 1804 the Navy Board wrote to the Admiralty to say that Leard had written to them to propose that they should immediately secure the purchase of 30,000 trees by paying down a proportion of their value. There could be no mistake in the number of trees (although Admiralty clerks making digests of the correspondence not unreasonably thought there was a mistake and reduced it to 3000, which has been further confused with the 3000 loads of timber referred to in later correspondence). The number was repeated in later reviews of the situation. A marginal note on the letter records that the Lord Commissioners of the Admiralty immediately responded on 31 July without further discussion, approving and giving orders that measures be taken for purchasing 30,000 trees.

On 29 August 1804 the Navy Board recommended that Leard be sent back out to Rijeka, and that, to give him additional official status in his relations with the Austrian authorities, he should be appointed British consul to Dubrovnik (although there was no suggestion that he should leave Rijeka to perform any duties there). The Admiralty passed on the recommendation to the Foreign Office, which agreed. So in September 1804 Leard was commissioned to return to Rijeka, where he promptly advanced Adamić £7200 as the down payment on 30,000 trees at 3 forints per tree and other sums to cover various expenses. Despite all the evidence to the contrary, the Navy Board was to argue that their final instructions to Leard did indeed authorise him to make down payments at one quarter of a notional value of only 1 guinea (£1.1.0 or about 13 forints) per tree i.e. about 3 forints per tree, but that they had limited this to only the number of trees as could be brought to Rijeka in the one year 1805. It is unclear as to whether Leard was somehow to have ascertained this in advance, or whether he was in effect only to pay this sum after delivery and pending some later final settlement of Adamić's account. Nor is it clear how Leard was able to access the funds to make these payments, without his having been authorised to issue bills (the equivalent of modern cheques) to be cleared through Austrian banks and charged to the Navy Board. The Navy Board had agreed that Leard himself was to be paid a salary of £400 per annum and a commission of 6 shillings on every load of timber delivered.

The War of the Third Coalition

In England the winter of 1804-05 was to be dominated by fear that Napoleon would invade England with the army he was assembling at Boulogne and that to effect this, the French and Spanish fleets would unite. In spring 1805 the French fleet in Toulon was able to slip out past the British blockade and to reach the Atlantic. Nelson left the Mediterranean in pursuit. In the meantime, England needed to find continental allies and to bind them into a new coalition against France. The British prime minister, William Pitt, was successful in persuading Austria and Russia to join the Third Coalition. Austria commenced hostilities in September in southern Germany, causing Napoleon to break up his camp at Boulogne and march away to campaign in Germany. Subsequent developments in 1805 involved Nelson's victory and death at Trafalgar in October and Napoleon's crushing victory over the Austrians and Russians at Austerlitz in Moravia in December, forcing the Austrians to sue for peace. Although, by the peace of Pressburg (or Bratislava) at the end of December 1805, Austria regained Trieste and kept Rijeka and the coast of Croatia, Venetia, Istria, Dalmatia, and the Bocca di Cattaro, as well as all the offshore Adriatic islands of Kvarner and Dalmatia were to be added to Napoleon's Kingdom of Italy.

Although all the main events of the war were far away from the Adriatic, it was not unaffected. In the first place, after Nelson left the Mediterranean to chase the French fleet in the Atlantic, few frigates or brigs of war could be left to convoy merchantmen. Only one British brig JALOUSE was left to make escort the diminishing number of merchant ships to the upper Adriatic. From the strategic point of view, it was hoped that the Russians, who had built up a large fleet at Corfu, would prevent any French moves across the Adriatic towards the Ottoman empire. Unfortunately, in the absence of the British frigates, the small fleet of Britain's other ally, Austria, proved too inadequate and inefficient to protect the merchant ships of Venice, Trieste or Rijeka from French privateers. Towards the end of 1805, after the French occupation of Trieste on 17 December and with the French besieging Venice, the Austrians had taken desperate last minute measures to save what remained of its navy and its trade. In early December orders had issued from Vienna to move the naval headquarters from Venice to Senj on the coast of Croatia, and by mid-December the commander, the French emigré L'Espine, had removed all the arms and stores that could be moved from Venice. But all such measures were nullified by the articles of the treaty of peace. The French forced the Austrians to agree to turn over to them all the ships of the small and neglected Austrian navy which had originally been built by the Venetian Republic, and to release from service all naval officers of Venetian origin. Venice itself, together with its important naval dockyard, the Arsenal, was to be evacuated by the Austrians by the end of January 1806.

The Austrian evacuation of Venice was completed on 19 January and the French promptly occupied it and took possessions of all those vessels of the Austrian navy, which had originally been Venetian. So Austria was left with only three brigs-of-war and some smaller craft and, more importantly, the French now had a naval force in the Adriatic to add to its privateers. It was not large, but it was enough to give the British concern in their assessment of the naval balance in the Adriatic. Above all there was the potential of the Arsenal for building Napoleon more warships.

Trieste remained occupied by the French for three and a half months until they finally left and handed it back to Austria on 4 May 1806. The big question as far as Trieste and Rijeka were concerned, even after the French had withdrawn from Trieste, was whether the Austrian authorities would feel free to allow merchant ships of Britain and Russia to use the port as long as they remained at war with France. It was also questionable whether such merchant ships would be willing or able, with or without convoy, to run the gauntlet between French-occupied territories to reach these ports, with the possibility of the newly-acquired French warships operating out of Venice added to the familiar risk of the French privateers. There were rumours that British ships would be excluded from Trieste and Rijeka by secret articles of the treaty of Pressburg.

Figure 12. Trieste, drawing by William Innes Pocock, 1813.

Trieste was in any case to lose much of its commercial importance. Austria had disadvantaged Venice by making Trieste a free port. Now that Venice was in French hands, the merchants of Venice, who had registered their ships at Trieste and trans-shipped goods arriving first at Trieste on to Venice, now promptly transferred their ships back to Venice. The Trieste registry of shipping in 1806 listed only 62 ships compared to 537 in 1805. From a British point of view, as long as the Austrian ports of Trieste and Rijeka remained neutral and open to either British merchantmen and the British navy, whatever the level of trade, they served as points through which communications with the Austrian court at Vienna could be kept open and French-held territory circumvented.

For the French to access and occupy their new territories in Dalmatia and at the Boka Kotorska by land, they had to cross neutral territories and marching down the steeply mountainous and virtually roadless eastern coast of the Adriatic for some 600 kilometers or 400 miles. The first part of that road took them through Rijeka. While neither the Austrians, Turks or Dubrovnik were strong enough or inclined to refuse the French demand to march across their territory, for easier communication and to supply their forces on the relatively infertile Dalmatian coast, the French needed to be able to sail across from Venice or Ancona or any of the other Italian ports under their control.

The Russian fleet sent to the Adriatic in the war of 1805 seized the Boka Kotorska before the French could arrive to take possession of it from the Austrians. This had repercussions in the north Adriatic. The French held the Austrians responsible for not having prevented the Russian seizure and exerted pressure on them to support their efforts to push the Russians out. In the first place this involved unimpeded transit for French forces over Austrian territory on the Croatian seaboard. Eliot, the British Ambassador in Sicily, wrote on 1 June 1806 that the Austrian emperor had been forced by the menaces of the French to consent to the passage of 40,000 French troops in two columns through the Austrian Dominions to Dalmatia for the purpose of driving the Russians out and probably also to invade the Ottoman Empire.

French pressure on Austria also involved denying the Russians and British access to the Austrian ports of Trieste and Rijeka. A proclamation issued in Trieste on 29 May 1806 declared that because of the situation at the Boka Kotorska had induced the emperor of Austria to take measures. All Russian and English vessels, without distinction, were prohibited entry into all

Austrian Ports in the Adriatic with immediate effect. Any British or Russian ship in port was to depart within three days unless impeded by bad weather. The prohibition had little effect as far as British trade was concerned. No British vessels of any description had arrived at Trieste since the previous November before the French occupation.

But the war of 1805 and the political situation described above, together with delays in completing the Louisa road, created considerable difficulties for Leard and Adamić. Leard was later to claim that they had cut down about 1700 trees making about 3000 loads principally of large timber. He had reported to the Navy Board in October 1805 that the French were building up forces in Italy. In the middle of November 1805 (the time that the French took Trieste) the sudden enemy advance had forced him and Adamić to abandon their work. Leard had been able to return to Rijeka in January 1806 after peace had been made between Austria and France, but he found (or later claimed) that the conditions of the peace prevented exportation of the timber and also imposed restrictions and very great difficulty on exporting naval stores even when cleared from neutral ports. He claimed that he and Adamić nevertheless found means, despite the opposition and intrigues of French agents, to send several cargoes of hemp and spars etc. to Malta at very moderate prices.[17] At the same time he kept the British ambassador in Vienna fully informed of the situation in Rijeka, and of the movement of French troops along the Croatian coast to Dalmatia.[18]

But whatever Leard was later to claim, little correspondence from him to his masters in the Navy Board can be found in their archives, and questions were beginning to be asked about his activity and the paucity of its results. In December 1806 the Admiralty asked the Navy Board what timber or naval stores had been procured by Leard since 1804. The Navy Board sent the Admiralty a list of five cargoes sent from Rijeka to Malta, four of which had been sent after Leard's return to Rijeka in autumn 1804, the most recent in April 1806, for which the Navy Board had only a bill of lading from Leard and no confirmation from Malta of its having been received. Although there were some consignments of spars and planks, there was no sign of the heavy timber. (Leard made claims for payment of two of these cargoes as late as 1811, quite separately from the account for the heavy timber. The Navy Board was unwilling to allow them on the basis that some of the supplies had been sent to Malta without Leard being asked to send them by the commissioner there, and that, in any case, these transactions had to be treated apart from that for which he was paid his salary).

Trade War 1806-9

By July 1806 the British government had decided to send back frigates and brigs to patrol the northern Adriatic. This was because is was feared that their Russian allies, while still at war with France, would soon withdraw from the war and could not be trusted to use its fleet in the Adriatic, based at Corfu and the Boka Kotorska, to prevent French moves against the Ottoman empire. But it was also because of growing fears that Napoleon was building warships in the Venice Arsenal. It was essential to blockade Venice and prevent any such ships taking to sea.

A small force of British frigates and brigs was ordered to the Adriatic by Admiral Collingwood, Nelson's successor as commander-in-chief of the British fleet in the Mediterranean. It arrived

---

[17] These would have included the consignment sent with the schooner HUNGARIA in April 1806. See note 8 above.
[18] Leard's petition to the Foreign Office in November 1811. See below

LORD COLLINGWOOD. FROM AN AUTHENTIC PORTRAIT.

Figure 13. Admiral Cuthbert Collingwood (1748–
1810). Book illustration based on an original
portrait.

in the upper Adriatic in September 1806 under the command of Captain Patrick Campbell on the frigate UNITÉ. Campbell soon decided it was practicable to station most of his squadron off the Istrian coast and in the approaches to Trieste. Even though neutral Austria had officially denied the use of their ports of Trieste and Rijeka to Russian and British ships, and although Istria was now occupied by the French, there were safe anchorages in its indented coastline, conveniently opposite Venice, and where he could find ways of obtaining fresh water and provisions.

The question of prizes i.e. captured enemy vessels and cargoes, and prize-money i.e. the money earned by the officers and crews of British naval ships from their sale was to bedevil the operations of the British in the Adriatic as in other seas. It could on occasion subvert the conduct of operations against the enemy, and complicate and embitter relations with friendly powers and neutrals. While on occasion the Admiralty and its courts, and senior officers, attempted to control it, everyone was compromised. The capture and sale of property belonging to or destined to the enemy whether carried on enemy or neutral ships defrayed the costs of naval operations to the Admiralty. The commanders of squadrons and the officers and crews of all ships in sight of a capture could claim their cuts to supplement their meagre pay and allowances. The more unscrupulous practitioners could become wealthy men and remain popular with their crews for whom the pursuit and capture of prizes was an important boost for morale in otherwise appalling conditions. Captains of the faster commerce-raiding frigates enjoyed considerable advantages over senior captains of ships-of-the-line who were frequently trapped in dull months of blockade duty outside the main enemy naval bases such as Toulon.

In theory the activity was carefully and strictly regulated. All captures had to be sent to ports where formal Admiralty courts could adjudicate on whether a capture was lawful and in accordance with the succession of Orders in Council which issued from the British Government as instructions as to the legitimacy of pursuit, search and seizure of the ships of which states whether enemy or neutral. On occasion the courts ordered restitution and compensation. Captains had agents in London and regularly took legal advice from specialist lawyers to protect their interests or to justify the extension of their almost piratical activity.

As far as the Adriatic is concerned, the question of prizes can be said to have first arisen with Patrick Campbell's arrival in September 1806. The activity of UNITÉ and the other ships of the new squadron was soon to have a devastating effect on the shipping and trade of the upper Adriatic. As well as the evidence in official records, valuable insights are provided by the personal diary of the Robert Wilson, a seaman serving as signalman on UNITÉ.

Campbell very quickly discovered that he had a problem in disposing of the plentiful prizes that his small squadron was ideally placed to detain or capture. Although there would occasionally be ships of 300 or more tons, or brigs of about 200, the majority of the small commercial craft engaged in coastal trade were of the trabacolo type with anything from only 15 tons to 100. Hardly any of these categories were armed and only needed crews of about 5-20 men to sail them in contrast to the large crews of warships which needed so many more men to handle guns.

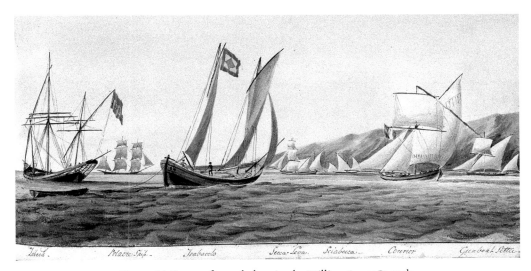

Figure 14. Types of vessel, drawing by William Innes Pocock.

The problem was how to send these smaller captures to a port with an Admiralty court for adjudication, and 'condemnation' to sale after evaluation of the ship and cargo by special surveyors. Malta, with the nearest court was 1400 kilometers away and Corfu the only port of any size on the route held by an allied power was 800 kilometers or 500 miles away on the route for Malta.

With a squadron of only four-five cruisers in the Adriatic, it could be risky to deplete the force the primary task of which was to prevent a French naval force from issuing out of Venice. After his first reconnaissance of Venice, however, Campbell seems to have decided that the risk from there was not great and that he could safely maintain a watch with only UNITÉ and one other vessel in the northern Adriatic to make periodic reconnaissance of the Italian side.

However, instead of sending all the prizes to Malta, the warships of Campbell's squadron took many only as far as Corfu where there was a market for ships. Even devoting most of his squadron to escorting prizes to Malta or only as far as Corfu did not satisfy Campbell or solve the problem, because UNITÉ went on capturing prizes while its sister ships were away and it was not convenient to put prize crews on them. Trieste and Rijeka were temptingly near. Although, under French pressure, the Austrian authorities had been forced to deny British and Russian ships access to them, these were neutral ports with British consuls or agents such as Leard to help smooth things. The British ambassador at Vienna, Adair, was delighted that the presence of British ships in the northern Adriatic gave him another outlet for his communications to the outside world. Leard was later to claim that he had been an important intermediary between the ambassadors at Vienna and Campbell and the English squadron.

Campbell with UNITÉ decided to approach Trieste and was off that port from late November until mid-December 1806. The journal of signalman Wilson gives us an excellent picture of what happened and suggests much more. The ship's officers went on shore after their arrival but not in uniform. Soon after several captured vessels and their cargoes were sold in Trieste. Campbell had found the solution to his problem. Mant, the UNITÉ's surgeon was thereafter to go on mysterious visits to Trieste and later to Rijeka. Wilson guessed at the true purpose of Mant's absences when he wrote in his journal in January 1807 that he believed Mant was their agent for captures etc.

Napoleon had in the meantime declared economic war against Britain. The Berlin Decree of 21 November 1806, announced a total blockade of the British Isles and prohibited the purchase or importation of goods produced either in Britain or its colonies into France and the associated territories of the French Empire. The so-called Continental System, to extend which Napoleon put pressure on his allies and friendly or neutral states, was meant to exclude British goods from the European markets and thereby to starve it of earnings (and coincidentally to provide markets for French goods which would enrich France). The decree marked an escalation in the economic war, which both sides had been waging on each other for many years. It covered all goods and not only armaments or contraband of war and all carriers whether from enemy, allied or neutral states.

The British government reacted to the Berlin Decree by the Order in Council of 7 January 1807. The rules laid down by this especially affected the ships of neutral states (as the order pointed out, enemy ports had already been subject to navy blockade and ships belonging to the enemy had been seized). No vessels were permitted to trade from one port to another if both belonged to or were in the possession of France or her allies, or were so far under their control that British vessels could not freely trade there. Any vessels conducting such trade could be captured and brought in, and, together with their cargoes, condemned as lawful prizes.

Campbell chose to interpret the order as giving him very wide latitude to control all ships coming and going from Trieste and Rijeka, on the grounds that these ports had been closed to British shipping for the previous six months. Campbell was to make much in future self-justification of a letter from Adair, the British ambassador in Vienna, of December 1806, which urged him to take immediate reprisals or counter-measures in response to the Berlin Decree. This might be supposed to have upset his arrangements at Trieste and Rijeka. But it would seem that he had by now established such practical (and indeed cordial) relations, with both the local authorities and some at least of the trading interests, that he could continue to dispose of prizes in both Trieste and Rijeka, even though the Austrian government at Vienna and its ambassador to London became increasingly strident in their complaints to the British government about interference with its shipping. One can only guess the extent to which Adamić might have been involved or affected by Campbell's activity, and whether he was one of Leard's associates in his dealings with Campbell.

The grip of the squadron of trade in and out of the upper Adriatic ports tightened considerably. Wilson recorded in his journal in March that scarcely a single vessel could pass the British warships without being examined, but that as well as damaging enemy trade, they were in a position to do favours to friends. For example, two gentlemen came on board UNITÉ from Trieste to ask permission for a brig to come unmolested from Rijeka to Trieste and that Campbell agreed. It is also clear from other entries in Wilson's diary that Campbell was in effect extorting protection money from the owners or masters of merchant ships in return for not interfering with them.

In early April 1807 one of the ships of Campbell's squadron, WEAZLE, captured two small Venetian trabacoloes of only 50 tons (S.ANTONIO DI PADUA and S.ANTONIO) moving from the island of Krk to Venice with timber for ship-construction at the Arsenal. It was most probably news of this last capture that led Campbell to move down from Umag on the north-west coast of Istria to the island of Lošinj (which, like the other islands of Kvarner, had been ceded to the French). Not only did the British now discover the advantages of the harbour at Mali Lošinj, but Campbell was on the trail of the supply of timber. Wilson wrote:

> 'Lussin was found to be a most beautiful island with a fine commodious harbour, deep and well-sheltered by the high hills on both sides of it, the entrance to which is quite narrow... Lussin is under no particular power but their vessels sail under Imperial colours; but the French had a Commissary resident on the island previous to our appearance. The manner in which we came to the knowledge of this island and its properties was by the WEAZLE chasing a trabacoloe right into the harbour and there capturing her. Captain Clavell of the WEAZLE was surprised to see so fine a place and moreover found it was quite defenceless. He accordingly communicated the intelligence to our captain... Our captain was so well pleased with the island altogether that he determined to make it a rendezvous for the future'.

With the British 'discovery' of Lošinj, the activity of the squadron during April-May 1807 moved south to the area between Istria and the French headquarters in Dalmatia at Zara. The day after his arrival at Lošinj, on 9 April, Campbell sailed up to the Austrian port of Rijeka for the first time. Wilson wrote:

> 'Fiume Bay is a very large and deep bay and much subject to gales'(the notorious bora). 'The town is but small and has a poor appearance'. 'The watering place without exception is certainly a very fine one. It is close to the bay side. You can fill your casks close to the salt water. When you come out of the salt water into the fresh it is enough to nip you in two being so cold; it is excellent water.'

On the evening of 11 April the English consul Leard (Wilson called him Laird) and another gentleman came and dined on board. Leard would have been a useful informant for Campbell on the question of where the French were obtaining the timber that WEAZLE had intercepted on the two Venetian trabacoloes. On 12 April UNITÉ preceded by its launch as a reconnaissance vessel moved down the coast of the Croatian mainland to Bakar and Sta. Maria (?) On 13 April Campbell found large quantities of oak timber cut down and laying in piles to be seasoned for use of the French to build ships of war at Venice (or possibly, according to another source,[19] for gunboats to be constructed by the French at Zadar) at a place called Les Essara, which Wilson described as part of the coast but which was more probably on the now French island of Krk, just across a narrow strait from the mainland of Austrian Croatia. It was an important find and UNITÉ's crew were soon loading timber onto trabacoloes at the place Wilson called Mosco or Mous (shown on British charts as Muschio about where Omišalj stands today). On 19 April UNITÉ returned to Rijeka where Leard and a Mr Sims (Leard's clerk) again dined on board, and on 20 April it was back in Lošinj harbour where it found WEAZLE with the prize brig ABRAMO captured in March and the two trabacoloes laden with timber from Krk. The next few days were spent transferring timber onto ABRAMO, which was then escorted away to Corfu on 23 April. There must have been so much timber that another brig GRACIOSO found in Lošinj harbour was pressed into service. A navy transport ALEXANDER arrived in May and might have been sent to take away any additional timber.

There is a mystery concerning this timber. At the beginning of 1812 when Leard was submitting claims for payment to the Admiralty, he included the cost of oak timber loaded on the above-named GRAZIOSO amounting to £384. Upon investigation of the claim, the Navy Board identified this as prize timber bought from Captain Campbell of UNITÉ but which on arrival at Malta had been found unfit for use and was returned to Adamić's agent. The Navy Board suggested further investigation of this item. The results of this enquiry have not been found, but the Navy Board accountants clearly suspected double-dealing. Had Leard and Adamić, finding themselves frustrated by the prohibition of the Austrian authorities, decided to sell some of the timber to the French? Was it really French property and therefore a legitimate capture for which Campbell could claim prize money? Even though it was found on the French-held island Krk and was unlikely to have been transported there from the mainland, it might have been cut down there by Adamić before the island was ceded to the French in early 1806. It is also possible that Leard and Adamić took the opportunity of UNITÉ's presence to send some of their own timber along with that which had belonged to the French. Why otherwise

---

[19]   Spiridion Foresti, the well-informed agent of the British on Corfu

would the timber have been returned to Adamić's agent? Or was it the unscrupulous Campbell who was making a fraudulent claim for prize money for timber that was at the same time being sold to the British navy?

Other items on Leard's 1812 claim, which were also challenged by the Navy Board investigators, seem to have concerned spars sent on the ALEXANDER and timber supplied to the carpenter of the UNITÉ. So it is clear that Leard and Adamić were using Campbell's presence and activity in Kvarner to circumvent the restrictions which the Austrian authorities, under French pressure, had imposed on them.

Campbell wrote to Admiral Collingwood in May 1807 to raise the issue of the legitimacy of seizing Austrian ships using the closed ports of Trieste and Rijeka and the use of Lošinj as a base. Collingwood advised him to respect Austrian neutrality. On the question of Lošinj, he wrote that soldiers for a garrison there could not be spared, but that, if the local people were friendly, the port could be used without the need for a garrison.

As the enemy squadron at Venice seemed unlikely to come out very far from Venice with British warships in the vicinity, UNITÉ withdrew towards the coast of Istria, to Lošinj and Rijeka for most of the month of July 1807. It is during this period that Wilson's journal illustrates the more relaxed side of the life of the British warships.

Whether or not the officers and crews of British warships were welcome in Trieste, they were certainly made to feel at home in Rijeka. On a previous and second visit of UNITÉ on 18-20 May 1807, Campbell had gone on shore and the English consul (Leard) had come on board, and there had been a dance on board UNITÉ for local guests. The visit on 11-20 July 1807 was even more festive as can be seen from Wilson's journal:

> 11 July. Mr Mant returned from town after which prize money was distributed to the crew (because he had again negotiated the local sale of prizes?)

> 12 July. 'Several boats came off from the shore full of people of both sexes to look at our ship. Five Imperial officers were asked on board and entertained by Captain Campbell'.

> 13 July. 'Some fine ladies were invited on board.... and highly entertained they were, for they left the ship in high spirits and sung some fine airs in praise of our frigate'.

> 14 July. 'Ship's company busily employed cleaning ship's decks to a degree of whiteness that nothing of the kind could excel and getting ship in order for company'.

> 15 July. 'Several ladies came on board with Captain Campbell. The ship's crew were all clean to receive them. Shortly after, the English Consul and another English gentleman came on board. The quarter-deck was adorned with colours for their reception and they were highly entertained.... Captain Campbell invited some gentlemen on board who were alongside in a boat viewing the ship; they partook of good cheer. The elder ladies with two of their daughters returned at 6 p.m.; the rest remained on board until nearly 11 and had a few country dances... All our officers were pretty jovial'.

16 July. DART arrived with a captured trabacolo and a French cavalry officer on leave who had been captured on board it. 'He was on his arrival on board treated with the greatest respect... An Englishman (Mr Ayres) and his wife (a fine German lady) were invited on board'.

17 July. 'A number of people came on board out of curiosity to see the ship; as for boats full of people there were a vast number, some with bands of music on board them, while passengers on board others sung'.

18 July. Preparations were made on board UNITÉ for a grand ball. The ship was decorated with flags and tables were set out with 'delicious viands'; there were chandeliers and reflecting lamps, sofas, chairs etc. There were about sixty guests, 'an assemblage of female beauty and manly gracefulness'. 'The band played most excellent, the dance was kept up without intermission until 12 o'clock; during the dance the company were regaled with jellies, lemonade, fruit etc. The French officer (prisoner) shared in the entertainment and the English Consul's wife kindly condescended to dance with him and he acquitted himself with much good grace, although he danced in his boots. After dancing the company retired to supper. Afterwards some songs were sung... producing much laughter, the utmost harmony and good order prevailing. A gentleman played on a violin to a degree of excellence that all who heard him were in raptures.... At the conclusion of supper the company began heaving bits of bread, lemon peel, etc. at one another jocundly. I was told it was the German fashion. After supper they danced again, and continued at that diversion until 4 or 5 o'clock on Sunday, 19th, when they all returned on shore and tired enough the ladies were and had lost the rosy colour of their cheeks'. The ship's officers went on shore with them.

But the situation was soon to change dramatically. In late July 1807 news reached the Adriatic of the Tilsit meeting between Alexander of Russia and Napoleon on 25 June. Russia was no longer at war with France or an ally of Britain and its large fleet in the lower Adriatic was potentially hostile. Russia had furthermore agreed to hand over Corfu and the other Ionian islands at the entrance of the Adriatic to the French. Collingwood was concerned that Campbell and his squadron in the upper Adriatic could be in danger and called him down to the lower Adriatic and Ionian Sea. But the danger was more imagined than real. The Russian fleet was in poor condition. Most of it left the Mediterranean, although a part of it went to Trieste as unwelcome but tolerated guests of the Austrian government. They added yet another object for the vigilance of the British warships in the upper Adriatic.

It was during this period from July to December 1807 that Campbell's earlier activity in the upper Adriatic came under scrutiny. Complaints from the Austrians were forwarded by the Admiralty to Collingwood. Collingwood also heard disturbing reports from other sources. He wrote to Campbell in October 1807 that, while at Malta, he had heard of the frequent practice of some ships cruising in the Adriatic of selling small vessels and cargoes which were the property of the enemy; of compounding for money with the masters of neutral vessels detained for having enemy property on board; and of sending others to Corfu where they were disposed of without condemnation and due proof of the legality of the capture. Such proceedings were illegal and had to stop.

Collingwood had been directed by the Admiralty to call on Campbell to state his case concerning his interference with Austrian shipping, which included the specific instance of his having compelled an Austrian ship of the port of Lošinj, the GRAZIOSO, to convey timber to Malta without the consent of the owners. Campbell claimed that the island Lošinj, where the owners resided, had been ceded to France and was no longer Austrian (even if the French had not effectively taken it over and the locals still found it more convenient to sail their ships under Austrian colours). The owner of GRACIOSO had carried no Austrian papers.

Collingwood was prepared to accept and support Campbell's case in this particular instance, even though he obviously knew of other irregularities that he did not report to the Admiralty. For the time being Campbell was off the hook but like the proverbial cat he had lost a number of his lives and Collingwood would be more wary and less accommodating in future.

Campbell was not the only person being subjected to suspicious scrutiny. The Admiralty and Navy Board were having growing misgivings about the failure of Leard to be able to supply timber. On 30 October 1807 the Navy Board wrote to the Admiralty reviewing the situation.[20] According to the most recent information received from Leard, about 2, 800 loads of timber had been cut down, for which he had paid on account about £7700. However, it was clear that the political situation in the Adriatic had changed and there was little probability that any of the timber could be brought away, or that the continued residence of Leard in Rijeka could serve any purpose. It was therefore recommended that Leard be ordered to desist from any further proceedings and that he should be recalled from his mission. All the timber which had been cut down and which had partly been paid for was to be left in the charge of Adamić. The Admiralty agreed. As an after-thought, the Navy Board further recommended on 9 November that the Admiralty request the Foreign Office to cancel Leard's appointment as consul to Dubrovnik, and this also was agreed. In November 1807 orders were sent to Leard to return to England. The Navy Board must have been shocked and irritated when Leard only replied to their letter on 16 February 1807, to say that it was essential that he remain in Rijeka to protect the timber, and that otherwise the French would reap the benefit of all his work. Besides this a quarter of his income depended on his commission on the timber when it was eventually delivered. So, despite the Navy Board's instructions, Leard stayed in Rijeka, but sent Mr Sims, his clerk, to England with his accounts. This provoked the Navy Board to inform Leard by a letter of 6 June 1808, that if he chose to stay in Rijeka, it had to be at his own expense as his salary was terminated with effect from 1 June 1808. As will be seen, Leard was to totally disregard this communication.

Campbell with UNITÉ passed back into the Adriatic at the end of January 1808, with orders to keep watch on the construction of French warships in the Venice Arsenal and the Russian ships-of-the-line at Trieste. UNITÉ sailed to her old base at Lošinj, arriving in late February, and immediately began to seize local shipping. Campbell was still up to his old tricks concerning the disposal of the smaller less valuable craft for which he was reluctant to spare men to serve as prize crews to sail them to Malta for the Admiralty court to adjudicate on their capture and evaluate them for prize-money. Some were scuttled but a brig had to be ransomed by her owners for a considerable amount of money.

---

[20] NA, ADM 106/2242

Figure 15. Sir Robert Ardair (1763–1855), oil painting by
Thomas Gainsborough (Baltimore Museum of Art).

Events in 1808 and into early 1809 were increasingly dominated by Napoleon's involvement in the Iberian Peninsula. It was apparent to everybody, including Napoleon, that Austria was building up its forces and was likely to go to war with him again when it was ready or when his commitments in Spain presented them with a suitable opportunity. On the other hand, pressure from France and Russia forced neutral Austria, in March 1808, to break off diplomatic relations with Britain and send away Sir Robert Adair, the British Ambassador. (He left from Trieste on UNITÉ). This meant that it was more difficult for UNITÉ to continue the unofficial access to Trieste and Rijeka it had enjoyed for the disposal of its prizes. It also meant that it was impossible for Leard and Adamić to export any timber from Croatia.

The other development at this time was the appearance in the upper Adriatic of British privateers, or at least of ships that may have carried British Admiralty letters of marque to authorise them to attack enemy merchant shipping and without which any such activity would have been deemed simple piracy punishable by death. Many of the privateers were Maltese flying British colours, while others were Sicilian (Sicily was in effect under British protection). Combined with the prize-taking of the British warships, their activity was to have a serious effect on the trade of the Adriatic ports, including Rijeka.

In 1808, the French were beginning to take more effective steps to deny the British warships use of the islands or restricted coastal waters, by building batteries and gunboats. On earlier voyages to Trieste, the British had found a convenient anchorage at Umag but without being able to land in the French-held harbour. A far better anchorage and base for operations had been discovered the long fine harbour of Mali Lošinj. To make their movements in this area

Figure 16. The harbour of Mali Lošinj.

more secure, at the end of April 1807, the British had attacked and destroyed a small fort the French had built and manned with French soldiers on a neighbouring small island which the British called S. Pietro de Nimbo (Sveti Petar or possibly Ilovik)[21] which seems to have been built to defend the sea lanes to Zadar and into Kvarner. However, without the British being able to leave a warship or a sufficient force on land to defend it, Lošinj could easily be retaken by the French in the periods between the visits of the British ships.

A new Italian frigate, brig and schooner of war, recently built in the Venice Arsenal, which UNITÉ encountered off Pula on 2 May 1808 were on their way to Lošinj, to take possession of it and deny its use by the British. Even after UNITÉ had captured the brig and chased the frigate and schooner into Pula, the captain of the frigate or corvette was persistent in following his orders. Even while UNITÉ was still at Mali Lošinj, he came onto the island of Lošinj to keep watch on the British. During the absence of all the British ships, it was learnt in July that 500 enemy troops had taken Lošinj and were fortifying it. Napoleon himself had written to General Marmont in March to deplore certain depredations of the British at Veliki Lošinj and to propose that 80-100 Dalmatians be placed there to prevent the British cruisers from disembarking. It is therefore likely that the determined efforts of the French and Italians to secure Lošinj were the result of orders from Napoleon.

Campbell and UNITÉ were to remain in the Adriatic until February 1809 when they were finally withdrawn. He had been the senior officer in the upper Adriatic since 1806. Collingwood had received further evidence of Campbell's malpractices, which he could no longer tolerate. In the meantime, there was another new arrival in the Adriatic in summer 1808. This was to be William Hoste, captain of the frigate AMPHION, who was sent to join Campbell's squadron. He also was to become obsessed with prize money and to copy some of Campbell's practices.[22]

---

[21] British maps of the time are inaccurate and use the wrong names for a number of the smaller islands.
[22] For various reasons, Hoste's reputation has been considerably inflated. Although he was in temporary command of the small British squadron of frigates and brigs at the battle of Vis in 1811, for most of the period he spent in the Adriatic from 1807-14, he served under a succession of superior officers and was never promoted above the rank of captain.

Figure 17. Sir William Hoste, c. 1833 by
William Greatbach.

The War of 1809

Napoleon's invasion in Spain in March 1808 had led to a popular general uprising of the Spaniards against the French in May, which in turn necessitated the commitment of large French forces and Napoleon's personal involvement in autumn 1808. His difficulties encouraged the Austrians to prepare for war and to negotiate with the British government from the middle of 1808, particularly for a large subsidy once Austrian military preparations were completed in March 1809.

Leard in Rijeka involved in helping the communications between the Austrians (and Count Hardenberg the ambassador of Hanover at Vienna who was mediating) and the British. Knowing how things were developing, he anticipated the outbreak of war by writing to the Navy Board on 1 March 1809. Ignoring their letters of 1807 and 1808, in which they had first ordered his return to England and then terminated his employment, he now announced that as the political situation was changing and that Austrian ports would soon be reopened to the British, he proposed to take up the question of the exportation of timber from where the French invasion of 1805 had forced it to be abandoned.

Leard enclosed a statement of how things had been left in 1805 with the amounts paid to Adamić between 4 November 1804 and 13 November 1805 on account towards the supply of 30,000 oak trees from military and private forests in Croatia and Slavonia. There were 3000 loads of timber, 500 of which had been cut down, sided and brought out of the forests to a deposit at Karlovac, while another 2500 had been cut down but left in the forests. For these Leard had paid Adamić on account, at different rates, £4160. But he had also made advance payment to Adamić of £7200 at the rate of 3 forints per tree for 30,000 trees. This was

30

eventually to be recovered from Adamić at the same rate per tree from the final payment for every load when they were eventually delivered to the place of shipment.

Leard, furthermore, claimed that he had been authorised to advance another £5000 to Adamić to cover the initial costs of establishments on the New Road. These included a stable and a timberyard at Karlovac near the New Road and the river Kupa, another timberyard at the port of Bakar, and 12 timber carriages. 24 horses had been bought but, when the French had invaded in December 1805, they had been sold and Adamić had given credit for these in his account with Leard. The balance of the £5000 that now needed to be advanced to Adamić was for three more stables on the New Road and another at the place of shipment. The £5000 were also to be recovered from Adamić by a deduction of 3 forints from the final payment of each load of timber delivered to the place of shipment. These payments to Adamić on account therefore totalled £16, 360 (over 200, 000 forints).

Leard now proposed, as soon as the Austrian ports were reopened and permission for exportation of the timber could be secured, that the 3000 loads should all be sided and brought down to the coast as soon as possible to prevent the timber decaying. Leard asked the Navy Board to arrange for ships to take it away. He was optimistic that the war would go well for the Austrians.

Austria did not declare war on France until 6 April 1809, followed within days by three advances by Austrian armies; the first under Archduke Charles into Bavaria; the second under Archduke John into northern Italy, and a third under General Stoissevich which crossed from the military borderland of Croatia into Dalmatia on 20 April. The war was to pass with remarkable

Figure 18A. Eugène de Beauharnais, c.1802–1804, oil painting by François Gérard.

Figure 18B. Auguste de Marmont (1774–1852), oil painting by Jean-Baptiste Paulin Guérin.

speed. Napoleon counter-attacked in Germany and drove back Archduke Charles, entering Vienna on 13 May. In northern Italy Napoleon's regent, his son-in-law, Eugene Beauharnais, had initially to retreat before Archduke John. But news of the French advance to Vienna led Archduke join to fall back into Hungary, with Eugene advancing behind him. In Dalmatia, the French commander, General Marmont, while holding back the Austrian advance collected the bulk of his forces in Zara, leaving small garrisons in the other fortified places.

In the Adriatic, the Austrian ports of Trieste and Rijeka were declared open to the British and the Austrians attacked the French garrisons in Istria (Hoste on AMPHION heard the Austrian cannons at Koper on 12 April). Pending the arrival of a stronger squadron of ships-of-the-line, the small force of frigates and brigs at the head of the Adriatic was reinforced and put under the command of Captain Jahleel Brenton, who arrived at Trieste with Lord Bathurst, the new British ambassador to Vienna on 18 April.[23] They were to watch Venice and the Russian warships at Trieste, and to check any attempts by the French to transport troops over the Adriatic. The Austrians were worried that Marmont's forces at Zadar might be ferried across to reinforce Eugene in Italy. The British squadron was also to assist the small Austrian squadron at Trieste, which was still under the command of Major General Count L'Espine. At the request of the Austrians, Brenton sent Hoste in AMPHION to cruise between Rijeka and Zadar to watch the French and to cooperate with General Stoissevich. Without difficulty the Austrians retook the islands: Krk on 6 May, Cres on 8 May. Brenton on his frigate SPARTAN made contact with the Austrians on Cres and ferried Lieutenant Colonel Peharnik and his troops to attack and capture Mali Lošinj on 9-10 May, despite resistance from a French garrison in new fortifications. The Austrians and British had regained a valuable base for further operations.

At about this time, according to Leard, Adamić tried to go to Vienna to obtain permission to export the timber, but news that Vienna had fallen and that the Austrian government had withdrawn to Buda, forced him to return.[24] Worse was to follow. As Archduke John withdrew towards Hungary, part of Eugene's French army advancing after him entered Trieste on 17 May. To the annoyance of Hoste and the other British captains, all of the prize vessels they had left there fell into the hands of the French. The small Austrian squadron at Trieste, consisting of two brigs and nine gunboats was able to extricate itself, moving first to Piran, and then, protected by British frigates, took refuge in Mali Lošinj, together with a large number of Austrian merchant ships. On 26 May, Captain Brenton on SPARTAN at Mali Lošinj wrote to Admiral Collingwood to report on developments. The Austrians were sending troops and gunboats to Senj on the coast of the mainland south of Rijeka. From the latest information, Marmont was closed up in Zadar.

However, hearing of Eugene's advance in Italy, Marmont at Zadar, instead of trying to cross the Adriatic, now moved to join his forces with those of Eugene, starting a lightening advance to the north on 14 May, easily breaking through the Austrian lines. Advancing on the inland road via Gospić and Otočac, but finding that the road to Karlovac was more heavily defended, he marched down to the sea at Senj and then up the coast towards Rijeka.

---

[23] Brenton's involvement in the events of 1809 is recounted in Memoirs of Life and Services of Vice-Admiral Sir Jahleel Brenton, ed. Henry Raikes, 1846
[24] The story of the activity of Leard and Adamić throughout 1809 is in the petition that Leard was to send to the Foreign Office in November 1811, now in manuscript collection of National Maritime Museum, Greenwich (NMM).

Figure 19. Admiral William Hargood (1726–1839),
oil painting by Frederick Richard Say.

On 26 May, Leard received a letter from the governor of Rijeka, Guiseppe di Klobuzistry, who still addressed him as British consul to the by now defunct republic of Ragusa. Because of the enemy advance, the Austrian authorities were removing government property from Trieste, Rijeka and Senj to the islands of Kvarner, only recently retaken from the French. The governor invited Leard to go with the Austrians taking refuge there and to mediate with the commander of the British squadron to give them protection and help in supplying them with food. At the time of the letter, Leard reckoned that Marmont's troops were already at Bakar, only five miles away. He left that same day with the last of the ships from Rijeka for Mali Lošinj, where he found that L'Espine had arrived the night before with some militia and artillery hastily withdrawn from Senj. There were also as many as 150 merchant vessels from Trieste and Rijeka.

On 28 May Captain Hargood arrived at Lošinj with three British ships-of-the-line ordered to the upper Adriatic by Admiral Collingwood in early April because of fears that the Russian ships-of-the-line in Trieste might decide to fight on the French side, and Leard was given assurances that the British ships would protect and support the Austrians. Hargood sailed on to Trieste in early July with the ships-of-the-line and the frigates, as commodore of the largest British naval force that had yet entered the Adriatic. But it was too late. The Russian warships withdrew into the inner harbour of Trieste under the protection of the batteries, now controlled by the French.

Leard and L'Espine at Mali Lošinj received news from Rijeka; firstly that Archduke Charles had won a victory over Napoleon an 21-22 May at Aspern-Essling on the Danube near Vienna; secondly that Marmont had left Rijeka on 1 June to march north to Ljubljana. L'Espine and Leard returned to Rijeka with 700 militia escorted by the British brig IMOGEN, and Austrian brig of war and 5 gunboats. They found that the governor had been arrested and left locked up, that the French had taken away property to the value of a million forints. Marmont had left his sick and wounded in Rijeka (including two generals, a colonel and several other officers) but had taken hostages to prevent them being killed by the country people. L'Espine now made them prisoners-of-war. Leard also found that a French colonel and four other officers, who had been billeted in his house, had obliged the person he had left in charge of it to provide them food for seven days, and on leaving had taken stores of food and wine and other valuables, having broken furniture and other property. He estimated the losses and damage at £150.

The recovery of Rijeka also meant that the British could deliver to the Austrians part of the large subsidy that had been promised. The loss of Trieste and the temporary loss of Rijeka to the French had given the British ambassador, Lord Bathurst, considerable concern that he would be able to deliver it. But he now sent Lord Walpole to Rijeka. In June the frigate LEONIDAS delivered a quarter of a million pounds sterling in silver. In July the brigs MINORCA and WEAZLE brought one and a half million dollars in silver bars.

Figure 20A. Benjamin Bathurst, British diplomat (1784–1809) (unknown artist).

Figure 20B. Archduke Charles of Austria (1771–1847) (by Jean-Baptiste Isabey, Louvre).

But again it was too late. Eugene, now reinforced by Marmont, had advanced to northern Hungary where he defeated Archduke John at Raab (or Gyor) on 14 June, before moving north up the Danube to join Napoleon for his decisive victory over the Austrians at Wagram on 5-6 July. Archduke Charles signed an armistice with the French on 14 July, after which peace negotiations dragged on until October.

In the meantime, Commodore Hargood and his squadron in the upper Adriatic was having a frustrating time in his dealings with L'Espine. After helping him to reoccupy Rijeka, the ships-of-the-line cruised between Venice and Trieste waiting to collaborate with L'Espine in an attack on Trieste. But on 2 July L'Espine informed Hargood that the attack on Trieste was deferred, as he did not have enough troops to hold it, and proposed an attack on Zadar. He then changed his plans repeatedly, asking Hargood to return to Trieste, then to Rijeka, and then to Trieste again. Soon after Hargood discovered that L'Espine had withdrawn towards Ljubljana.

After the armistice Leard and Adamić decided to go to the Austrian government, now at Buda, to seek permission to export the oak timber. The journey took from 25 August until 15 September.[25] On the way they visited the army camp of Archduke John, who assured them that he was preparing a force to go to defend the Adriatic coast, in the likely event of hostilities recommencing, and that he had replaced the ineffective L'Espine (whom Leard suspected of treachery). At Buda, Lord Bathurst gave similar reassurances that the Adriatic coast would not be surrendered by the Austrians to the French. Having obtained permission to export the timber, Leard and Adamić returned to Karlovac, but heavy rain, which had flooded the low land north of Karlovac, led to further delay.

In the upper Adriatic, it was now clear that the continued presence of Hargood and the ships-of-the-line was serving no purpose and they were recalled to the blockade of Toulon. Before leaving, the squadron was at Rijeka about 25 September. (Adamić was later to claim that he had provided Hargood with supplies and information).[26] As Brenton with SPARTAN had already left in early June, Hoste, who was on shore in Rijeka recovering from fever in the house of a family of Flemings,[27] was left in charge with his frigate AMPHION and the brig ACORN.

Austria signed the humiliating peace of Vienna (Schonbrunn) on 14 October, which included the surrender of Trieste, Rijeka and Croatia west of the Sava. (They were to be absorbed, along with Istria, Dalmatia and Dubrovnik, within Napoleon's Illyrian Provinces). On 4 November L'Espine summoned Hoste to a meeting in Rijeka to inform him that two general officers had arrived to put the treaty into effect and to stop all further relations with the British. The port was to be closed to the British in readiness for its delivery to the French. Hoste gained a few days by demanding notice in writing, giving himself time to embark all the British property. However, when he sailed away on 7 November, he retaliated against the Austrians by seizing a brig of war and 2 gunboats, rather than leaving them to be handed over to the French. He would only allow them to sail to Malta or Sicily. He forced them to accompany him to

---

[25] The exact dates are known from the claim Leard was to make in 1812 to the Navy Board for their travelling expenses.
[26] NA, FO 7/112, Adamić-Foreign Office, 30 Jan. 1814
[27] In a letter dated 23 April 1810, Hoste was to write that he had passed past Rijeka and signalled the family of friends. The ladies who had nursed him waved back with their handkerchiefs.

Mali Lošinj where their Austrian officers sold them to Maltese merchants. Their cannon and military stores were sent to Kraljevica, where the last two brigs of the Austrian navy were sold to American merchants.[28]

Leard was sent news of the peace by Lord Bathurst, and warned by the governor of Rijeka that the French had put a price on his head, he went on board a ship at Rijeka five days after the news arrived. Four days later communications with the shore were forbidden, and he was unable to settle his affairs or take away all his possessions before having to leave.

Leard also claimed that a party of French soldiers was sent to Kastel, about 40 miles from Rijeka to Karlovac and about half way to the forests where the timber had been cut, where he had stayed several times (between 1805-09) to be out of the way of enemy troop movements to and from Dalmatia, and also for managing the business of the timber. These soldiers burned and destroyed all the furniture, and his stock, books, papers, mathematical instruments and other property to the value of £750. The French also sequestered and disposed of his house and garden in Rijeka, which he valued at £1150.

Travels 1810-12

From 1810-12, the story of the British navy in the Adriatic largely concerns the story of its use of the island of Vis, the attempts of the French to drive them away from it, and the measures taken by the British to defend it and ultimately to garrison it in April 1812.[29] Vis was the base from which the British continued to watch French attempts to build new warships and put them to sea from the Venice Arsenal. It was also the base for British navy cruisers, together with a growing number of privateers, to attack enemy trade along the coast of the new Illyrian Provinces. Moreover, a new emphasis was placed on smuggling British manufactured goods and colonial produce from the eastern Mediterranean, through the Adriatic and the Ottoman Balkans, to the markets of the Austrian empire and beyond. Although, in general, the French authorities attempted to maintain the continental blockade against the importation of British goods, the shortages of various products in the territories under their control often led them to condone or even collude in the illegal contraband traffic.

John Leard appears to have gone to Malta, where he persuaded one of the British navy commissioners to use his services to procure timber from Turkish Albania in 1810-11.

In Rijeka, Adamić, as one of richest and most important merchants, was soon involved in the chamber of commerce established by the French,[30] who were soon seeking his help. Adamić was given the important concession of farming the state monopoly of salt in the Illyrian Provinces. In a contract of April 1810 concluded between himself and the governor-general, Marmont, Adamić was engaged to supply the state with over one and a half million litres of salt.[31] But supplies from local and continental sources had to be supplemented with salt from overseas, the supply of which was controlled by the British. It was under these circumstances that General Bertrand, the new governor-general of the Illyrian Provinces in 1811, even

---

[28] NA, ADM 1/415 Collingwood-Admiralty, 29 Dec. 1809
[29] The author of this research has written about the British occupation of Vis elsewhere.
[30] See Žic, op cit.
[31] See Pevec-Stele, op. cit, p. 226

Figure 21. Croatia 1809–13.

allowed Adamić to enter into negotiations with the British. The main questions concerning Adamić's dealings with the British concern the extent to which he used the opportunity to advance other business interests which the French would not have welcomed, and the extent to which he became a British secret agent and involved in what the French would have considered treasonable activity.

After the war of 1809, a British diplomatic agent called Johnson had been left in Vienna to establish a secret network of agents and to liaise with discontented elements in the Austrian court and army. Napoleon had insisted that a large number of officers serving in the Austrian army, who came from other countries with which he was at war or which were hostile to him, such as Savoyards from the kingdom of Sardinia, should be dismissed from the service. Prominent among these was a senior officer of Irish origin, Laval Nugent, who was well connected at court. Johnson and Nugent started to secretly recruit other dismissed officers and to send them across the Ottoman provinces to the Adriatic, from where they went on to Sicily to serve under Lord William Bentinck, the commander-in-chief of the British armies in the Mediterranean. Nugent himself passed backwards and forwards between Vienna, Sicily and London, on secret missions to negotiate Austria's eventual re-entry into war against Napoleon and to secure British support for an insurrection in the Illyrian Provinces. British agents were also to negotiate with the prince-bishop or vladika of Montenegro to encourage

Figure 22. General Henri Bertrand (1773–1844)
(unknown artist).

him to attack the French in the area of the Boka Kotorska. The principal go-between was to be Colonel Danese, a Dalmatian who had served the Venetians, Austrians and French before being involved in an insurrection against the French in Dalmatia in 1809, after which he had fled into Bosnia and then became one of Johnson's agents.

One of the earliest indications that both Leard and Adamić were involved in the secret network is given in a long letter which Danese in Scutari (Skohdra or Skadar, just within Ottoman Albania near Montenegro and French-held territory around the Boka Kotorska) wrote in coded Italian on 25 December 1811 to Johnson in Vienna.[32] Danese had arrived there at the end of November after a long and difficult journey via Slavonski Brod and Sarajevo, with the object of going on either to Vis, Malta or Sicily. He reported to Johnson on the situation he had found at Scutari and what he had heard there. This included news from the neighbouring pashalik to the south which included Durazzo, where Leard had been caused much trouble because of the intrigues of Breujer, the French consul in Scutari, and had been violently forced to depart. Also that Adamić had gone to London but would soon return to Malta. Danese did not need to identify Adamić, so it can be assumed that he was already known to Johnson, and the inclusion of the reference to him in the letter suggests that he was of interest to Danese and Johnson for reasons other than his trading activity. The most conclusive evidence of Adamić's complicity, however, was in his own later admission that, during the French occupation of

---

[32] Decoded into Italian, the letter is in the Fremantle collection (BRO).

Figure 23A. Laval Nugent (1777–1862) (unknown artist, Trsat Castle, Rijeka).

Figure 23B. William Bentinck (1774–1839), by C.H. Gifford.

Rijeka, he had supplied important information, and assisted Johnson with letters, messengers and passengers.[33]

Having had to leave Albania, by November 1811 Leard was back in London, where he petitioned the Foreign Office for compensation for his losses in 1809. He also had the temerity to send claims for payment for his services and detailed accounts to the Admiralty. These were received by the Admiralty on 4 January 1812 and passed on to the Navy Board, which then appears to have set up a special committee to examine in detail Leard's claims against both the Foreign office (passed on to the Admiralty) and themselves.[34]

In its final report to the Admiralty of 27 April 1812, the Navy Board tried to be fair to Leard. He could not be blamed for the various political changes and the delays in the construction of the Louisa road. On the other hand, none of the timber had ever been delivered, although Leard had advanced a very considerable amount of money to Adamić and was now claiming £900 as his own commission (which in 1804 had been estimated would be about £600 a year in addition to his salary of £400). Leard had disregarded their orders to wind up the business and return home in 1807 and their subsequent decision to terminate his salary from 1 June 1808. His claim for his losses in 1809 had been after the termination by the Foreign Office (at the request of the Navy Board) of his consulship. Nor did they see why Leard should be compensated for the loss of his house in Rijeka, which, in their view, he should never have bought.

In an item by item examination of Leard's accounts, the Navy Board disallowed many, particularly those concerning expenses after 1 June 1808. It proposed further investigation of

---

[33] NA, FO 7/112, 30 Jan 1814, Adamić-Castlereagh
[34] Taken together, the petition to the Foreign Office, the Navy Board's notes and their report to Admiralty of 25 April 1812 constitute a primary source for the story of the timber project from 1803-11. The former are in the NMM, the latter in NA, ADM 106/2257).

some items, including the question of Captain Campbell's prize money for timber, and a fine that the French had imposed on Adamić, presumably for his involvement in the timber project, of £200. When Leard had been sent to procure timber in Albania in 1810-11, the commissioner in Malta had authorised Leard to draw on the Navy Board up to £2500, but he had used this to make himself back payments of his salary, lodging and expenses from 1 June 1808 until 31 March 1810, even though he was paid £400 a year for his services in Albania in 1810, as well as commission on the timber delivered. Not surprisingly the Navy Board did not consider that Leard had served them well or deserved compensation. If anything, he owed them money.

Quite surprisingly, on 27 April, the Admiralty decided to pay Leard his commission on the 3000 loads of timber that had been cut but not delivered, but all claims for costs after 1 June 1808 were to be refused. Whatever other balances due from Leard were to be recovered if possible[35] Even though Leard continued to lobby them for more, the Admiralty was probably prepared to make this payment to Leard so as to keep him out of the new contract that they had just negotiated directly with Adamić, which they fully expected would result in the delivery of the timber for which Leard was claiming his commission.

Evidence concerning Adamić's movements and activity in 1811-12 can be pieced together from a variety of sources.[36]

It is known that Adamić had left Rijeka by November 1811. His absence was noted in the records of the chamber of commerce, and in correspondence between General Bertrand, the governor-general of the Illyrian provinces, and Napoleon concerning the development of dockyards at Trieste and the construction of warships there (Adamić was named as the only merchant capable of contracting for this). All the evidence indicates that Bertrand had authorised Adamić to go to Malta, or even to London, to negotiate with the British to allow him to import salt.

In fact, Adamić had already arrived in Malta by early September 1811. The British merchants of Malta were involved in the very profitable business of sending British manufactured goods and colonial produce through Salonika and the Ottoman provinces in the Balkans, via Sarajevo and Slavonski Brod, to the Austrian empire and beyond. Adamić was later to claim that he had himself been the first to be involved in the establishment of this trade through Turkey, and that after 1809 he had established a branch of his business in Malta under his son-in-law.[37] He clearly knew of, and was engaged in promoting the new possibilities that the island of Vis had to offer. The chairman of the committee of British merchants of Malta, Jameson Hunter, had already, in April 1811, been pointing out to the British authorities on Malta the importance of the contraband trade to the Adriatic coasts, which was only possible if the British secured Vis by sending a garrison there.[38] The committee had received information about the island not only from captains Campbell and Hoste, but also from Leard, who had recently been there. Hunter also recommended that vessels from enemy ports could be given British licences to bring goods to Vis, including hemp, cordage spars etc., and smuggle back from Vis to the

---

[35] NA, ADM 1/156, 98.2
[36] Including the records of the chamber of commerce in Rijeka, which recorded his long absence from Rijeka. See Æic, op. cit.
[37] NA, FO 7/112, 30 Jan. 1814, Adamić-Castlereagh.
[38] NA, ADM 1/4698, letter dated 25 April 1811

mainland contraband British and colonial goods which the Maltese merchants would take there.

On 14 September 1811, Hunter petitioned the British civil commissioner on Malta, General Oakes, on Adamić's behalf.[39] Adamić had arrived at Malta in order to lay the foundation of a very extensive commerce with the ports in the possession of the enemy and needed licences from the British for this purpose. British regulations (Orders in Council) of March 1809 had permitted ships to go to enemy ports provided at least two thirds of their cargo <u>by volume</u> consisted of British or British colonial produce. Hunter argued that the authorities in Malta should not enforce this rigorously, but allow licences for vessels carrying two thirds of their cargoes in British goods <u>by value</u>. This would facilitate the proposed commerce by enabling Hunter to select those of the ports of the enemy where the continental blockade against British goods was less rigorously enforced. Hunter expected to dispatch within the following six months 100 British or Maltese vessels of 200-300 tons with British goods, valued at no less than half a million scudos, which would be smuggled into enemy territory. The value of the goods exported and those imported (naval stores and grain) would probably yield 150,000 scudos in customs duties at Malta, without taking into account further customs duties on goods sent on to England.

The full significance of Hunter's proposals and their relevance to Adamić become clearer after General Oakes wrote on 2 November to the Colonial Office in London enclosing Hunter's petition, and informing them that Adamić, not having been able to resolve his business in Malta, was proceeding to London and would be the bearer of the letter, which at Adamić's request, explained his mission. The Colonial Office referred the questions raised by Oakes's letter and Hunter's petition to the Board of Trade, which responded on 23 January 1812.[40] Insofar as Adamić wished to have licences to export salt from Sicily to the Illyrian Provinces, application had to be made to the Sicilian government. As far as licences to export or relay goods from Malta to enemy ports was concerned, the authorities in Malta could grant such licences on condition that two thirds of the cargo in bulk consisted of British goods, while the remaining third could consist of goods produced or manufactured in either friendly countries or even enemy countries, if these had been imported to Malta via another British port. As had already been clear to General Oakes, it was apparent that Adamić's real purpose was to export salt from Sicily. As Sicily was a friendly country (it was under British protection), it was covered by this last condition. The Board of Trade agreed that the two thirds and third of cargo could be calculated according to value rather than by bulk. This meant that more salt, which was more bulky but less valuable than other goods, could be carried in any vessels that Adamić might employ to bring it to the Illyrian provinces. But he would have to win the agreement of the French authorities, either publicly or covertly, to let the British goods enter the ports of the Illyrian provinces in defiance of Napoleon's Continental System (to impose which on Russia, the emperor was preparing his famous 1812 campaign). It is unlikely that Bertrand, in allowing Adamić to negotiate the importation of salt, had envisaged that it would be at the cost of such a large breach in the continental blockade of British goods. It is more likely that Adamić was prepared to smuggle the British goods, either in the same ships

---

[39] NA, CO 158/17
[40] NA, BT 3/11

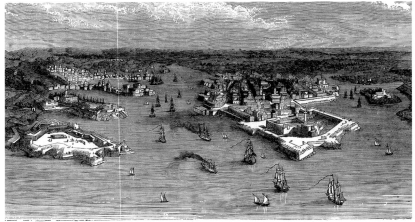

VIEW OF THE TOWN AND FORTIFICATIONS OF THE ISLAND OF MALTA.

Figure 24. The fortifications of Valletta, Malta, illustration from *L'Illustration*, 575 (XXIII), March 4, 1854.

Figure 25. Malta, the entrance to Valletta (Museum of the Order of St John).

bringing the salt, or relayed in other vessels from Vis. In either case, although there were risks, large profits could be made.

In addition to the letter he had been given by General Oakes, Adamić was given another letter of introduction dated Malta 12 October 1811 by the somewhat eccentric commander of the British navy schooner ORTENSIA, a Lieutenant E. Blaquiere, addressed to Wellesley, the secretary of state for foreign affairs.[41] Repeating information which had probably been given him by Adamić, and which Adamić could confirm, he claimed that the French were building warships in an arsenal they had established in the Ombla at Dubrovnik using timber from Albania. (The fact that John Leard in London wrote to the Foreign Office on 23 November to report the same intelligence, suggests the possibility that Adamić had arrived in London by

---

[41] NA, FO 70/45

that date, that they had met, and Adamić had given Leard the same information. On the other hand, Leard claimed he had received it by letter from a gentleman who had recently arrived at Malta from Albania.[42] The fact that the letter brought by Adamić to the Colonial Office from General Oakes was only passed on to the Board of Trade on 2 January 1812, would indicate that he arrived in London towards the end of December 1811).

The other information in Blaquiere's letter, all of which could be confirmed by Adamić, concerned the political and military situation in the Adriatic, the need to fortify Vis, the possibility of the Montenegrins attacking the French in support of an insurrection at the Boka Kotorska, and the problem of the acts of piracy and violence committed by Maltese privateers. A number of vessels laden with naval stores for Malta had been kept in port in the Adriatic for fear of their being seized by these privateers. (Could they have belonged to Adamić?) Other privateers had committed robbery and rape on the island Lošinj. It is probable that Blaguiere had received much if not all of this information from Adamić (who was later to claim in his own defence that he had persuaded the British to stop the activity of the privateers).

In January 1812, soon after his arrival in London, Adamić was in touch with the Foreign Office to tell them that Austria wanted trade with England via the Adriatic and the Black Sea. Zagreb, Slavonski Brod, and Semlin (near Belgrade) and Alt Orsova on the Danube would be made free Austrian ports. The Foreign Office wrote immediately to Vienna to ask their officer there to check this with the Austrian government.[43]

The Timber Contract of 1812

The other subject that Adamić was now to raise with the British government was the vexed question of the oak timber for the British navy. General Bertrand was unlikely to have sanctioned this (any more than the provision of political and military intelligence or the smuggling of British contraband goods), although General Oakes had suggested in his letter of 2 November 1811 that Adamić had suggested to him that a deal could be made with the French if the British made concessions over the supply of salt.

The contract between the Navy Board and Adamić of 12 March 1812 cannot be traced, but its terms can be reconstructed from correspondence concerning it both from that time and later. The Navy Board had advanced large sums of money through Leard to Adamić and had an obvious interest in ensuring that they saw some return for it. In 1807, when they instructed Leard to return to England, they had told him to leave the timber in Adamić's care. They clearly saw the value in having direct dealings with Adamić rather than through the mediation of Leard, who was excluded from the negotiations.

According to the calculations of the Navy Board accountants, the net amount advanced to Adamić was £12,192. This was now to be recovered from him by deductions of £2 per load of timber from the agreed price per load whenever the Navy Board's officers in Malta paid him for the cargoes delivered there, until the whole of the debt was liquidated. The Navy

---

[42] NMM, Rowley papers. Adamić was to propose that some of the timber he was to provide the British navy should come from Albania, and this, together with the fact that Danese on his arrival in Albania heard that Adamić had gone to England, reinforces the suspicion that Adamić had visited Albania and that he was Leard's informant.
[43] NA, FO 7/99, Foreign Office-King, 24 Jan. 1812

Figure 26A & B. Somerset House; the Navy Board occupied the south wing. A. aquatint by Samuel Ireland, 1791. B. engraving for Dugdale's *England and Wales Delineated* (1845).

Figure 27. The courtyard of Somerset House, by Thomas Rowlandson and Auguste Charles Pugin.

Board also inserted a penalty clause to the effect that, if Adamić was unable to provide enough timber to pay off the entire debt, they reserved the right to send agents to take possession of the timber that had been cut, and of the grounds, stables, carts which had been purchased with the money advanced to him, up to the value of whatever balance remained.[44]

It is clear from the correspondence that some the timber in question, which Leard was obligated to take possession of and deliver, was that which had been cut in the forests near Karlovac, now in French-controlled territory, although the Navy Board letters confusingly refer to it as being in Slavonia. Some later correspondence refers to timber in the forests of Croatia, Slavonia and Carniola, and there can be some doubt as to what exact areas they were talking about. There must be some doubt as to whether Adamić could have hoped to export timber from the Illyrian Provinces, with either the agreement or complicity of the French authorities there. (It is clear from later developments that they did not approve). The Louisa road had finally been completed in December 1811, with the agreement of the French authorities, by the Hungarian society that had started it, making it easier to move timber down to the coast.[45] But Adamić was definitely considering other possibilities, less subject to agreement by the French. One was Turkish Albania, where Leard had been procuring timber in 1810, and which there is evidence that Adamić himself visited in 1811. The other possibility which Adamić was definitely considering was that of supplying timber from what is actually Slavonia, which were then in Austrian Croatia, by transporting it down the Danube and via the Black Sea.[46] (Later references in Navy Board correspondence, to Adamić having had establishments both at Karlovac and Slavonski Brod, suggests that timber was taken down the Sava to the Danube).[47]

Before the contract was signed, in a letter 4 March 1812,[48] the Navy Board informed the Admiralty that it had accepted Adamić's proposals, which were summarised as being to deliver the timber procured in Croatia and Slavonia, with a quantity of masts, to the naval arsenal at Malta, by transporting it via the Danube and the Black Sea; and also to supply the arsenal

Figure 28A. Somerset House: stairs leading to the Navy Boardroom.

Figure 28B. West India Dock for sugar & colonial crops, by Thomas Rowlandson and Auguste Charles Pugin (Metropolitan Museum).

[44] NA, ADM 106/2266, Navy Board-Admiralty, 17 Feb. 1815
[45] Pivec-Stele, op. cit., pp. 85-91
[46] NA, FO 7/112, Leard-Foreign Office, 29 July 1814, enclosing Adamić-Leard, 28 July 1814
[47] NA, ADM 106/2266, Navy Board-Admiralty, 17 Feb. 1815
[48] ADM 106/2256, Navy Board-Admiralty

Figure 29. The Rhinebeck Panorama, showing London between 1806 and 1811 (Museum of London).

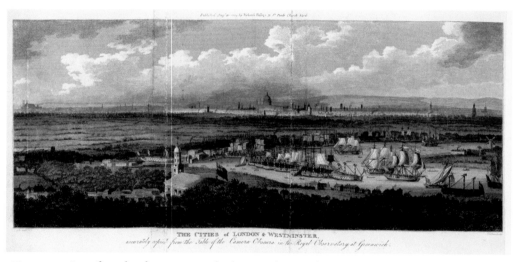

Figure 30. View of London from Greenwich, showing the Deptford Dock Yards, 1809 (Royal Museums, Greenwich).

with timber and other naval stores from Albania and the coasts of the Adriatic. Lord Bentinck (commander-in-chief of the British armies in the Mediterranean and ambassador to the court of Sicily) was to be asked to grant Adamić licences for any vessels from Sicily that he might employ to take Sicilian (salt) and British produce to Goro (Grado?) in Italy and other ports on the formerly Austrian and Albanian coasts, and to return to Malta with Italian and Illyrian produce, consisting of hemp, timber, spars or plank, and, for appearance, some corn, rice, silk quicksilver (mercury) and cream of tartar(!). (This was presumably to allay the suspicions of the French, although it was clearly difficult if nor impossible to load and unload supplies of timber in secrecy). The officers commanding the British Squadron in the Adriatic and at Vis were to be instructed to give protection to this traffic and allow passes to the small craft and fishing boats of under 50 tons coming under whatever flags from Italy or Illyria with (clearly smuggled) naval stores, provisions etc.

The Admiralty consulted the Board of Trade on the question of licences. It was advised that, while the governor of Malta had full powers to grant them to enable Adamić to fulfil his contact with the Navy Board, it was not recommended to grant licences from Sicily. So it would seem that, after all, Adamić may not have been given any help by the British government in London to take salt from Sicily to the Illyrian Provinces. The Admiralty, however, did ask the Foreign Office on 22 March 1812 to instruct Liston, the British ambassador to Constantinople, to use his influence with the Ottoman authorities to facilitate the export of timber from Albania. The Foreign Office, no doubt realising how little control the Ottoman government had over the local pashas in Albania, wrote the same day to Spiridion Foresti, their Greek representative in the Ionian islands, to ask him to seek protection for Adamić from the powerful Ali Pasha of Joannina, and also from Ibrahim Bey (pasha of Scutari) and Caplan Pasha (pasha of Croja, whose territories included Durazzo and Tirana).[49] By an interesting coincidence, their letter probably crossed with one to them from Foresti dated 30 March 1812, in which he informed them that a new channel for trade had been opened up by agents of trading houses in Vienna to take British goods disembarked at Durazzo overland to Austria and Germany.[50] It is possible that Adamić was involved.[51]

Adamić's Return to Rijeka, 1812

Adamić was later to claim that he was away in England for two years.[52] The evidence indicates that he was away from Rijeka for at least a year, perhaps a year and a half. The next items found in British archives are two letters from Adamić to Lord William Bentinck, the commander-in-chief of the British armies in the Mediterranean and ambassador to the court of Sicily (which was under British protection).[53] Both are in Adamić's own handwriting, in Italian and difficult to read or interpret in isolation

The first is dated Palermo 21 July 1812. It must be presumed that Adamić had returned from England to Sicily to pursue his negotiations to export Sicilian salt to the Illyrian Provinces. The letter thanked Bentinck for a note he had sent him the previous day and a letter to recommend him to the British commander at Vis (British troops had finally been sent to garrison the island at the end of April 1812). He was writing on the delicate matter of the queen of Sicily (a daughter of the empress Maria Theresia, whose intrigues had made her an embarrassment to Bentinck and the British government) and pleaded her cause, regretting the difficulties that had arisen.

Adamić's second letter to Bentinck was written on 6 August 1812 from Vis, where he had just arrived in time to meet Admiral Fremantle who was on the point of leaving the island on a cruise. Adamić had been in Albania, where he had found considerable British trade. The pashas of Scutari and Durazzo wanted a British consular office to facilitate this trade.

---

[49] NA, FO 42/13.
[50] idem
[51] See below for Adamić's letter to Bentinck, 6 Aug. 1812
[52] NA, FO 7/112, Adamić-Foreign Office, 30 Jan. 1814
[53] UN, Portland collection

Admiral Fremantle was aware of this and had praised Danese, who was representing British interests in Albania until such time as Bentinck might appoint a consul. The rest of the letter concerned a certain Mr Stolz,[54] who had been able to pass through Turkish territory with no difficulty from the Turkish customs officials in bringing out weapons. Adamić had asked that Danese be charged with their delivery to an armed British ship and with the supervision of the timber that was to be delivered to Malta. It is not clear where the weapons were coming from or where they were to be taken, although there is a hint in a letter from King, a British diplomatic agent in Vienna (who was later to be implicated in a plot to cause an insurrection in the Illyrian Provinces)[55] to the Foreign office in September 1811, concerning the availability for purchase of 200,000 stand of arms (muskets), and that he should be able to arrange for the shipment of 50,000 from Durazzo or Salonika.[56]

This letter, Adamić's presence on Vis, and the question of the arms must be put in context. Not only had the British garrisoned Vis in April 1812, but news of the possibility of in insurrection against the French in the area of the Boka Kotorska, with support from the Montenegrins, had brought Admiral Fremantle to Vis at the beginning of July with a strong expeditionary force to assist any such attack on the French. However, having sent Colonel Danese to Scutari to liaise with the Montenegrins, Fremantle was not convinced that the threat to the French was serious. In addition to this, Bentinck had at the same time sent letters to Fremantle to cancel the expedition, having been told by Nugent, who had just arrived in Sicily from Vienna, that according to a recent agreement between Napoleon (preparing to attack Russia) and Austria, any such attack on the French would be viewed as a hostile act by the Austrian government.

It can only be a matter of speculation as to what Adamić's involvement could have been in any of this. What is possible is that in July 1812 he could have met Nugent (with whom he was to have a close relationship much later) in Sicily. In July or early August, he most probably met Danese, either in Albania or Vis. He definitely met Admiral Fremantle on Vis. Johnson, the spymaster, who was the essential link, had arrived in Albania after a long journey from Vienna to in June, and come to Vis in mid-July, although it seems from Adamić's letter that he had left Vis again before Adamić's arrival.

How much did the French know or discover about Adamić's movements, activity and contacts? They obviously knew about, and had approved, his mission to negotiate with the British for the supply of salt to the Illyrian Provinces, but they were beginning to have their suspicions about his other activities. It was difficult to keep them secret, especially as the French had their own networks of agents and spies. When Adamić visited Malta on his way back from London, he discovered that the contract he had signed in March to supply the dockyards with timber, which he had understood was to be kept a secret, was common knowledge.[57] The French had known about his earlier provision of supplies to the British navy (as we have seen, an item in Leard's accounts was the fine the French had imposed a fine on Adamić because of it), and could not be expected to approve any further such dealings.

---

[54] Captain Stolz had been established as an agent at Slavonski Brod in Jan. 1813 (British Library, Aberdeen papers Add. 43074).
[55] See below
[56] These incredibly high numbers must have been exaggerated, although Johnson was also to write of 'an immense quantity of arms'. NA, FO 7/99, King-Foreign Office, 14 Sep. 1811, also FO 7/111, Johnson-Foreign Office, 16 June 1811
[57] NA, FO 7/112, Adamić-Leard, 20 July 1814

Figure 31. Admiral Thomas Fremantle
(1765–1819).

In his absence, in July 1812, the French revoked the concession they had granted Adamić in April 1810 to provide the Illyrian Provinces with salt. The state 'Regie' would take direct responsibility for the supply and sale of salt. This decision does not seem to have been related to his not having supplied the full amount for which he had contracted, nor because of his relations with the British. But his associates in Rijeka had been very concerned at the possibility of Adamić suffering serious losses through making large purchases of salt before he received news of the decision.

In November 1812, Adamić arrived in Venice, where he was arrested and interrogated. He claimed that, because he had been sent on his mission by the governor-general of the Illyrian Provinces, he was prepared to give an account of his activities to him only. He was released but again arrested in Ljubljana, the seat of the government of the Illyrian Provinces, and taken to Trieste, where he was put in the castle and again interrogated by the police. It was suspected that he had assisted the movements of Danese in Dalmatia or Albania. He was released again on 27 November. Back in Rijeka, he complained to the governor-general that the 52 days that he had been under arrest had ruined him and undermined his credit. He claimed that his mission to England had been successful not only in the business of the salt, but in persuading the Admiralty to suppress the activities of privateers and to lift the blockade for all unarmed ships. If the lies being spread about him were not officially denied, he threatened that he would withdraw to Austria or Italy. One of Adamić's associates claimed that, after Adamić had denounced 42 privateers to the British admiralty, he had learned at Malta that they had sworn to take revenge, and that he had therefore taken a Sicilian ship to Vis to avoid them. At Vis, he had indeed met Danese, who had told him that the British were preparing an attack at the Boka Kotorska, and so, wishing to avoid Dalmatia, he had gone to Venice.[58]

---

[58] Pivec-Stele, pp. 236-37, based on reports and a letter in the Archives de la Guerre, Paris

The story was not altogether implausible. Adamić probably did complain to the Admiralty about privateers (Lieutenant Blaguiere's letter of introduction to the Foreign office had mentioned that privateers were preventing ships with naval supplies for the British from leaving Adriatic ports). However, whatever action the Admiralty took against their abuses was as much because of complaints from many other persons and sources, including senior British naval officers. Nor was the visit to Vis so easily explained, and the Admiralty most certainly did not begin to allow free movement of unarmed ships without licence.

Whatever the truth of the matter, Adamić may not have suffered as much as he was later to claim, either financially or in restrictions on his freedom of movement (which he was to claim prevented his going to Austrian Croatia to send timber to the British by the Danube). There is evidence to indicate that the French authorities needed him so much that, within a week of his return to Rijeka, they were asking him for help in sending supplies to Dubrovnik and Kotor.[59] But clearly, he could no longer take the same risks as long as the Illyrian Provinces remained under French control, and may indeed have felt obliged to leave Rijeka, abandon all his houses and estates, and retire to Austria.[60]

The Aborted Insurrection, February-April 1813

It is therefore uncertain whether Adamić was resident in Rijeka during the first half of 1813, when developments leading to the expulsion of the French from the Illyrian Provinces were accelerating.

There had been numerous proposals and preparations for insurrections against the French, many involving Laval Nugent, other exiled or discontented Austrian army officers, even some of the junior archdukes of the Austrian imperial family, the bishop of Zagreb and the network of Catholic priests. However, when a potentially serious insurrection almost broke out in early 1813, it came as an almost complete surprise, both to the British on Vis and Lord Bentinck in Sicily.

Although after 1809 there were no formal diplomatic relations between Britain and Austria, there were unofficial British agents, known to the Austrian authorities, such as Johnson, who maintained informal relations with the Austrian court and authorities, while also involving themselves in more secret dealings with persons such as Nugent to undermine French influence and to persuade the Austrian emperor, now Napoleon's father-in-law, to go to war with France again. More dangerously, they were involved in conspiracies, involving Austrians, to cause insurrections in the neighbouring French-controlled territories. After Johnson's departure from Vienna in March 1812, the British diplomatic agent at Vienna involved in such activity was John Harcourt King.

On 18 Mar 1813, Johnson, who was suffering from pulmonary problems, left Vis to go to Palermo in Sicily to try to recover. On 25 March, a messenger arrived at Vis with an urgent letter from King in Vienna dated 16 February, which, in Johnson's absence, was handed to Admiral Fremantle. However, parts of the letter were in cipher and Johnson had left no

---

[59] idem
[60] NA, FO 7/112, Adamić-Foreign Office, 30 Jan. 1814. There appear to be contradictions in Adamić's letters as to whether he could or could not leave the Illyrian Provinces.

Figure 32. British brig off Pula, February 1813, drawing by William Innes Pocock
(National Maritime Museum).

code books at Vis. Fremantle could only send the letter to Lord Bentinck in Sicily, where it arrived on 3 April. Johnson was immediately consulted and the letter decoded. To the horror of Bentinck and Johnson, the letter, now over six weeks old, was to inform Johnson that an insurrection was to break out at the beginning of April. It was essential that British warships be stationed near Rijeka, about the end of March, with arms and ammunition and some field cannon. It was highly desirable that Bentinck spare 1500 or 2000 troops to act in unison with the rebels in taking possession of Rijeka. Neither Bentinck nor Johnson had received any earlier information about the insurrection. Bentinck could only send a copy of the decoded letter to Admiral Fremantle at Vis to ask him to do whatever he could to assist the insurrection as and when he heard anything more about its having broken out. Bentinck had no troops to spare but sent arms and ammunition to Vis to be taken from there to the insurgents.

However, the insurrection, which was to have broken out simultaneously in the Tyrol and Vorarlberg, parts of north Italy and the Illyrian provinces, and to have involved various Austrian officers and the Archduke John, had been nipped in the bud, even before it began, by Metternich, the Austrian foreign minister. Metternich already had his suspicions of what was going on, and did not want any unwelcome or premature complications with France. On 22 February 1813, King sent Danelon (formerly vice-consul in Trieste, who also lived for a time in Rijeka),[61] with unciphered copies of dispatches to the British ambassador in St. Petersburg. The dispatches were stolen in Moravia by thieves who were without doubt agents of Metternich. Early in March there were numerous arrests, Archduke John was reprimanded by the Emperor, and King was told to leave Vienna. Nugent was not directly implicated in the insurrection and did not arrive back in Vienna from a visit to England, returning via Spain and Sicily, until April. Johnson wrote to the Foreign Office on 21 June to explain that news of

---

[61] NA, FCO 7/111, Johnson-Foreign Office, 5 Oct. 1813

the insurrection on the east side of the Adriatic had brought him back to Vis, but it had been deferred because of news of the arrests in Vienna of some of the persons concerned.

It was a curious episode, which may go some way to explaining the attack that Admiral Fremantle was to make on Rijeka on 3 July 1813. Even though he knew of the collapse of the planned insurrection in March-April, and though he had no encouragement or prompting from Johnson, he may have hoped that an appearance in strength by the British naval squadron at Rijeka might stimulate a rising against the French. Even if it did not, together with other attacks on French batteries along the Adriatic coast, the destruction of Rijeka's defences would prepare the way for intervention in later developments. From April 1813 he was convinced that he must shift the focus of his attention and more of the activity of his squadron to the northern Adriatic, particularly to Rijeka and Trieste. If they fell, the French would have greater difficulty in holding on to Dalmatia, Dubrovnik, and Kotor.[62] In a letter Fremantle was later to write to Lord Melville at the Admiralty in October 1813, he was to claim that, anticipating that Austria would go to war with France, he had taken all the places on the coast between Rovinj and Karlobag, and destroyed all their batteries, in order to facilitate communications when it happened.[63]

The British Attack on Rijeka, July 1813

It is a thankless and usually impossible task to undermine cherished and attractive popular traditions,[64] but sometimes the true and substantiated versions of history can be as interesting and entertaining. In the case of the British attack on Rijeka, there is no evidence that Karolina Belinić or any other beautiful lady of Rijeka interceded with the commander of the British squadron to persuade him to spare the town (and none that he ever intended to destroy it). Nor was the commander of the squadron William Hoste, who was the captain of a frigate, and never promoted to admiral. At Rijeka, two of the British naval officers involved were senior to him: Admiral Fremantle, who accompanied and commanded the squadron, and Charles Rowley, captain of the ship-of-the-line EAGLE. There is no reason to believe that John Leard was anywhere near the Adriatic at the time, and, although a master in the British navy, he never commanded a ship 'Master of the Navy', which probably never existed.

On the other hand, a detailed account of the attack can be assembled from Admiral Fremantle's official report and the logbooks of the British warships involved. Admiral Fremantle later obtained various French reports on the raid, which he kept in his private papers,[65] so any exaggeration or partiality on either side can be balanced out.

Whatever Fremantle's real intentions, the squadron that he brought to Rijeka was very strong, with more than enough firepower to do very serious damage to the town, and excessive if his only military objective was to disable the batteries that guarded it. So there is some mystery about the timing and purpose of the attack, which has probably given rise to the legends. The

---

[62] UN, Portland Papers, Fremantle-Bentinck, 29 April 1813
[63] NMM, Fremantle-Melville, 10 Sep. 1813.
[64] These are summarised in Žic, op. cit.
[65] Now in the Buckinghamshire county record office (BRO). There are discrepancies between the numbers given in documents on both the British and French sides. The figures given in the following account are those that seem most reasonable or best corroborated.

Figure 33A. Karolina Belinić, popularly believed to have saved Rijeka by petitioning the British commander.

Figure 33B. Poster for the film *Karolina Riječka*, 1961.

squadron consisted of three 74-gun ships-of-the-line, MILFORD, EAGLE and ELIZABETH, the frigate BACCHANTE, and brig HAUGHTY, with a combined armament of over 250 guns.

However, British warships were seldom exposed to the risk of being seriously damaged by shore batteries, especially if they had facilities for heating and firing red-hot shot, which could cause fire if imbedded in their timbers. The common practice was to open fire at a relatively safe distance, and to send the ships boats to disembark marines and sailors to attack the batteries on land.

Fremantle first consulted Hoste, who knew Rijeka well, and who was sent to reconnoitre the town.[66] The British squadron entered Kvarner on 1 July 1813 and in the evening of 2 July anchored about 4 miles from Rijeka. There was a storm during the night of 2-3 July, with heavy rain, thunder and lightning, but the gales were not strong enough to scatter the British squadron. There were 4 batteries at Rijeka mounting 15 heavy guns. The warships opened fire on them at 9.20 on the morning of 3 July. In the exchange of fire, some damage was sustained by EAGLE and HAUGHTY. Marines and sailors under Rowley and Hoste were landed from boats to storm the batteries at about 11.00 a.m. Having captured the first two batteries, at the entrance to the river at the east end of Rijeka, they entered the town, but encountered musket fire from the windows of houses and a field cannon placed in the centre of the main street.

---

[66] Hoste letter to his mother, 10 July 1813, included in his published letters.

Figure 34. Scene from the opera *Karolina Riječka*.

The French (they were in reality about 350 Croat soldiers, supported by customs officials) were forced to retreat to the square, taking the cannon with them, and occupied a large house. A boat from the MILFORD brought a carronade (a lighter, but powerful at short-range, type of ships gun), which when fired against the end of the house, obliged the French to abandon any further resistance and to flee in all directions. The remaining two batteries (one of which would have been that at the Capuchin monastery at the west end of the town) were quickly occupied, and the British were in control of Rijeka by the end of the morning,[67] having landed about 400-600 men.[68] There were very few casualties on either side, even though the French estimated that the British ships had fired 300 shots to silence the batteries.

The British spent the remainder of 3 July and most of 4 July removing property from the town. Fremantle claimed that, although the town had been stormed, not an individual in the town was plundered, and nothing was taken away, except what was afloat or in the government stores. The British found nothing in the treasury, the contents of which had been removed to Karlovac, but found the warehouses of the unpopular state monopoly or Régie, full of salt and tobacco. The salt warehouse was thrown open for local people to pillage. It seems that it was about 3-4000 country people from outside the town rather than the townspeople themselves who availed themselves of the opportunity. The Austrian consul dissuaded the British from setting fire to the tobacco warehouse. The barracks and powder magazine, and the military storehouse installed in the lazaretto also contained considerable amounts of military equipment and supplies. 59 iron cannon found in the town, only some of which were

---

[67] Fremantle's official report is in the NMM, Pellew papers.
[68] French estimates.

mounted, were spiked and made totally useless. 8 brass 18 pounder cannon, and the field piece, together with 500 muskets and 200 barrels of gunpowder, were taken away on the ships. One French report spoke of the removal of 100 beds for soldiers. The records of the health office about local sailing vessels and seamen seem also to have been removed. Those persons, who had been found guilty of trafficking in contraband, were released from the prisons, and all goods that had been seized as contraband were taken away from the customs house.

Fremantle did not encourage pillaging by his own men, and ordered the local authorities to close the liquor shops to reduce the possibility of disorder. However, the merchant ships in port or in the river were fair game, and Fremantle would have made himself very unpopular with his own men if he had disappointed their hope of prize money. Of the 90 vessels, twelve, laden with oil, and the flour, grain and gunpowder taken from the government stores, were taken away to Vis escorted by the brig HAUGHTY. About half, being small, were handed back

Figure 35. The British bombardment of Rijeka (the Adamić sugar refinery can be seen on the left).

Figure 36. The British bombardment Rijeka with Učka mountain and the sugar refinery. The batteries at the mouth of the Riečina are unprotected and unmanned.

Figure 37. HMS BACCHANTE at Deptford 1811, commanded by Hoste in the bombardment of Rijeka (National Maritime Museum).

to their owners, but the remainder were burned.[69] The British warships also took away cows and a hundred sheep, but these were paid for, and soon slaughtered and eaten.[70]

According to one French account,[71] during the night of 6-7 August (it must have been either 3-4 July or 4-5 July, given that the British squadron set sail between 4-5 a.m. on 5 July),[72] someone cut signals from the cables on one or more of the British warships. The local authorities who remained in town heard of this, and fearing reprisals, they went to the British commander (Fremantle, but possibly Rowley) to express regret (perhaps Karolina Belinić accompanied them). The commander agreed not to take revenge on condition that he be brought the four volumes of Montesquieu's 'L'Esprit des Lois', a history of Rome, the letters of priest Panganelli (Panigarola?), a round hat, a packet of gold braid, and some ducks!

After the British had left, various French officials wrote reports about the incident, with some attempting to exaggerate the violence and barbarity of the attack. One report pointed out

---

[69] Fremantle's account. According to a French report, only 10-12 vessels were burned.

[70] Logbooks of HAUGHTY, NA, ADM 51/2362, and EAGLE, NA, ADM 51/2420

[71] Report to d'Abrantes, governor-general of Illyria, dated Trieste, 8 July 1813, from the commissaire général of police, based on a second report from Marinitsch, the commissaire of police at Rijeka. The date given for the cutting away of the signals was the night of 6-7 July, but by that time all the ships of the squadron had left. Now in BRO, Fremantle collection.

[72] The logbook of MILFORD, Fremantle's flagship, NA, ADM 51/2595, and EAGLE indicate that MILFORD and BACCHANTE weighed anchor and set sail towards Kraljevica between 4.00-5.30 a.m. on 5 July. EAGLE followed them at 8.00 a.m.

that the British had seized a rope warehouse belonging to Adamić, who had been absent, and had emptied it not only of rope but also of an elegant boat belonging to him. His employees had not pointed out that they were private and not public property. The inference confirms that the British were only targeting public property. They may indeed have been unaware that the warehouse belonged to Adamić, but one might conjecture that, if they knew it was his and that he had been working for the British (which Fremantle did, having met him on Vis the previous August), the attack on his property was to remove suspicion from him.

According to the same report, Hoste, who was well-known in Rijeka, had rather injudiciously visited the Vierendek family (the Flemish family who had nursed him back to health), but they could not be blamed for they were loyal. However, this and other French reports referred to suspicions that there were many British spies in Rijeka, and others whose conduct had revealed them to be British sympathisers. The police were now trying to identify these, as well as the many local people who had engaged in pillaging the warehouses.

On 5 July, the British warships proceeded from Rijeka to Kraljevica, where (according to French accounts) they did not touch the shipping. Captains Hoste and Markland landed with men to destroy the batteries, which were found abandoned, the 10 guns having been spiked and the ammunition thrown into the sea. The British could only burn the gun-carriages and blow up the fortifications. Fremantle also landed, and unlike Hoste, who had made various demands, listened to the appeals of the mayor and priest. Some local peasants asked Fremantle for permission to pillage the grain stores but he refused.

Ships boats went up to Bakar, where they found 13 vessels scuttled, only one of which could be recovered. Hoste seems to have been in charge. French reports said that when the town council appealed to him, he threatened to have them shot if they tried to control the pillaging (perhaps by local people). He seized stocks of food without paying for them, took away three boats belonging to inhabitants, and left marines to ensure that the pillaging continued.[73]

After this Fremantle ordered the squadron to disperse to various stations. On 7 July, Captain Rowley in EAGLE attacked and destroyed the five-gun battery at Farassina (Porozina) at the north-west corner of the island Cres.

One person on the British side who disagreed with Fremantle's attack on Rijeka was the spymaster Johnson on Vis, which makes it less likely that it was meant to spark off an insurrection against the French. The two men did not like each other and had frequent disagreements. In February 1813 Johnson had written to the Foreign Office, claiming he had established a line of communication between Vis and Austria by which messages could reach him in nine days. To achieve this the letters or messengers had to come through Rijeka, with safe houses and contacts in Rijeka to help with horses or vessels to reach Vis. With the French authorities in Rijeka hunting for British agents in the aftermath of Fremantle's attack, these communications were put at risk. Johnson wrote from Vis on 26 July to Bentinck's office in Sicily (Bentinck himself was on campaign in Spain) to complain that the attack had done more harm than good, especially as Rijeka had been his principal channel for communications with Austria, and the seizing and destruction of the merchant vessels at Rijeka had also damaged

---

[73] From French reports in the BRO, Fremantle collection.

the contraband trade of Vis. The people of Rijeka were paying dearly for the salt that had been distributed by the British officers to the poor.

Johnson may have been exaggerating. On 2 August he asked Fremantle for a pass to allow a vessel to carry dispatches from Rijeka to Vis.

There seems to have been another casualty from the British raid, about whom Johnson wrote on 12 July.[74] The Austrian consul in Rijeka (probably Baron Lederer) had left Rijeka to come to Vis, possibly on a British warship returning from the attack. For whatever reasons he had left his post, Johnson's opinion was that he would be the more culpable the longer he stayed on Vis, and that he should go back to Austria via Klek (at the Turkish outlet on the Adriatic coast), the Neretva valley and Bosnia. The consul may have known just how close the outbreak of war between Austria and French was to be.

Nugent liberates Rijeka, August 1813

After his return to Vienna in mid-April 1813, the British expected General Laval Nugent to stay there only a short time and to go again to Sicily.[75] At the end of May-early June both Fremantle and Danese waited for him to come overland to the Adriatic coast at Scutari. Nugent did not arrive, because he had been caught up in the rapid developments taking place in Austria and Germany.

After his disastrous campaign in 1812 in Russia, Napoleon had raised a new army in France with which in 1813 he attempted to check the advance into Germany of the Russians, now allied with Prussia. Both sides were exhausted and agreed to an armistice from 4 June-20 July, brokered by Metternich, the Austrian foreign minister, who still hoped to negotiate a general peace settlement and keep Austria out of the war. But Metternich realised that renewed war between Austria and France was probably inevitable and that time had to be gained to strengthen the Austrian army.

During the armistice, the Russian Tsar Alexander was at the castle of Reichenbach in eastern Silesia (then in the kingdom of Prussia, now in Poland). With the support of Count Stadion and the pro-war faction of the Austrian court, and probably with the prior approval of Metternich, Nugent went to Reichenbach to meet Lord Cathcart, the British ambassador to St. Petersburg, who was accompanying the tsar. Nugent arrived at Reichenbach on 20 July, the day the armistice had been due to expire, although in the meantime, Metternich had agreed with Napoleon an extension until 10 August to allow for peace negotiations, which had began in Prague on 10 July. On the assumption that the peace negotiations would break down and the Austrians would enter the war against France, Nugent presented Lord Cathcart with his plan for joint action between Austrian forces and the British troops and squadron in the Adriatic. On 22 July, subject to the approval of the Austrian government, Cathcart agreed to put at Nugent's immediate disposal £20,000. Nugent was to immediately raise and equip two battalions consisting of 5000 Croatian soldiers, to be subsidised for three months at £5000 per month. With these he was to cross the Sava and invade the Illyrian Provinces as soon

[74] BRO, Fremantle papers, Johnson-Fremantle, 12 July 1813. Fremantle on MILFORD had returned to Vis that same day.
[75] NA, FO 7/100, Nugent-Foreign Office, Durazzo 29 Mar. 1813.

Figure 38. A caricature of Napoleon, published Berlin 1813 and sent by Adamić to Fremantle.

as war broke out, which was expected to be on 16 August. The British government would thereafter assist the raising and equipping of a further 4 battalions.[76] Nugent sought and was given Metternich's agreement at Prague on 27 July.[77]

The first news of what was happening reached Vis in a letter from Nugent dated Vienna 11 June 1813, in which he told Johnson how great a blow the armistice had been to his plans. However, he expected that Napoleon would be too demanding, and believed that it was still possible that war would break out. He needed to stay in Austria to see how things developed. He would go first to Gitschin, in Moravia, where the Austrian emperor and court had moved (conveniently close to the tsar at Reichenbach), but would then come down to Sarajevo, where he hoped to be met by Danese.[78]

Nugent's next letter to Johnson, dated Vienna 21 June, reached Vis on 2 August. Nugent was more optimistic that war would break out. Metternich and Stadion had met the Tsar, and the Austrian army was being prepared for war. Johnson immediately copied part of the letter to Fremantle, told him that they would soon receive an official request from the Austrian government for the co-operation of the British forces in the Adriatic, and asked for a pass for a vessel to go to Rijeka to bring back dispatches.[79] The message which was brought back to Vis from Rijeka on 5 August was a letter from Nugent dated Brandeis (Bohemia) 10 July. 'They' (the Austrian government as Nugent had not yet met Cathcart) were giving Nugent three battalions drawn from the Croatian (Grenzer) regiments[80] to advance to the Adriatic coast via Karlovac and meet the British naval squadron at Senj. He suggested that Fremantle seize Mali Lošinj before 16 August and to go to the coast to wait for him as soon as it was heard that he had crossed the frontier into Illyria, which he hoped would be on 16 August. If the enemy

---

[76] NA, FO 65/86 Cathcart-Foreign Office, 26 July 1813
[77] idem, 6 August 1813
[78] UN, Portland papers, Nugent-Johnson, 11 June 1813, enclosed Johnson-Smith, Palermo, 26 July 1813
[79] BRO, Fremantle papers, Johnson-Fremantle, 2 Aug. 1813 enc. Nugent-Johnson, 21 June 1813.
[80] Weil: Le Prince Eugène et Murat, 1902, says that Nugent was given two battalions of the Varasdin-based Franz-Karl regiment and two squadrons of Radetzky hussars, but elsewhere that Nugent had only one battalion of the Warasdiner-Kreutzer regiment and one squadron of the Radetzky hussars, amounting to only 1000 men to which he hoped to add deserters from the French. The British were to complain that Nugent never had the forces for which they had agreed to pay the subsidy.

Figure 39A. William Cathcart, by Henry Meyer, after John Hoppner (National Portrait Gallery).

Figure 39B. Klemens von Metternich, oil painting by Thomas Lawrence (Royal Collection).

were to hear that the English had disembarked on the coast, it would help to undermine their resistance.[81]

If the date on the copy of Nugent's letter is correct (it is doubtful whether a letter sent after the 20 July arrival of Nugent at Reichenbach could have reached Vis by 5 August), it appears that Cathcart may have been misled into supplying funds for troops which already existed and had already been put at Nugent's disposal. This would also explain how Nugent could be ready, in less than a month after his visit to Cathcart, to invade the Illyrian Provinces in mid-August. On his way south from Reichenbach and Prague, he only left Vienna for Zagreb, where his troops were already assembled, on 10 August.[82]

As Fremantle was away from Vis on MILFORD, Johnson immediately took a small boat to go to find him and tell him the news and to seek his agreement to Nugent's proposals. Johnson replied to Nugent on 7 August that the admiral had agreed to rendezvous with Nugent on the coast (even though it seems Fremantle had been reluctant to commit himself). It appears from Fremantle's letterbooks that there was then ensued one of those unseemly squabbles between the admiral and the secret agent that could have prejudiced everything. Fremantle demanded to see all of Nugent's letters to Johnson, but Johnson refused. An angry exchange of letters continued until 17 August.

The peace negotiations in Prague had achieved nothing by the end of the extended armistice on 10 August. Austria declared war on France on 12 August, and Nugent and his forces crossed

---

[81] BRO, Fremantle papers 235/1, Johnson-Fremantle, 15 Aug.1813 enc. Nugent-Johnson, 10 July 1813
[82] NA, FO 7/100, Nugent-Castlereagh, Vienna 10 August 1813.

the Sava at Zagreb on 19 August to invade the Illyrian Provinces and march to liberate Rijeka. He reached and took Karlovac on 20 August before the French could assemble their forces, mainly Croatian soldiers from the southern grenzer regiments of the Krajina, who now began to desert in large numbers and whole battalions to Nugent.[83]

On Vis, despite his quarrel with Johnson, Fremantle had not been inactive. On 13 August, Colonel Robertson, the governor of Vis and commander of the garrison there, informed Fremantle that he could spare 450 troops for operations elsewhere, while leaving sufficient to defend Vis.

The British on Vis expected Nugent to reach the coast at Senj, and Johnson had asked Fremantle on 15 August for an armed vessel to go there with two other agents to meet Nugent when he arrived. Early on 18 August Fremantle sailed north from Vis with two ships-of-the-line, MILFORD and TREMENDOUS, and the frigate HAVANNAH. Later that same morning, boats from the two ships-of-the-line were sent off manned and armed. MILFORD and TREMENDOUS sailed on to Brijuni off the west coast of Istria, where two other ships-of-the-line, ELISABETH and EAGLE joined them on 23 August (the frigate BACCHANTE and brig WIZARD also arrived at Brijuni on 26 August). The night of 21-22 August was stormy (WIZARD was obliged to return to Vis for repairs) but early in the morning of 22 August a boat came out from Senj to HAVANNAH, which had been left cruising the entrance to Kvarner. It brought the news that the French governor at Senj had quitted the town during the night and gone off towards Zadar. HAVANNAH moved in towards Senj where it saw the Austrian flag on the castle. The fort fired a salute, which the frigate returned. The Croatian garrison had changed sides. The French were trying to withdraw troops from Dalmatia but, finding HAVANNAH at Senj, did not dare continue towards Rijeka, and their Croatian soldiers quickly deserted.[84]

The five boats from MILFORD and TREMENDOUS which had left on 18 August joined HAVANNAH at Senj, and on 25 they moved to the northern end of the Island of Krk. That same day, Fremantle, with MILFORD and EAGLE moved into Kvarner from Brijuni and were seen by Nugent's troops near Kraljevica. It was at midday on 25 August, when he was 6 miles from the north end of the island Cres, that Fremantle received two messages. One was from Baron d'Aspré, the officer commanding Nugent's advance guard. He had occupied Kraljevica where he was expecting Nugent to arrive shortly. The enemy were at Bakar, falling back towards Rijeka.[85] Baron d'Aspré had also brought a letter from Colonel Church, the British officer assigned by Lord Cathcart to accompany Nugent. Church's letter had been written at Bosiljevo (west of Karlovac, where Nugent was later to build a castle) on 23 August. Presumably because they had met so little serious opposition, Nugent and his forces were marching along the recently finished Louisa road and could be expected to arrive at Rijeka on 26 August.[86] At 6.00 a.m. on 26 August 1813 observers on board MILFORD saw the Austrian troops march into and

---

[83]   Nugent informed Cathcart that he crossed the Sava on 13 August (NA, FO 65/86, Nugent-Cathcart, Karlovac 22 Aug. 1813), but it is clear from letters from Colonel Church, a British officer whom Cathcart had assigned to accompany Nugent, that there were delays imposed on Nugent by senior Austrian officers and that they only crossed the Sava on 19 August (NA, FO 65/86, Church-Cathcart, 20 August 1813 and British Library, Bunbury papers, Add. 37051, Church-Bunbury at War Office, 20 August 1813).
[84]   UN, Portland papers, Nugent-Cathcart, Rijeka 31 Aug. 1813 and NA, WO 1/314 Nugent-Campbell, 26 August 1813.
[85]   BRO, Fremantle papers, 40/5/3
[86]   idem, 39/7

Figure 40. The Louisa Road into Rijeka.

take possession of Rijeka without opposition.[87] The French garrison and the retreating French forces from Karlovac had evacuated the town during the night.

Adamić's return to Rijeka, autumn 1813

On 26 August, the very same day that Nugent and his troops entered Rijeka, Adamić at Merslavodizza (Mrzla Vodica, about 20 kilometers east of Rijeka near the Louisa road) lost no time in writing in English to Fremantle to welcome him. He told the admiral about his troubles with the French, explaining that these were the reason for his having had to keep away from the coast, to avoid any suspicion that he was communicating with the ships of the squadron. He now considered himself free of any such restrictions. He was going to Zagreb to see some of the leading authorities and in a fortnight would return to Rijeka, when he hoped to meet Fremantle. In the meantime, he placed his house (home or business house?) at the disposal of Fremantle and his squadron, and had ordered his nephew, Anderlich, to be of service. He sent, enclosed with his letter, other letters to be forwarded to Vis, Malta, Messina, Gibraltar and London, to encourage the resumption of the English trade.[88] It had indeed been one of the arguments used by Nugent with Lord Cathcart that the capture of Rijeka would open up the trade route to Austria and Hungary.[89]

There were, however, problems concerning the early resumption of trade. The war was not over. Over the next two months, Nugent and his troops were engaged in liberating the towns of Istria, supported along the coast by the ships of the British squadron (beginning with Mali Lošinj on 28-30 August, Novigrad on 4 September, Rovinj on 5 September). In most places the Croatian soldiers of the garrisons readily deserted the French, but to the north, between Trieste and Ljubljana, there were the stronger forces, consisting of French and Italian soldiers, of the army of Eugène Beauharnais, Napoleon's viceroy in his kingdom of Italy, which were checking the advance of the main Austrian armies. The garrison of Rijeka had withdrawn up

---

[87] Logbook of MILFORD, NA, ADM 51/2595
[88] BRO, Fremantle collection, D/FR 38/4/21
[89] NA, WO1/314, Nugent, Rijeka-General Campbell, Ionian islands, 26 Aug. 1813.

the road to Trieste to the area of Lipa, where it was soon reinforced. Rijeka itself was not safe from French counter-attack.[90]

Admiral Fremantle landed in Rijeka on 26 August and met Nugent for the first time. Although there were doubts on the British side about the quality of Nugent's soldiers and much criticism of other Austrian generals, they were very impressed with Nugent. Fremantle was enthusiastic in his efforts to support Nugent's campaign. He immediately sent ships of squadron to the Ionian islands (EAGLE with Colonel Church on 31 August) and Sicily (HAVANNAH on 1 September) to ask for more British troops and arms and ammunition. Fremantle undertook to defend Rijeka with his warships and to put marines into the town so that Nugent could use his own men elsewhere. Fremantle would make Rijeka his headquarters because of the ease of communication with Nugent, and of access to water and provisions.[91] On 9 September Fremantle wrote to his wife in London that he was living in a fine large house on the shore with only 50 marines the town, the entire Austrian force being outposted from the town. In the event of their suffering reverses, the Austrian soldiers would have to retreat into Rijeka under the protection of MILFORD.[92]

A first French counter-attack took place on 29 August but Nugent was able to repulse it and attack the enemy positions at Pasja and to occupy Lipa (both on or near the Trieste road north-west of Rijeka). The French attempted to concentrate their forces by drawing in their garrisons from Istria and bringing down reinforcements from the north. Despite continuous desertions of their Croatian soldiers, Nugent's troops were heavily outnumbered.

On 10 September Fremantle wrote from Rijeka directly to Lord Melville at the Admiralty in London to explain how, despite having received permission to return to England in response to his own earlier requests for transfer, the importance of the developments had convinced him that he should stay in the Adriatic. He sent Melville a detailed account of the military situation, and the disposition of the squadron, accompanied by a sketch map. He was staying with MILFORD at Rijeka, so that, if Nugent's posts were forced by the enemy, he could retreat to Rijeka under the protection of its guns. The presence of a party of marines in the town enabled Nugent to use all his troops elsewhere.

But when the main enemy attack came on 14 September, Fremantle was unable to stop them recapturing Rijeka. Faced with the advance of the Italian general Pino with 7-8000 enemy soldiers, Nugent, rather than put himself into a trap, wisely withdrew with most of his force of about 2000 men westwards to Kastov in Istria. On the morning of 15 September 4000 enemy troops were observed descending the hills behind Rijeka. With only a few of Nugent's hussars and his marines left in the town, Fremantle decided it could not be defended and took the marines back on board MILFORD. The logbook of MILFORD records that at 12.10 in the morning enemy troops marched in and took possession of Rijeka. MILFORD weigh anchored, make all sail, and withdraw from Rijeka to a position 3 miles away.[93] There must have been considerable panic in Rijeka as it was nearly completely abandoned by the population, with 59 vessels from

[90] A detailed account of the military activity is given in Weil, op. cit.
[91] UN, Portland papers 2572, Fremantle-Montgomerie (Bentinck's deputy in Sicily), 31 August, and Fremantle-Admiralty, 4 September 1813 (quoted Ann Parry: The Admirals Fremantle, 1971).
[92] The Wynne Diaries, ed. Anne Fremantle, 1940
[93] Logbook of MILFORD, NA, ADM 51/2595

the river taking away the women and children. However, the enemy, finding that Nugent had gone into Istria, soon left the town, leaving only a small detachment. This was captured the next morning when Nugent's hussars, who had withdraw to Kraljevica, re-entered the town.[94]

Fremantle must have decided (perhaps after prior consultation with Nugent) that Rijeka was safe, or that his presence was more necessary elsewhere. That same day, 16 September, Fremantle sailed away to Pula (where the British together with Austrian soldiers, had captured the islands and turned the guns of the fort on the peninsula landwards) and then up the coast of Istria to Koper to join forces with Nugent in besieging Trieste.[95] But before he left Rijeka Fremantle wrote to Adamić. As he had concluded that the French had entirely evacuated the neighbourhood, and it was necessary for someone to look after British interests, he asked Adamić to act as temporary British consul in Rijeka, until such time as someone more properly authorized by the British government was sent out. He asked Adamić to inform Baron Lederer about his appointment (Lederer had been the Austrian consul in Rijeka and now seems to have been appointed governor). Fremantle also asked Adamić to finish supplying MILFORD with the supplies that had already been agreed, and after his departure to send him any information of interest which he heard at Rijeka.[96]

There were to be a number of letters over the next few months from Adamić to Fremantle.[97] However, there is an early indication that Fremantle had not been as obliging as Adamić may have hoped. This concerned the problems with Adamić's long-standing commitment to supply the British navy with timber. Adamić wrote on 20 September 1813 to Johnson (the spymaster, for whom he had acted as an agent), to complain that he was encountering difficulties in fulfilling his contract, and could not understand Admiral Fremantle's refusal to help him, unless it was because he was receiving malicious reports from persons employed in the naval dockyards at Malta. Johnson received the letter in Prague and forwarded it from there on 5 October to the Foreign Office to be passed on to the Admiralty. Johnson knew nothing about the contract but stated that Adamić was in financial difficulties, had been obliged to suspend his payments, and was nearly bankrupt. He could only guess that Adamić, being unable to fulfil the contract, was looking for excuses for further delay. Johnson recommended that the Admiralty consult Joseph Danelon, acting as British consul-general to Trieste but resident in Rijeka until Trieste was liberated from the French, who also had experience of supplying timber.[98] (Johnson had other reasons for recommending Danelon. He had himself recommended Danelon to Lord Aberdeen, the ambassador-designate to Vienna, for his appointment to Trieste. Most probably because of his dislike of Fremantle, after he received Adamić's letter, he wrote to Lord Aberdeen to object that the admiral had had no right to appoint Adamić as consul in Rijeka, which was, moreover, insignificant as a commercial centre).[99]

---

[94] Fremantle's account of these events is in NMM, Pellew papers 16, Fremantle at Pula-Pellew, 18 Sep. 1813.

[95] Idem. Fremantle met Nugent at Pula, where these movements were agreed between them.

[96] A copy of Fremantle's letter is enclosed with Adamić-Foreign Office, NA, FO 7/112, 30 Jan. 1814.

[97] BRO, Fremantle papers. Some of these concern payment of bills on Fremantle's behalf, passes for ships, and news of major developments elsewhere. All of the letters were written in Rijeka (Adami} did not accompany Fremantle at any stage of his movements leading up to the surrender of Trieste). There is other correspondence concerning Adamić's services. Writing to Fremantle, from Vienna in November, his secretary mentioned a carriage he had bought from Adamić.

[98] See above. Danelon had been associated with Leard in 1803 in identifying sources of timber. He was also the courier carrying the dispatches that were stolen by Metternich's agents in February 1813.

[99] British Library, Aberdeen papers Add. 43074, Aberdeen-Danelon, 7 Oct. 1813 and Johnson-Aberdeen, 29 Oct. 1813.

The reasons for Adamić's complaint become clearer in the comments of the Navy Board on the correspondence dated 10 December 1813.[100] There had been a serious outbreak of the plague at Malta, which made it dangerous and difficult, given the imposition of strict quarantine regulations, for ships to go there. Adamić had clearly hoped that he could take the timber only as far as Vis, either for onward shipment to Malta or for use in the small dockyard which Fremantle had established there. The Navy Board considered that the danger of the plague had subsided and access to Malta was again permitted. Any difficulty Adamić had met with in his dealings with their officers at Malta could only have been because of their insistence that he observe the terms of his contract.

One of the more important letters from Adamić to Fremantle was dated Rijeka 12 October 1813. EAGLE had returned to Rijeka (from the Ionian islands via Vis with arms and ammunition for Nugent, the Austrian archduke Francis, with wife and retinue, as well as Croatian soldiers from French garrisons in Dalmatia who now wished to serve under the archduke and Nugent). Adamić, together with Mr Golden, Fremantle's commissioner for supplies, had loaded EAGLE with wine and the bread which was provided under a contract supervised by Adami}. However, Adamić suggested that Fremantle should in justice and equity give (the contractor?) some special consideration ('qualche abbuono') because of the difficult circumstances under which he had suffered costs in the last withdrawal.[101]

Fremantle replied to Adamić on 29 October, the last day of the blockade and siege of the town and castle of Trieste by the British squadron and Nugent's forces begun on 5 October. He had been so occupied with the siege that he had not had time to deal with the various letters he had received from Adamić. But on two points, he had to give negative answers. He could not give Adamić blank papers to be made out as passes for merchant ships using Rijeka. Respecting the supply of provisions, although he had appointed Adamić temporary consul, he could not authorise him to spend one shilling on the public account.[102]

If Adamić was disappointed or offended by Fremantle's response to his requests, a subsequent letter to Fremantle dated 11 January 1814 was written with good humour. He enclosed a caricature of Napoleon he had been sent from Berlin through his daughter in Vienna. Napoleon's hat was formed by an eagle with a clipped wing; his face by dead bodies; his collar by streams of blood; the star on his coat by a cobweb; and his epaulets by hands.[103]

The End of the War

After the fall of Trieste, the war passed into northern Italy, with the British squadron transporting Nugent with Austrian and British troops (mainly from the garrison of Vis) to the delta of the Po. The recovery of Trieste and later of Venice was to diminish the importance that Rijeka had enjoyed when it was the only Austrian port through which British communications and trade could pass. The course of the war had taken the British squadron away from Rijeka, and with the end of the war in 1814, most of its warships and officers would shortly be

---

[100] NA, ADM 106/2262, Navy Board-Admiralty.
[101] BRO, Fremantle papers D/FR.38/4/36.
[102] NMM, Fremantle letter book IGR/15.
[103] BRO, Fremantle papers D/FR 38/5/23.

withdrawn from the Adriatic altogether (including Admiral Fremantle in March 1814, Rowley and Hoste, all rewarded with Austrian honours).

As already seen Johnson had opposed Fremantle's nomination of Adamić's nomination as consul in Rijeka. Fremantle himself had told Adamić that his nomination was only on a temporary basis until the British government sent someone else. In November 1813 Fremantle was informed by Lamb, the British chargé d'affaires at the British embassy in Vienna, that the Austrian government would not recognise Adamić's appointment, and suggesting that Danelon, appointed by Lord Aberdeen, could also cover Rijeka. Throughout 1814-5 there was to ensue a period in which various people were in competition for remunerative posts or pensions, which they hoped that the end of the wars and the return of peace would bring them. The situation was complicated by political questions affecting the ports of the north-eastern Adriatic, for example, whether the Austrians would consider Trieste more important than Venice or Rijeka, and whether Rijeka would be the port of Hungary. These considerations would determine where the British would place their senior consul-generals and subordinate consuls and vice-consuls.

Adamić made his own bid for consideration for establishment as a permanent consul-general in Rijeka in a letter of 30 January 1814 addressed directly to the British secretary of state for foreign affairs, Lord Castlereagh, with which he enclosed the end of year return of ships flying British colours (they were all from Vis or the Ionian islands).[104] He argued that there was the need for a consul-general to cover the entire Adriatic coast south of Rijeka, including Dalmatia and Albania, in the same way that the consul-general in Trieste was now responsible for Istria. He recalled that Leard had been (even if only nominally) consul to Dubrovnik. If Leard was not to return in this capacity, he argued his own case for consideration and summarised the services which merited it: the provision from 1801 of supplies to the British navy, including the contract for timber and supplies to Hargood's squadron in the 1809 war; his involvement in the trade through Malta, his visit to England to negotiate contraband trade to the Adriatic, and also his initiatives in opening up communications and English trade with Austria through Turkey; his arrest and the losses he had sustained under the French; and the assistance given to Johnson and his secret agents. He did not seek the appointment for the sake of any salary or emolument, but because of his affection for Great Britain. The Austrian government had authorised him to serve as a British consul and had been pleased by his appointment by Fremantle.

One can only guess at Adamić's reaction when his old associate, John Leard, arrived in Rijeka in July 1814 to replace him as British consul.

---

[104] NA, FO 7/112. The detail of Adamić's account of his activities has already been given in the above text. There is no evidence of any other contact between Adamić and Viscount Castlereagh. It was customary for government officials to address correspondence not to ministers but to the senior civil servant in the ministry concerned. In the Foreign Office this was the under secretary of state, at this time William Hamilton. As in the case of letters addressed to government ministers today, Adamić's letter to Castlereagh may never have been seen by Castlereagh himself but would have been dealt with at a lower or more appropriate level. It is nevertheless possible and indeed likely that Adamić had some direct dealings with, or may have met, the other ministers and senior officials he mentions in his letter e.g. Lord Bathurst, the President of the Board of Trade (who, as ambassador to Austria, might already have met Adamić when Leard and Adamić visited Budapest in 1809).

Leard's return to Rijeka, July 1814

In view of the circumstances of the earlier cancellation of Leard's appointment as nominal British consul to Dubrovnik, it is strange that the Foreign Office should have decided to use him again. However, Leard was shameless in losing no opportunity to promote himself and his own interests, and resolute in ignoring any impediments he might have found in his way. Moreover, Leard was intelligent and he no doubt persuaded the Foreign office that he would be of use to them, especially given his familiarity with Rijeka and his indisputable experience of maritime and mercantile matters.[105] Although the protocol of his appointment now required it, Leard was never again to address a letter direct to the Admiralty or Navy Board but always to or through the Foreign Office in London. But the Navy Board did not forget how Leard had failed and defied them, and rejected any applications he addressed to them through the Foreign Office to act as their agent.

But it was not only Leard who was under a cloud as far as the Navy Board was concerned. It is ironical that the first instructions that Leard was given were to call Adamić to account on the question of the contract for timber. These were given to Leard on 9 July 1814 when, on his way to take up his post in Rijeka, he delivered letters from the Foreign Office to Lamb, the chargé d'affaires at the British embassy in Vienna. What is of interest is the question of whether Leard still had any close, friendly or loyal relations with Adamić, or if, rather as poacher turned gamekeeper and true to his own character, he was now ready to betray his old associate's interests to advance his own.

On 29 July Leard to the Foreign Office and Lamb in Vienna enclosing copies of the letter that Adamić had sent to him the previous day. Adamić claimed that, despite all the difficulties and restrictions he had suffered after his return to Rijeka in 1811, his people had been able to send, from Austrian Croatia by the Danube and the Black Sea, about 2000 loads of timber, which should have liquidated about £4000 of the £12,192 which, according to the 1812 contract, he owed the Navy Board. As conditions were now better, he proposed to resume the delivery of timber. According to his contract he was to be paid prices up to £15 per load for timber delivered at Malta, from which was deducted £2 per load to liquidate the debt. It cost him £3 per load to ship the timber to Malta. Adamić now proposed to deliver the timber to Rijeka, as had originally been proposed (in 1803-04), but according to a new contract and at revised prices. He admitted that the revised prices might seem high, compared with those calculated at the beginning of the undertaking, but losses on rates of exchange (particularly on bills drawn on London compared to cash) and labour costs had to be taken into consideration. (Leard pointed out in his letter to Lamb that Adamić had agreed to lower the prices, according to the principles of the proposed revised contract, if the exchange rate changed in favour of sterling).[106]

There was no immediate response to this correspondence. In other letters of 1814 Leard was busy putting forward his own claims to be the senior consul on the Austrian coasts (with a network of consulates to come under him). He also advised British navy officials at Malta

---

[105] Although often self-serving, Leard's letters to the Foreign Office are in good clear handwriting (possibly copied by someone else from drafts), well argued and informative.
[106] NA, FO 7/112. In his letter to the Foreign Office, addressed to William Hamilton, the under secretary, Leard mentioned that Nugent had passed through Rijeka on his way to Vienna and sent greetings.

about the availability of treenails (wooden nails or spikes for securing planks) either from Albania or the neighbourhood of Rijeka. In this he tried to promote the interests of a Mr J. L. Lampel, who gave estimates of costs, while at the same time asking the Foreign Office for approval to appoint Lampel (described as a respected resident of Lošinj, who had served with Leard in Albania and Dalmatia) as vice consul at Rijeka.[107]

The Navy Board had not taken kindly to Adamić's attempt to revise his contract. On 17 February 1815 they wrote to the Admiralty that they had terminated the contract and appointed a Mr Samuel Follet, one of their officers who was then at Malta, to go to Trieste or Rijeka without delay, and on behalf of and in the name of His Majesty's Government and the Lord Commissioners of the Admiralty, to take possession from Adamić of all the property for which money had been advanced to him. This property was in trees, timber, grounds, stables and carts. It was to be recovered up to the value of £8027 14s 9d, this being calculated as the remainder of Adamić's debt to the Navy Board. They further requested that the Foreign Office should ask the British ambassador in Vienna to assist Mr Follet by seeking the agreement of the Austrian government to the steps being taken and the co-operation of its governors in the districts in question. The trees were understood to be in forests in Slavonia, Croatia and Carniola, and the buildings in Karlovac and Brod.[108]

There is curiously no further trace of Follet. It would seem that he never arrived but was replaced by a certain Mr Monk of the commissioner's office at Malta, who died before being able to undertake or complete his mission. In January 1816 the Foreign Office forwarded to the Admiralty a letter from Leard (dated 23 December 1815) asking to be allowed to replace the late Mr Monk in the performance of the service concerning Mr Adamić's contract.

Leard followed this with an extraordinary letter dated 19 May 1816 in which he presented yet another summary of the history of the project to supply timber since 1803. He added the information (not included in earlier explanations received from Adamić) that of the 3000 loads of timber that had been cut down, a part that had been brought out of the forest to the New Road near Karlovac had been burned by the French in 1809, another part had been lost in floods of the Kupa river, and the remainder had most probably lain so long exposed to the weather as to be seriously damaged. (It was clearly not going to be easy for any agent sent out by the Navy Board to recover any part of it in repayment of Adamić's debt to them). Leard went on to suggest (as he had already proposed, not only to Robert Gordon at the British Embassy in Vienna in July 1815, but also to Prince Metternich on a visit with the Austrian emperor to Rijeka) that there should be an agreement at government level, instead of or indeed in preference to a contract with Adamić or any other merchant, for the supply of timber to the British navy.

It was going to take some time for the Navy Board to digest these proposals. It was not until 26 October 1816 that, referring to the Foreign Office's letter of January, the Navy Board not surprisingly offered its opinion that it would not be expedient to employ Leard to supervise the winding up of Adamić's contact.[109] There was no response recorded in the Navy Board's

---

[107] NA, FO 7/112, Leard-Foreign Office and enclosures. From latter correspondence it appears that Lampel was appointed.
[108] NA, ADM 12/174 Digest cut 98, and ADM 106/2266.
[109] NA, ADM 106/2271, Navy Board-Admiralty. The delay was most unusual, unless the Foreign Office's letter had been

archives to Leard's letter to the Foreign Office of 19 May. Leard had followed this in June by submitting, through the Foreign Office, competitive proposals from a Mr Nicolo di Lussani, another Rijeka merchant, for the delivery of oak timber from Hungary to the mouth of the Danube in the Black Sea as well as to ports in the Rijeka consular district between Istria and Karlobag. The Navy Board turned these down on the grounds of the difficulty and expense of loading and transporting timber from the mouth of the Danube, and that the quantities in question from Rijeka were too small (although they amounted to 10,000 loads) to merit their sending out an agent to superintend its shipment.[110] The irrepressible Leard was soon but equally unsuccessfully applying to be transferred from Rijeka to Trieste, having heard that the senior but much older consul there was about to retire.[111]

Whatever the lack of progress on the question of Adamić's obligations or continued involvement in any business concerning the provision of timber from the Austrian empire in 1816, there was a spate of correspondence[112] and rapid development in 1817.

On 25 January 1817, the Foreign Office forwarded to the Admiralty another letter from Leard regarding timber supplies dated 1 January. The exportation of timber from imperial and private forests had been made easier by a recent decree and the Austrian authorities had told Leard that they wished to encourage it, given the impoverished condition of the country after the war. Because of the scarcity of return cargoes for British ships bringing goods to Rijeka, some merchants had shown interest in taking back timber. Leard recalled that, during his earlier period of residence in Rijeka, enquiries had been made on behalf of the Spanish and French and these were now likely to be renewed. The Spanish had earlier tried to take out timber from Carniola via Trieste but had given up because of transport difficulties. The new Louisa road now made it easier to bring timber out of Croatia and Slavonia.

On 9 July 1817, the Foreign Office forwarded to the Admiralty yet another letter from Leard dated 18 June concerning timber. Contrary to the opinion he had expressed in his letter of the previous May that the timber left lying on the ground for nearly 12 years would have decayed, Adamić and an Englishman, Mr Samuel Haire, had just returned from the forests near Karlovac with samples of the timber which showed that it had hardly decayed at all. This demonstrated how good the timber would be for naval purposes, and also proved that Leard had been right in recommending it for its high quality in 1803.

The Navy Board informed the Admiralty on 1 August 1817 that it had (finally) decided that it would be expedient to take measures to bring back to England some of the timber cut down in 1805. But they could not entrust this to either Leard or Adamić, neither of whom had given satisfaction in the past. They proposed to send out to Rijeka a Mr George Smith, their own under secretary and Mr Gill, the foreman of the new works at Deptford (navy dockyard), to decide on the quality of the timber. The instructions to Smith also told him to take possession of the property in the hands of Adamić which the failed mission in 1815 of Follet and Monk

---

mislaid or there was a mistake in the date given in the transcription into the Navy Board's letter book.
[110] NA, FO 7/130, Leard-Foreign Office, 29 June 1816 and Foreign Office-Leard, 20 Aug. 1816
[111] NA, FO 7/130, Leard-Foreign Office, 30 Oct. 1816
[112] While the consular correspondence Leard-Foreign Office has been published (Ivan Crkvenić: Britanska konsularna služba no našoj obali i britanski izvoz drveta preko Rijeke tokom prve polovice XIX stoljeća, Pula, 1958, quoted Žic, op. cit.), it does not seem to have been cross-referenced to the Navy Board archives which shed a rather different light on these developments.

had been intended to recover from him and which was still considered by the Navy Board to be theirs because of the money advanced to him in 1805. Leard and other consuls in the Adriatic were given instructions by the Foreign Office to give them every assistance.[113]

Leard informed the Foreign Office on 19 September 1817 that Smith and Gill had arrived in Rijeka and that they were to proceed the next day, accompanied by Leard, to Karlovac. But Smith and Gill had already reported the results of an inspection of timber in the dockyard at Venice. The lord commissioners were puzzled and asked the Navy Board for clarification of the instructions given to Smith and Gill. These, when provided, turned out to be those concerning their mission to Rijeka.[114] It can only be assumed that they had been told that some of the timber had been sent by Adamić and/or Haire for use in shipbuilding in Venice.

Leard reported to the Foreign Office on his visit to Karlovac on 1 October.[115] With military escorts to defend them from possible attack from bandits who crossed the frontier, they had gone into the military forests towards Bosnia where trees had been cut down in 1805 and the private forests where Adamić had reserved trees and others from which supplies of timber might be drawn for many years. Gill had cut samples to be sent to the Navy Board. But Leard also observed that most of the trees that should have remained from those cut down in 1805 had been removed for their own purposes by the French in the period 1809-13. He had similarly discovered that other trees, cut down in a private domain near Kastel in Carniola under his own direction, had also been removed by the French. By Leard's summary calculation, of the 30,000 trees which it had been hoped would be cut down, the 2052 cut down in the military forests and the 280 cut down in the private domain had very largely been lost. (It was going to be difficult for Smith to recover Adamić's debt to the Navy Board by taking the timber he had cut down, and he was, according to Leard's letter making his own report to the Navy Board that same day, 1 October 1817).

The Last Timber Contract 1818-20

Smith appears to have decided, as the Navy Board had in 1812, that the best way to recover the money that Leard had advanced to Adamić so many years before was to enter into a new contract that would incorporate the debt. Leard wrote to the Foreign Office on 15 October 1817 to report that Smith had agreed a contract with Messrs. Adamić and Haire to deliver to naval dockyards in England 20,000 loads of timber within three years.[116] The agreed price was £11-13 per load according to dimension to include £4 for transportation to London. Gill and Haire were returning direct to London to report to the Navy Board; Smith was returning via Livorno. Leard could not resist suggesting that the timber should only be shipped at rates fixed by the Navy Board as return cargoes for British ships visiting Rijeka, so as to cut whatever profit margins the contractors might have allowed themselves for freighting the timber to England, and to prevent their use of non-British ships. He also sent with Smith a letter to the Navy Board to remind them of how long and well he had served them. He followed this up with a further letter to the Foreign Office dated 19 October again offering his services to the Navy

---

[113] NA, ADM 12/185, Digest cut 98.2/98.3 and ADM 106/2274, Navy Board-Admiralty, 7 Oct. 1817.
[114] NA, ADM 12/185, Digest cut 98.3 and ADM 106/2274, Navy Board-Admiralty, 7 Oct. 1817.
[115] FO 7/137 copied Foreign Office-Admiralty, 27 Oct. 1817.
[116] FO 7/137.

Board as an agent to supervise the new contract, with whatever remuneration or allowances the service might be deemed to merit.[117]

Just when it seemed everything had been settled, there were to be further complications and crossed wires which could have threatened the Adamić and Haire contract. Robert Gordon at the British embassy in Vienna was now enthusiastic about the idea that Leard had suggested to him in July 1815 for a direct arrangement or contract between the British and Austrian governments. On 18 October 1817 Gordon wrote to Leard to say that he had been instructed by the British government to raise the possibility of a contract for oak timber with the Austrian government in Vienna and that Smith's journey had been only to collect information.[118] Leard needed little encouragement and, in the flurry of letters that ensued, his fertile mind had provided all the arguments in favour of a government-to-government contract, facts and figures, costs etc. Any such contracts would be limited to the huge forests of the military border where the soldier-farmers of the grenzer regiments, now there was peace, could provide their manpower and wood-cutting skills, and draught animals, all of which would result in lower prices than could be offered by any merchants. If the Austrian government did not go ahead with some agreement to sell large numbers of fully-grown trees which were surplus to its own requirements (Leard reckoned that half a million could easily be spared from over a million fully-grown trees), they would decay and be wasted.

The Austrian government appears to have shown little enthusiasm for the proposed contract and to have denied such a superabundance of trees.[119] By 19 December 1817 Leard had heard that the Navy Board would decline any other proposals from private individuals for contracts for timber other than that agreed with Adamić and Haire.[120] Leard still hoped that, even though a government-to-government contract could not replace that between the Navy Board and Adamić and Haire, some such arrangement could supplement it. However, it is clear that he had received no response from London. In the same letter of 8 January 1818 in which he reported that Mr Gill, now appointed the Navy Board's agent in Rijeka, had gone with Adamić to Karlovac to commence the felling of trees, Leard expressed the hope that his various letters had been received.[121]

At long last, the undertaking into which Adamić had entered in 1803-04 to provide timber for the British navy was to be achieved. There were some further problems involving Leard, who tried unsuccessfully to nominate himself to replace Gill as the Navy Board's agent in 1818. One problem concerned anchorage charges levied by the Rijeka port authorities in January 1819 on H.M.S. WEYMOUTH (indicating that the British navy was using its own ships to take away the timber). These included disputes in 1819-20 between Leard and Adamić and Haire over the payment of consular fees on the cargoes of timber loaded onto British merchant ships and for attesting their signatures on bills drawn for their payment. While the Foreign Office and Admiralty agreed that consular fees should be paid to Leard, it was decided that the Navy Board should pay them and not Adamić and Haire. If there were any other problems, they might have been resolved by further visits to Rijeka by George Smith, the assistant secretary

---

[117] Idem. Copied Foreign Office-Admiralty, 13 Nov. 1817
[118] Idem. Various letters Oct.-Dec. 1817, Leard-Foreign Office and between Leard and Gordon.
[119] Idem. Gordon-Leard, 21 Nov. 1817
[120] Idem. Leard-Gordon, 19 Dec. 1817
[121] NA, FO 7/139

of the Navy Board, who, on his return to England in 1820 was highly commended for the successful results of the mission he had undertaken since 1817 to procure supplies of timber.[122] The Navy Board had finally declared itself satisfied.

Indeed, this time the timber was actually delivered as planned. By the end of 1818 only about 2300 loads out of the 20,000 agreed in the contract had been brought to Rijeka for shipment, but by 3 January 1820, 5500 loads had just been loaded onto as many as 14 vessels at Rijeka and Bakar. In September 1820 ships loading timber at Bakar were even honoured by the visit of Archduke Franz-Karl, the emperor's second son, who was on an official visit to Rijeka. Leard's end of year consular report for 1820 informed the Foreign Office that 33 British ships had taken timber to British navy dockyards in England. The Adamić-Haire contract, barring some relatively small items, was completed.[123]

From 1821, the export of timber from Rijeka was directed to the French naval dockyards. Leard made a last attempt to undermine the possibility of Adamić entering any further contract for timber for the British navy by recommending that business could be undertaken directly with his sub-contractors. However, by this time, Adamić had probably decided that it was easier to do business with the French,[124] and the Navy Board had discovered that vast amounts of good timber could be found in the recently extended British empire.

Figure 41. The Pool of London in the 1820s (the Customs House is on the right) (by Robert Havell).

---

[122] NA, ADM 12/196, Digest cut 69.1a and ADM 106/2279, Navy Board-Admiralty, 25 Feb.1820.
[123] NA, FO 7/165, Leard-Foreign Office, 1 Jan. 1821.
[124] There was to be an attempt to revive the proposal for an agreement with the Austrian government, to help it repay debts to Great Britain, in 1823, in which Adamić was called to Vienna (NA, FO 7/178, Leard-Foreign Office), but it seems not to have resulted in further exportations from Rijeka of timber for the British navy.

Epilogue

Throughout the 1820s, reports from Rijeka from the ageing Leard dwindled in number and size to the regulation half-yearly returns of shipping and consular fees. These show that not only was there little British trade with Rijeka but that there were few ships from other countries, and that in these years, largely because of the lack of a lazaretto with quarantine facilities, trade was going to other Austrian ports, mainly Trieste. Leard died in Rijeka on 11 April 1831 aged about 74, less than three years after the death of his old associate, Andija Ljudevit Adamić.

Figure 42A. Andrija Ljudevit Adamić, identified here as 'Deputy from Fiume' (Rijeka).

Figure 42B. Laval Nugent, who was buried in his residence of Trsat Castle, Rijeka.

Figure 43A & B. John Leard and his wife.

Figure 44A & B. Paintings of Rijeka: A. from the sea and B. of the waterfront showing the Adamić Sugar Refinery.

Figure 45A & B. Adamić Sugar Refinery, by A.C. von Mayr.

Figure 46. The Sugar Refinery Palace, today the Town Museum.

Laval Nugent acquired and restored the castle of Trsat above Rijeka adding a Doric temple dedicated to heroes.

Figure 47. Trsat Castle before Nugent's restoration.

Figure 48. Trsat Castle in 1837 with Doric Temple.

Figure 49. Trsat Castle today.

Malcolm Scott Hardy 2005 (illustrated 2023)

Part 2:
The British and Vis:
War in the Adriatic 1805-15

Introduction: The British and the Adriatic

The first question to address is why the British considered it necessary to establish a presence in the Adriatic in the period 1805-15. Prior to this there had been an occasional British navy vessel there but no regular squadron.

The reasons can be summarised as:

1. The global strategy that dictated that the extension of French power and influence anywhere had to be checked and contained;
2. The need to keep open routes to communicate with and give support to Britain's allies by subsidies, supplies of arms or by naval or military diversions;
3. The imperative of preventing the French from acquiring ship-building capacity and ships and being able to assemble them so as to give them even only a temporary advantage which could pose a threat to British naval supremacy;
4. Economic warfare to disrupt the enemy's trade and to ensure access to markets for British and colonial products, which Napoleon was trying to exclude from European markets with his 'Continental Blockade';
5. The procurement of timber and other naval supplies for the construction and repair of ships;

The encouragement of dissidents and of revolt against French rule.

Some preliminary treatment must now be given to these factors before looking at the story of the British presence in detail.[1]

***

British involvement in the Mediterranean had been initially in the Western Mediterranean in the attempt first to capture and afterwards to blockade the French naval base at Toulon and then to save the ailing kingdom of Naples from the progress of the French armies down Italy. It failed to save Naples or prevent the completion of the French conquest of mainland Italy but it did keep the French out of Sicily until the end of the wars thanks to the British navy, a British garrison and political control of the decadent and treacherous Bourbon monarchy.

It was Bonaparte's attack on Egypt in 1798-99 that focused attention on the Eastern Mediterranean. Certain aspects of the French defeat deserve particular attention here. The British recaptured Malta (which had been taken by the French from the Knights of Malta) and then held on to it themselves, thus offending their ally Tsar Paul of Russia who had accepted the invitation of the Knights to be their protector. On the other hand the Russians and the Turks had taken the Ionian Islands which, although constituted as a self-governing republic, remained effectively under Russian control. As long as Sicily, Malta and the Ionian Islands were held and defended by the British and Russians and as long as Britain and Russia remained allies, French expansion out of or east of the Adriatic could be blocked. It was the

---

[1]   See Appendix 1: Sources for bibliography. The best account of British involvement in the Mediterranean during part of the period, examining political and diplomatic, and naval and military aspects, is in Mackesey, P: War in the Mediterranean 1803-10

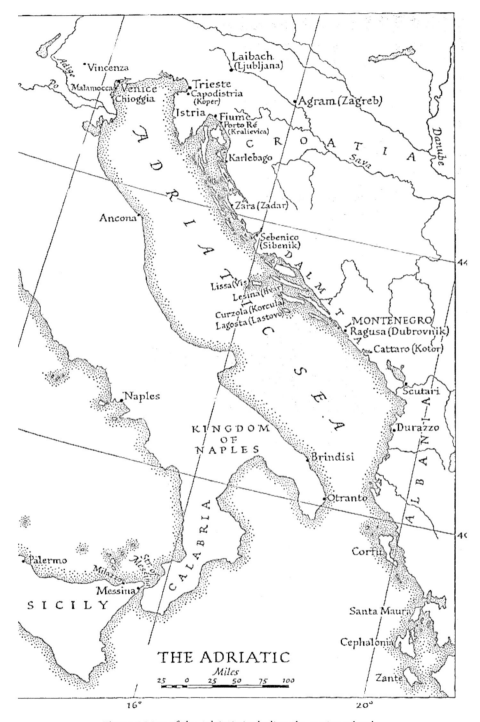

Figure 1.Map of the Adriatic including the Ionian Islands.

This View of LA VALLETTA, taken from the
is most humbly Inscribed by Permission, to
then Commanding the ALLIED FORCES in MALTA;

GARGUR BATTERY during the SIEGE in 1800,
Brigadier GENERAL THOMAS GRAHAM,
by his humble Serv.t, Major Ja.s Weir

Figure 2. Valletta, Malta, during the British siege of 1800, drawn by Major Weir.

failure of Britain to honour its commitment by the Treaty of Amiens of 1802 to give up Malta which gave France a grievance and was a cause of the renewal of war in 1803.

Both Bonaparte's Egyptian campaign and the subsequent short-lived alliance of Tsar Paul with France before his assassination in 1801 raised a perceived threat to British dominion in India. It is incredible today that this could have been taken seriously by any of the parties concerned. An attack on India was definitely projected by Tsar Paul and Napoleon. It is one of the reasons why history has written off Paul as a madman. The same logic has not been applied to Napoleon who also entertained the same megalomaniac dream. The Napoleonic legend has somehow left the conviction that his willpower and ability could have brought it to fruition, despite the fact that the ill-conceived and disastrous 1812 Moscow campaign would have paled before the difficulties of an attack on India, whether overland or by sea from a Red Sea base. The British were in any case far over in the north-east or the south of India (where France's ally Tippoo Sultan was defeated and killed in 1799). The historical tradition that British Government policy could have been determined by this fear smacks more of Kipling's Great Game in the late nineteenth century, when Russia had advanced into central Asia and the British in India to the Himalayas and distances had been reduced by steamships and railways. But true admirers of Napoleon (and no doubt Napoleon himself) have believed him at least the equal of Alexander.

The real fear that informed British policy and was to influence its decisions with regard to the Adriatic was not for India but for the Ottoman Empire. Even though for most of the French wars Turkey was either neutral or leaned towards France out of its fear of Russia, Britain (and indeed Russia, which was at war with Turkey for much of the period) did not want to see the collapse of Turkey if this meant that France could take the lion's share of the spoils. Much of Britain's diplomatic effort was to persuade Russia that this would be the case.

As long as the eastern side of the Adriatic was not in French hands the danger of French conquest of European Turkey in the Balkans seemed remote. Although Bonaparte had destroyed the Venetian Republic in 1797 he had allowed Austria to acquire its territories including Istria and Dalmatia by the Treaty of Campo Formio. Combined with the coast of

Croatia between Istria and Dalmatia this provided a buffer zone between France and Turkey held by Austria. So far there was no reason for British activity in the Adriatic. The turning-point came in 1805 when Austria was defeated at Austerlitz, pushed out of the Second Coalition and forced by the Treaty of Bratislava to cede Istria and Dalmatia, which became parts of Napoleon's Kingdom of Italy. This in turn led to the first limited activity of the British fleet in the Adriatic in association with the Russians. Worse was to come when, by the Treaty of Tilsit in 1807, Russia surrendered the Ionian Islands to Napoleon, giving him a bridgehead across the Strait of Otranto. The further defeat and humiliation of Austria in another war in 1809 at the battle of Wagram and the Peace of Vienna (or Schonbrunn) gave the coast of Croatia to France. With the exception of the coast of Turkish Albania this left the Adriatic a French lake.

Throughout this period there can be no doubt that Napoleon seriously considered the invasion of European Turkey. Along with the diversion caused by the start of the Peninsular War in Portugal and Spain, it was partly due to the success of the British navy in cutting his communications and supplies across the Adriatic that it did not take place. Both sides continued to woo the largely independent pashas in Albania and Bosnia.

These were the changes to the strategic position that drew the British into the Adriatic to check and contain the extension of French power and influence.

***

Britain's principal ally in the region was Austria. A recipient of large British subsidies it was repeatedly defeated and humiliated by Napoleon. The final humiliation came in 1809 when, encouraged by British intervention in the Spanish Peninsula, it again went to war against France. Although it achieved some success against the French in Dalmatia with the help of the British squadron, the crucial battles were again on the Danube. Its crushing defeat at Wagram followed by the Peace of Vienna and the marriage of Princess Maria-Louisa to Napoleon meant that Austria was henceforth at best a cautious neutral and at worst the reluctant ally of France. It became the policy of Austria under its new foreign minister Metternich (formerly its ambassador in Paris) to avoid any embarrassing or compromising situations that might provoke Napoleon. Even after the 1812 debacle in Russia, Metternich played the honest broker for a general peace during the 1813 armistice while biding his time and preparing for war.

Even before they lost them in 1809, the Austrians had closed their Adriatic ports of Trieste and Rijeka to British ships to placate the French. While not having an official diplomatic representation at Vienna from 1809-13 the British maintained a network of unofficial 'confidential agents' in Austria who were known to and kept in touch with Metternich. The French had insisted on a secret clause in the Treaty of Vienna whereby officers in the Austrian army who originated in countries under French rule whether Italian or from the new Illyrian Provinces, which included Istria, Dalmatia and a large part of Croatia, had to quit the service. These together with other political refugees and dissidents opposed to Napoleon swelled the numbers seeking service with the British. In 1811 even a member of the imperial family, the Archduke Francis of Austria-Este, left Austria and became a focal point for emigré officers and intrigue under the protection of the British army commander-in-chief and minister to the court of Sicily, Lord William Bentinck. Although it was possible for Austrian or British agents going to or from Vienna to avoid French-occupied territory by travelling via Kolberg on the

Baltic Sea coast of Prussia, alternative routes were by the Adriatic or the Ottoman Balkan territories. The British also needed to keep open lines of communication for the supply of bullion and arms in the event of Austria being induced to re-enter the war against France. The continuing commanding presence of a British naval squadron in the Adriatic provided for this eventuality.

While Austria was the most important real or potential ally in the region, it was important to give some support and reassurance to the regional Turkish pashas of Albania who feared punishment by the French if not by the Sublime Porte in Constantinople if they collaborated with the British.

Last but not least there was Russia. Although after Tilsit in 1807 Russia was meant to be in alliance with France and an enemy of Britain, by 1811 it was clear that its relations with France were deteriorating and that Napoleon was preparing for war. At war with Turkey from 1806-12, its armies were in Moldavia and Wallachia and fighting on the Danube to the east of Belgrade. It was aiding a Serbian insurrection against the Turks which affected areas not far inland from the Dalmatian coast. And there was Montenegro, the remarkable prince-bishop or vladika of which, Pietro Petrovich, had already, together with a Russian fleet, temporarily occupied the Bocca of Kotor and advanced on Dubrovnik in 1806. In 1812 the British were receiving strong but not altogether convincing indications that the Montenegrins were prepared to attack the French in Dalmatia if British help were forthcoming. Appeals also came from the Russian army on the Danube for money, supplies and the support of the British fleet, if it marched across the Balkans to the Adriatic for a diversionary attack on the French through north Italy while Napoleon was marching on Russia.

The British could not rule out and did not wish to discourage any of these possibilities. It must however have always been clear that at the end of the day even relatively wealthy Britain, which had been disbursing huge sums of money to its principal allies, could not back all proposals and certainly not on the scale demanded by their originators. But for most of the period in question, the need to keep its options open and to be in a position to support all its potential allies was another strong reason for a British presence in the Adriatic.

**

The major and constant preoccupation informing British naval strategy was that of maintaining numerical superiority over the fleets and squadrons of France and its satellites and allies wherever they might be encountered. The fear was that, as France conquered more territories and forced other powers into alliance, it would acquire more warships and ship-building capacity. It was essential to deprive France of the advantages of such increases in naval power as quickly as possible or to prevent the assembly in any one place of the enemy fleets. This situation had arisen in the cases of the navies of the Netherlands, Denmark and Spain in the days of Nelson. The destruction of a large part of the combined French and Spanish fleets at Trafalgar in 1805 seemed to remove the threat and to guarantee British naval supremacy. But two new threats arose almost immediately afterwards.

In 1797 when Bonaparte had taken Venice, the Venetian navy was about half the size of the French navy and a fifth the size of the British navy. But much of it was in disrepair. The French took the pick of the larger ships. About half of the remainder of the Venetian fleet, along with Venice itself, was acquired by the Austrians. Despite further gains when the Austrians and Russians captured Ancona in 1799, Austria so badly neglected its navy that by 1805 it did not have enough seamen to man even the sadly reduced force it could put to sea. By the Peace of Bratislava Austria had to hand over to the French all the ships which had originally been built in Venice and to release from its service all the officers of Venetian origin. More seriously from the British point of view, Venice was handed over to the French. While he had stripped and damaged the famous Arsenal before handing it over to the Austrians in 1797, Napoleon now planned to use its ship-building capacity to augment his fleet.

A serious disadvantage of Venice was that the waters of the lagoon at its entrances were too shallow to allow large ships of war to put to sea fully armed. Guns had to be taken aboard elsewhere or methods devised to help float out ships ready armed. Until the end of the wars it became necessary for the British fleet to keep a constant watch on Venice and a ship-of-the-line cruising nearby large enough to take on any warship which the French might slip out. (There were also reports, which were however soon discounted, that the French intended to use and develop the capacity of the shipyards of Dubrovnik at Gruž).

The second danger came from a less-expected source. A Russian squadron had operated in the Adriatic and seized the Ionian Islands in 1799. In 1806, with British encouragement and support, another large squadron from the Baltic had reached the Mediterranean. Operating from Corfu it was active in the Adriatic in blockading the French as they took over Dalmatia from the Austrians. It acquired a further base in the Bocca of Kotor. Although there were from this time British warships in the Adriatic, the strength of the Russian squadron there reduced the need for a strong British presence.

The blow came with the Treaty of Tilsit in 1807. Not only did Tsar Alexander hand over the Ionian Islands for immediate occupation by the French but also his agreement with Napoleon left at large a strong Russian squadron of doubtful neutrality (which had even been given the British signal books). It became a major preoccupation of the British navy to track the movements of the ships of the Russian squadron. Most tried to make their way back to the Baltic but six of them including four large ships-of-the-line put into the now neutral Austrian port of Trieste. Here they remained, becoming increasingly unseaworthy and under suspicious British surveillance, until Trieste fell to the French in 1809.

From time to time French warships would slip out of Toulon and through the blockade imposed by the British fleet from its base at Port Mahon in the Balearics. British ships would then have to search high and low for them throughout the Mediterranean to prevent them from uniting with French ships elsewhere and thus acquiring a temporary superiority over any nearby British force. It was always possible that the French ships would make for Corfu or enter the Adriatic to join up with others in Ancona or from Venice and thus gain a temporary advantage endangering the British squadron in the area and allowing the transportation of French troops against Turkey or Sicily. Constant vigilance was necessary and from 1809-13, as Britain had no allies in the Adriatic, the presence of a British squadron there seemed essential. Although the French naval force in the Adriatic was progressively destroyed by action and accident, right up until 1815 there were alarms over the movements of surviving frigates.

***

Economic warfare against the enemy in the form of blockades of ports, the seizure of merchant ships and their cargoes, and the issue of letters of marque to license privateers to conduct a form of regulated piracy was not new to the French Revolutionary and Napoleonic Wars.[2] But Napoleon's grand concept of the continental system to exclude British goods from European markets, as proclaimed in the Berlin decrees of November 1806 and the Milan decrees of December 1807, posed a particular challenge to the British. They retaliated by a succession of Orders in Council instructing the ships of the British fleet to stop, examine, detain or confiscate ships carrying goods to or from enemy ports. While thus depriving the enemy of essential supplies and disrupting trade in his produce, a system of licenses allowed other ships to carry and smuggle through British and colonial goods to neutral and friendly countries and even (with the frequent connivance of the French authorities themselves) into French-controlled territory. Heligoland served as an important centre for this traffic in the North and Malta in the South. Maltese and Sicilian merchants carried British goods to Salonika from where they were taken overland to the territories of the Austria empire.

In the Adriatic the primary objective of the British was to deprive the French in Dalmatia and the Ionian Islands of supplies and to destroy trade across the Adriatic or along its coasts. Not only the ships of the British squadron but also Maltese and Sicilian privateers (and even Dalmatians sailing under the British flag) were constantly preying on the small local ships. The French sought vainly to protect them by the use of convoys escorted by gunboats that hugged the coast or passed among the Dalmatian islands under the protection of forts and batteries.

The commerce raiding, especially that conducted by the privateers, often amounted to no more than licenced piracy, to the extent that British navy commanders were so outraged as

Figure 3. Types of vessels in use in the northern Adriatic, watercolour by William Innes Pocock
(National Maritime Museum).

---

[2] It is important to distinguish between 'privateers' whose status was recognised and had the protection of law, and 'pirates' who were outlaws and if caught by either side could be hanged.

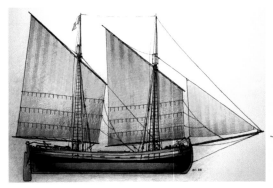

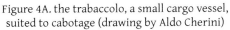

Figure 4A. the trabaccolo, a small cargo vessel, suited to cabotage (drawing by Aldo Cherini)

Figure 4B. A model of a chebec, a swift merchant vessel, typical of the northern Adriatic.

to arrest them. But the practice of awarding prize money in the British navy, no matter how rigorously regulated, also had a corrupting effect. While primarily intended to defray the cost of maintaining the navy and to improve the morale and fighting spirit of ships' crews, it could also make the fortune of otherwise poorly paid officers. The most popular officers were inevitably those who took most prizes, the captains of frigates who were constantly cruising instead of serving in un-remunerative blockade duties. However, as everyone took a share, from the Admiralty, to the commander of the squadron, the officers and crews of the ships directly involved, and even of those in sight of the capture, everyone was compromised. Senior officers might deplore the embarrassment which interference with the ships of neutral or friendly powers could cause them or the extent that the pursuit of prizes could deflect their captains from other duties. The most rapacious of these latter included the celebrated Captain William Hoste whose reputation must always be sullied by his obsession with prize-money. In theory the rules and regulations were well-defined and strictly enforced, with a special Admiralty court established at Malta to determine in every case whether a ship and its cargo had been legally detained and could be 'condemned'. On occasion individual officers were ordered to make restitution of ships and cargoes, and claims for compensation for wrongful seizure went on for years after the conclusion of the wars. Officers such as Hoste were constantly endeavouring to stretch the rules and, aided by agents and lawyers, to challenge the constraints placed upon them. Some at least of the resentment of naval officers against privateers arose from their relative freedom from constraint in making captures. Given the mountainous character of the eastern coast of the Adriatic, the lack of roads and dependence on coastal shipping, the effect on the economy of Istria, Croatia and particularly Dalmatia was devastating.

The second objective of ensuring that British goods could find their way inland from the Adriatic was less easily accomplished. Although some local merchants and ship-owners made their fortunes by carrying British goods under licences issued by the British naval commander, this could hardly compensate the local economy for the losses suffered from the commerce raiding. It involved its own risks not only from arrest and confiscation by the French authorities on land but also from French privateers. Nor were the merchants of Malta ever persuaded that routes inland from the Adriatic could supplant the longer, well-established and to their minds safer route via Salonika. While the licensing system involved various deceptions to evade

French control, its practitioners could just as easily seek to cheat the British by using the licenses to supply the French with non-British goods. One can sense the disappointment and resentment of British captains when they recorded in their log-books how they chased and detained merchant ships only to discover that they carried licenses issued by their admiral. The destruction of enemy trade, the deprival of supplies to the enemy and benefits to British trade were nevertheless advanced as an added justification of the British naval presence in the Adriatic when other reasons had diminished in importance.

***

A maritime nation was in constant need of suitable timber, tar and rope to both build its ships and keep them in good repair. Over the centuries most of these supplies came from the Baltic. But the navy in the Mediterranean with its dockyard at Malta needed a source closer at hand. Despite the serious deforestation of the Adriatic coast by the Venetians, there were still good supplies of timber to be had from inland Croatia and Albania. One of the leading merchants of Rijeka went to London secretly and at considerable risk (after Rijeka had been ceded to the French in 1809) to negotiate such supplies for the British navy with the Admiralty.

***

Lastly there was the prospect of insurrection against French rule by the local inhabitants of the regions around the Adriatic. Whatever the benefits of French rule and its advantages over the ancien regime, there was a host of malcontents. In general the business classes in the towns were relatively happy, but the representatives of the older establishment (in the aristocracy, officer cadres and clergy) and the peasantry remained loyal to or nostalgic for the old order. The drain on the local economy by taxation combined with the effects of the British blockade. Above all, French conscription and the removal of units of the armed forces for service far afield, especially on the disastrous Russia campaign of 1812, were much resented. Towards the end people simply decided that it was unwise to stay on what was clearly the losing side.

There were always numerous emigrés, from archdukes to generals, exiled officers and priests or impoverished noblemen, who were constantly trying to interest the British government in London or its representatives abroad in schemes to stir up revolt in French-held territory. They did not all aim at the restoration of the old order. At one point the British were trying to reconcile proposals for an insurrection to restore Austrian rule in Italy with separate proposals from Italian nationalists. The temptation was clearly to give priority to defeating the French with whatever allies could be found without worrying unduly over what happened thereafter. All the conspirators had one thing in common. However little they stood in need of the support of British ships and armed forces, they all wanted money, whether by being taken into British service, in pensions or funding of their schemes. It was assumed that the financial resources of Britain were inexhaustible.

Although some of the senior officers in the British army viewed the emigré Austrian officers as worthless adventurers, both the British government in London and Lord Bentinck in Sicily sought ways of using them, whether to serve in Spain, to officer a new Italian Levy raised from prisoners of war for the liberation of Italy, or to foment discontent and mutiny in the regiments of the Croatian military frontier that were in French service down the Adriatic coast. The various plots of revolt refined by the 'confidential agents' and their contacts were to range from Montenegro, the Illyrian Provinces, Venetia and North Italy, to the Tirol, Vorarlberg and Switzerland. Claims were repeatedly made that they involved or had the tacit support of the Austrian emperor and archdukes and of the archbishop of Zagreb, whose clergy would be actively involved. To sustain the plots it was necessary to maintain communications through the Adriatic with a network of agents and contacts.

***

It would be wrong to assume that all of these reasons for British involvement in the Adriatic went to form a coherent British policy. There was little effective coordination abroad of the efforts of the British navy, army, and diplomatic and secret service. Despite the best efforts of senior officers to keep each other informed, there were jealousies dividing the services, and uncertain lines of command, which inevitably led to failures in communication. Above all there was the slowness of communication. The upper Adriatic was over 3000 miles away by the roundabout sea route from London, a distance almost equivalent to that to North America or the West Indies. The reports of the naval commander in the Adriatic were relayed via Malta to the commander-in-chief of the navy in the Mediterranean based on Port Mahon and sent on by him through the Straits of Gibraltar to the Admiralty in London. At best this could take about six weeks, at worst two months or more, and as long again for a reply to come back from London.

Similarly, the army commander in the Adriatic reported either to the army command in the Ionian Islands (after Zante, Cephalonia and Santa Maura were captured from the French in 1809-10) or to Lord Bentinck in Sicily as Commander-in-chief of the British army in the Mediterranean, who himself reported to the War Office. At least Bentinck combined his military command with the diplomatic functions of minister to the court of Sicily in which latter capacity some of the 'confidential agents' reported to him. But he was constantly struggling with court intrigue and the task of constitutional reform in Sicily and was repeatedly absent, either to seek political support in London or on campaign in Spain.

Admiral Fremantle, the commander of the squadron in the Adriatic, was to complain repeatedly that he received no strategic or political guidance from London, although Admiral Pellew, his immediate superior as commander-in-chief of the navy in the Mediterranean, was supportive of whatever initiatives he felt able to take. Fremantle was exasperated that the few communications from the Admiralty, which Pellew forwarded to him, included terse and petty complaints that he had incurred unnecessary expenditure.

Given the speed and global nature of modern communications, it is necessary to consider just how difficult it was for anyone to be able to collect enough accurate and up-to-date information to have a good overview of the situation. With the benefit of hindsight the historian can hazard a guess as to what combination of factors determined events. At the time most decisions were uninformed or ill-informed gambles.

Britain was continuously involved in a global war with France and her allies and satellites for more than twenty years with only one short interval in 1802-3. The situation and the reactions that it demanded were in constant change. The Adriatic was never a major theatre of operations. The critical campaigns involving the greatest commitment of men and resources were elsewhere. From 1810 the major theatre of operations, as far as Britain was concerned, was the Iberian Peninsula. From 1811 Napoleon's ill-conceived project against Russia was to determine that his remaining campaigns were to be in the North. The Adriatic, within the overall situation, could only be a side-show of minor significance. After 1815, Istria, Croatia and Dalmatia were to remain under Austrian rule until 1918. British intervention contributed towards that result, although it cannot be argued that it would have been otherwise without it.

The defence of Lissa: A safe harbour

In the war between Britain and France, the Adriatic saw various developments in 1808 in the lull during which Austria, encouraged by Britain, was preparing for a renewal of war with France, a war which was to break out in 1809 and make the Adriatic a more important theatre of operations. These developments included the consolidation of French control and defence of the harbours and islands of the eastern Adriatic seaboard, and the related and consequent need of the British warships operating in the Adriatic to find safe anchorages and bases for their activity.

Even though the French had held Istria and Dalmatia after their defeat of Austria in 1805, had soon after added Ragusa (Dubrovnik), and obtained the Bocca di Cattaro (Boka Kotorska) after

Figure 5. The Adriatic in 1806

91

Figure 6. The Adriatic in 1809, showing French territorial gains.

Napoleon's alliance with Alexander of Russia at Tilsit in 1807, their control over many areas, particularly the islands, was tenuous. There were also breaks in the coastline which they did not hold: Austria still had the ports of Trieste and Fiume (Rijeka) and the coast of Croatia from Fiume down almost to Zara (Zadar) in Dalmatia; and the territories of the Ottoman Turkish province of Bosnia reached the sea at the mouth of the River Narenta (Neretva) between Dalmatia and the seaboard territories of the old Republic of Ragusa. 1808-9 was to see the strengthening of French control, following the withdrawal in 1807 of the Russian fleet which had encouraged and sustained local revolts against the French and temporarily seized various of the islands.

While the few British frigates and brigs of war, which were almost constantly cruising in the Adriatic, could keep to the sea for long periods of time, either by carrying adequate stores when leaving their base at Malta or being re-supplied by special transport vessels, they needed safe anchorages to shelter from bad weather, carry out emergency repairs which could not wait until their return to base, and where the warships, which frequently cruised separately, could rendezvous. Finding sources of fresh water was also important, as was having somewhere where prizes and their cargoes taken in attacks on enemy shipping and commerce could be collected, transferred or disposed of.

The small British squadron in the Adriatic had since August 1806 been commanded by Captain Patrick Campbell in the frigate UNITÉ. His principal functions were to observe and report on the progress of the French shipbuilding programme in the Arsenal of Venice, maintain communications with the Austrians through their port of Trieste, interfere with enemy communications across the Adriatic, and as a highly profitable incidental activity, to seize or

Figure 7. British frigate of 38 guns.

destroy any enemy merchant shipping. On the UNITÉ's cruise up the Adriatic of April-June 1808, we know from the diary of one of the seamen on her, Richard Wilson, that the French were beginning to take more effective steps to deny the British warships use of the islands. Both Fano and Merara, in the lower Adriatic to the north of the French held island fortress of Corfu, were found to have been occupied and fortified by the enemy. Pola (Pula) in Istria had also been refortified after the earlier destruction by the British of a battery there. New small ships of war constructed in the Venice Arsenal for the French and Italian navies were beginning to take to sea, especially numerous gunboats which could operate more effectively in the narrow channels between the islands.[3]

On earlier voyages to Trieste, the British had found a convenient anchorage off Umago (Umag) on the north-west corner of Istria but without being able to land in the French-held harbour. Until March 1808 when the Austrians had finally been forced by Napoleon to break off diplomatic relations with Britain and deny all access whether official or unofficial, UNITÉ had been able to use Trieste for the illegal disposal of prizes or cargoes. A far better anchorage and base for operations had been discovered in April 1807 in the long fine harbour of Lussin Piccolo (Mali Lošinj) on the island of Lussin (Lošinj) just south of Istria. But the island could easily be reached from the Istrian mainland by short crossings to and between the islands, and without the British being able to leave a warship or a sufficient force on land to defend it, it could easily be retaken by the French in the periods between the visits of the British ships.

---

[3] (For full details of sources and explanation of abbreviations see Appendix 1: Sources) Wilson diary in Thursfield, H. G. (ed.): Five Naval Journals, 1951, pp. 224-25

Figure 8. Istria and Kvarner (Umago lies between Pirano and Cittanova, Lussin is bottom right).

Figure 9. Piccolo Lussin/Mali Lošinj, engraving by Jacob Emil Schindler.

An Italian frigate, brig and schooner of war, which UNITÉ had encountered off Pola on 2 May 1808, had been bound from Venice for Lussin, to take possession of it and deny its use to the British. Even after UNITÉ had captured the brig and chased the frigate and schooner into Pola, the captain of the frigate or corvette persisted in following his orders. Wilson noted in his journal on 10 May, while UNITÉ was still at Lussin, that the captain of the Italian frigate had come onto the island of Lussin to reconnoitre the British. The British brig of war

Figure 10. Auguste de Marmont (1774–1852), oil
painting by Andrea Appiani.

MINSTREL (with the diarist Richard Wilson) left UNITÉ at Lussin on 13 May to take prizes to
Malta. It was only on 10 July when UNITÉ and MINSTREL met again at the island of Lissa, that
Wilson noted that 500 enemy troops had taken Lussin during the absence of UNITÉ when it
was taking further prizes to Malta, and that they were fortifying it. Napoleon himself had
written on 20 March 1808 to General Marmont, commanding his forces in Dalmatia, to deplore
the depredations of the British at Lussin-Grande (Veliki Lošinj) and to propose that 80-100
Dalmatians be placed there to prevent the British cruisers[4] from disembarking their men. It is
therefore likely that the efforts of the French and Italians to secure Lussin had been ordered
by the Emperor himself.[5]

It is against this background that the island of Lissa (Vis) began to take on greater importance
in British consideration of their needs and strategy in the Adriatic.

***

[4] 'Cruiser' at this time was used to designate the smaller and faster warships such as frigates and brigs which were
used for patrol duties and were not 'ships-of-the-line' for use in battles between fleets. They were usually engaged in
battles with one or two other ships of the same size. The sea battles near Lissa have been of particular interest, given
the number of cruisers involved, with their greater and faster capability to manoeuvre.
[5] Wilson diary, pp. 224-29, 237 Napoleon's letter is in Marmont, Viesse de (A. F. L.): Mémoires du Maréchal Duc de
Raguse, Paris 1857 UNITÉ logbook (ADM 51/1808)

It is difficult to establish when and by whom in the British navy the great advantages of Lissa as a harbour and base were first observed. It is possible to study the British sources, such as the diary of Richard Wilson, the reports of the captains of the British warships and their logbooks on the one hand, and local records on the other. The priest of Lissa, Canon Doimi, wrote a detailed account of events on the island that has been much used by historians of Dalmatia. While he is most often right about the names of the British ships and officers, he confuses them and his chronology is seriously at variance with the movements of the warships as recorded in their logbooks, sometimes by more than a year. It is therefore probable that his account was written retrospectively some years after the events he described. [6]

Although British ships would have been aware of the existence of the island of Lissa and have sighted it as they passed up the Adriatic on their way to the port of Trieste, they may not have known of the excellent harbour of Port St George which lay in a long deep inlet on its northern side. In 1804 Nelson had sent Captain Thomas Staines in the sloop CAMELEON on a secret mission to track down enemy privateers, which had involved exploring parts of the eastern coast of the Adriatic not normally touched by British warships acting as convoy escorts to Trieste. The logbook of CAMELEON records that it anchored on 10 November 1804 in Port St George (possibly the first British warship to do so) and that Captain Staines and the sailing master spent 12-13 November surveying the harbour. As frequently happened when a warship touched land, members of the crew ran away and search parties were sent on shore to track down the deserters before Staines left Lissa on 15 November. Austria had acquired Lissa after the suppression of the Venetian Republic in 1797 and had no doubt inherited Venetian administrative structures and officials. In 1804 Austria was a friendly neutral and was soon to be an ally of Britain in the war of 1805 against France. In any case, it is unlikely that anyone would have wished or been able to deny a British warship access to the island.[7]

Austria ceded Istria, Dalmatia and the islands, and the territories of Ragusa to France by the treaty of Bratislava in December 1805, although it took some time for the French to move in and assert their authority. It was in this brief interlude that a Chevalier Tinseau presented his memorandum to the British government in March 1806 recommending the seizure and occupation by British forces of Liesina or Lesina (Hvar). Tinseau mentioned that Lissa had a good harbour in Port St George. As a footnote, Tinseau considered the disadvantages of occupying Lissa instead of Lesina. These were that the entry to the harbour faced the wrong way for the most favourable winds; there were very few inhabitants, no existing establishments for troops or ships, no fortifications, and very little food. The only advantage was that it could be defended with fewer troops because it was smaller. However, Tinseau recommended that, although Lesina should be the primary objective, the British should also seize and occupy the islands of Lissa, Brazza (Brač) and Curzola (Korčula).[8]

The British government decided not to act on Tinseau's advice and the French had in any case quickly made Lesina one of their principal strongholds. From the point of view of the British government, the problem with permanently occupied bases was that they tied up both scarce warships and troops for their defence, required the expense of fortification, and were

---

[6]   Doimi is used by Foretic, D: Vis u medjunrarodnom zbivanju, 1956, and Pisani, P: La Dalmatie de 1797 à 1815, 1893
[7]   Nicolas, Sir Nicholas Harris: Dispatches and Letters of Admiral Lord Nelson, Vol. V, 1 Sep. 1804. CAMELEON logbook (ADM 51/1487)
[8]   Chevalier de Tinseau: Mémoire sur la Dalmatie et ses Isles, dated 10 March 1806 (FO 42/8)

Figure 11. Lesina/Hvar harbour, photographed in 1908.

much more likely to provoke enemy attack than the casual use by British warships of islands not held in strength by the enemy. The only recommendation in Tinseau's memorandum on which the British seem to have been willing to act (although it is one of the most obscure episodes in the documents of the time) was for the temporary seizure (without permanent occupation) and destruction of the fortifications on the Tremiti Islands 65 miles to the west of Lissa near the coast of Italy, although the attempt to achieve this was unsuccessful.[9]

Although the French had moved quickly to secure the islands nearer to the mainland, including Lesina and Curzola, it is unlikely that they could do much to secure the more distant island of Lissa. As early as April 1806 a ship of the Russian naval squadron based in the Bocca di Cattaro visited the port of Lissa, bombarded the town, removed some old Venetian cannon from a tower in the harbour and took away some prisoners. They subsequently did the same at Comissa on the west side of the island. It is not clear whether their prisoners were French or locals in French service, nor whether the Russians left any force on the island until their withdrawal from the Adriatic after the Tilsit agreement of July 1807. In 1806-07 the Russians successfully ousted the French from Curzola but an attack on Lesina and landings on the mainland in support of local revolts against the French were not successful.[10]

It was in this period that we have the next references to British warships visiting Lissa. WEAZLE and ESPOIR bringing a convoy of prizes taken in the northern Adriatic reached the island of Lissa on 16 November 1806 where they watered at the little port of Comissa on the west side of the island. It was easy access to excellent fresh water at Comissa that was to make it a regular port of call. Wilson in his journal frequently refers to the case of a seaman called Michael Welsh who seems to have been a member of a prize crew who deserted on this occasion. Welsh was captured by the French, either on Lissa or when attempting to reach the mainland, where they forced him to work on the new fortifications at Zara.[11]

---

[9] AMBUSCADE logbook June-Sep. 1806 (ADM 51/1631). Wilson diary, entry for 23 Sep. 1806
[10] Pisani, op. cit., pp.272-280
[11] ESPOIR logbook (ADM 51/1623). Wilson diary, entries for 10 Dec. 1806 and 19 June 1807

After the Russians and French made peace at Tilsit in early July 1807, the Russians soon left those Dalmatian islands that they held. General Guillet in command at Lesina had been ordered by Marmont to reoccupy Brazza and other islands where the inhabitants had collaborated with the Russians and had armed vessels as privateers against the French. Guillet took revenge with executions on Solta on 20 August and on Brazza on 24 August, and some arrests on Lissa. Canon Doimi recorded in his memoirs that the inhabitants there had been encouraged to buy off the general with anything they had of value.[12]

According to Doimi, in January 1808, a General Monfalcone in French service visited Lissa. He promoted a local magistrate to be a government commissioner responsible for raising a force of pandours or militia to be commanded by a former Venetian officer, Carlo Alessandri, who arrived one month later. But this was as far as French control of Lissa was to go. Alessandri and his small force were to prove powerless to prevent the visits of British warships or the use of the harbour of Port St George by numerous privateers or pirates.[13]

On 13 May 1808, while still at the island of Lussin and just before the French were to reoccupy that island in his absence, Captain Patrick Campbell of UNITÉ wrote to Admiral Lord Collingwood to recommend the occupation and fortification of Lissa:

> 'I take the liberty of strongly recommending to your Lordship, taking possession of the island of Lissa which your Lordship will see by the Chart lays in a most excellent situation for preventing the communication between the Upper and Lower parts of the Adriatic. It has one excellent Port; by building a small Blockhouse at its entrance, which is very narrow; and with a garrison of about a hundred or two Men, would with our Men of War, cruizing in the Adriatic resist any force the Enemy could easily bring against it, the land about it being very high and inaccessible from the Sea except in a perfect calm: the inhabitants may amount to about 3,000. As there is a want of Hemp and other Stores at Malta, the Imperial (i.e. Austrian) Small Vessels that trade in the Gulph (Gulf of Venice i.e. the Adriatic), would bring there, whatever quantity were wanted (indeed the proposition has been made to me by several Merchants) as they cannot clear out for any but an Austrian Port, with that article; and our transports might lie in safety to load and carry it to Malta. I am certain a thousand tons, or more, of that article might be procured in the course of a twelvemonth'.[14]

There had always been strong interest on the part of the British navy in securing new or alternative supplies of shipbuilding materials. The Austrian merchants to whom Campbell referred were presumably those of Trieste and Fiume, ports which, together with the coast of Croatia, were still parts of the Austrian Empire (the merchant Adamić in Fiume was to long continue to supply the British navy, even years after Fiume had also passed to the French in 1809). Collingwood forwarded the letter to the Admiralty under cover of a letter of 24 June 1808 from his flagship OCEAN off Cadiz in which he commented:

> 'I have received a letter from Captain Campbell of the Unité recommending the possessing of the Island of Lissa in the Adriatic as a place of rendezvous for the trade

---

[12] Pisani, op. cit., p. 285
[13] Foretic, op. cit., p. 531
[14] enclosed Collingwood-Admiralty (ADM 1/414, no. 144)

Figure 12. Admiral Lord Collingwood. Succeeded Nelson as
commander-in-chief of the British fleet in the Mediterranean.
Oil painting by Henry Howard, after a painting by Giuseppe
Politi (National Portrait Gallery).

which might be opened with the Ports in that Sea, if the ships had such a place of
rendezvous: - as I never saw this place I cannot give an opinion on the eligibility of it,
but I have not encouraged it, because it frequently happens that places unoccupied and
not drawing the attention of the Enemy are more useful than when establishments are
made on them, the expense of which in a precarious establishment would be greater
than any advantage from it would compensate, and whatever works were erected,
it would probably require a squadron for its defence: - I transmit an Extract from
Captain Campbell's letter, in which he states the probable advantages, - and which
I apprehend, surrounded as it is by Enemies, would all vanish the moment it was
regularly possessed.'[15]

Canon Doimi claimed that 1808 saw more and more visits by English warships and he names
UNITÉ, AMPHION, ACORN (as AICHORN), and VOLAGE, the ship-of-the-line MAGNIFICENT
as arriving in June 1808, and an unnamed frigate which put in for five days for repairs and
repainting in October 1808, with only the captain landing and going for a walk. But it is clear
from the logs of the ships he mentions that the frigate AMPHION of 32 guns, although first in
the Adriatic in June 1808, did not anchor at Port St George until 5 February 1809; ACORN sloop

---

[15]   ADM 1/414, no. 414

of 18 guns did not arrive in the Adriatic until June 1809 (first at Port St George on 5 December 1809); VOLAGE corvette of 22 guns until 1810; and MAGNIFICENT 3rd rate ship of the line of 74 guns did not arrive at Lissa until the end of March 1811. Even Patrick Campbell's frigate UNITÉ of 40 guns, which was in the Adriatic until leaving for good in early February 1809, appears never to have entered Port St George even though it made its rendezvous off Lissa with the other ships in Campbell's small squadron. This leaves MINSTREL sloop of 24 guns under Captain Hollinsworth, which certainly took on water at Comisa in June-July 1808 and used Comisa as a base from which to sail north to try to seize merchant shipping among the islands. It sent such prizes as it captured back to Comisa and possibly also to Port St George. With the reoccupation by the French of the island of Lussin Piccolo at about this time, the British needed to send their prizes to a new collection point. (A glimpse of how the arrival of British seaman affected the lives of the local people is given in the dairy of Richard Wilson, who came to Comisa with MINSTREL. Walking alone on the hills above Comisa he tried to buy food and drink, but the local inhabitants in their fear of him closed their doors and windows. When he had finally forced his way into a house and had been given water, he offered payment but it was refused by the adults and he gave money to a child).[16]

While there are strong reasons to doubt Doimi's chronology, he also recorded the arrival at the port of Lissa in late 1808 of a number of privateers in English service under masters who had Italian names and of two flying Sicilian colours, and that when UNITÉ arrived at Lissa in March 1809, the captain invited the captains of the privateers to his ship and ordered them to call back all of their armed boats which had been sent out for piracy, threatening that he would otherwise burn their ships. According to Doimi, this intervention saved the traffic of small ships on the poor coasts of Dalmatia and Puglia. If Doimi is right about the date, by early February 1809 UNITÉ commanded by Patrick Campbell had left the Adriatic never to return. It is more likely that it was the British frigate AMPHION (commanded by William Hoste, who was an even more dedicated prize-seeker and resentful of any competition or ruses by merchant seamen to deprive him of a capture) which first visited Lissa on 5 February 1809 and was back again on 18-19 March. The AMPHION's logbook for the first of these dates described the harbour and noted how best to anchor there for future reference.[17]

From this point on over the next two years, the island of Lissa became increasingly important to the British, not only as a convenient though informal base or place of rendezvous for its warships and their prizes, but also for the many Sicilian, Maltese and other privateers and smugglers who flew British colours and were engaged not only in attacking all local shipping both large and small, but also in defying French efforts through the 'Continental System' to stop the importation to the mainland of British and British colonial goods. Smuggling of contraband and the profitable business of supplying Lissa with food for this greatly enlarged population inevitably involved Dalmatians despite severe penalties imposed by the French authorities.

The war between Austria and France that began in April 1809 and ended, after the defeat of Austria at the battle of Wagram, with the treaty of Vienna or Schönbrunn of 14 October 1809, increased the importance of Lissa. The British naval squadron in the Adriatic was substantially

---

[16]   Foretic, op. cit., p. 531. AMPHION logbook (ADM 51/1909 and 2097). ACORN logbook (ADM 51/1872 and ADM 51/21439). VOLAGE logbook (ADM 51/1792 and 1954). UNITÉ logbook (ADM 51/1935). Wilson diary, pp. 234-6
[17]   Foretic, op. cit., p. 532. AMPHION logbook (ADM 51/2097)

reinforced to be able to support the Austrians and it had soon assisted the Austrians to take possession of the islands in the Gulf of Guarnerolo (Kvarner) south of Istria, including Lussin, which again became a convenient base for British warships. But the British navy could not prevent the French from capturing Trieste and could not affect the outcome of the war as it was determined by the French army's victories far to the north. The treaty of Vienna not only gave the Kvarner islands including Lussin back to the French, but also ceded Trieste and Fiume, inland Istria, and the Croatian coast from Fiume down to Dalmatia. Except for the small gaps where Ottoman Turkish territory reached the coast at the mouth of the Narenta/ Neretva river and between Ragusa and the Bocca di Cattaro, the entire northern section of the eastern coast of the Adriatic, together with all the offshore islands, was in French hands (as were the entire Italian northern and western coasts of the Adriatic). Napoleon immediately consolidated his gains by the creation of the Illyrian Provinces. While this was with military considerations in mind (the possibility of an attack on the Ottoman territories in the Balkans and to act as a check on any future hostility from Austria), it is clear that Napoleon also had clear economic objectives: to seal off the territories of the Austrian Empire from any further importation of British goods and to develop overland routes for France's own commerce with the Ottoman Empire.[18]

The British responded to the challenge. British goods still reached the Austrian Empire from Malta via the long and dangerous overland route from Salonika over the Turkish provinces in the Balkans to Sarajevo and Slavonski Brod on the Sava river border with Hungary, and from there to Budapest and Vienna. But as long as the British navy could dominate the Adriatic, merchant ships could use Lissa as a convenient base for sending on British goods into Turkish territory by the Narenta/Neretva river or to arrange for them to be smuggled into or across French territory.

***

Against this background, it is clear that Napoleon attached considerable importance to the capture of Lissa whenever the buildup of his naval forces in the Adriatic made an attack possible. For years the shipbuilding facilities of the great Arsenal of Venice had been dedicated to building new warships for the French and Italian navies. As it was impossible for heavily armed ships to pass over the sandbars at Venice to reach the open sea, rendering it of little value as a military base, Napoleon had given orders for the development of Ancona as his main military port in the Adriatic and it was there that he attempted to concentrate his Adriatic squadron. As well as such frigates and brigs as were slowly produced by the shipyards of the Venice Arsenal, there were also the badly decayed ships remaining from the Russian Adriatic fleet, which had been trapped at Trieste and were finally handed over to the French in 1809, some of which were not totally beyond repair. Otherwise the reinforcement of Napoleon's naval force in the Adriatic involved a kind of relay race whereby frigates and other smaller vessels slipped out of Toulon and relieved those guarding Corfu, which in turn tried to reach Ancona, Venice or Trieste.

---

[18] For a full account of British involvement in the war of 1809 see Mackesey, P: War in the Mediterranean 1803-1810, 1957. On the origins and economic purposes of the Illyrian Provinces see Pivec-Stele, M: La Vie Économique des Provinces Illyriennes 1809-1813, 1930

It was not until October 1810 that Napoleon sent orders, through his viceroy in Italy Eugene Beauharnais, for the French squadron in Ancona to attack Lissa. By this time the Italian squadron based at Venice and Ancona consisted of vessels of the French and Italian (or 'Venetian') navies and amounted to 5 frigates, 2 corvettes and 6 brigs, which on 6 August 1810 had been placed under the command of capitaine de vaissaux Bernard Dubourdieu.[19] The number of British warships in the Adriatic was always variable and the frigates, brigs and sloops of which it consisted seldom sailed as a squadron but sailed separately singly or in pairs to observe the enemy whether in Trieste, Venice and Ancona, or to attack enemy shipping wherever they could find it. There was no British squadron of warships that had the particular duty of guarding the island of Lissa. Captain William Hoste was one of the senior post captains in command of a frigate. He was usually in charge in the intervals between the periods when more senior officers came to take command in times of particular crisis. Even when Hoste was left as the captain in command of the two or three frigates and one or two brigs which at this time made up the Adriatic squadron, he did not always fulfill the role of commodore answering directly to the admiral commanding the British fleet in the Mediterranean but was often subject to the orders of the commodore commanding the British squadron lower down the Adriatic which had the continuous role of blockading the French fortress island of

Figure 13. Captain William Hoste. Most famous of the British naval officers serving in the Adriatic but never an Admiral. Drawing by William Greatbach (National Maritime Museum).

---

[19] For the French, Italian and Illyrian navies see Pisani, op. cit., Vol. 2, pp. 405-07, Pivec-Stele, op. cit., pp. 189-95, and Safanof, N: Ratovi na Jadranu 1797-1815, 1988 pp. 246-48

Figure 14A. Eugene de Beauharnais, portrait by Jean Duplessi-Bertaux.

Figure 14B. Bernard Dubourdieu (1773–1881), led the French raid on Lissa in 1810 and was killed at the Battle of Lissa, 1811.

Corfu.[20] These comments are a necessary corrective to the often repeated mistakes in histories written in Dalmatia and the former Yugoslavia which at worst add up the names of all British warships that visited the Adriatic to make up a huge permanent fleet,[21] and which subscribe to the myth of Hoste (much promoted by his family and biographers) that he was the only senior officer in the Adriatic throughout the whole period, with the rank of commodore or even admiral.

Given that the few British frigates and brigs were usually away from Lissa on separate missions in different parts of the Adriatic, the danger to the island of an attack by a French squadron was very considerable. It was almost entirely a matter of chance whether ships of the two squadrons would meet each other at sea or whether they would find each other either at Ancona or Lissa. Hoste on his frigate AMPHION regularly looked into Ancona once or twice a month to check the state of the French squadron, and as late as 6 October 1810 had been chased away by ships of the enemy squadron. [22]

---

[20] In the British navy 'captain' and 'commodore' are not ranks but indicate effective commands. An officer with the rank of Post Captain could command (or be the 'commodore' of) a squadron, a ship-of-the-line, or frigate, while an officer with the rank of Lieutenant could be the 'captain' of a frigate or smaller vessel.
[21] Both Pisani and Pivec-Stele, op. cit., say that there were 22 British warships in the Adriatic between 1809-13 without explaining that they were not all there at the same time, and give the impression that the French navy was hopelessly outmatched in the number and size of ships (although Pisani does recognise that the real superiority of the Brish navy lay in its training and seamanship). The British navy was very economical in the use of its warships and seldom assigned more ships than were necessary to match the forces which the enemy could put to sea.
[22] AMPHION logbook (ADM 51/2097)

Dubourdieu left Ancona on 17 October with a squadron consisting of three frigates, two corvettes, and two brigs and carrying a battalion of 500 troops of the 3e leger italien regiment.[23] They reached Lissa on 22 October, without being seen by any British warship or finding any in the vicinity of Lissa. The squadron approached the entrance of the harbour of Port St George flying British colours (using the enemy's flag was a common trick practiced by both sides), then raised French colours and sent in 500 men on their boats to seize the merchant shipping anchored there and to pillage the warehouses. Reports of the damage inflicted by the French squadron at Lissa vary very considerably and the numbers given in various sources are difficult to interpret. Dubourdieu claimed he had burned 62 vessels of which 43 were laden, had taken 10 privateers with a total of 100 cannon, restored 10 ships to Napoleon's subjects, 14 Illyrian, Neapolitan and Italian, and taken 100 prisoners.[24] It is not clear if any one number includes another. The Viceroy Eugene, writing to Napoleon from Ancona on 27 October, conflated the damage to 68 ships and 100 cannon.[25] On the other hand, Canon Doimi recorded only that three prizes, which had been captured earlier by the British, were sent by the French to Spalato, and two privateers and a contrabandier were burned.[26] This is reflected in a letter from William Hoste to his father on 16 February 1811 in which he complained of the prize money he had lost (he would have been much less concerned for any loss of privateers).

> 'The vessels the French took at Lissa were 3 detained ships (neutrals) captured by my squadron and were valuable: they are lost in toto'.[27]

Whatever the truth of the matter, the figures indicate the level to which the French believed that British-sponsored activity at Lissa had risen.

In the afternoon sails were sighted to the south and Dubourdieu, fearful lest they be those of British warships returning to Lissa, promptly took his squadron back to Ancona and sent the vessels captured or released to Spalato (Split). Napoleon was to be displeased with Dubourdieu, especially for having abandoned Lissa and allowing the British to return to it. In a letter of 4 November to Viceroy Eugene he wrote (using yet another number for the privateers captured):

> 'Je suis mécontent que D. n'ait pas emmené les seize corsaires qu'il a trouvés à Lissa et qu'il ait abandonné l'île'.[28]

But the predicament of Dubourdieu recalled the comment of Chevalier Tinseau in his memorandum of 1806 that once inside the harbour of St George it was not always easy to work one's way out. Without fortifications or a force outside at sea superior to anything that

---

[23] For accounts of the French attack on Vis see Erber, T: Storia della Dalmazia, Zadar 1886-92, Pt. IV, pp. 7-10, Pisani, op. cit., Vol. 2, pp. 409-10, and Safanof, op. cit., pp. 168-69. An English account is given in James, W: Naval History of Great Britain, 1837, Vol. V, p. 88

[24] Quoted in Erber, op. cit., p. 8

[25] Quoted in Erber, op. cit., p. 9

[26] Pisani, op. cit., p. 410. James, op. cit., appears to base his figures on Dubourdieu's claim and gives 30 vessels taken (including 10 privateers mounting a total of 100 guns), 64 burned of which 43 were laden, and 100 prisoners taken. Pivec-Stele, op. cit. p. 206 gives 44 ships burned, 12 privateers taken or destroyed and 14 'French' ships released.

[27] Hoste, W: Memoirs and Letters, 1833

[28] Quoted Erber, op. cit. p. 9 and Pisani, op. cit. p. 410

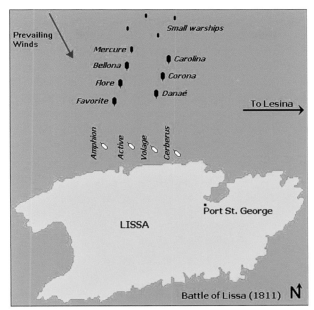

Figure 15A & B. Battle Lissa 1811. A. Map, created by Ruhrfisch; B. watercolour by Nicholas Pocock (Tate).

was sent against it, the harbour would be a trap. Had there been any British warships at Lissa insufficient to attack Dubourdieu's squadron when it arrived , their only choice would have been to take to sea rather than seek refuge in the undefended harbour. Hoste was to write to his father from Malta on 4 January 1811 that from French reports of the raid 'one would suppose that Lissa had been fortified and garrisoned, whereas there was not the shadow of resistance, nor the means to resist'.[29]

---

[29] Hoste, op. cit.

Dubourdieu's raid on Lissa immediately had repercussions. The British realised that Lissa had become too important for them to lose (activity there immediately resumed at a high level). It would have to be defended against any further French attempts to capture it, either by committing more warships to the Adriatic squadron, by the construction and garrisoning of fortifications, or a combination of both. In the short term, and while the long debate over exactly what was needed went on between the British government, army and navy, the only hope was that the British navy could maintain a force in the Adriatic capable of coming quickly to the defence of Lissa and sufficient to take on anything that the French might send against it. It is ironical that the French were unable to take the next opportunity offered to them. On 27 November 1810 two of the British warships, Hoste's frigate AMPHION and the corvette VOLAGE collided and damaged each other in heavy seas while watching Ancona. Both had to be sent to Malta for repairs. [30]

On 2 February 1811 Napoleon sent orders to Viceroy Eugene for a further attack on Lissa and its occupation. But it was decided that this would have to await the arrival of two more French frigates, FLORE and DANAE, which left Corfu on 23 February 1811 (having been replaced there by new arrivals from Toulon), sailed via Gravosa (Gruž, the port of Ragusa), and arrived at Ancona on 5 March. Dubourdieu's reinforced squadron of four frigates, two corvettes, a brig, two schooners and a xebec embarked troops and set sail for Lissa late on 11 March 1811. As luck would have it, AMPHION and VOLAGE were back at Lissa on 7 March joining the frigates CERBERUS and ACTIVE and Hoste was again in temporary command. Even now this force was reduced from 8 March when AMPHION and VOLAGE cruised away to the south towards the Tremiti Islands and Pelagosa (Palagruža). But they returned to Lissa on 12 March in time to be able to meet Dubourdieu's squadron on 13 March and win the celebrated battle of Lissa, unusual in being an all-frigate/corvette action. Almost by accident Hoste was given the enduring claim to fame on which his otherwise exaggerated reputation has been built.[31]

Hoste soon departed from Lissa on 25 March 1811 for Malta and then for leave in England, leaving others to resolve the problem of what to do about the further defence of Lissa, although he is credited with having drafted plans for shore batteries to guard the mouth of the harbour of Port St George before his departure.[32] (As already seen, Captain Campbell had made proposals as early as May 1808). The French frigates which had escaped from the battle of Lissa had sought shelter under the French forts on Lesina, where they landed the Italian soldiers they had brought from Ancona, and then in the harbour of Gravosa at Ragusa, but were still considered a threat.

***

[30] Hoste, op cit. p. 184
[31] The Battle of Lissa has received much attention in many publications, so a full account of it is not repeated here. See note 1 above on its significance and accounts in James, op. cit., Vol V, p. 90. Pisani, op. cit, Vol. 2, p. 415. Safanof, op, cit., pp. 171-78. Pocock, T: Remember Nelson, 1977. Even given the numerical superiority of the French squadron, this author believes that, at this stage of the wars, British seamanship was so superior as to guarantee victory for the British squadron. Hoste happened to be in command. The result would probably have been the same if the British squadron had been commanded by another officer.
[32] Pocock, op. cit, p. 184

The defence of Lissa: Delays and surveys

Captain Charles Rowley of the ship-of-the-line EAGLE 74[33] cruising off Corfu had been placed in overall command of the Adriatic squadrons in February 1811. It is thanks to the survival of both his official and private letter-books, those of the commander-in-chief of the Mediterranean fleet from June 1811, Admiral Sir Edward Pellew, and the records of the British Admiralty and War Office, that we can follow the development of the long debate on what to do about the defence of Lissa as the army and navy tried to shift the burden of responsibility from one to the other.[34]

It is important to understand the context in which the debate took place. The reluctance of the British government and armed forces to commit troops or ships to the defence of permanent bases was largely due to the chronic shortage of manpower caused by the length of the wars and the ever-increasing demands for men. Bases required garrisons that locked up military forces. Within the Mediterranean, the British now had their two important bases of Gibraltar and Malta, both of which required about 5000 troops. From 1806 Britain was committed to the defence of Sicily, with its long coastline and the short distance from the Italian mainland over the straits of Messina. At one point after the French conquest of Naples, the garrison of Messina rose to as many as 20,000. By the treaty of 1808 between the British government and the Bourbon monarchy of Sicily, because of the need to redeploy British forces to Portugal and Spain at the beginning of the Peninsula War, the British guaranteed a minimum British

Figure 16A. Admiral Sir Charles Rowley (1770– 1845), portrait by George Sanders.

Figure 16B. Admiral Edward Pellew (1757–1833), portrait by Samuel Drummond (Royal Albert Memorial Museum and Art Gallery).

---

[33] The number given after a warship is of the number of guns carried. It also indicates the type of vessel. Ships-of-the-line carried more than 70 guns, and 74 was the standard at this time; frigates over 30 guns; and brigs over 15.

[34] See Appendix 1: Sources

force of 10,000 men to stay in Sicily to supplement the Sicilian armed forces. Of the maximum of about 30,000 troops that eventually reached the Mediterranean, two thirds were bound up in the defence of military bases, leaving only some 8-10,000 deployable for offensive action. These were sent out of Sicily with the greatest reluctance, and from 1808 the first call on them had to be from Spain.[35]

Much the same was true of the British navy, many of whose warships were either committed to the defence of the bases or to the blockading of enemy ports. In 1808 the British Mediterranean fleet numbered 80 vessels of which about 25 were ships of the line. Given the large number of men needed to serve the guns quickly and effectively, a third rate ship of the line of 74 guns needed between 600-700 seamen and marines, a fifth rate frigate of 32-40 guns between 200-300, and a sloop or brig of 16-18 guns between 90-120. The total number of men in the British Mediterranean fleet was about 28,000.[36]

Both sides tried to raise men from other sources. There were a surprising number of officers and men in the British army from France, Switzerland or Corsica who had served in the former French royalist army and left France after the revolution.[37] Sicilians were enlisted into the British army, especially to man the British army's gunboats, which were to play an important role in the Adriatic towards the end of the war.[38] It was always hoped that troops might be raised locally, whether in Albania or Dalmatia or Croatia. But both the British and the French were to find that there was no great enthusiasm to fight other peoples' wars especially if it involved leaving home. Nothing did more damage to the acceptability of French rule in Dalmatia than the attempts at compulsory conscription into the regular army that stimulated a number of revolts. General Marmont, governor of the Illyrian Provinces from 1810-12, claimed he had greater success in organizing a national guard of about 10,000 men to defend the coast.[39]

On the naval side, besides the numerous Sicilian and Maltese privateers flying British colours and carrying British letters of marque, the crew of any British warship would include a high proportion of seamen from other countries, whether pressed men taken from American merchant shipping, Finns, or (by French estimates of 1813) some 6,000 Illyrian seamen who were in British service. These last may have been attracted by the better pay offered by the British, an attractive alternative to unemployment or possible compulsory service on the losing side.[40]

After Admiral Collingwood had advised against the occupation of Lissa in 1808, he had been reluctantly persuaded (and found himself having to persuade an even more reluctant commander of the British armed forces in Sicily) that there was a good case for seizing from the French some of the Ionian islands, not only to counter the possibility of a French invasion of the Ottoman Empire using their fortress base of Corfu, but also to help the British to make

---

[35] Mackesey, op. cit., p. 15
[36] Mackesey, op. cit.., p. 16
[37] See for example Grouvel, Francois Marie Leon Robert: Les Corps de troupe de l'émigration francaises 1789-1815, 1957
[38] To make matters more complicated, the gun-boats were technically part of the Sicilian navy, with the British officer who commanded them holding a commission from the King of Sicily.
[39] Marmont, op. cit., Vol. 3, pp. 386-89. Pisani, op. cit., Vol 2, p. 395 gives a less positive picture.
[40] Pivec-Stele, op. cit., pp. 194-95

it even more difficult to pass in or out of the Adriatic. Corfu was too strong to be attacked, but it was hoped that the local Greek population would help to drive the French from Cephalonia and Zante and the neighbouring islands of Ithaca and Santa Maura. Collingwood hoped that British garrisons would not be needed after the Ionians had been helped to organise their own defence. The islands fell easily to the military forces that the British navy transported to them from Sicily in October 1809, but though the local inhabitants seem to have been delighted at their arrival, they did nothing to assist the operations and showed neither enthusiasm nor ability to organise their own government or defence. Despite the doubts of the British commander in Sicily that he could spare the troops, the invading British force had to stay to garrison the islands (their occupation was to last until 1864 when they were handed over to the Kingdom of Greece). This situation was to stiffen the resistance of the army commanders to any proposal that they should also occupy Lissa.[41]

***

When Captain Rowley of the EAGLE 74 arrived off Corfu at the beginning of April 1811 to take charge of the British warships blockading Corfu and cruising in the Adriatic, his first concern was to find out where the French frigates that had escaped from the battle of Lissa had taken refuge. He himself was off Ragusa from 4 April with two brigs DELPHINE and EPERVIER. These were described as fire brigs in the journal of a young officer of marines who was on EAGLE[42] and indeed Rowley's order book includes orders dated 4 April to Captain Stephens of the brig IMOGEN to reconnoitre the ports, towns and inlets and assess the possibility of burning enemy vessels with fire-craft. Other orders of the same date to Stephens suggested that he first search for the French frigates in Pola, then in Trieste and Venice. On his way north Stephens was to take orders to Lissa to Captain Moresby of the brig ACORN (the only British vessel left there) to tell him to cruise off the small island of Cazza (Sušac to the southeast of Lissa) and occasionally to stand towards Lissa to deter the enemy from taking it but to be cautious of superior force. But on 7 April while Rowley was still off Ragusa, IMOGEN brought the news that the French frigates were already within Gravosa or Santa Croce, the well-protected harbour of Ragusa itself. Rowley therefore rejoined the rest of his squadron blockading Corfu on 10 April but immediately sent Captain Murray Maxwell in the frigate ALCESTE to reinforce and take ACORN under his command to defend Lissa. However on 13 April when Rowley received news that the French frigates at Ragusa were ready for sea and destined for Lissa with troops, he also ordered up Captain Brisbane in the frigate BELLE POULE. He replaced BELLE POULE with LEONIDAS (Captain Griffiths) on 27 April with orders not only to defend Lissa but also to check the enemy in conducting trade or in collecting a force. LEONIDAS was replaced on 23 June by ACTIVE (Captain James Alex Gordon) which had arrived back from Malta, when the orders he sent up to Lissa again put Captain Maxwell of ALCESTE in command. He pointed out to Maxwell that his earlier orders to Griffiths had allowed for some part of the squadron to annoy the enemy's coastal trade, but it was now the wish of the commander-in-chief of the Mediterranean fleet to prevent the enemy from establishing himself on Lissa and preventing the Royal Navy from using it, and harassing the enemy had to be a secondary object. 'As I have no orders to take possession (of Lissa) I can give none'.[43]

---

[41] Mackesey, op. cit., pp. 354-55
[42] Journal of Captain Matthews, Royal Marines, manuscript in the National Maritime Museum, Greenwich (NMM). This diary usefully supplements information in the EAGLE logbook and in the Rowley papers on EAGLE's movements.
[43] Rowley's orders to the ships in his squadron are in his order books (ROW 6) included in the Rowley papers in the

Figure 17A. Sir Murray Maxwell (1775–1831), etching by Richard Dighton (National Portrait Gallery).

Figure 17B. Captain James Alexander Gordon (1782–1869), engraving by an unknown artist.

This bewildering series of changes reflected Rowley's difficulties in ensuring the defence of Lissa as his frigates and brigs were recalled to England or needed to go to Malta for essential repairs. To maintain an adequate naval force to defend Lissa was not easy, and there were inevitably periods when that force was reduced. On 5 May BELLE POULE and ALCESTE were as far north as Parenza (Porec) where they sank the French brig of war SIMPLON. Fortunately the French were not able or ready to exploit such weakness. As Rowley reported on 19 May 1811 to his superior, Admiral Sir Charles Cotton (who had taken over the command of the Mediterranean fleet after the death of Collingwood in March 1810), the French frigates were still at Santa Croce but withdrawn for even greater safety some 5-6 miles up a river above Santa Croce (the Ombla inlet). They were disabled and suffering desertions, to prevent which the troops landed at Lesina had been sent to Santa Croce.[44]

At this stage Rowley joined his voice to those others that were already urging improved defence of Lissa. On 24 May 1811 he wrote to Admiral Cotton that a line-of-battle ship had to be kept in reserve to watch the French and to enable the frigates off Lissa to cope with any single force sent to take possession of Lissa. It was clear that the enemy was resolved to raise a navy in the Adriatic. The British navy needed a port to procure water and at which to shelter in the event of damage from action or weather. If Lissa were lost they would have to go to the Albanian coast that was difficult of access in winter. He recommended that some establishment be made on Lissa, which was in the centre of the Adriatic, had an excellent

National Maritime Museum, Greenwich (NMM)
[44] Rowley's letters to senior officers (ROW 6) in NMM. The French troops were landed on Lesina from the French frigates which survived the Battle of Lissa. They were to have occupied Lissa.

Figure 18. Admiral Sir Charles Cotton (1753–1812), by Henry
Meyer (National Portrait Gallery).

harbour, plenty of water, and the 'partiality of the Inhabitants to the English' . Its defenceless
state meant that the enemy could land and become masters of the heights above the harbour.
It should be garrisoned by some British troops, as it otherwise needed a squadron in the upper
Adriatic to guard it.[45]

There had also been correspondence initiated in December 1810 involving the Admiralty and
Admiral Cotton and the British merchants of Malta concerning the utility and importance
of a contraband trade with the enemy on the coasts bordering the Adriatic. The reply dated
25 April 1811 from James Hunter, chairman of the committee of British merchants at Malta,
was unambiguous. Such a trade was only possible if possession were taken of Lissa and troops
stationed there. The merchants had received information about the island from captains
Campbell and Hoste, and from Mr Leard (formerly British consul in Fiume but now consul
at Valona in Albania) who had recently been at Lissa. There were about 4,000 inhabitants
who would welcome the change. The island would be easily fortified at small expense and
tenable by a small force. If licences were issued for protecting enemy vessels coming to Lissa
permitting them to bring goods to the island and to receive there goods which were imported
to Lissa under English colours, there would be the same good results as had already followed
the decision to permit the same kind of trade from Malta. Furthermore, maritime supplies
such as hemp, cordage, spars etc. were abundant on the shores of the Adriatic.[46]

---

[45] ROW 6, NMM
[46] 45 Letters received by Rowley from Admirals Cotton and Pellew are in ROW 8 (NMM)

In June 1811 Admiral Cotton was replaced as commander-in-chief of the British fleet in the Mediterranean by Admiral Pellew (although Rowley only received Pellew's communication of 4 June informing him of this on 7 September, a very long delay even by the standards of the time).[47] Rowley was writing again to his commanding admiral on 1 July urgently requesting instructions regarding Lissa. He reported that Captain Griffiths of LEONIDAS during his short time at Lissa in May-June had erected a small battery in the mouth of the harbour of two 18 pound guns on a rock outside of and commanding the entrance to Port St George. This is the first reference to attempts to build shore fortifications, in contradiction of a persistent tradition that it was Hoste who first envisaged or initiated such defences (reinforced by the fact that the rock, earlier known as Ubriachi or 'drunkards' was later called Hoste island), and it is clear from later correspondence that it was Captain Maxwell of ALCESTE who continued the work begun by Griffiths. Rowley added in his report that the enemy had forbidden all communication between Lissa and the mainland but that a great quantity of British goods was landed from Lissa on small boats. On the other hand the islanders were short of grain. From the information that Rowley had received from captains Brisbane (BELLE POULE) and Griffiths (LEONIDAS), 3-400 marines would prevent the enemy from taking Lissa. [48]

Things were moving but painfully slowly because of the slowness of communications, especially given that the respective navy and army commanders at the various levels were writing or copying correspondence to each other and to the next level up the chain of command. On the side of the navy, there was the change of command in the Mediterranean from Admiral Cotton to Admiral Pellew on 4 June 1811. The naval commander-in-chief was usually in the western Mediterranean at or near the Spanish base of Port Mahon on the island of Minorca in the Balearics, from where he could direct the blockade of Toulon or drop down to defend Sicily. It could take as long as a month or more for his communications to reach the British squadron blockading Corfu. (What is extraordinary from a modern point of view is that naval and military officers, despite their numerous other duties, almost always wrote replies if only to acknowledge receipt immediately after receiving a letter, usually on the same day or the day after, whether or not there was a ship ready or any other means of sending them). [49] On the side of the army, the situation was much more complex, given a whole series of changes in the command structure taking place in 1811. Lieutenant-General Sir John Stuart, the commander-in-chief of the British army in Sicily, resigned in January but had to stay at his post until a replacement was sent out from England. It was decided to replace him with Lieutenant-General Lord William Bentinck, who was now to be not only the commander-in-chief of all the British land forces in the Mediterranean but also the British minister resident in Sicily responsible for relations with the Sicilian court. He did not arrive in Sicily until 28 July 1811 (although, being immediately confronted by a crisis at court, he almost immediately returned to England to seek additional powers, only returning to Sicily in December).[50] He was to be supported by a second in command, Major-General Frederick Maitland. Two generals in the Mediterranean who were senior to Bentinck had to be removed, so there were a number of

---

[47] 44 ADM 1/4698, Promiscuous H, no. 1100, PRO
[48] ROW 6, NMM
[49] Navy letters were usually endorsed with the date of receipt or also give the names of the vessels by which they were sent. Otherwise orders and letters from superior officers were usually acknowledged in replies that gave the dates that they were sent and received.
[50] Bentinck's papers are in the Portland Papers at the University of Nottingham.

Figure 19. Lord William Bentinck. Commander-
in-chief of the British army forces in the
Mediterranean and British Minister to the Court of
Sicily. Portrait by Thomas Lawrence.

changes which gave the senior army officers both in Sicily and the Ionian Islands the excuse to drag their feet on the question of army commitment to the defence of Lissa.

Admiral Cotton passed on Rowley's arguments for the occupation of Lissa to Sir John Stuart, the outgoing army commander. Stuart, who was making a last visit to inspect the British forces in the Ionian Islands, wrote to Rowley on 29 July 1811 to say that although he himself could not decide the question, Rowley should correspond with Colonel Smith who was in command in the Ionian Islands on the southern island of Zante. Smith also wrote to Rowley suggesting that, if Rowley could arrange transport, he was willing to send an officer of Royal Engineers to Lissa to conduct a survey. On receipt of these letters, Rowley immediately replied on 6 August that if Smith could arrange for the officer to be sent up to Santa Maura, he would send a ship to collect him from there and himself take him to Lissa or send a vessel with him as soon as VICTORIOUS arrived from Malta to strengthen his squadron off Corfu.[51]

> 'My own knowledge of the Island of Lissa is only from official reports - but which are from such respectable and well informed officers that I have little (missing word) in hazarding my opinion that a force of 5 or 600 men would secure the island against any attempt the French would venture to make - as the island will always be considered a Rendezvous for our navy, and consequently it would prevent any great force collecting or coming over from the adjacent islands.

---

[51] ROW 6, NMM

Figure 20. Hudson Lowe (1769–1844), British
commander on the island of Santa Maura, portrait by
R.C. Seaton.

Captain Maxwell has built a fort in the entrance of the harbour and from his description
I should conceive it was judiciously placed and I think the Engineer Officer whom you
mean to send should be warned against expence and extensive plans.

The kinds of defence for such an Island are strong positions near the sea coast to molest
landing and to secure themselves till they receive succour from a man of war and the
sooner the defence of it is begun the better'.[52]

On 8 August Rowley confirmed to Smith that he had sent IMOGEN to Santa Maura to collect
the engineer officer.[53] Rowley's friend, Colonel Hudson Lowe (whose reputation, after
distinguished service in the wars, was somewhat tarnished by his unsympathetic treatment
of Napoleon when he was in command on St. Helena) was then in command at Santa Maura,
and their less formal correspondence gives another dimension to the discussion of the Lissa
problem. Rowley repeatedly urged Lowe to accompany himself and the engineer officer to
Lissa '... besides as Lissa is to be garrisoned, and as the whole blame will be attached in the
House of Commons if the plan fails, I should like you to see the situation. You know I am no
great admirer of engineers and diplomatic gentlemen in the defence, or attack of irregular
situations... Keep the business of Lissa a secret as well as what I have said respecting your chief
[Sir John Stuart?]'. [54]

---

[52] ROW 4, NMM
[53] ROW 4, NMM
[54] The Lowe papers are in the manuscript collection of the British Library. Letter Rowley-Lowe, 8 Aug. 1811, Add

For whatever reason (probably the late arrival of VICTORIOUS), there was further delay in sending the engineer officer to Lissa. On 24 August 1811 Rowley, still at his normal station off the island of Fano just north of Corfu, wrote a letter to be delivered by Captain Bennett, Royal Engineers, to Captain Maxwell of the frigate ALCESTE at Lissa, asking him to give Bennett every facility and information. Maxwell was to report his opinion again not only on the advantages of Lissa to the British government but on the size of a garrison for its defence, the need for a flotilla of gunboats and how many, whether there was water at Port St George and at what other places, the means of provisioning a garrison, the number of inhabitants, the produce of the island and its revenues, the means of supplying the inhabitants with the necessaries of life, for how many months it produced grain for its own population, and if it were possible to increase the produce by introducing and substituting grain in lieu of wine.[55] On 25 August Captain Stephens of IMOGEN was again instructed to take Captain Bennett on board and to take him to Lissa and back, although in the event (as Rowley was to report to Rear-Admiral Boyle on 31 August) it was to be the sloop KINGFISHER 18 (Captain Ewell Tritton) which took Bennett to Lissa on 26 August, Rowley himself having given up the idea of going because of signs of activity in the French squadron at Corfu.[56]

***

There were parallel developments at almost exactly the same time in London. On 22 August 1811 Captain William Hoste, who had arrived back in England in June to bask in the glory of the victory at Lissa of 13 March, wrote to the Admiralty:

> 'The Island of Lissa has on the N.E. side of it an excellent harbour, it has been frequented by the British Ships of war and Privateers - the French have occupied the coast of Dalmatia and the littorale, and its advantages whether considered as a port for our Cruizers or as a Depot for the British and Maltese merchants introducing their manufactures & merchandize to the Enemies country, are incalculable. - nothing can place the necessity of some port to repair to, in a more striking point of view than the situation of the British Squadron after the action in March last. If Lissa had not been open to receive us, I do not conceive it possible to have saved the Squadron. The ships were all so damaged in their masts and rigging (let alone their hulls) that the slightest gale would have carried them away; and the consequence would have been a dead lee shore without any anchorage for the wind the day after the action blew a severe gale from the N.E. which would have drove us over to the coast of Apulia, whilst the French Squadron would have sheltered themselves in any of their numerous ports. The coast of Dalmatia opposite to Lissa is not like that of Istria, which is a roadsted from one end to the other. I think a Martello Tower[57] built on the emminence at the head of the harbour to secure it from a 'coup de main' with a Garrison of 3 or 400 men would

---

20110
[55] ROW 4, NMM
[56] ROW 6, NMM
[57] In 1794 when British forces were assisting a revolt against the French in Corsia, they were given great difficulty by a round tower at Cape Mortella ('Cape Myrtle') which was able, which only three light and medium guns, to keep at bay and damage a British warship of 74 guns. The British were so impressed that they used the model of the tower for their own coastal defences in England, Ireland and Canada, but miss-spelling the name as Martello. These round towers were very simple with very thick walls and a strong roof-vault, on top of which there were one or two heavy guns.

whilst you possess a naval superiority, keep it quite secure from any attack from the opposite coasts of Dalmatia or Apulia, and its centrical situation for a Squadron or as I said before for the mercantile Interests are obvious. . . . In possession of Lissa the whole coast of the enemy would be kept in constant alarm, and their convoys which go now inside the islands would be liable to be attacked at any time from thence, as the signal post I raised there commands a complete view of the coast of Dalmatia.- If I am rightly informed it employs two frigates and a sloop now to protect the Island against a surprise from Spalatro, from whence it might be taken in their absence by a single Gun Boat'.

The Secretary to the Admiralty did not send an extract from Hoste's letter to Lieutenant-Colonel Bunbury at the War Office for the information of the Secretary for War, Lord Liverpool, until 8 October 1811. A further copy was to be sent on 13 November together with papers received from Admiral Pellew 'if not already sent'.[58] Despite the claims of his admirers, it was not Hoste's submission that was to be critical. The reports sent to the Admiralty by Admiral Cotton enclosing Rowley's observations had already been passed on to the War Office. On 22 August 1811, the same day that Hoste wrote his letter, Lord Liverpool wrote to Lord Bentinck:

'I herewith transmit for your Lordship's information, the Copy of a Letter addressed by desire of the Lords Commissioners of the Admiralty, to this Department enclosing Communications from Sir Charles Cotton and Captain Rowley, upon the Subject of the Island of Lissa, which is strongly urged upon the Attention of His Majesty's Government, as a Naval Station of much Importance to the British Squadrons in the Adriatick; as well as being very favourably situated for Commercial purposes, and likewise for maintaining a communication with the Coasts of Italy, and of the Ceded Provinces of Austria.

Having given full consideration to the Suggestions which have been urged in favour of the Occupation of Lissa by a British force, I feel it adviseable to recommend this Measure to your Lordship's early Attention, provided that you find the Works which may be requisite for the defence of the Island (and particularly of the Harbour) are not likely to be attended with a serious Expence, or to require any considerable Body of regular troops for their protection.

In the Instructions addressed to Your Lordship upon the .... of June last, I pointed out the Light in which His Majesty's Government regarded the security of Sicily as of paramount Importance to any other present Object in the Mediterranean; and this Impression continues unchanged, the General Principle that the British Forces in that Sea should be kept as much as possible concentrated, must be always borne in mind; but considering the Naval, as well as political Importance of Lissa, the Smallness of its Size, the Attachment of its Inhabitants to the English, and consequently that in all Probability, a very small Body of regulars under a judicious and active Commandant,

---

[58] WO 1/727, PRO. ADM 1/421, PRO. Pocock, op. cit. p. 184: 'the British decided to implement Hoste's idea for fortyfying Port St George....'. Hoste's widow, who published his memoirs in 1833 (much used by subsequent historians), borrowed heavily from the journal of his friend and admirer, the chaplain on BACCHANTE, Rev. W. J. Yonge. He recorded their arrival at Lissa on 19 Aug. 1812 after Hoste had been on leave in England: 'The island is to be fortified by us, owing to the suggestion of Hoste to that effect'. Hughes, Quentin: Military Architecture, Beaufort 1991, also attributes responsibility for the Lissa fortifications to Hoste

may be sufficient for its defence; I am induced to authorize your Lordship to detach troops from Sicily, or from the Greek Islands, for the purpose of garrisoning Lissa, and putting it into acceptable State of defence, provided that your Lordship's Enquiries shall confirm the idea that the Island will not demand for its protection so considerable a Detachment as might materially weaken your force in more important Situations.

In case you shall find it expedient to occupy this Island, I beg to call your Lordship's Attention to the Expediency of facilitating a Commercial intercourse with every port of the Adriatick, to as great an Extent as possible; and also to the Means it will afford for procuring for His Majesty's Government the fullest information respecting the Affairs of the Austrian Dominions, and of the whole of Italy.

It only remains for me to add that your Lordship would probably be enabled to derive considerable Aid in the Defence of Lissa, from the Well affected Inhabitants, who might be armed and employed either as Militia or on board of Gunboats; and it has been reported that if it proves necessary, a small Corps of Dalmatians worthy of Confidence, might be readily formed and maintained at a very low Rate of Expence'.[59]

So here, including all the usual provisos, was the authority for the occupation of Lissa. It only now remained for the letter to reach Bentinck and for the necessary decisions to be made concerning the forces and defensive works that would be needed. It was to take another 8 months until almost the end of April 1812 before any British army forces reached Lissa.

There must have been earlier signals that the proposals to occupy Lissa would be approved in London. It is clear from later correspondence that Lord Bentinck after his arrival in Sicily in July left instructions regarding Lissa before his hurried departure again for London on 4 September. On 1 August 1811 Admiral Pellew on HMS CALEDONIA off Toulon wrote to Rowley (in a letter which Rowley was not to receive until 27 September):

'As it is in contemplation the Island of Lissa with a British Garrison, should any troops be sent thither, it is desirable that you should render them every aid in forwarding them thither, and that in such event you afford the island every assistance and protection by the ships under your orders in the upper part of the Adriatic, making it their Rendezvous for watering and refit, and giving such support by their occasional presence as may render the position respectable in the View of the Enemy'.[60]

Pellew added in the same letter that Rear-Admiral Thomas Fremantle was appointed to be Flag officer at Palermo in Sicily in charge not only of the squadron based there but also of Rowley's Adriatic squadron. (A separate letter from Pellew to Rowley concerning Fremantle's appointment written on 6 August 1811 somehow overtook Pellew's letter of 1 August and was received by Rowley on 11 September).[61] The other information in Pellew's letter of 1 August was that VICTORIOUS 74 (which Rowley was waiting for off Corfu to be able to send a ship with the officer of engineers to Lissa) was being sent to Palermo to be under Fremantle 'who

---

[59] WO 6/57, PRO
[60] ROW 8, NMM
[61] ROW 8, NMM

Figure 21. Admiral Thomas Fremantle, commander of
the British naval squadron in the Adriatic, 1812–13.

has received my instructions to assist in the conveyance of the proposed Garrison to Lissa by appointing Captain Talbot [of VICTORIOUS] to that duty '.

On the same day, 27 September 1811, Rowley was also to receive another letter from Pellew dated 9 September, in which he seems to be much more guarded, and which was clearly a response to Rowley's of 1 July asking for instructions about Lissa:

> 'Your representations respecting..... an Establishment on the Island of Lissa will be duly attended to: Instructions for placing a Garrison on that Island have I understand been given to the C-in-C [Commander-in-Chief] of the Forces in Sicily'.[62]

***

While these communications were making their slow way to Rowley, the situation developed more quickly at the local level. Rowley sent Captain Bennett of the Royal Engineers from Fano on 26 August up to Lissa together with a letter to Captain Maxwell asking him also to provide more information about the island.[63] Maxwell had anticipated this need for extra information and carried out a reconnaissance of the whole island that he reported to Rowley in a letter of 22 August.[64] He had found only two places where the enemy could land (besides the harbour of Port St George and Comisa 'which are both now in a state of defence') which were small

---

[62] ROW 8, NMM
[63] ROW 4, NMM
[64] Copy in papers of Admiral Pellew in the National Maritime Museum, Greenwich, PEL 14, NMM

fishing bays at Port Manica 5 miles to the south and Port Chiavi 4 miles to the north of Port St George. The roads from either of these places were unfit for moving cannon, being only foot tracks among rugged rocks, but mountain guns might be brought on the backs of mules to the heights commanding the harbour. Maxwell was convinced that the enemy intended some night to land some 2-3000 men from open boats as the crossing was only a 2 1/2 hours sail distance.

'Two martello towers, one on Mt. Hornby, and the other on Whitby Hill (respectively east of the mouth of the harbour of Port St George and behind and south of the main settlement of Lucca within the bay, both now named after British naval captains who had fought in the battle of Lissa), together with the two eighteen pound batteries we have already built on Hoste's Island (and) with Camessa Castle, which, during the summer months, commands all the water upon Lissa, and a force of 200 or 250 marines I will be bold to say would maintain it against any number the enemy could send'. The garrison could be provisioned and withdrawn if necessary by the squadron.

Maxwell also reported that the two French frigates and corvette at Ragusa were ready for sea and threatened to raise the British blockade of the coast between Zara and Spalato by the 3 gun boats which ACTIVE had captured from the enemy (off Ragosniza - Rogoznica on 27 July) and some of the boats from the warships. Maxwell had now sent ACORN to reinforce them. The manning of the gun boats, garrisoning Hoste Island and Comisa Castle, keeping lookouts on Mount Gordon and Whitby Hill (named after British captains in the March 1811 battle of Lissa), together with the boats watching the opposite shore, kept the frigates ALCESTE and ACTIVE short of men.

On receipt of Rowley's letter asking for more information on Lissa, Maxwell wrote a further letter on 29 August to answer Rowley's specific questions and to summarise and comment on the findings of Captain Bennett who had by now completed his survey.[65] Bennett thought that because of the natural strength of the island 500 men would be enough, although Maxwell thought less. It would be best to have marines. It would be useful to have gunboats, of which 8-10 would suffice. Port St George had no water in the summer months except what could be kept in cisterns. These could be enlarged and new ones dug for the garrison as winter rains were abundant. A store of provisions would be necessary although cattle and grain would be available from the mainland and the neighbouring islands. The number of inhabitants was 4000-5000. They produced only wine; grain was needed from elsewhere. 'Nothing would please them more than seeing a British Garrison'. (Maxwell had explained in his letter of 22 August that, having consulted the principal landowners, he had agreed to prohibit any trade in wine from the enemy islands to encourage the sale of Lissa wine 'which has always had the reputation of being the best in the Adriatic', and to protect the export of sardines). The revenue raised on the island 'under the mild Government of Austria was not so productive as under the grasping one of the French, which was not regulated by the people's means to pay, but by its own craving exactions.... but could never be much'.

Both of Maxwell's letters were in Rowley's hands by the 3 September when KINGFISHER brought Captain Bennett back to him off Fano. Rowley immediately wrote to Colonel Lowe at

---

[65]   PEL 14, NMM

Zante (temporarily commanding there in place of Smith?) to say he was forwarding Bennett with his report, that although it seemed to be the strong opinion of Maxwell and Bennett that the defence of the island would be better if entrusted to marines, it would not be possible to find the 3-400 required out of the fleet. A store ship would have to accompany any troops sent to Lissa to keep them provisioned. Rowley dutifully added that there should be as few works as possible to avoid expenses (the familiar refrain in most of the communications concerning Lissa).[66]

Captain William Bennett's report addressed to Colonel Smith was dated 4 September 1811 aboard KINGFISHER and referred to the orders he had been given on 12 August:

> 'The Harbour of St George is situated on the North East side. Captain Maxwell of the Alceste Frigate has constructed a Battery in the small Island, at the Mouth of the Harbour, and to complete its security, Batteries will also be required on the points St George and Argentina, which form its Entrance.
>
> The Bay of Comissa on the opposite side of the Island is open and unsafe Anchorage, it is protected by an old square Tower in which Captain Maxwell has mounted four Guns. This work will require some Repair, and a Battery will be necessary on the ground to the left to complete the security of the Bay.
>
> There are also two small Coves, called Port Chive and Port Manica, which it will be adviseable to secure by Batteries. The rest of the coast is a continuation of rocks rising abruptly from the sea, and in general is inaccessible. In the event of Lissa being taken possession of by the British, it is natural to imagine that the jealousy and attention of the French will be most strongly excited, and situated so distant as it is from any of our possessions, and surrounded by the Enemy, it is obvious a very strong Garrison would be required for its defence, without the certainty of constant naval assistance, and the Island is not capable of affording accommodation for any considerable Force, nor does it produce any means of subsistence.
>
> I have conceived it out of the question to.... propose for Lissa any work of such nature and strength as to be capable of containing a Garrison, and being defended for a time against a superior force, in the hope of succour. Your instructions besides cautioning me against extensive and expensive plans, and the Island affording little means for the construction of works of any kind.
>
> From a consideration of these circumstances I am of opinion that the safety of Lissa must chiefly depend on the constant presence of the Navy. If the Senior Officer of the Squadron in the Adriatic had positive orders to consider the Island under his protection, I should think a small Garrison of three or four hundred Men, with about 12 Gun-boats, would cooperate with great advantage together with the assistance which may reasonably be expected from the Inhabitants, and in the possibility of the Enemy's succeeding in forcing a landing the Retreat of the Troops to the ships at a point agreed on with the Naval Commander might I conceive be effected without difficulty'.[67]

---

[66] ROW 4, NMM
[67] WO 1/310, PRO

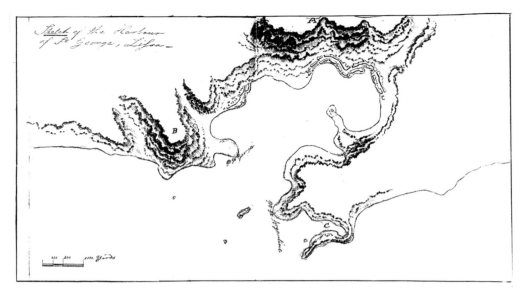

Figure 22. Captain Bennett's sketch map of the port of St. George, October 1811 (University of Nottingham Portland (Welbeck) Collection).

Lowe at Zante wrote to Rowley on 6 September to inform him that Bennet had arrived back there that morning. His report with Rowley's communication (of 3 September) was being forwarded immediately to Messina for the deliberation of the new commander of the forces whose reply might soon be expected. From what Captain Bennett had said about the Lissa, it seemed likely that it could be rendered secure by the means suggested by Rowley and Bennett. 'The square tower with few guns on it at Camiso Bay he represents as very strong and this point d'appui may perhaps render superfluous the construction of another'.[68]

It was Colonel Smith who himself wrote two days later on 8 September 1811 a letter taken on BLACK PRINCE (an army vessel) from Zante to the adjutant-general in Sicily, Major-General Campbell:

> 'In consequence of Sir Charles Cotton's application to Sir John Stuart, I was directed to correspond with Captain Rowley commanding the squadron in the Adriatic and also to send an Engineer Officer (Captain Bennett) to examine and report on Lissa'.

The opinion of both Rowley and Bennett was that 400 men and a few gun boats would be sufficient if the navy supported. Such a small force would need a strong work for their defence if the navy were drawn away although 'Captain Rowley is under no apprehension of this'. There would be some difficulty in victualling the detachment and transports would be required for the purpose. Bennett had given this as his reason for agreeing with Rowley in preferring marines to troops because they could be supplied from cruising vessels (it would be bureaucratically more complicated for the navy to supply the army with food from its ships). The nearest enemy post was Lesina at 10 miles and Spalato at 30 miles where a French general

---

[68] Lowe Papers, Add 20110, BL

was stationed. Nor was the island very far distant from the coast of Italy and it would need constant support from the naval force. Smith needed advice on the description of the troops and the commanding officer if the detachment had to come from his division of the army in the Ionian Islands. Instructions given to the officer of army gunboats should define how far they should be subject to the naval commander as one would always be present. (In this Smith was prescient: no such instructions were given and command of the gunboats was to become a source of friction).[69]

The first of Admiral Pellew's communications to Rowley, that of 4 June 1811, informing him he had taken over command of the Mediterranean fleet, reached Rowley at Fano on 7 September. On 15 September Rowley confirmed receipt of this and wrote another letter on the same day summarising the developments concerning Lissa and enclosing Maxwell's reports. Rowley drew attention to the conclusion of Maxwell and Bennett that it would be better to use marines. He had thought it best to inform Colonel Smith that the fleet could not provide these until they were sent from England. In the meantime the army would have to supply the 4-500 men and 10-12 gunboats.[70] Pellew received Rowley's letter off Toulon and on 14 October forwarded it and its enclosures (with a covering letter in which he raised no objections) to the Admiralty, where it was received on 13 November and copied on to the War Office.[71]

***

Bennett's report had a much rougher passage. Colonel Smith had sent it to the adjutant-general who was presumably meant to bring it to the attention of the commander-in-chief, Lord Bentinck. But Bentinck had left for England at the beginning of September and it went to the new second-in-command, General Frederick Maitland, on 18 September. While remarkably short, Bennett's report might have been expected to find favour, given that it put the onus on the navy to supply marines and defend the island with its ships, and, other than the construction of a few batteries, it did not recommend the construction of anything more substantial such as martello towers or forts. But General Maitland, who seems to have been an irascible Scotsman, was determined to find fault and raise difficulties.

Some of Maitland's criticisms concerning Bennett's report were justified. It had been very brief and gave the impression of being superficial and Colonel Smith, in suggesting that the tower of Comisa could be the main point in the defences, had clearly misunderstood the situation. In forwarding and commenting on the report in notes addressed to Bentinck written from 17-21 September, Maitland wrote in a very negative sense, although if his main point was to minimise the army's input, he curiously did not take up the point about the preferability of Navy marines:[72]

> 18 Sept Letters are just come from Col Smith who commands in the Greek Islands; they are about the Occupation of Lissa - a Brief Report of the Island which appears to be without any Work of Defence, except one old Tower on the Side of the Island opposite to where the Harbour is - there are four landing Places (I will enclose a copy)

[69] WO 1/310, p. 281, PRO
[70] ROW 6, NMM
[71] ADM 1/421, no. 852, PRO
[72] WO 1/310, no. 269, PRO

The Island has no means, <u>but Water</u> - It is plain that this Island cannot be safe, cannot be held with<u>out</u> the presence of the Navy - an Enemy's Garrison ten Miles distant, and others very near - I much fear we shall sacrifice any Garrison we can <u>now</u> afford. It will be absolutely necessary to construct two or three <u>Redoubts</u> - perhaps the Island mentioned and the two points of the Harbour might answer. There appears to be no cover for troops which must be made for a fixed Garrison - The <u>poverty</u> of the Island seems to make it unfit for Chief aim you had in view'-

On 18 September 1811, General Maitland also replied to Colonel Smith:

'I have received the Letter with the Inclosures which you addressed to Lt. Genl. Lord Wm Bentinck relative to Lissa.

His Lordship did leave with me directions to occupy that Island; at the same time he did so without knowing what means the places could afford.

The Report which you have sent made to you by Capt Bennett Roy. Engineer is very short and is not sufficient in many points - What is the Size of the Island? The (Distance/by Calculation, not a survey but from the Eye and having walked or rode over it) from the Tower at Comissa Bay to the Harbour? What the size and capability of the small Island at the Entrance? - Are the extreme points of the Harbour favorable for uniting with the Island upon a small plan of defence? - Could we construct a Redoubt for 200 Men on each of these points with four heavy Guns in each? And another of the same force on the Island, with a good Ditch and pallisades? - What the nature of the Ground on these spots, is it Rock or loose soil? Can you procure Pallisades easily in the Greek Islands or from the Continent opposite you?

Nothing less than such a plan, as I have now given you the Outline of, would answer any good purpose. These three Redoubts keeping Picquets at Comissa and the two coves to alarm might protect the Garrison during a short absence of the Squadron, perhaps for a Week or ten days.

But it is obvious, and I wish it to be clearly understood by Commodore Rowley, that if we garrison Lissa, we can only do it as a dependency upon the support, and the <u>constant support</u> of the <u>Squadron</u>.

We cannot send them six hundred Men for the three Redoubts, but probably there could always be some addition from the Navy in the Harbour, and Merchantmen and Inhabitants -

In our present strange Position we can spare nothing from Sicily, and the Garrison of Lissa (if it takes place) must be from your Division. It must be partly English and partly Foreign, with an intelligent Officer who ought to be English - we can supply no Gun boats. The Navy must undertake all the means of Defence upon the Water, unless you find that your Division of Gun Boats can be spared.

I am not yet prepared to make the Order positive. I want more Information.-

Pray transmit a copy of this letter to Commodore Rowley and request to have his remarks and his assurance how far he will be responsible for the support of the Navy, and whether the Navy can give any and what assistance in constructing such works as I have mentioned.

How many Inhabitants are there and can they be had from good-will or for hire to work at Fortifications? - Is there limestone in the Island? It would be very desirable to give the scarp a demi revêtement - Have you any Camp Equipage (Tents) and how many?

The most we could allow for Lissa at present would be four hundred and without artillery men -

PS. Capt. Bennett should have given a rough sketch of the Island shewing distances as near as he could and a particular one of the Harbour shewing distances and commanding Ground. I shall expect this from Capt. - who has lately been ordered to go there and <u>then to come with his Report</u> to Messina.'[73]

It seems that Rowley may also have written direct to Bentinck, because Maitland wrote direct to Rowley on the same day 18 September, acknowledging a letter from Rowley to Bentinck and pointing out that he had asked Colonel Smith to send him a copy of Maitland's letter to him, which answered the questions Rowley had raised or sent through Smith. 'We cannot afford to lose men'. It was necessary for the Navy to play its part.[74]

The other rather puzzling thing in Maitland's letter to Colonel Smith was the reference in the postscript to another captain of Royal Engineers who had already left (from Sicily?) on 18 September and was on his way to report on Lissa, even before Maitland had seen and found Captain Bennett's report wanting. The solution to this is in a personal letter from Colonel Hudson Lowe on Santa Maura to Colonel Smith dated 20 September:

'Captain Smith has shown me the letter of the Chief Engineer, whose instructions appear to be nearly the same as those you gave Captain Bennett. I have of course explained to Captain Smith that his mission had been anticipated upon, though I should not be much surprized if he was again directed to be sent up, as Capt. B's report is merely an opinion on the island without being a description of it to enable other persons to form their opinions... '[75]

Lowe was right in his surmise. Colonel Smith in Zante received Maitland's letter to him of 18 September and forwarded a copy to Rowley on 29 September:

'Captain Smith who can be easiest spared has been ordered by the General to Lissa for the purpose of making a more circumstantial report which he is himself to be the bearer of to Messina'.

---

[73] WO 1/310, no. 301, PRO
[74] ADM 1/421, no. 894, PRO
[75] Lowe Papers, Add 20110, BL

Colonel Smith had ordered BLACK PRINCE to take Captain Smith to Lissa and she had proceeded to Santa Maura that very evening. He suggested that it would save time if a ship of the squadron could take the engineer officer to Messina.[76] Colonel Smith also sent a personal note up to Santa Maura for Lowe to whom he confessed his personal embarrassment with the situation:

> 'The opinion on Bennett's report seems to be pretty much what you had predicted. I am sorry for it on his account as he seems annoyed by it. He has written to me to say he can give all the information required, requesting that he might be allowed to proceed to Messina and Smith stopped - but as the General at the same time he wrote his last letter knew that the order for Captain Smith to proceed to Lissa had reached me after Bennett's return, and repeats it, I cannot with all the inclination in the world, venture to detain him - besides he seems to be a stiff old Gentleman and might say something very unpleasant'.[77]

Colonel Smith asked Lowe to look at the copy of the letter from Maitland which he was forwarding to Rowley and to edit it or suppress it all if he saw fit, and to give Captain Smith any direction in the colonel's name. While BLACK PRINCE was at Santa Maura, Lowe wrote two letters to his friend Rowley on 5 and 7 October, in the first of which he tried to explain Captain Smith's mission and to reassure him:

> 'BLACK PRINCE, one of the army flotilla vessels who is now here to carry up Captain Smith of the Engineers to take another look at the island of Lissa, Captain Bennett's report not having appeared to Lt. Gen. Maitland sufficiently full and explanatory. In other respects his intention is pretty decided about occupying the island and I should hope the present delay will be the last. Colonel Smith's communication and General Maitland's letters will inform you of all particulars'.[78]

Meanwhile, back on Zante, Captain Bennett felt it necessary to insist on submitting to Colonel Smith on 6 October the information on Lissa which General Maitland had found lacking in his report:

> 'It appears from General Maitland's letter that my report has not given him the information he requires. I can explain points he deems necessary.
>
> Lissa is a fortification by nature. If the four points I mentioned are secured, the rest of the coast is inaccessible.... I stated that the presence of at least one warship is essential and did not consider it necessary to enter into detail of works for the small garrison to retire into.... If General Maitland expects the case that the island would be left by warships for seven to ten days, the works suggested might protect the troops till the return of the navy to take them off, but they would not assist in the defence of the island - they would divide and weaken our small force.... If a landing were effected, the enemy would have no difficulty in getting over in a week as many troops and supplies as he wished and to establish himself firmly.

---

[76] ADM 1/421, no. 894, PRO
[77] Lowe Papers, Add 20191, BL
[78] Lowe Papers, Add 20110, BL

I enclose a rough sketch of the Harbour of St George. It is too extensive to admit of all points being secured by three redoubts. The points St George and Argentine which I fixed on for sea batteries to secure the harbour are not calculated for redoubts, the former is low and completely commanded, the latter so confined that I hesitated whether there was sufficient space for a battery which I should be particularly anxious to accomplish, as it would see into the small bay marked C where a landing is practicable.... These two points are composed of rock.... The ground all round the harbour rises abruptly from the water's edge – the hgt of the Hill A[79] I suppose 5-600 ft. at B 4-500 the ground between the points & all round the harbour varies from 1-300. The small island at the ent. is a rock which may be 250 yds x 50 & completely commanded. It does not appear to me connected to a system of defence other than for a sea battery. High ground at A & B too distant from each other & diff. in level too great to all works constructed on them any mutual defence. B most favourable for a work to protect 3-400 men for the time Gen. Maitland mentions.

A small fort or possibly a more capacious & complete redoubt which might obtain some flank defence by demi-bastions or redans with a strong tower in the interior appears to me most feasible plan. Sketch will show disadvantages & point out the doubt whether the comm. with the ships might not be prevented supposing the Enemy in poss. of the small island & every other part of the coast & harbours.

Island between 10-12 miles long & 4-5 broad, 6-8 miles St George-Comisa. Only a track for mules & 1-2 other narrow paths. Interior high & abrupt hills, complete rock covered in pts. with a thin soil just suff. for cult. Vine. Island produces nothing else worth noting. There is not a single village. 3-4000 inhabits. live in small places at St. Geo. & Comissa. Only spring is at Comisa from whence ships watered. For supply troops at St. Geo. necessary to make terraces & cisterns.

 There is little material for the construction of works. Lime is at present obtainable from adjacent islands is enough for the inhabitants but when the enemy knows we are carrying on works, he will prevent it. There is limestone on the island but no kilns to burn it or firewood.... About 40-50 masons might be procured from the inhabitants to work at fortifications. Their pay is half a dollar a day (one Spanish dollar was worth about five shillings).... Palisades cannot be procured in the Greek Islands but from the continent.

PS. The best defence is to prevent a landing. Gun boats which could lie in small coves and would afford great protection and is a species of force well-adapted for this situation.'[80]

Bennett's letter appears to have been forwarded to Messina where it was marked received on 13 October. There are marginal comments (the underlining suggests General Maitland):

---

[79] On Bennett's sketch map Hill A is Whitby Hill south of the harbour and Hill B is Hornby Hill east of the entrance to the harbour.
[80] Portland Papers, no. 6339

'Capt. B trusts all his defence to his success in preventing a landing. It does not follow that because an Enemy may effect by Surprise a landing he therefore can afterward leisurely bring over what he wants and when he plans'.

By the time these comments were made, Maitland had received Lord Liverpool's letter of 22 August from the War Office in London giving Bentinck covering authority to occupy Lissa. In Bentinck's absence, Maitland replied on 2 October:

'Ld. B left instructions with me to attend to this service. I immediately directed an officer of Engineers (Captain Smith) to proceed there and report. I have not yet received his report. But I have received a letter and some papers upon the subject from Col. Smith to which I returned the enclosed answer (Maitland-Smith of 18 September). When there is a garrison on Lissa, the enemy will be more anxious to dislodge us. There must be some redoubts that a handful of men are not left in a trap. A garrison not dependent on the RN is beyond what we could spare'.[81]

**

BLACK PRINCE with Captain Smith and the letters from Lowe, Colonel Smith and General Maitland reached Rowley off Fano late on 8 October 1811, and on 9 October Rowley immediately wrote letters to all concerned.

There was an added complication insofar as Rowley now had a new superior officer to whom to explain the situation. He had written to Admiral Fremantle on 19 September to tell him that he had heard unofficially that Fremantle was in command off Sicily. On 29 September he had written to Admiral Pellew to say that he had received Pellew's letter of 1 August ordering him to place himself under Fremantle's command. He now wrote on 9 October to Fremantle to inform him that Captain Smith had arrived and enclosing copies of the letters received the previous night from Maitland, copies of the reports from Maxwell at Lissa received on 3 September and copied on to Pellew, and of the letters from Pellew of 1 August he had received on 27 September ordering him to assist in the transportation of troops to Lissa. With all of these he enclosed a copy of his reply to Maitland in which he referred him to Fremantle respecting the Navy guarantee of the safety of any garrison he might put on Lissa, enclosed a copy of Captain Maxwell's report on Lissa and extracts from the orders he had himself received from Pellew, and assured him of every assistance being given by the ships off Lissa in erecting any forts that might be required, while pointing out that while gunboats would be the principal arm of defence they could not be provided by the Royal Navy in the Mediterranean.[82]

At the end of his letter of 9 October to Fremantle, Rowley was to transmit news of an alarming nature that was to highlight the danger to Lissa and the risks that the protracted correspondence and delays in taking action were bound to incur. Even while Captain Smith had been on board EAGLE with Rowley discussing his mission to Lissa, there had arrived a Maltese privateer two days out of Lissa and carrying a letter 'in cypher' from Captain Maxwell dated 6 October saying that he expected to be attacked as the French had assembled 3,000 troops on the opposite coast and requesting that another frigate be sent to reinforce him.

---

[81] Lowe Papers, Add 20110, BL
[82] ROW 6, NMM. ADM 1/421, no. 894, PRO

Since the battle of Lissa in March had temporarily thwarted his plans to seize the island, Napoleon could not be expected to give up all hope or intention of further attempts to take it. There were still the two frigates and corvette which had escaped from the battle and taken refuge in Ragusa, and the possibility of his Adriatic squadron being reinforced and regrouped with new ships launched at the Venice Arsenal or frigates slipping into the Adriatic past the British warships blockading Corfu. Any such naval force might be strong enough to challenge the British ships defending Lissa and help to defend a military force which could be transferred in small boats from the nearby French-held islands or the Dalmatian mainland (the main danger which the various reports on the defence of Lissa had addressed).

Already in his letter to Rowley of 22 August 1811, Maxwell had told Rowley that he believed that the enemy intended to land 2-3000 men on Lissa at night from open boats. He had boats watching the opposite coast that had presumably observed enemy activity, as well as no doubt having various reports from the local boat-owners who were smuggling provisions from the islands and mainland out to Lissa. In the same letter he reported that the three French warships were ready to sail and threatened his blockade of the Dalmatian coast from Zara to Spalato. He did not suggest that the frigates could protect the landing of the troops, perhaps because the possibility was obvious. It was apparent to Rowley who, in his first official letters of 27 September to his new superior Fremantle at Palermo, pointed out the danger of enemy ships at Corfu slipping out to join those at Ragusa and attacking Lissa.[83]

All these dangers, of frigates from Corfu, frigates from Ragusa, new ships from Venice, and a military force on boats from Dalmatia were soon to materialise but in so uncoordinated a way as to cast doubt on any French master plan to link them (although as has already been often observed, delays in communications and in controlling the movement of ships at sea undermined most such endeavours). The two French frigates (FLORE and DANAE) and corvette (CAROLINA) left Ragusa after sheltering there 6 months on 20 September, but instead of supporting an invasion of Lissa from Dalmatia headed north and arrived at Trieste on 8 October. It has been suggested by the historian Pisani that their escape was thanks to a diversion by the Dalmatian flotilla which attracted British attention to Lesina.[84] But the activity in preparing boats and assembling men on the mainland coast and the nearby islands which was observed by Maxwell in late August would only have served to focus his attention on the very seaways which the frigates had to use. Nor if this activity was only a ruse to help the frigates could it explain why the activity continued well after the frigates had escaped.

The situation as seen from the British side tells a rather different story. Rowley responded immediately on 9 October to Maxwell in response to the ciphered message brought by the Maltese privateer. There was a mistake in the second word of the cipher that made it unclear whether Maxwell believed or did not believe that Lissa was to be attacked as the French had 3,000 troops opposite him. Rowley told Maxwell that French frigates were ready to sail from Corfu but that they were probably not bound for Lissa, as an expected French convoy from Ancona to Corfu would be escorted by two of the frigates that had left S. Croce (the harbour of Ragusa).[85] Somehow Rowley had heard of movements of the French frigates from Ragusa before he had news of them from Maxwell, but his information was wrong. While they had

[83] PEL 14, NMM. ROW 6, NMM
[84] Pisani, op. cit., p. 416
[85] ROW 4, NMM

indeed left Ragusa, they were all at Trieste. In any case Rowley, assuming that the French frigates had gone on elsewhere, did not consider Maxwell's situation at Lissa to be so serious as to justify urgently sending up reinforcements. In a second letter to Maxwell of 10 October, Rowley enclosed copies of the letters from General Maitland and Colonel Smith and briefed him on his reply to the general, but said nothing about Captain Smith proceeding to Lissa.[86]

But Rowley was to receive a batch of three more letters from Maxwell dated 2, 10 and 15 October that arrived at Fano on 18 October.[87] The first explained what had happened with the French frigates from Ragusa. The British sloop ACORN had been off the island of Arcangelo (Arkandel near Mali Drvenik), which was the ideal position, not too distant from Lissa, to help the British gunboats to blockade the Dalmatian coast, but had run aground. While ACORN was being dragged off, the French frigates from Ragusa were seen off Arcangelo going north, their presumed destination being Pola. Any threat they had presented to Lissa had passed, at least for the time being.

It was the second and third letters from Maxwell of 10 and 15 October that were to give Rowley more concern. For several years the French had been known to be building not only frigates and smaller warships but also heavy ships-of-the-line in the Venice Arsenal. As many as five ships-of-the-line were on the stocks in Venice in 1808 being built for the French and Italian navies. But such large ships took a long time to build and the British cruisers in the Adriatic had been able to disrupt the supply from Croatia of timber for their construction. But now in autumn 1811 the first of these battleships, RIVOLI of 74 guns, was ready for sea. Because of the shallowness of the channels leading from the Venice lagoon to the sea, it was not normally possible for warships to pass through them with the weight of guns, and they had to be armed elsewhere. With RIVOLI the French were not prepared to risk it being caught unarmed by a British warship after it had passed out of the Venice lagoon. They tried to take it out already armed with all its guns by using a 'camel', a construction built under and up the sides of the battleship to float it higher in the water so as to clear the sand banks. Maxwell's letter of 10 October brought the alarming news that the French were trying to put the RIVOLI to sea, but also the welcome news that RIVOLI had been damaged in the attempt and had been taken back in. Maxwell repeated his earlier warnings of French preparations to attack Lissa and enclosed his assessment of the strength of the French naval forces in the upper Adriatic. Maxwell's letter of 15 October claimed that, as all other French preparations for an attack on Lissa were completed, RIVOLI had been ordered to sail 'sink or swim'.

It was the possibility that RIVOLI might be successfully put to sea that determined Rowley that he would have to leave his regular post off Fano and go to Lissa himself in EAGLE 74 as only a ship-of the-line could be expected to take on another ship-of-the line. As recently as 17 October in a long letter to Fremantle concerning the British blockades of Corfu and Venice and the question of Lissa (it would not be difficult or expensive to build or enlarge cisterns at Port St George to increase the supply of water for the fleet), Rowley had sounded no alarm.[88] It was the receipt of Maxwell's letters on 18 October that seems to have changed his mind. Presumably because his message to Fremantle had already left and he could send a further

---

[86] ROW 4, NMM
[87] ROW 4, NMM
[88] ROW 6, NMM

message more easily to Malta than to Sicily, he wrote to Admiral Boyle at Malta on 19 October, saying that, having received a letter from Maxwell, he was sailing for Lissa.[89]

Rowley in EAGLE reached Lissa on 24 October. By 28 October in orders he gave to Maxwell he was satisfied that there was no immediate danger from the damaged RIVOLI and that he proposed to return to blockade Corfu. As General Bertram had concentrated 2-3000 troops on Lesina, Brazza and Cazzola (i.e. Curzola) to take Lissa and had assembled boats at Citta Vecchia (Stari Grad) on Lesina, Maxwell was ordered to continue to prevent the enemy taking Lissa.[90] (It has not been easy to identify this General Bertram, otherwise called Beltaume or Beltamme, but it is most probably General Bertrand, the new French governor of the Illyrian Provinces, who later accompanied Napoleon to St. Helena, normally based at faraway Laibach (Ljubljana) but visiting Dalmatia in September-October 1811).[91] The brig IMOGEN was to join Maxwell until the return of the frigates UNITÉ and ACTIVE and was to be sent with the sloop ACORN and 2-3 privateers to stand off Citta Vecchia and blockade the enemy's boats whenever the wind or weather was fair enough for them to cross over to Lissa. ACORN was otherwise to remain off Arcangelo to blockade coastal traffic. The frigate ALCESTE was to move around Lissa which 'will give countenance to the islanders and confidence to the privateers (a portion to be kept at Lissa)'. Maxwell was warned not to be caught in Port St George by a Borea (the violent north wind now called a bura).

Despite having declared his intention to return to Corfu, Rowley was still at Lissa when he wrote to Fremantle on 31 October to report that he had visited Lissa for the first time and was impressed. Captain Smith (who had presumably gone up to Lissa with Rowley, had finished his survey on 30 October and sailed for Messina on IMOGEN on 31 October) was to deliver the letter and give Fremantle his views and a copy of his survey. Pending a decision Rowley would stay off Lissa, although it would be impossible for all the squadron to guard it indefinitely. He also reported to Fremantle that RIVOLI had been damaged in an attempt to put her to sea with a camel and needed repairs. 'The enemy seem determined to take Lissa'.[92]

On 2 November Rowley ordered Captain Bligh in the sloop ACORN to station himself off Arcangelo with two Maltese privateers RIVIOLI and ESPERANZA. Rowley had heard that 12 rowboats of a new type of construction had arrived at Zara from Venice and would probably be moving down the coast.[93] Then (as he was later to report to Fremantle and Pellew on 16 November in letters written when he was back at his regular position off Fano) Rowley changed his mind again, leaving Lissa at 8 p.m. on 5 November, feeling that the island was secure under the charge of Maxwell in ALCESTE and with ACTIVE, UNITÉ (back in the Adriatic but now commanded by Captain Edwin Henry Chamberlayne) and ACORN cruising off the island of Arcangelo to molest the coasting trade of Dalmatia. After reconnaissance, it had been decided that the enemy strength was not enough to take Lissa. The arrival of EAGLE had forced General Beltaume to disembark the troops and cannon he had collected at Lesina for an attack on Lissa and to take defensive measures. Lissa did however still bind up frigates and limited their freedom of action.[94]

---

[89] ROW 6, NMM
[90] ROW 4, NMM
[91] Pisani, op. cit., p. 346
[92] ROW 6, NMM
[93] ROW 4, NMM
[94] ROW 6, NMM

On his way down from Lissa to Fano, Rowley wrote a long personal letter to his friend Hudson Lowe at Santa Maura which he sent on by BLACK PRINCE while he was taking on water at Valona on the Albanian coast:

'Shortly after receiving your letter by Captain Smith, I was obliged from information to make the best of my way to Lissa, where I arrived exactly in time to save the Island as General B had embarked all his Troops and Guns in small boats. Total about 2500 soldiers. In consequence of Eagle's appearance and a Ruse de Guerre, the General thought it wiser to look to his own possessions than making new ones, and disembarked his troops and placed his cannon in battery. They are now employed fortyfying all their islands and therefore till they have secured themselves I do not think Lissa is in danger, particularly as I have 3 large frigates and a small Post Ship round it. But I cannot permit the whole of these ships to be employed in nothing else.... without Gen. Maitland decides to garrison it, it must be abandoned and when it is, the French will garrison it in such a manner as to prevent you taking it. Whatever I thought of its advantages previous to my seeing it, which were numerous, it is trifling to what I think of it now. There is no expense in my opinion that would not be worth GB's while to undergo them to forego the advantages of possession. While you possess the superiority at sea, you would with this island be enabled to paralyze all his naval force in the Adriatic and would annihilate the commerce in the upper part of the Adriatic as well as fan the flame of discontent in the northern part of Italy, Venice, Dalmatia etc. and in a commercial pint of view there cannot arise a doubt.

With respect to the defence required, it would be necessary to have a respectable work for a cittadel beyond a coup de main and one or two other works - the plans of which you will see Captain Smith having them - As to the possibility of landing except in one or two places - it is all nonsense, they may land wherever they like, if they have no opponents, and where they will have the success of landing will depend as it does always on the courage of the Besiegers being better than the besieged.... If you garrison Lissa it ought not to be less than 600 to 1000 men as the closeness of it to the other islands will always induce the French Rascals to be hazarding little embarkations, which a respectable garrison will prevent or if they attempt large embarkation, they cannot do it without a marine force and that they will not dare hazard.

I have given out that prisoners cannot be made of those who are found on the seas in unarmed boats without protection and for the avowed purpose of ransacking a poor set of miserable people (that have been obliged to submit to the fostering arm of GB) for three days, which General B has promised to his soldiers on capturing the island. Maxwell had hinted something of the kind previous to my coming up, and the General said it was not a Gentlemanlike mode of warfare. What he will say when he is told that I am resolved I have not an idea, but he like a Frenchman said that while the English were saving those who surrendered, he should be able to get on shore 6 or 700 and that they should pillage and ravish male and female for three days. Many have deserted. The Italians swear they will not go. Dalmatia has not a French soldier in it, as they are all sent to the island of Lessina'.[95]

---

[95] Lowe Papers, Add 20110, BL, dated Valona, 10 Nov. 1811

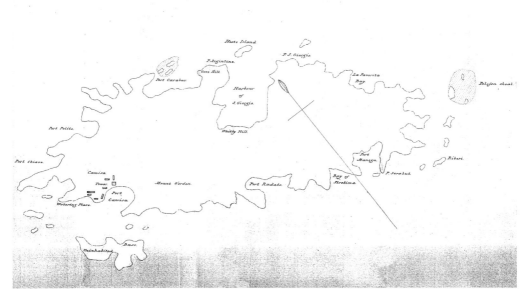

Figure 23. Captain Smith's map of Lissa, October 1811. He may not have surveyed the whole island in person as Comissa (Komiža) is misplaced. (Nottingham University Portland (Welbeck) Collection).

While at Valona on 9 November Rowley also wrote to Colonel Smith at Zante to inform him that Captain Smith had left Lissa on 31 October for Messina on IMOGEN. At least 800-1000 men would be necessary for Lissa. This size of garrison would give confidence to the islanders, who could raise a militia of at least 1000, and all of whom had their own muskets. The closeness to the mainland would ensure a supply of grain and cattle.[96]

***

When Rowley arrived back at Fano he received a letter on 15 November from General Maitland dated 9 November. The second report on Lissa by an officer of Royal Engineers signed by 2nd Capt. F. (Frederick) Smith had reached army headquarters in Sicily on 7 November. Maitland now agreed that Lissa should be garrisoned by 1000 men, but he declined taking any active step until Bentinck arrived back from England. Rowley promptly reported this new development to Admiral Pellew on 16 November.[97]

Captain Smith's report[98] was indeed a very thorough piece of work with which it would have been difficult to find fault, although parts are in a poorly punctuated shorthand style which is not always easy for a modern reader to understand. It was accompanied by carefully drawn

---

[96] ROW 6, NMM
[97] ROW 6, NMM
[98] Portland Papers, 6342/1-3, marked as received 7 Nov. 1811

maps of the island. In his description of the island, he considered the possibility of landing in every bay and found more where it would be possible than the four identified by Captain Bennett:

> 'Bay of Andato or Rudo. Rudato - landing place where boats could land troops.
> Bay of Maniga - troops from Lessina with an E wind could land in this bay - 4 miles from St George.
> Carolen Bay (Carobar on his map?) - vessels of 200 tons may anchor in safety except with E by S wind.
> Bays of Chiave and Polito - landing possible but road to St George very bad.
> La Favorita Bay - Just on outside of St George's Harbour to S. Most likely point from which to reach heights commanding St George's Harbour.'

The population of St George was calculated at 2,900 of which 1,000 might be called upon at any moment. Their general occupation was fishing and the cultivation of the vine. At Comisa there were 1,800 inhabitants, engaged in fishing from June-September, 800 of whom would be ready to take up arms. All the inhabitants were in possession of fire-arms and would defend their country. As far as local military forces were concerned, there was no provincial corps established. Under the Venetian government there had been some guards to assist the governor to enforce taxes. A corps of militia might easily be formed.

None of the roads were fit for passage of even the lightest guns, although by dint of great labour they might be conveyed from the landing places to the towns. The roads could be repaired to allow passage of 6 pounders but would have to be completely remade for heavy ordnance. If the enemy landed at Comisa they would have to climb up to pass over to St George and the space was confined so that troops with light guns on the ridge could hold an enemy at bay. There was a signal post on the Comisa side of the island set up by Captain Maxwell.

As far as the soil was concerned, the hills were rocky while in the valleys there was red earth that could produce corn for consumption (as it once did for a population of 13,000) but it would cause hardship to compel replacement of the vine. The island now had no corn, which was imported from Ancona and the Italian coast, and there was little pasturage involving only a few sheep and the rare bullock, cattle being in general brought over from Dalmatia. The boats of the islanders consisted of 30 bracciera and 60 smaller boats.

There was only one spring at Comisa from which water was brought by boat to St George where the houses only had tanks. There was no timber fit for building but some for burning. There was limestone all over the island and sand in most of the creeks.

When it came to describing the defences of Lissa, Captain Smith was very complimentary about the improvements which Captain Maxwell had been able to make in the previous few months and which in Smith's description suggest the unorthodox application of maritime skills:

> 'The Harbour of St George is defended by two batteries placed on Hoste's Island, one of two guns on traversing carriages both defending the entrance and one of them Carober Bay. The other of 1 gun similarly mounted and defending the interior of the harbour

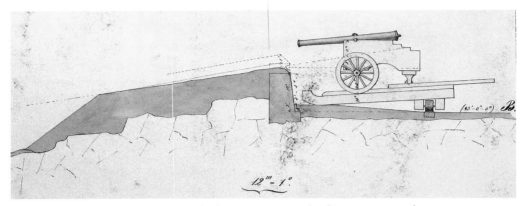

Figure 24. A traversing cannon in the battery on Hoste Island. From Austrian drawings in 1854. Although from 40 years after the British had built the batteries, little has changed.

Figure 25. Comisa (Komiža) in a nineteenth century view with the Venetian Tower. The important spring that served as a watering place for the British warships is inside the harbour to the left. (Fisković Collection).

completely and seeing into Carober Bay. Magazines for these two batteries have been formed with great judgement cut out of the Rock and a covered communication made to them, these batteries are very ingeniously formed, the parapet is of Earth and revetted in the interior with stone. The traversing carriage moves round a beinguette (?) 2 feet below the crest of the parapet and four feet wide within which the work (?) is sunk 4 feet deep giving perfect cover to the men who work the carriages by blocks and tackles with the greatest facility and security. A barracks for about 80 (?) men and two officers is nearly completed under the South side of the island. This however is not a means of defence but erected for the ease of those stationed there.' (Dalmatian accounts most probably based on the recollections of Canon Doimi relate that in the course of 1811 the English completed fortifications on Hoste Island where 40 soldiers were under the command of a cadet; and that in March 1811 they constructed 2 batteries and a barracks with cisterns where they placed a midshipman with a small garrison on a small island called after Hoste).[99]

Comisa. There is a square tower built 300 years ago near the water side. Towards the town side it is 49 and on the other only 40 feet high. In the tower floor an 18 pounder is mounted and in the upper one 18 pounder and one six pounder. The parapet is in barbette and casemated embrazure to the land fronts. The guns towards the sea fire on every part of the bay and would prevent any vessels taking shelter there. The tower is 32 feet square and the parapet 5 feet thick. The domed Roof only foot and 1/2 thick.

Project for the Defence of Lissa

Works so constructed as to impede an enemy's entering into the Harbour with whatsoever Force, but also to take up or defend those points which were he to occupy he would prevent those vessels getting out that might be in the harbour.

With 5-600 men properly situated it would be absolutely impossible for the French to take the Island so long as GB maintains her naval superiority in the Adriatic. Want of provisions would be most severely felt by them and if the attack were in summer we would control the water at Comisa. The difficulty of erecting their batteries in such a soil would lengthen the defence that with the Navy they would be forced to surrender.

Hoste's Island is admirably calculated to defend the Harbour but as from its being occupied the French would never attempt to force into the anchorage, but by landing elsewhere take a post that would enable them to render the works on the island perfectly untenable. It becomes absolutely necessary that we should occupy that Post as our first Consideration. The Enemy established on Hornby Hill would with a few field pieces completely silence the fire of Hoste's Island and making a lodgement for musketry at point St. Giorgio which is almost directly under it, he would prevent our vessels getting through the wider passage. Merchant vessels certainly would not attempt it. We should occupy the hill with a Redoubt of a respectable construction.

Possession of the hills near Argentine Point - Hoste's Island would be within musket shot and [the enemy] would take all that side of the harbour. I propose to erect for Cove Hill a blockhouse of sufficient strength to oblige an enemy to make batteries for its reduction - difficult given the soil and no place between Polita and Carober Bays where heavy guns could be landed. In landing guns at Carober they would be exposed to works on Hoste's Island and partially to fire from Cove Hill.

Our hold would be considerably strengthened by a redoubt on Whitby Hill at the head of the Harbour which would see the entrance and from an elevated position - too high for a sea battery - a couple of guns would completely cover and protect the mercantile

---
[99] Pisani, op. cit., p. 417. Foretic, op. cit., p. 630

part of the town and render it impracticable for them to force into the anchorage. It is a critical point with relation to the bays of Marnica and Rudato to the South and as it is to Chiave and Polito to the North it presents a retreat and a rallying point to the Troops and Militia. Within reach of affording succour to any of the landing places which advantage Hornby and Cove hills do not possess. If taken its possession would not help him against them.

Hornby redoubt would be capable of the longest resistance - propose work to have ditch and counterscarp shell proof magazine and cisterns with a barracks in the interior covered by the parapet from fire. The hill is rocky and I apprehend the Escarpe will stand without a revetement. Should it however be intermixed with earth or the Rock be of a loose nature a very trifling and certainly not an expensive revetement may be given it. The lime may be burnt on the spot, the greatest delay in collecting earth for the parapet which must be brought from the adjoining plains.

The same advantages hold good to Whitby Hill (i.e. lack of soil to help the enemy construct batteries).

Calculating on the assistance of a militia, 150 men would be sufficient for the Hornby Redoubt, 80 at Cove Hill, and 40 on Hoste's Island. 100 men would be adequate on Whitby Hill but it would have to be large enough to hold 300 as, besides the militia who would retire there, there would also be the 30-40 men from Comisa.

The Block House at Cove Hill would be 40 feet long and 20 feet wide and shot proof towards the interior. It would be surrounded by a ditch and palisade raised to 20 feet (using the earth which would arise from quarrying stones to form a small covertency (counterscarp?) and strengthening it with palisades). The cost, not including the value of the timber (Rowley had said that timber could be brought from Durazzo at a reasonable price) would be 2000 dollars (about £1000 pounds sterling) and could be completed in 6 weeks. The work could be proceeded with shortly after Hornby Redoubt was commenced as there were at present 50 masons and 15 carpenters on the island and the number might be increased as soon as the island was occupied.

The barracks including officers' quarters on Hornby Redoubt would cost 1200 dollars not counting the timber. It was difficult to calculate the cost of Hornby Redoubt before the nature of the soil had been ascertained but calculating the quantity of masonry at 1 1/3 dollars per cubic yard it would amount to 4800 dollars and 1200 for the arch of the magazine. Smith reckoned it would take 3 months to complete the work. He assumed that the island's revenues would entirely defray the cost of Hornby Redoubt, for which 8 x 24 pounders and two 8 inch mortars would be sufficient ordnance.

Smith's report involved a considerable increase both in the number of men and the number, size and cost of the proposed works over any of the previous proposals. Maitland's purpose in insisting on a second survey may have been to stall for time, or to kill off the proposal for the occupation of Lissa by ensuring that a realistic assessment of the needs and costs would be far more than could be accepted. On the other hand, given that he wrote to Rowley accepting the estimated need for 1,000 troops only two days after the arrival of Smith's report, it is possible

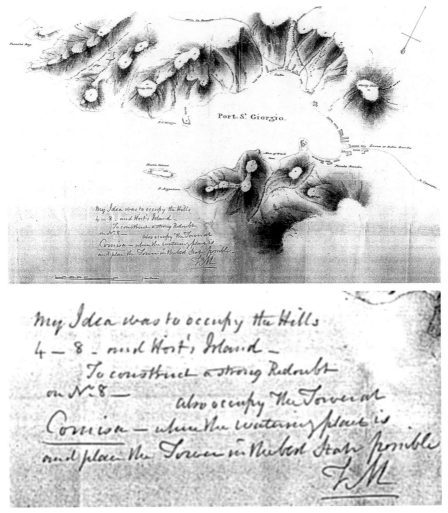

Figure 26A & B. Captain Smith's map of Port St. George, October 1811 with the hills numbered and named according to English conventions, e.g. Hornby Hill, Cove Hill etc. The note at the bottom (B.) is initialed F.M. (Frederick Maitland). (University of Nottingham Portland (Welbeck) Collection).

that, as a cautious Scotsman, he had suspected the inadequacy of the earlier optimistic estimates. Whatever the case, the political pressure to retain and exploit Lissa was building up and it would become difficult even for Maitland to argue for its loss or abandonment to the enemy for want of troops or because of the cost of the works.

Almost ironically, the surviving map of the surroundings of the harbour of St George carefully drawn by Smith is annotated:

> 'My Idea was to occupy the Hills 4 - 8 (the next summit on the ridge behind Hornby Hill and Cove Hill) and Host's Island - To construct a strong Redoubt on No.8 - also occupy

the Tower at <u>Comisa</u> - where the watering place is and place the Tower in the best State possible'.

The handwriting is not that of Captain Smith but is recognisable. The initials are FM (Frederick Maitland)![100]

***

The problem in late 1811 was that none of the senior officers in the Mediterranean, whether navy or army, were able or willing to break the deadlock. Admiral Pellew off Toulon received Rowley's letter of 15 September enclosing Maxwell's report on Lissa and including the news of Bennett's survey and sent it on to the Admiralty on 14 October where it was received on 13 November.[101] But in his reply to Rowley of the same day (received by Rowley on 21 November and quoted by him to Maxwell at Lissa on 7 December) he wrote:

> 'I have also transmitted to them (the Lords Commissioners of the Admiralty) the satisfactory information of Captain Maxwell regarding the island of Lissa.... the proposition for putting a British garrison there is already in the hands of Lord William Bentinck. I shall take no measures on that subject unless directed by the Admiralty'.[102]

Pellew next received (brought to him by REDWING) a copy of Rowley's letter of 9 October to Fremantle with copies of his correspondence with Maitland. Pellew wrote to Fremantle on 6 November to protest that Maitland had to be disabused of the some of his notions concerning the navy, especially that crews of ships could be used to supplement garrisons. Pellew then copied the entire correspondence to the Admiralty on 14 November where it arrived on 13 December.[103]

When Pellew received Rowley's letter of 16 November to tell him that he had heard from Maitland that he agreed to a garrison of 1000 for Lissa but would not take any steps until Bentinck returned from England, he could only repeat in his reply of 1 January 1812 (only received by Rowley on 15 February 1812) that everything depended on Bentinck:

> 'With respect to Lissa, nothing will be undertaken without the direct arrangement of Lord Wm. Bentinck whose return to Palermo will provide for that or any other measure regarding the military services of the Adriatic upon which you will receive ample information through Rear Admiral Fremantle'.[104]

Fremantle in the meantime at his post at Palermo was closer to Maitland at his headquarters at Messina and tried to persuade the general to take action. But Maitland was adamant. He had to await the return to Sicily of Bentinck. Whatever he had written to Rowley on 9 November about agreeing to supply 1000 troops for Lissa,, using but not mentioning Captain Smith's report, he wrote on 15 November to Lord Liverpool at the War Office in London:

---

[100] Portland Papers, 6350
[101] ADM 1/421, no. 852, PRO
[102] ROW 8, NMM and ROW 4, NMM
[103] ADM 1/421, no. 894, PRO
[104] ROW 8, PRO

'I have not undertaken to garrison Lissa. The smallest garrison would be 600 men and Rowley thinks 1000. In the present circumstances we are not able to detach this number. There would be heavy expense with constructions of some works of defence and barracks. The island is a rock and without water except a small supply at Comissa 6-7 miles from the principal harbour.... There are 7-8 landing places exposed to attack.... needs a respectable garrison to be safe. Fremantle is satisfied that at present we cannot with Discretion detach the necessary Force'.[105]

Fremantle was not happy with the situation. In his private correspondence with a Major-General Donkin in Messina, he must have expressed his frustration as Donkin wrote to Fremantle on 29 November that Maitland was 'sensitive to the opinion of a Navy officer being taken over an army officer'. Another letter in Fremantle's papers, but lacking the name of the person to whom it was addressed or a signature (and therefore probably a copy of one of Fremantle's letters to the same Donkin), complained about Maitland: 'My dear General, The Navy have reason to complain of the general conduct of General Maitland.... Maitland is saddling us with all responsibility'.[106]

Hudson Lowe at Santa Maura was also trying to help and advise his friend Rowley. On 6 December in a report about various matters to General Campbell he slipped in that 'Captain Rowley seems very impressed indeed with the importance of Lissa not only as a harbour for the shipping, but as a means for extending our political influence'. But in writing to Rowley himself on 16 December he warned him that 'I know not yet what may be the determination of the subject, but presume nothing decisive will be done until Lord W. Bentinck returns'.[107]

Everything clearly had to await Lord Bentinck's return.

***

In this further period of delay there were the usual alarms over reported dangers, many imagined and some very real. On 1 November Hudson Lowe wrote to Rowley that the British 'confidential agent' at the court of Ali Pasha of Joannina had arrived at Santa Maura and told Lowe that he had recently heard from and communicated with Rowley via Valona about a French expedition against Lissa that was being fitted out at Trieste. Lowe wrote that this particular individual was an opponent of the occupation of Lissa and was proposing the seizure of the Bocca di Cattaro instead, although Lowe dismissed him as being rather an agent of Ali Pasha than of the British government.[108]

Almost any movement of the French seemed to be directed against Lissa. One exception was the French attempt to send a convoy from Trieste via the coast of Italy to supply Corfu, which Rowley had been anticipating, but it was escorted not by the French frigates which had escaped in September 1811 from Ragusa to Trieste (one of which, FLORE, sank on 25 November trying to reach Venice) but by another force of frigates which the French had managed to put together. On 27 November Rowley on EAGLE 74 met them and captured the frigate CORCYRE

---

[105] WO 1/310, PRO
[106] Fremantle's papers are in Buckinghamshire Record Office, Aylesbury. Letters to Donkin in 39/12/1
[107] Lowe Papers, Add 20110, ff. 200 and 208, BL
[108] Lowe Papers, Add 20110, BL, f. 185

40 and chased the frigate URANIE and brig SCEMPLONE or SIMPLON into Brindisi.[109] The French move had not represented a threat to Lissa but was a reminder that the navy had other concerns and that the French were still able to put together naval forces in the Adriatic. The British had thought SIMPLON sunk in action off Parenzo on 5 May, but the French had been able to refloat and repair it.

Only two days later on 29 November 1811 Captain Murray Maxwell in ALCESTE, with the other ships with which he was defending Lissa (the frigates ACTIVE and UNITE and the sloop KINGFISHER), intercepted three French warships which had been sighted approaching from the south by the telegraph post on Whitby Hill above Port St George. A French frigate THETIS had been able to reach Corfu to relieve the French warships there. The frigates PAULINE and POMONE and the armed store-ship PERSANNE loaded with 120-130 guns then slipped out of Corfu towards the north (according to Rowley's report on 16 November). In the ensuing action off the island of Augusta (Lastovo), sometimes called the second battle of Lissa, POMONE and PERSANNE surrendered, and PAULINE escaped badly damaged to Ancona.[110] It was naturally at first assumed that the French squadron was intended for another attack on Lissa. Hudson Lowe at Santa Maura on 26 December informed General Airey (who had just taken over from Colonel Smith in command of the Ionian Islands) that the three French ships were supposed to have been bound for Lesina with 165 guns and 300 soldiers. One suggestion of the true purpose of the French squadron was (from the British point of view) just as sinister, that is that it was trying to reach Trieste with the guns on PERSANNE destined for the heavy battleships being finished in the Venice Arsenal.[111]

The movement of the French ships made Rowley concerned for Lissa. On 7 December he wrote to Maxwell that because of the movements of French ships in all directions he should withdraw his men from Lissa back to their ships, which should be collected together to cruise around the island.[112] On 11 December he ordered Captain Talbot in VICTORIOUS 74 who had just joined him off Fano to go up to Lissa and take command of ALCESTE, ACTIVE and ACORN and stay there until a decision had been made by Bentinck regarding its occupation by British troops. If there was no immediate danger to Lissa, he was to reconnoitre Venice, Trieste, Ancona and Pola. But by 18 December Rowley was able to report to Pellew that he had heard from Maxwell that, as he had heard of the loss of the French frigate FLORE off Chiozza (Chioggia) and that URANIE in Ancona was unable to sail, he had decided not to withdraw his men from the batteries he had built on different points of Lissa. He commended the efforts of Maxwell and his men who had for the last 9 months prevented the enemy from taking Lissa.[113]

1811 had been a disastrous year for the French and Italian navies in the Adriatic. At the end of the year they had few frigates left: THETIS at Corfu, DANAE at Trieste (CAROLINE was laid up out of service), URANIE and PAULINE at Ancona. There were also five brigs at Trieste and

---

[109] ROW 6, NMM, letters to Fremantle 28 Nov. 1811 and to Pellew 18 Dec. 1811
[110] Accounts in James, op. cit., Vol V, p. 181. Pisani, op. cit., Vol. 2, p. 416. Safanov, op. cit., p. 179. ROW 6, NMM, letter to Fremantle 18 Dec 1811
[111] Safanov, op. cit., p. 180. This is improbable. The guns must have been light than those needed for a ship-of-the-line. James, op. cit., adds that POMONE was also carrying 42 iron and 9 brass guns, together with 220 iron wheels for gun-carriages, which suggests that the guns were for field artillery. The question remains as to how Corfu could spare the guns, where they were being sent, and for what purpose. It has been suggested that they were for a French invasion of the Ottoman Empire but this is also implausible.
[112] ROW 4, NMM
[113] ROW 4, NMM and ROW 6, NMM

Venice and SIMPLON at Ancona. Everything now depended on what could be produced by the Venice Arsenal. There were two frigates being built and of the line-of-battle ships RIVOLI had been launched and was being repaired, and CASTIGLIONE and MONT ST-BERNARD were almost ready. There was another report dated 23 November addressed by Leard (who had been British consul in Durazzo but forced to leave in late 1811 by French intrigue), not to anyone in command in the Adriatic or Sicily, but to Wellesley, the Foreign Secretary, by whom it was passed on to the Admiralty, that the enemy was developing a new arsenal for warships at Gravosa, the harbour of Ragusa. The letter was eventually forwarded by Pellew on 9 March 1812 and received by Rowley on 20 April. Rowley was soon to dismiss the report on 26 April as improbable as the necessary materials were not available at Ragusa thanks to the British blockade and agreements with the Albanian pashas not to supply the French with timber.[114]

Lord William Bentinck finally arrived back in Sicily on 7 December 1811 after an absence of over 3 months. He was one of the more outstanding personalities of the period. Not only a professional soldier, he was a liberal with a highly developed political sense (he was to impose a constitution for Sicily against the opposition of the court at Palermo, cherished the idea of the liberation of Italy without the restoration of the ancien regime, and was later as governor-general of India to attempt to introduce the Indians to the benefits of British government). The number of problems requiring his attention in 1811-14 were both serious and numerous, but he had extraordinary energy and resolution. He had no difficulty in sharing the opinions of Rowley and Fremantle about the importance of Lissa not only as a naval base or centre for smuggling but as a key point from which to foment disorder and support revolt on both sides of the Adriatic. In the brief period he had been in Sicily in July-August 1811 before the crisis with the court led him to return to England to seek support for a stronger line, he had already been active in establishing a network of agents and in secret negotiations involving junior members of the Austrian royal family and Austrian and Italian emigrés, with a view to undermining the French position in Italy and the Illyrian Provinces. Indeed at a secret meeting in Palermo on 28 August immediately before his departure for England between himself and General Maitland and one such Austrian representative, the list of points agreed included the occupation of Lissa.[115] So it was not surprising that he soon confirmed his readiness to occupy Lissa to Admiral Fremantle (with whom he was on good terms). Fremantle was able to write to Rowley on 18 December 1811 (a letter delivered to Rowley on 14 February 1812 by the VENUS sloop pilot vessel) that he was concerting measures with Bentinck for the garrisoning of Lissa.[116]

In the meantime there was no lack of concern that the French might be able to strike at Lissa before any British troops arrived or it was made impregnable. Captain Talbot of VICTORIOUS having taken over command of the British ships at Lissa appears to have written to Rowley on 24 December that there were still enemy troops on the adjacent islands. Rowley wrote back on 24 January 1812 from off Cephalonia that if the troops had been withdrawn, he was to cruise to attack the enemy's trade.[117] Spiridion Foresti, the British diplomatic agent in the Ionian Islands, who often picked up reliable intelligence from the mainland wrote to the Foreign Office on 29 February 1812 from Zante (and would probably have informed others locally)

---

[114] ROW 8, NMM Pellew-Rowley 9 March 1812 and ROW 6, NMM Rowley-Pellew dated Lissa 26 Apr 1812
[115] Portland Papers, 5570, also in FO 70/44, PRO
[116] ROW 6, NMM
[117] ROW 4, NMM

Figure 27A. Captain John Talbot (1769–1851), commanded the British ships in the action against the RIVOLI. Portrait by Catterson Smith (National Maritime Museum).

Figure 27B. HMS WEAZLE, 18 gun brig. Watercolour by Nicholas Cammillieri (National Maritime Museum).

Figure 28. The battle between the new French ship-of-the-line RIVOLI and HMS VICTORIOUS with their escorts near Pola. Oil painting by Thomas Luny (National Maritime Museum).

Figure 29. HMS WEAZLE in action against French gunboats in Bassoglina Bay (Zaljev Marina west of Trogir) in April 1812. (National Maritime Museum).

that the French had evacuated all the small islands in the Adriatic to concentrate a force about Ragusa of 600 men which would be sent to occupy Lissa.[118] Whether there was anything in this report or whether or not Talbot received Rowley's letter of 24 January, he must have

---

[118] FO 42/13

decided that Lissa was under no threat from the islands, as he moved north with VICTORIOUS accompanied by the brig WEAZLE 18 (Captain Andrew) and arrived off Venice on 16 February. RIVOLI 74 had finally been repaired and put to sea fully armed and escorted by three brigs MERCURE, JENA and MAMELUKE in an attempt to cross to the fortified harbour of Pola in Istria. In the chase that now ensued, WEAZLE was able to destroy MERCURE on 22 February and chase off the other two brigs. VICTORIOUS attacked RIVOLI on 23 February and forced her to surrender off Point Legnian only 7 miles north of Pola.[119] RIVOLI was taken by VICTORIOUS to Lissa where according to Canon Doimi their appearance to the north initially caused panic on 26 February and the battery on Hoste Island was prepared for action.[120]

Rowley off Corfu heard of the victory in dispatches from Talbot brought down by WEAZLE and on 9 March reported it to Fremantle.[121] But almost immediately after he heard that another two French ships-of-the-line at Venice, ST. BERNARD and RIGENERATORE were trying to come out of Venice. Rowley in EAGLE moved north to check the situation arriving at Lissa on 18 March and writing to Fremantle on 18 March than he proposed to keep VICTORIOUS there until relieved by the frigate APOLLO when it could sail with RIVOLI to Malta to refit.[122] While Rowley was at Lissa the sailing master of EAGLE, W. White, collected enough information to make a chart with soundings of Port St George and its approaches (which was dated March 1812 and addressed direct to the Admiralty when Rowley was at Malta in May).[123] Rowley left Lissa on 19 March, was off Pola on 22 March, Rovigno on 3 April, Umago on 7 April and Sansego (Susak island south of Istria) on 12 April. He wrote to Fremantle on 20 April from Lissa that the enemy had abandoned their plans to bring out more ships from Venice.[124]

The possibility of enemy ships-of-the-line coming out of Venice was to remain a danger until the end of the war in 1814 and from now on ensured the presence in the upper Adriatic not only of frigates and brigs to observe any movement but also of British ships-of-the-line to encounter them as soon as they came out. This in turn was to increase the importance of Lissa as the base of a much-enlarged British naval squadron.

The defence of Lissa: Occupation and fortification

Bentinck moved into action over Lissa on 10 February 1812 when he wrote to Lord Liverpool at the War Office that he had appointed Lt. Col. Robertson of the Sicilian Regiment to the command of Lissa. Bentinck proposed to send 600 men to Lissa but the exact composition was yet to be determined.[125] On the same day Bentinck wrote detailed orders for Robertson that did give some information on the troops he was to command. What is curious from a modern point of view is that an officer might hold his commission and rank in one regiment and then be given command of troops from an entirely different regiment. This was to some extent because during the French Revolutionary and Napoleonic Wars the British Army recruited or co-opted and paid for numerous formations of foreign troops over which it appointed

[119] Accounts of the action in James, op. cit, Vol. V. Pisani, op. cit., pp. 417-18. Safarov, op. cit., pp.181-82
[120] Foretic, op. cit., p. 629. The British sailors killed in the action were buried on Lissa next to those who had been killed in the Battle of Lissa (Foretic, idem).
[121] ROW 6, NMM
[122] ROW 6, NMM
[123] ROW 3, letter to Admiralty dated 18 May 1812. Chart of Port St George now in NMM
[124] ROW 6, NMM
[125] WO 1/311, p. 67

British officers. Although Robertson had been commanding a regiment raised in Sicily, Bentinck now gave him 630 men from other regiments including 200 officers and men from the 35th Regiment of Foot, a regular British regiment that had been stationed in the Ionian Islands since their capture in 1809. The rest of Robertson's force was to be made up of 400 Corsican Rangers and an officer and 30 artillerymen of the Royal Artillery, a captain of Royal Engineers and a commissary.[126] Robertson's force was to be even more mixed than this when the Adjutant-General in Sicily, Major-General Campbell, drew up a detailed description on 25 February. 200 of the Corsican Rangers were replaced by 100 Swiss troops of Roll's regiment and 100 Calabrian Free Corps. Only three gunboats and a light armed bow-boat from the army flotilla were to accompany the force to Lissa.[127]

Bentinck's orders to Robertson made it clear that the Royal Navy and the local habitants were to complement the army contingent as means of defence. The other points in Bentinck's orders included:

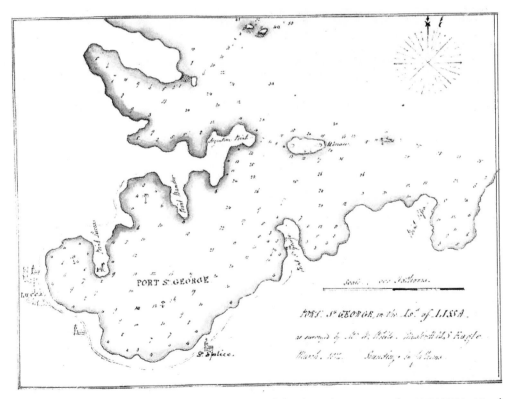

Figure 30. Chart of Port St. George with soundings made by the sailing master of HMS EAGLE in March 1812 and copied into his sketchbook by William Innes Pocock. (National Maritime Museum).

---

[126] Portland Papers, 3474
[127] WO 1/311, p. 83. See Appendix 4: Ships and Soldiers

Figure 31A. Lt. Colonel George Duncan Robertson, appointed commander at Lissa in February 1812.

Figure 31B. Captain of the 35th Regiment of Foot which provided the main body of soldiers sent to Lissa in April 1812. Caption reads 'from Colonel Luard's "Dress of the British Soldier"'.

'4. To secure your position, an off. of Engineers furnished with sufficient instructions and means will be stationed under yr command and authority to construct work as the ground will best receive and on a scale as nature of service will require.

5. To keep up constant communication with Navy. Need for mutual good understanding and harmony.

6. Left to yr judgement in what manner inhabitants can be organised and trained for defence. Early part of yr plan to prepare them as an auxillary force. 500 stands of spare arms will be placed at yr disposal.

7. You will leave the inhabitants to arrange their own civil concerns. You are to consider yrself head of Civil Government but to interfere as little as possible allowing them to go on according to their own customs.

9. Free exercise of religion.

10. A council of about 12 prominent inhabitants.'

Robertson's force assembled at the Ionian island of Cephalonia. From there it was to be taken in transports to Lissa escorted by the brig IMOGEN. Rowley had know this from communications from Fremantle he had received when still off Fano as early as 17 February when he wrote to

Figure 32. Uniform of the De Rolls Regiment, a company of
which served at Lissa.

Talbot on VICTORIOUS at Lissa: 'I am daily in expectation of the Arrival of the Imogen with the Troops'.[128]

But there was to be yet one more alarm. Fremantle at Palermo wrote on 13 March that he had for three days been anxious as an account had been received of the escape of two ships-of-the-line and two frigates from Toulon. He was afraid they were gone to the Adriatic.[129] Robertson on Cephalonia wrote to Bentinck on 28 March:

> 'On 25 March we were proceeding from hence when we received intelligence that a French squadron had escaped from Toulon. We returned to our anchorage and will wait until we can proceed in safety to Lissa. All troops are embarked in good health'.[130]

The troop transports escorted by IMOGEN finally reached Lissa on 25 April where they were awaited by Rowley in EAGLE 74 with Captain Taylor of the frigate APOLLO (Talbot in

---

[128] ROW 5, NMM
[129] Wynne Diaries, ed. Anne Marie Huth Fremantle, Oxford 1935, abridged edition 1952
[130] Portland Papers, 4716

VICTORIOUS 74 with RIVOLI had left for Malta after his arrival), Captain Maxwell in the frigate ALCESTE and Captain Andrew in the brig WEAZLE. After all their efforts to ensure the safety of Lissa over the previous year, the delays, frustrations and alarms, Rowley and Maxwell must have been greatly relieved. (Yet historians have forgotten them and given all the credit to Hoste). Rowley reported to Fremantle on 26 April:

'Imogene arrived yesterday with troops for the garrison of Lissa. I shall remain until they are landed and settled on the island in a day or two. Weazle is to convoy the transports which brought the troops from Cephalonia back to Zante...'[131]

Colonel G. D. Robertson sent his first report from Lissa to Bentinck on 26 April:

'I have the honor to report to Your Lordship that the Convoy did not arrive here untill yesterday; we put back four times to Cefalonia in consequence of contrary winds. This is much to be regretted as we have lost a great part of the cool season for going on with our works, and much opportunity of collecting water. I have this day taken possession of the Island with some little form. The Inhabitants have received us with the utmost satisfaction and I have reason to suppose that they will render us every assistance that we can expect from them... The Apollo Frigate is to be stationed here for our protection. I propose landing the Troops tomorrow and shall lose no time in going on with the utmost exertion with our Works. No time shall be lost in getting our Stores out of the Transports in order that they may return to Sicily.

The only information that I can give your lordship at present is that from all accounts the Inhabitants on both sides of the Adriatic are exceedingly discontented with the French. They have evacuated the neighbouring Islands with the exception of very small Garrisons of provincial Troops left for the protection of the Forts'.[132]

Robertson was right. The real danger to Lissa had passed. Any hopes that the French might have entertained of capturing Lissa had waned with their serious naval losses in 1811-12 and, in preparation for Napoleon's invasion of Russia, troops were withdrawn from the Illyrian provinces. In a sense, coming so late, the British garrison on Lissa and the fortifications that were now to be constructed were superfluous. But the presence of the army on Lissa did free the navy commanders from further serious concern for the safety of their base, from which they could from now on launch increasingly serious attacks on the enemy's coasts in support of Bentinck's more aggressive policy of sponsoring revolts against French rule.

**

The official reports of the arrival of the British troops at Lissa and of how it affected life on Lissa can be supplemented by the very vivid and detailed descriptions of Canon Doimi and in the private journals of various of the British officers who were based there, although as usual many of the dates and details in Doimi's journal (repeated by generations of Dalmatian

---

[131] ROW 6, NMM
[132] WO 1/311, no. 351. Canon Doimi recorded the arrival of the British troops and the ceremony and parade with which Robertson took possession of Lissa , but the detail of numbers and officers' names is only partially confirmed by the official British records. Some of the officers he names arrived later. Doimi's account is repeated in: Foretic, op. cit., p. 630. Pocock, op. cit., p. 184

historians) are at variance with those in British official records. However, from this point on this account of the British involvement with Lissa must be limited to the measures taken for its defence in terms of the naval and military forces dedicated to it and the fortifications and ancillary works which were constructed.

Doimi's account (as edited by Foretic) is that as early after their arrival as 27 April 1812, Colonel Robertson as governor, accompanied by Engineer Captain Henryson, climbed the hill where Fort George was to be built and laid the foundation stone with his own hand. A tower called Bentinck was also built nearby while Fort Wellington was built on the other or east side of the harbour with barracks and a well (where the Austrians were later to build a battery of 8 cannon). Henryson had a subordinate officer and 10 sappers and the works, although complicated, progressed fast as many masons, stonecutters and carvers were attracted from Italy, Istria, Pula and the Dalmatian mainland.[133] The historian of Napoleonic Dalmatia, Paul Pisani, using the same sources says that along with Fort George, three large towers were built called Bentinck, Wellington and Robertson and that 'une quantité d'ouvriers terrassiers et maçons vinrent d'Italie, d'Istrie et de Dalmatie, et tous les travaux furent achevés en peu de mois'.[134] Although the physical structures, to some extent altered during the Austrian period, survive to this day and still bear the same names, the British records tell a rather different story about their construction.

Captain Henryson did indeed go out immediately after his arrival to survey the ground and wrote a report to Colonel Robertson on 27 April. His conclusions were different from those of his predecessor Captain Smith. Smith had recommended that the principal and most expensive redoubt should be on Hornby Hill to the east of the entrance to the harbour, but Henryson decided that the main works (Fort George) had to be near but not on Cove Hill (where Smith had proposed a block house) and protected from behind by two martello towers (Bentinck and Robertson). There was to be a smaller fortification on Hornby Hill (Wellington). As the report was only written on 27 April and as it proposed a different location for the fortification to be known as Fort George from the fortifications at Cove Hill of Smith's report, it is hardly likely that Colonel Robertson rushed the same day to lay a foundation stone.

> 'Having examined the ground, the hill immediately on the point on the right hand entering the Port (Point Argentine in the earlier maps and descriptions) is the only spot from where a proper command of the entrance and Hoste's Isle can be had and affording a safe
>
> comm.(-unication?) with the sea side. I propose a redoubt be built there. As the hills gradually rise above each other and because of the proximity of the two nearest the ground proposed for the redoubt it is absolutely necessary to construct at least 2 advanced works. The steepness of these hills forming small ravines close to the proposed redoubt and therefore covered from its fire is another strong reason for additional works. The Enemy could otherwise construct first works of attack within 200 yards of the front of defence. As the hills are steep and pointed no other than very

[133] Foretic, op. cit., p. 361
[134] Pisani, op. cit., p. 418. Pisani also describes the optical telegrah system linking Port St George with Comisa. (see also Safanov, op. cit., pp. 183-84)

lofty works can see to their basis. I propose Martello Towers which require few men to garrison them and are less expensive.[135]

The hill [Hornby Hill] forming the point on the opposite side of the harbour (although the summit is 1/2 mile away from the entrance and a mile from the other side proposed for the redoubt) is so commanding because of its height and should not be entirely neglected. A small musketry work may suffice which could be built in a few days.

To give temporary security to the troops I recommend that a Field Line [a trench] be roughly thrown up in advance of the proposed redoubt as marked aaa on the accompanying sketch [probably the two lines on the surviving plan of the entrance of the harbour running from the redoubt to the end of Point Argentine].

As the two advanced towers can be built in a short time to such a height as to render them respectable musketry posts together with the Field Line they will occupy and secure the ground so effectually as to leave no apprehension I conceive from any sudden attack unless executed by a very superior force indeed. The Field Line would be a temporary work. I propose that it be constructed by the Troops in Fatigue.

The construction of the redoubt and towers will be more expensive than usual owing to the small number of artificers in the Island, the number of houses building and in consequence the exorbitant wages the former receive. The great distance and the scarcity of materials (except stone) will tend to heighten the expence.'[136]

Colonel Robertson sent a further report to Bentinck on 14 May 1812:[137]

'I have the honor to report to your Lordship that immediately on our landing we lost no time in commencing Field Works, and throwing up Field lines, to cover ourselves against any sudden attempt of the enemy, every man was employed and in three days they were finished; I am not in the least uneasy. We have commenced building the principal redoubt and Martello Towers and are making tolerable progress considering the difficulties we have to encounter, the articles necessary (particularly water) have to be brought at a very great distance.

I have the honor to enclose your Lordship the report of the officer of the Royal Engineers, and also a rough sketch where our works are to be placed. As soon as the Officer receives his mathematical instruments a correct Plan of the Island and Works shall be sent to your Lordship. [It seems strange that Henryson had brought no instruments with him on what was an urgent mission, or that the works were begun without drawings that could be copied to Bentinck. The sketch map survives but no

---

[135] One of the junior officers with the 35th Foot, Ensign Hildebrand, wrote in his memoirs (probably many years later) that the towers had to be constructed later because of the vulnerability of the redoubt: 'The harbour at Lissa had been entirely unprotected by fortifications or forts, the remedy of which, however, was immediately set about under the direction of a Captain of Royal Engineers, but when finished was found to be so commanded by the neighbouring heights that it was necessary to add several Martello Towers, which certainly restored the required protection (none on the land side) to a great degree' (typescript copy in National Army Museum, Chelsea). It is clear from Henryson's report that he planned the towers from the outset.
[136] Portland Papers, 4722, sketch map 4721
[137] WO 1/311, no. 371

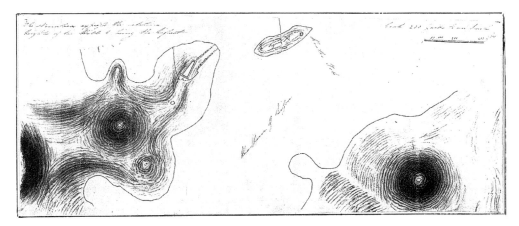

Figure 33. Captain Henryson's sketch map of the entrance to Port St. George, April 1812, showing the sites he chose for the fortifications. (University of Nottingham Portland (Welbeck) Collection).

properly measured plans of the forts, as opposed to sketches, have been found and were possibly never made]. The labourers here are very scarce and the articles dear, particularly timber, which will make our works become expensive but every possible economy will be used. [The lack of timber on Lissa had been repeatedly pointed out in earlier reports and correspondence, so it is surprising that none or an insufficient supply had been brought from Albania as Rowley had suggested].

The last Reports from Venice say that after the taking of the Rivoli, the French were so disheartened that they dismantled the ships of war in that port, discharged their artificers, and marched their crews to the Danube, but we are not certain of this information: one of the frigates here will shortly look into that place.... The Enemy in the Island of Lessina is much alarmed at our being so near, and is very busy in throwing up works for his protection.

The L'Achille, Apollo, Alcemene, Weazle and Imogen Ships of war are here. I have received the greatest assistance from the navy, they most kindly got all our heavy guns upon the Height'.

A further letter from Robertson to Bentinck on 8 June 1812 reported:

'The principal work [Fort George] is begun and the Martello Towers are in great forwardness, particularly the advance one which will shortly be finished... The Inhabitants are greatly attached to us and the whole of them have voluntarily offered to take the Oath of Allegiance to His Britannic Majesty. I hope very shortly to have a good militia formed of 500 men'.[138]

His next report of 14 June did not mention the fortifications but was concerned with other dangers to the security of Lissa, such as the efforts of the French to cut off the island's supply

---

[138] WO 1/312, no. 33, enclosed Bentinck-Bathurst 13 July 1812

of provisions, desertions by some of the Corsican Rangers and the increasing number of mouths which needed food.

> 'Supplies of provisions depend on the Continent and the Neighbouring islands - we have lately been most amply supplied. The French have therefore fitted out armed vessels and have captured many of the provision boats. I sent out gun-boats to protect the provision boats... The gun boats fell in with the Enemy's and after a good deal of firing beat them off... The measures of the French have occasioned such misery on both sides of the Adriatic that great numbers of the inhabitants are coming to Lissa for protection. I was under the necessity of putting a stop to their coming.'[139]

Captain Henryson gave Robertson an update on the progress of the works on 6 July:

> 'In excavating for the stone with which to build the front wall of Fort George I find (contrary to my first expectation) that the rock inside the intended Walls is much easier removed than elsewhere in the neighbourhood and that in consequence it becomes necessary to lower that ground considerably in order to procure a sufficient quantity of stone: this unexpected circumstance obviates the necessity of constructing the Fort so narrow as represented in the Plan I laid before you on the arrival of the Troops here. I submit another plan for the fort adapted to this last and other circumstances of the ground. The Profile or Section I am sorry I cannot as yet determine, not knowing how much the ground can be lowered nor in consequence how high the walls may require to be raised.
>
> The arch of the most advanced Tower from Fort George (called Bentinck's Tower) is nearly finished and the Walls are 20 feet high. The Tower nearest the Fort (Robertson's) is 10 feet high and in a respectable state of defence as a musquetry post. The Third Tower (on the opposite side of the Harbour's mouth) is built as high as Robertson's. I propose leaving these two last mentioned towers as at present until the construction of the Fort is more advanced.
>
> The Front Wall of Fort George is built 8 feet high. Its construction has not advanced with the celerity the other walls will, from its being of cut-stone. I hope the barracks and wall of the Fort (to a defensible height) will be executed before the commencement of the ensuing winter.'[140]

In his next letter to Bentinck of 8 July, Robertson referred to the changes in the shape of the principal work and enclosed the officer RE's reasons for it and his progress. Perhaps his concern that things were not going as well as he could have hoped is betrayed by his claim the works were 'getting on as rapidly as can be expected'. The endorsement on the letter refers to 'a letter with a plan shewing an Alteration in the shape of the new work' but no such plan has been traced.

Robertson was still having problems with his Corsicans: a further nine had deserted on the provision boats returning to the mainland and another seven had been caught and punished.

---

[139] idem
[140] Portland Papers, 4725 a and b

Figure 34. Admiral Thomas Fremantle, print from a
portrait by Edmund Bristow.

He thought that at least another 60 Corsicans (out of the total of 200) were unreliable and that
he would have liked to send them to serve elsewhere because of the bad impression they were
making on the islanders and on the mainland.

The other event that Robertson reported, which was to considerably affect the further history
of the British in the Adriatic, was the arrival at Lissa on MILFORD 74 of Rear Admiral Thomas
Francis Fremantle.

***

In his letter of 14 May 1812, Robertson had reported that the Montenegrins with a number
of Russian officers had attacked the French at the Bocca di Cattaro and that another attack
was to be made on 25 May. The news fitted in with the background of the numerous clashes
between the Montenegrins and the French of the previous few years and various other reports
and negotiations which Bentinck had been conducting concerning local uprisings against
the French to be perhaps linked with an attack by the Russian army on the Danube across
the Balkans on the French in Illyria and Italy. Admiral Fremantle immediately and without
seeking the prior approval of his naval superiors agreed with Bentinck in early June to sail
from Sicily (departing from Palermo on 13 June) to Lissa with a substantial military force
(1200 men from the Ionian Islands under Colonel Moore of the 35th Regiment of Foot) to
support any such attack on the French or mainland uprising.[141] But when Fremantle arrived at

---

[141] PEL 15, NMM, Fremantle-Pellew 10 June 1812 enclosing Bentinck-Fremantle 8 June 1812 and Robertson-Bentinck

Lissa on 4 July with the first 400 soldiers of this force, he was soon to decide that the reports of an insurrection on the mainland had been exaggerated and premature, and a letter from Bentinck which reached him at Lissa on 23 July informed him that Bentinck had been warned that any British support for an attack on the Illyrian Provinces at that time could bring Austria into war with Britain. He had therefore directed the rest of the troops which had been meant to follow Fremantle to Lissa to Spain and was recalling those who had accompanied Fremantle.[142] In replying to Bentinck on 24 July Fremantle confirmed that there was little immediate likelihood of a rising in Dalmatia:

> '... without 1000 Men we can at the present moment have no reasonable hope of carrying the Natives with us. Within a few miles of us, [at] Lessina there are 700 Croatians [i.e. soldiers of the so-called Croatian or Grenzer (Border) regiments raised in the military districts of southern Croatia ceded to the French in 1809, which had high proportions of resettled Serbs] ... at Spalato they have a thousand of the same description, and except Ragusa and the Bocca di Cattaro there are no native French troops... Bonaparte has published a decree bearing the date 25th of June making it death to any who supply this Island with provisions'.[143]

Despite the collapse of the project that had brought him to Lissa, it was soon decided that Fremantle should stay there with an enlarged squadron. He was to be in charge of naval operations and various joint operations with the army until almost the end of the war in 1814. He is in many ways, along with Charles Rowley, one of the more attractive personalities on the British side (and certainly more sympathetic than his subordinate officer, Captain William Hoste, whose reputation was later so assiduously cultivated by his widow and family as to overshadow that of Fremantle, Rowley and many other officers who deserve credit). While Fremantle was imaginative and generous, especially in his protection of the interests of the local inhabitants (most particularly on the island of Curzola (Korčula) in whom he took an exceptional and protective interest), he was easily exasperated. At worst he could be considered querulous, impatient and over-critical, with little skill in handling people. But he seems seldom to have nursed grievances for long, his tempers soon passed over, and he was more often than not the party to the quarrel who tried to be conciliatory. At Lissa he had well-documented disputes with Robertson and Hoste, as well as with the secret agent Johnson. On most of these occasions he had good reason, not only because his arguments on various issues carried more weight but also, as he was easily the most senior officer by rank with the greatest responsibility, he was not unreasonable in expecting others to defer to his judgement and wishes. Except for these cases, there is every reason to believe that Fremantle was liked and respected by his superiors such as Pellew and Bentinck, and the fellow-officers whom he commanded such as Rowley.[144]

The frustrations of living at close quarters with each other in such a restricted and relatively uncomfortable place as Port St George no doubt made outbursts of bad temper inevitable. But the essential underlying problem was that of divided responsibility and parallel lines of command. Robertson as the officer commanding the troops and governor reported to

---

14 May 1812
[142] Bentinck-Fremantle 1 July 1812, Fremantle Papers, 39/3/11, also quoted Parry: The Admirals Fremantle, p. 106
[143] Portland Papers, 2556-7, also quoted Parry, op. cit.
[144] Parry, op. cit. Wynne Diaries. Pocock op. cit

Bentinck and often had the temerity to report (wrongly) on naval matters. Fremantle was on good terms with Bentinck, shared his views of the political potential of the situation, and corresponded with him, although he was strictly speaking only responsible to Admiral Pellew and the Admiralty in London. On many questions the original orders given by Bentinck to Robertson were not clear as to the relationship of the army and navy and their respective responsibilities other than that he should maintain good relations.[145] Inevitably (as Colonel Smith had foreseen) the question of who should determine the use of the gunboats from the army's Sicilian flotilla became a bone of contention between Fremantle and Robertson,[146] as did such questions as to whether port dues should be levied on ships arriving at Lissa (to defray the cost of the civil administration which Robertson headed).[147] Fremantle was convinced that it was essential to keep it a free port to increase the flow of contraband goods in defiance of Napoleon's continental system. With Hoste (who had returned to the Adriatic in command of the new frigate BACCHANTE), the disagreement concerned Hoste's rapacity and unscrupulousness in seizing prizes and interfering with local ships to which Fremantle had granted licences, and was exacerbated by Hoste's arrogance and resentment at having both Fremantle and Rowley as his seniors and superiors.[148] Bentinck had given the Irishman Johnson responsibility for maintaining a network of spies, agents and contacts throughout the region. While Johnson needed the navy to supply the ships to transport them, he insisted on reporting only to Bentinck in Sicily and kept Fremantle in the dark about many developments in which the admiral would inevitably need to become involved and in which he had a strong and legitimate interest.[149]

So it is not surprising that Fremantle was quickly to develop his own ideas concerning the land defences of Lissa and to find himself in disagreement with Captain Henryson, although the first of the problems to arise regarding the respective responsibilities of the navy and the army predated his arrival.

In his report to Colonel Robertson of 27 April 1812 on his survey for the proposed fortifications, Captain Henryson had made no reference to Hoste Island and this is almost certainly because, the fortifications there having been built by Captain Murray Maxwell and his men, it was considered a naval preserve. Indeed, Maxwell and his frigate ALCESTE had still been at Lissa and he had a pressing claim for compensation for the work and materials that he and his crew had put into the defence of Hoste Island. As early as 30 April, only a few days after their arrival, Captain Henryson was reporting to Colonel Robertson that, in compliance with his orders, he had established the value of the materials and labour involved in the construction of the barracks, roads and two batteries on Hoste's Island. He had asked Maxwell for the total

---

[145] See above, dated 12 Feb. 1812

[146] See above Smith-Campbell 8 Sep 1811 and note 65

[147] Fremantle's frequent complaints to Bentinck about Robertson are in Portland Papers e. g. 2555 (Robertson 'knows as little of trade as his Corps legislative do of reading and writing'), 2559/1, and 2565/1. Fremantle Papers, 12/8-10, 39/12. Wynne Diaries, July 1812 ('Col. Robinson's Corps Legislative is quite a comedy'). Parry, op. cit., pp. 107-8. Robertson also wrote to Bentinck about his difficulties with Fremantle: Portland Papers, 4742 ('I regret to say I still continue to have unpleasant correspondence with the Admir. – on trifling subjects. I will follow yr. Advice & try to avoid unpleasant discussion')

[148] See Pocock, op. cit., pp.186-7. Hoste kept all the written exchanges between himself and Fremantle, now in: Hoste Papers, MRF 88/3, NMM

[149] Fremantle Papers, 235/1. Wynne Diaries, p. 367, 18 Mar. 1813 ('The Unity sailed for Messina with Mr Johnson on board – hope I shall never see his face again')

Figure 35. HMS BACCHANTE, the newly built 38 gun frigate in which Captain William Hoste returned to the Adriatic and Lissa in August 1812. (National Maritime Museum).

of the bills for materials and been told by Maxwell that he had spent £1500. 'Above all from the time necessary to sink the two batteries into the rock, I believe the labour worth £500'.[150]

On 12 May Robertson sent the details of Maxwell's claim to Sicily for consideration by Bentinck and confirmed that the navy had put the island and its works into his possession.[151] The subsequent story demonstrates the inherent problems in any overlap between the army and the navy in their respective fields of activity. On receipt of Robertson's letter, as Maxwell in ALCESTE had left Lissa for Malta, Bentinck wrote to General Oates in Malta on 11 June 1812 asking him to settle with Maxwell 'as per the usage of the service'. General Oates replied to Bentinck on 4 July that he was wholly unacquainted with the usage of the service and had no authority to give warrants for expenses. He could only refer to Captain Maxwell who had sent him a letter that he was enclosing for Bentinck.[152] The main points of Maxwell's case were that he had used material taken from prizes and that he was personally responsible to his officers and men for the loss of prize money. The value of the works could easily be established as additional works were being constructed by the commanding engineer (i.e. Henryson).[153]

---

[150] Portland Papers, 2841 and 4718 (copy of 2841)
[151] Portland Papers, 2842
[152] Portland Papers, 4317
[153] Portland Papers, 4318

Bentinck referred the case to Admiral Pellew in a letter of 1 August 1812 that reached the admiral off the mouth of the Rhone on 23 August.[154]

'Some time after the occupation of the Island of Lissa by H.M. land Forces, I received a communication from Lieut. Colonel Robertson, the officer in command, acquainting me that Capt. Maxwell RN had delivered to his charge certain works on Hoste Island which had been constructed by Capt. Maxwell, during the period that he commanded HMSs at that Station. Lieut. Col. Robertson also forwarded a statement of the value of these works, as estimated by the officer of Engineers amounting to £2000 viz. £1500 for the materials and £500 for the labour, and suggested to me that the amount of this valuation should be paid to Capt. Maxwell....

As I was unacquainted with the circumstances under which the expence was incurred, I referred the subject to Lieut. General Oates at Malta, where Captain Maxwell then was, and I have received in explanation a letter from Captain Maxwell... From this it appears that Capt. Maxwell has a claim for the value of the materials (the labour as I understand having been performed by the men of the squadron) which has been estimated at £1500.

It now therefore only remains to decide whether this amount shall become a charge against the Navy or the Army Accounts, and as the expense was incurred before my part of the Army was on the station, I am induced to refer the matter in its present stage for your consideration'.

But the question was not resolved by Pellew. On 27 November 1812 a Mr Harrison of the Treasury in London sent a letter that Bentinck received on 23 January 1813. It enclosed a letter from Maxwell and asked that Bentinck send the result of his referral of Maxwell's claims to General Oates. Maxwell's letter of 11 October 1812 from 12 Clements Inn, the Strand, London, addressed to the Lords of the Treasury recounted the story of the fortifications on Hoste island and, despite some obvious exaggeration and special pleading, adds some extra detail to the information from other sources:

'Early in 1811 I was given a squadron to protect Lissa. I saw it was necessary to defend the entrance to Port St George and formed two batteries upon which we mounted 3 x 18 pdrs. with traversing carriages and also built a barrack capable of containing 80 men. The materials I either bought or appropriated from furniture and cargoes of several small vessels captured by the squadron and were unfit to be sent to Malta for adjudication. Officers and men consented to this upon my promise of indemnification. The works were scarcely finished when the French Gen. Bertram sent with 3000 troops and 150 sail of small craft from Dalmatia to town Lessina (9 miles from Lissa). The good effects of our voluntary contributions and incessant labours... I landed marines of the squadron at Hoste's Island - and I was able to go with the ships to prevent the enemy moving across - which would not have been possible if we had been obliged to stay in harbour for its protection. We captured and destroyed a large number of

---

[154] PEL 12, p. 117, NMM

the enemy's craft and defeated the squadron going from Corfu to Trieste. After four months Bertram's army was obliged to break up at Lessina.

The materials cost £1500-2000 beside the labour of our men and a mason hired to build the barracks. The RE officer said the works were absolutely necessary and delivered over in a perfect state to Col. Robertson. I hope to be repaid'.[155]

No evidence has been found that Maxwell was ever repaid.

Even though Maxwell had handed over Hoste Island to Robertson, Admiral Fremantle still considered it to be naval territory. As far as other essential questions concerning the ability of the British to hold and exploit Lissa were concerned, from such common concerns as the encouragement and protection of the boats bringing in provisions, the water supply, and the storage of provisions and supplies, to those more particularly of the navy in the establishment of a dockyard for the repair of the ships, Fremantle was soon asserting his authority.

In his letter from Lissa to Bentinck of 24 July, three weeks after his arrival, he wrote:

'I have been impressing on Col. R the placing of our stores and provisions in a state of security and under the guns of the forts, Hoste Island is not more than a cable's length from the point, and completely commanded that must be our principal depot and whenever the forts are finished the place cannot be carried except by regular siege and the enemy would need command of the sea to supply them with guns, supplies etc.'[156]

Fremantle did not expect to stay long on Lissa. He received a letter from Admiral Pellew to say that he was to use his own discretion in either remaining at Lissa or returning to Sicily.[157] By 6 August he had decided that he would leave Lissa and drafted comprehensive orders for Rowley to take over command again as Senior Officer of the Adriatic squadron. They reveal how much he had achieved in the month after his arrival, including a further fortification of his own on Hoste Island.[158]

'Whereas I have thought it necessary to purchase a piece of Ground well calculated for the purposes of repairing or refitting the King's Ships, which has occasioned infinite labours, it is my direction that the Senior Officer of the Ship or Ships in the Port of St George's do take charge of the said Arsenal, and follow the directions I point out, leaving to him to improve the same as time or circumstances will permit, attending always to the Tank, which should be kept full for the month of May.

Having built with much fatigue a Tower on the Rock at the entrance of the harbour I have to direct that the said Tower be attended to and kept in repair if necessary to do so...

---

[155] Portland Papers, 2839
[156] Portland Papers, 2556
[157] idem
[158] ADM 1/424, no. 413

The Transports being entirely under the control of the officer commanding His Majesty's Ships, he will attend, as occasion will require, to any applications of the Commandant of the place, in sending for supplies, and a Transport will always remain at Lissa to be ready for a contingency...

Lissa is not, until further orders, ever to be left without a King's Ship in the Port for its protection....

A good look out is to constantly to be kept on Mount Gordon, and Mount Whitby...

Care is to be taken of the Transport laden with Ordnance Stores which it is to be presumed the Commandant will take the earliest opportunity of removing from on board ship to places of greater security as well as to get rid of the expence of the Ship, whenever that Transport is cleared, she is to be sent to Messina or Malta as most convenient.'

But Fremantle was not to leave so soon. On 17 August 1812 he received orders from Admiral Pellew dated 14 July to stay at Lissa.[159] He replied to Pellew on 21 August enclosing the orders he had drafted for Rowley that he would now put into execution himself.[160] He had paid £50 for the ground for the dockyard which already had buildings on it suited for warehouses and a hospital. He described his tower on Hoste Island:

'I have also built a round Tower Eighteen feet high, and as many in Diameter on the little rock at the entrance of the harbour - this I thought necessary, as it is scarcely above the water's Edge: this was done entirely by the Crew of the Milford... I send plans of the Harbour of Comissa, forts and Dock Yard, for your Information; whenever the Fort is completed I shall consider the Island as secure against a Coup de Main: it will require a regular siege to dispossess us provided a Naval force is here sufficient to defend the Coast against the landing of heavy artillery and stores'.

Later in the year when he wrote to Admiral Pellew on 24 October,[161] as well as having built himself a little cottage in the dockyard, Fremantle was employed in making a tank to contain 1200 tons of water for the summer season. He was finding out more about other places to procure water, especially important given the additional thousands of sailors of the navy, as well as the soldiers and merchant seamen, who were either living or regularly visiting the island. The price of water was a dollar (about 5 shillings) a ton if bought. Captain Taylor of APOLLO made a detailed report of the springs at Comisa with a view to improving the supply.[162]

In the meantime, Captain Henryson had been pursuing the army's works. On 24 July he wrote to Colonel Robertson.

---

[159] Formal orders from Admiralty were forwarded by Pellew on 6 Aug 1813. Fremantle letter book, NRA 20664, NMM
[160] idem and PEL 16, NMM. Portland Papers, 2559/1 Fremantle-Bentinck ('I am to remain here, this will not break my heart'). Further formal order from Pellew dated 6 Aug. 1812 followed:
[161] PEL 16, NMM
[162] Fremantle Papers, 40/7/1

'The Bomb-Proof Arch of Bentinck Tower is completed and the top of the Tower levelled so that I hope work will be finished in a few days. The other two towers are very nearly completed as musquetry posts.

The Front Wall of Fort George is nearly terminated and the side walls are in a good state of progress. In short the whole of the works from the great exertions of the people employed under my command advance so much more rapidly than I could have expected. I am confident the troops will be in barracks before winter.'[163]

They were still accommodated in bell tents (according to the memoirs of Ensign Hildebrand of the 35th Regiment of Foot). On 3 September 1812 Robertson wrote again to Bentinck:

'The fortifications are getting on most rapidly. I hope to have the barracks finished for the Troops by the end of the month. The Magazine and cistern are in forwardness. Notwithstanding the troops are necessarily much exposed the garrison is extremely healthy'.[164]

This optimism compares with Fremantle's comment in his own letter to Bentinck of 22 August 1812:

'By letter from Pellew of 14 July I am to remain here, this will not break my heart.... The fortifications here are going on tolerably rapidly and now that the port is again declared free we have an abundance of supplies both of corn and cattle'.[165]

Robertson's later letters to Bentinck in 1812 reveal little about the progress of the fortifications. On 27 September 'The works are getting on rapidly and the garrison is in good health'.[166] On 29 November he was reporting more desertions by the Corsicans and even by some of the Swiss, although the size of the enemy garrisons on the neighbouring islands were now so small as to no longer pose any threat to Lissa. 'The Enemy islands in the neighbourhood have hardly any garrison. 30, 50, or 100 men is the most and there are no Frenchmen'.[167] Indeed, as the British had always hoped, the soldiers of the Croatian or Grenzer regiments (who now constituted, along with soldiers of Napoleon's Army of Italy under French senior officers, the only forces on the islands and along the coast of the mainland) began to desert (like so many Illyrian seamen before them) to the British on Lissa. Robertson was to be given permission by the War Office of 15 June 1813,[168] transmitted to him by Bentinck, to form these deserters into a new corps of the British army. By August 1813 he would have made a modest increase of the British forces on Lissa of 141 soldiers in a 'new levy', that consisted of Italians and probably Italian-speaking Dalmatians in a detachment of the Italian Legion which Bentinck had been forming in Sicily for an attack on Italy, but also of the predominantly Serbian soldiers of the Croatian regiments in a unit now called the 'Illyrian Light Infantry'.[169] But at this stage of the

---

[163] Portland Papers, 4741

[164] Portland Papers, 4742

[165] Portland Papers, 2559/1

[166] Portland Papers, 4743

[167] Portland Papers, 4744

[168] WO 6/57, Bathurst-Bentinck 15 Jun 1813 in response to Bentinck's letter of 20 Apr. 1813 (WO 1/33, no. 337) enclosing Robertson's of 16 Mar. 1813 (WO1/33, nos. 341 and 345)

[169] Fremantle Papers, 38/6/7

Figure 36. Curzola/Korčula showing the British tower to the left of the town. Detail from a Panorama of Dalmatia by Giuseppe Rieger (Fisković Collection).

war in 1813, Lissa was in no danger, the British were attacking everywhere along the coast, and hundreds of the soldiers of the Croatian regiments who had either been captured or had surrendered or deserted were simply shipped by the British to serve with the Austrian army against the French in Istria, at Trieste, or in north Italy around the mouth of the Po.

In January 1813 Fremantle and Robertson were able to cooperate on a joint navy and army attack from Lissa on the nearby islands of Augusta (Lastovo) and Curzola (Korčula) that were captured relatively easily and without strong or sustained resistance on 29 January and 3 February.[170] Captain Henryson had landed with the troops on the island of Augusta but on 27 January wrote back to Fremantle at Lissa that he himself was returning to Lissa because of some works he was supervising at Comisa. He judged the French fort on Augusta that the British troops were now about to attack so strong that it could hold out for at least a month and, if the defenders were resolute, two months or until provisions failed. 'Robertson has uniformly rejected my opinions (I believe from personal enmity) and even refused 4 Calabrese to escort me to reconnoitre the fort'.[171] In the event the small garrison of the French fort surrendered it in two days.

Having taken Curzola, Fremantle signed a detailed agreement with the inhabitants, whereby he more or less established a British protectorate under his own personal guarantee.[172] One of the provisions of the agreement was that the inhabitants of Curzola should build a tower on the hill of St. Blaize (Sveti Vlaho) above the town to command the strait between the island of Curzola and the Sabioncello (Pelješac) peninsula. The tower was designed by one of Fremantle's naval captains and built thanks not to the exertions of the local inhabitants but to those of the crews of the many British warships that Fremantle regularly routed past the island.

[170] ADM 1/426 no. 172 and WO 1/313 pp. 277-82
[171] Fremantle Papers, 38/6/21
[172] ADM 1/426, Fremantle-Pellew 17 Feb 1813

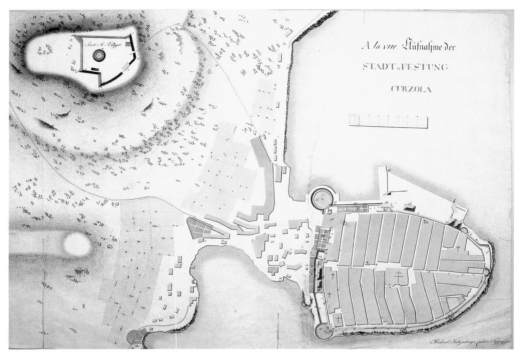

Figure 37. Plan of Curzola/Korčula showing the fortifications of San Biaggio (Sveti Vlaho), including the British tower on the hill above the walled town. From the 1835 Austrian survey of fortifications (Kriegsarchiv, Vienna).

Henryson was to protest that he had not been consulted in a letter which he sent to Colonel Robertson dated Lissa 17 February 1813:

> 'As a work of intended Military defence has been commenced I understand in the island of Curzola (occupied by a detachment of Troops under your command) without my direction or knowledge, and therefore of course without your concurrence, I have the honour most strongly to recommend you to Order the undertaking to cease 'til I receive your Orders on the subject, and am enabled to execute any fortification you may wish in the island according to the usual Rules or Customs of the Service and the principles of my profession'.[173]

Robertson passed the letter on to Admiral Fremantle, who did not hesitate to send a strong and indignant reply to Robertson on 19 February 1813, in which Henryson's advice and conduct on Augusta was not forgotten:[174]

> 'It is painful for me to animadvert on the letter you have put in my hands from Captain Henryson RE. The work at Curzola is undertaken <u>under the terms of a Convention between me and the inhabitants of that place at their own expence</u> the terms of that

---

[173] Fremantle Papers, 235/1. It is possible that Henryson had failed to provide Fremantle with plans. Fremantle Papers, 38/6/32, Henryson-Fremantle 9 feb 1813: 'Illness Mr Bains has prevented me sending plans I promised'.
[174] idem

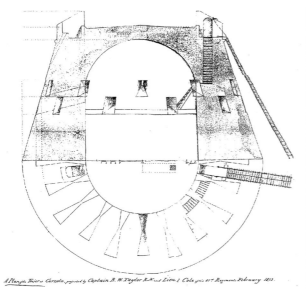

Figure 38A. The original design of Curzola Tower by Captain Taylor of the navy and Lieutenant Cole of the army, neither of whom were trained engineers. (Buckinghamshire Record Office).

Figure 38B. Korčula Tower today.

Convention... [are] entirely unknown to Captain Henryson and the Tower is essentially necessary for the defence... reference to the Captain of Engineers must have caused considerable delay and under the present people will be constructed in much less time, and I am warranted in this opinion when I look round me to see that Captain Henryson after being 11 months here, and having expended £6000 sterling has not at this day a single Gun in an embrasure, the powder and ammunition still on board a Transport kept expressly for the purpose at the expence of nearly £300 sterling a month.... Captain Henryson left you on actual service, <u>because his business called him here</u> this [?] public declaration at Augusta before the principal Officers with his prediction that the Troops would be made prisoners, is a sufficient reason why I have no confidence in him. The mischievous tendency of Captain Henryson's letter could have 3 objects

- to impede public service
- to discredit the faith of the nation by a breach of the Convention
- to set at variance the 2 professions

I shall not fail representing his conduct to his superiors.'[175]

There is only one further document found in the various British archives consulted concerning the British fortifications at Lissa. On 8 March 1813 Captain William Bennett RE, the same officer whose first army report on Lissa in 1811 had been found so inadequate by General Maitland and who was now the principal officer of Royal Engineers in Sicily, responded from

---

[175] Henryson left Lissa on 3 May 1813 to return to Sicily. WO 17/2744 (7) Monthly Returns, RE, Medit., PRO

Palermo to an enquiry he had received from Lt.-General Gother Mann (who since July 1811 had been Inspector-General of Fortifications).

> 'I have the honor to inform you that the Fortifications constructing in the Island of Lissa are nearly finished, as far as it is at present intended they should be, the Commander of the Forces (Bentinck) having desired that those works should be closed short of the original project. The Fort to be only completed as a Musquetry Post, 2 of the Towers are already finished but the other will remain half built. The expence has caused his Excellency's decision -

> The Islands of Curzola and Augusta (adjacent to Lissa and the coast of Dalmatia) lately taken possession of by a detachment from Sicily, contain no Fortifications of any consequence the small Town of Curzola is surrounded by a very old Wall flanked by round Towers but completely commanded by the adjacent hills - In Augusta there is a large Tower on the summit of a high hill commanding the Town but it is only adapted for Musquetry'.[176]

So the story of the British fortifications on Lissa ends with the all too familiar theme of a project begun too late with many misgivings, which ran over schedule and over budget, before being given up before it was finished as being unnecessary and too expensive.

***

There was, however, to be one last threat to Lissa, potentially the most dangerous. In early June 1813 news reached Lissa of the outbreak of plague in Malta in May.[177] As so many ships at Lissa came from Malta, including Royal Navy ships, every precaution had to be taken to impose quarantine and avoid contagion. In all the plans for fortifications, cisterns, dockyards and barracks, no-one had made provision for a lazaretto which, according to the usage of the time could serve for quarantine and the airing of goods from the ships. The situation caused one of the last arguments at Lissa between the admiral and the colonel. Hoste Island found a new function in stopping ships, which were prohibited the use of the port, from forcing their way in and as a place where naval stores could be exposed to the air. There must be no contact for fear of contagion between the sailors on Hoste Island and the soldiers at Fort George on the other side of the channel.[178] The spymaster Johnson, who was blaming Fremantle for an attack he had made on Fiume in June 1814, gloomily predicted that, together with the plague (and French success in persuading the Bosnian pashas to stop British trade via the Narenta), it had put an end to trade from Lissa with the mainland. 'If the plague continues, we shall not be able to provision or keep possession of Lissa'.[179]

The plague, which was in this outbreak to cause over 5,000 deaths in Malta, was everyone's enemy. A member of the 'service militaire' (Auddan?) on Lesina wrote on 27 June to M. Bouillerot, commandant d'armes à Spalato et arrondissement:

---

[176] WO 55/611
[177] Fremantle Papers, 39/7
[178] Fremantle Papers, 38/6/29
[179] Portland Papers, 2956/1, Johnson to Joseph Smith (Bentinck's secretary)

'A fishing boat with an English officer and 3 seamen arrived this morning at. 4.00 a. m. at the left battery as postman of a letter for the commandant. I sent an officer to tell him that I could not receive any communication (parlimentaire) and he must go to Spalato or Ragusa. He replied that his mission was to warn us that a ship (trabacolo) from Malta refused entry at Lissa was bound for Spalato. I enclose the letter. He said with truth that he could not go to Spalato because of contrary wind'.[180]

A second letter was sent on the same day by the Sub Délégué of Lesina (Snirvich?) to the Duc d'Abrantes (General Junot, the Governor-General of the Illyrian Provinces) to report that on receipt of Robertson's letter, they had immediately sent a boat to Spalato to warn the military commandant and the Council of Health. Another boat with an officer of the Garde Nationale and a detachment of troops was sent to make the ship pass into the Lazaret of Spalato. It could not overtake the trabacolo but followed it until it was seen to enter the port of Spalato. They had however received information by telegraph from Milna that the trabacolo was commanded by a Jerome Babarovicz of Milna who claimed that his crew were all healthy. Robertson had also assured the French that there was perfect health at Curzola and Lissa.[181]

Whether the plague, as Johnson feared, did deter the Dalmatians from sending provisions to Lissa, is doubtful. The French authorities were already aware of the extent to which the trade with Lissa undermined their own health precautions. Fremau(?), Lt. commandant la

Figure 39A. Jean Andoche Junot, Governor of the Illyrian Provinces, May–July 1813.

Figure 39B. Joseph Fouché, who succeeded Junot in July 1813, portrait by Claude-Marie Dubufe, after an original by René Théodore Berthon (Palace of Versailles).

---

[180] Fremantle Papers, 39/14
[181] idem

Figure 40. Port St. George Harbour. Martello Towers are seen on the hills to the left and right of the harbour (Fisković Collection).

Figure 41. Port St George/Vis Harbour today showing the sites of the British fortifications.

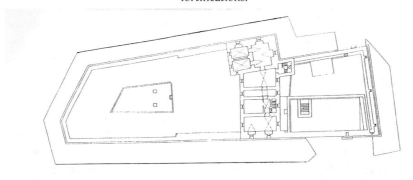

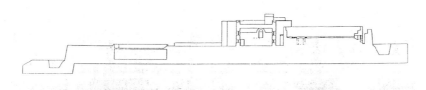

Figure 42. Plan and elevation of Fort George. Modern drawing based on originals. Changes were made in the Austrian period although projects that would have resulted in its complete replacement by a new and larger fortress were never realised.

Figure 43A. Fort George from the approach to the harbour, 2012 (author's photo).

Figure 43B. Fort George entrance, 2013 (author's photo).

gendarmerie de l'arrondissement, wrote a secret report, dated Spalato 15 March 1813, to Bouillerot, chef de Bataillon commandant d'armes et arrondissement de Spalato. On his last inspection of Lesina, he had discovered that most of the inhabitants went to Lissa two or three times a week, with the permission of the local authorities. The délégué of Lesina claimed he was authorised by the Governor-General to send people to Lissa to gather intelligence, under cover of their taking corn, and that the number of people to whom he issued permission was limited. Fremau was sceptical:

'In all these voyages, the laws of quarantine are not observed. One goes to Lissa, and after the sale of corn, comes back the next day or the day after that. There is a risk to the security and health of Lesina. I have given orders to the gendarmerie to redouble surveillance on those who go, with or without permission. But it is almost impossible to catch anyone'.[182]

The danger of plague persisted. As late as June 1815, Robertson, only a short time before the final withdrawal of the British from Lissa, was re-assuring the British authorities that Lissa was free of the plague. The Superintendent of Quarantine at Malta wrote on 28 June 1815:

'By a letter from Col. Robertson dated 12 June who commands in Island of Lissa, I am happy to state that no contagious disease existed on that island at that period, and from judicious precautions adopted early in May last for preventing the Introduction of Plague we have been induced to diminish the quarantine from that island from 40 to 15 days for men of war & 25 for merchant ships'.[183]

It seems that mainland Dalmatia was not so fortunate. Hoppner, the new British consul in recently-liberated Venice, reported to the Foreign Office on 3 June 1815 that there was plague at Macarsca and the Narenta and fear of it spreading along the whole coast of Dalmatia. As late as 16 December 1815, he reported that fresh symptoms of plague had reappeared in Dalmatia and that the whole of the coast had been placed in strict quarantine. By this time, the British had left Lissa and the other islands they had occupied.[184]

Life on Lissa

Having followed the story of the British involvement with Lissa from the military point of view and using official reports, it is now necessary to try to redress the balance by considering the more human side of how the British lived, how the lives of the inhabitants were affected, and how they related to each other.

Life on Lissa for the British, their conditions of life and how they reacted to them, and how they related to the local inhabitants, can be seen in the range of official and private records that have survived.

Lissa does not seem to have been particularly unhealthy. Colonel Robertson in his reports to Lord Bentinck repeatedly assured him that the troops were in good health, despite (but possibly because of) having no barracks and living in tents. Despite the scare in 1813 when it was feared that ships would bring the plague from Malta to Lissa, there seem to have been no deaths from it on Lissa.[185] One person who definitely left Lissa because of ill health was the spy-master Johnson, but his health had been undermined by difficult journeys by little-known routes over the highest of the Albanian mountains. Nor in the fighting were casualties high on either side, particularly towards the end when the Italian and Grenzer regiment soldiers left in isolated garrisons surrendered after little more than token resistance rather than die for

---

[182] Fremantle Papers, 39/14/1-13
[183] PEL 16, NMM, R. Grimes to Capt. Vincent of TRIDENT
[184] The plague reached Dalmatia from Bosnia. Wherever it had originated (almost certainly within the Ottoman Empire), the outbreak on Malta was serious and British concern was of it spreading from there.
[185] See Defence of Lissa above, p. *

a lost cause. On the side of the British navy, as was usual except in the relatively infrequent clashes between warships of the same size and armament such as the March 1811 battle of Lissa and the February 1812 fight between VICTORIOUS and RIVOLI, most deaths were the result of accident, usually from falls and drownings. Captain Taylor of the frigate APOLLO, one of Admiral Fremantle's favourite captains, who was involved in the capture of the islands of Augusta and Curzola, fell out of a ship's boat and was drowned off Brindisi.[186] A more sensational but tragic accident occurred in Port St George on Lissa when the unexplained discharge of a ship's gun blew to pieces young midshipman Charles Anson, grandson of a famous English admiral.[187]

Quite apart from the disputes between Admiral Fremantle and Colonel Robertson, Captain Hoste, and Johnson, the secret agent, the British officers differed greatly from each other in their education, interests and reactions to the situation in which they found themselves. Hoste was possibly one of the most dissatisfied and the letters later published by his widow interspersed with extracts from the journal of his friend and crony the ship's chaplain Yonge, who shared his prejudices and resentments, contain numerous negative references to Lissa and its inhabitants.[188] Fremantle was much more interested in the welfare of the local inhabitants, and his dispute with Hoste, however complicated by jealousy on either side, was essentially because Hoste was not sympathetic to the interests of the local merchants and smugglers

Figure 44. Port St George with the Franciscan Church on the other side of which Fremantle established his dockyard.

---

[186] Fremantle Papers, NMM, NRA 20664, Letter Book, no. 92, Fremantle-Pellew 5 Mar. 1814. It has been estimated that out of the total of 103,000 deaths in the British navy over a 10 year period, combat accounted for only 6.5%, the vast majority being caused by illness and accidents such as falls and drownings (Masson, Philippe: Histoire de la Marine, Paris 1981, Vol. 1, p. 419 referring to study by M. Lewis).

[187] Hoste Memoirs, pp.115-17

[188] See, for example Hoste Memoirs, 31 Aug. 1810 and p. 100, 19 Aug. 1812

Figure 45. The Franciscan church today.

Figure 46A. Admiral George Anson (1697–1762), who circumnavigated the globe and served as First Lord of the Admiralty during the Seven Years War. Midshipman Charles Anson was his grandson. Portrait in pastels by Francis Coates (Shugborough Hall).

Figure 46B. The Anson family seat of Shugborough Hall.

who with British encouragement and licences from Fremantle were risking their lives and livelihoods to take British goods to the mainland and bring provisions back.[189] (Rowley had also sympathised with the islanders in the danger they were running).[190] Hoste, always on the lookout for loopholes in the regulations to justify taking prizes (his private correspondence is full of letters to lawyers on the subject),[191] believed (very probably with some reason) that they were abusing the Admiral's trust.[192] In their worst dispute on the question, Fremantle insisted on compensating the local merchant himself when Hoste refused to give back the cargo he had siezed.[193] Fremantle, over and above his naval duties, shared with his friend Bentinck some political sensitivity, which Hoste seems to have singularly lacked.[194]

---

[189] Hoste Papers, MRF 88/3, NMM
[190] Lowe Papers, Add. Mss. 20110, f. 196, Rowley-Lowe
[191] Hoste Papers, MRF 88/4, NMM
[192] Hoste Memoirs, p. 133, 21 Feb. 1813. Hoste went over Fremantle's head and wrote directly to Admiral Pellew.
[193] Hoste Papers, MRF 88/3, NMM
[194] See, for example, Wynne Diaries, Dec. 1812

Figure 47. The tombstone of Midshipman Anson on Vis (author's photo).

However, in fairness to Hoste, he could be sympathetic to the local inhabitants. In the earlier period when he was in command of the British squadron in the Adriatic, he reported to the then commander of the Mediterranean fleet, Admiral Lord Collingwood, that he had supplied the inhabitants of Lissa, who were facing famine, with corn from a prize he had taken. Collingwood, in a letter dated 26 March 1809, approved of Hoste's action:

> 'I have received your letter of the 6th February informing me that in consequence of an urgent request from the Governor and inhabitats of the Isalnd of Lissa who were in great distress for want of Corn – you have disposed of the Cargo of a French brig laden with that article to the inhabitants. From the particular circumstances of this case, which you have represented, I approve of your having done so and do full justice to the sentiments which induced you to it...'[195]

Lissa had few social amenities to help fill the time between the performance of duties. It had nothing to compare with the rounds of parties and balls which officers could enjoy when they returned to Malta or Sicily, and which Fremantle was to find in Trieste after its recapture from the French in 1813.[196] Fremantle devoted some of his time on shore to building himself a house, organising a dockyard, but had enough surplus energy to spare to resent having to leave the local government and most official dealings with the local notables to Robertson, which explains the enthusiasm with which he took Curzola, after its capture in February 1813, under his personal protection. Some official entertainment of the local notables did take place, sometimes on board ship, and for which Fremantle organized a band, presumably made up of sailors. Fremantle's letters and diaries give some idea of the efforts made to make social exchanges with the local community on Lissa and particularly on Curzola.[197]

> '7 July 1812. The Canonica & Actamesa dined with me; occupied in the Dock Yard all this morning, the poor lord priests removing their effects.' (Fremantle rented church

[195] Hoste Papers, NMM, MRF 88/1-5
[196] Wynne Diaries, 16 Nov. 1813
[197] idem, for dates given

property for a dockyard on the headland next to the inner harbour of Port St George from the church).

'20 Sept. 1812. My band is now quite perfect, they not only are a military band, but play pieces of music with violins and violin cello, my horns are capital, and the trumpeter speaks music'.

'11 Feb. 1813. Had a gay ball on shore (on Curzola), some tolerably looking damsels there. My band with their Instruments, deserted to the enemy, the devil go with them'.

'12 Feb. 1813. 'A grand ball given by Taylor (Captain Taylor of APOLLO), one remarkably pretty Venetian woman of the party, amused myself very much'.

'15 Feb. 1813. Gave a ball to all the Inhabitants which went off well – it was on shore, danced two dances with Madm. Boschi, who dances well – dined on Apollo'.

'30 March 1813. Called on several Ladies with Mrs Lower (the wife of Captain Lowen, the army officer left in charge on Curzola), had coffee four times, pass my evening at the Boschi's where I stayed supper...'

It is uncertain whether such entertainments swayed loyalties, especially as both sides could play the same game. General Marmont as French governor of Dalmatia had wooed the upper and middle classes with rounds of parties and balls that had been popular. Certainly Doimi remembered how the arrival of MAGNIFICENT at Lissa earlier in March 1811 had caused a sensation because the captain had invited the dignitaries for a feast on board, followed by the performance on deck of a tragedy.[198] Such entertainments were certainly a good way to establish less formal relations with the local inhabitants and to relieve the feelings of boredom and isolation from which the British officers could suffer. Fremantle, who was clearly sensitive and volatile by nature, complained in his private letters and diary of boredom, the limitations of the all-male company of his fellow British officers, and the boorishness of many of his junior officers.[199]

'24 oct 1812. Dined with a small party. Was made angry by my brats all being drunk'.

'Dec. 1812. I never have felt myself more uncomfortable since I left England, as I have done all this month, first there is no society that is at all worth cultivating, and nothing to be done at sea, no communication with England, and little to amuse – I employ myself getting on with my house which is certainly the most comfortable in all the Island, but still that can only employ me a part of the day – There are no French troops in the neighbourhood, but it is not our policy to distress the poor Natives'.

Rowley was a well-educated man with wide interests. We have the packing list of his books,[200] and know from his private correspondence that his friend Hudson Lowe on Santa

---

[198] Foretic, op. cit. Doimi says it took place in March 1809, but MAGNIFICENT was at Lissa only at the end of March 1811.
[199] idem, dates as given
[200] ROW 4, NMM

Maura sometimes sent him books. The secret agent, the Irishman Johnson, although in his dealings with Fremantle a presumptuous and difficult man (Fremantle was greatly relieved when Johnson left Lissa), was a linguist and a bibliophile (the catalogue of his book collection survives in the British Museum).[201] He had protested vigorously when, after spending several years in Vienna, he was ordered to stay on Lissa.[202] Whatever the limitations of life on Lissa, it is conceivable that such men could always find things to interest them or to fight off boredom. Fremantle was determined to make the most of it, although even he was twice on the point of leaving before turns of events persuaded him it would be better to stay. Others, as Hoste wrote in a letter to his father in England, could only find solace in cricket.

> 'We have established a cricket-club at this wretched place, and when we do get anchored for a few hours, it passes away an hour very well. I have not been at Malta, nor seen anything but these almost savage islanders since I left it in the beginning of March'.[203]

Whether any of the British positively enjoyed being on Lissa is doubtful. It no doubt depended on what expectations there were of conditions of service, and how it compared with the unpopular, monotonous and less profitable (with regard to prize-money) posts in fleets blockading the French ports, or the unhealthiness of the West Indies.

There are numerous instances in the official and private correspondence and journals of Fremantle and even more particularly of Captain Charles Rowley to their always wanting to pay the fair price. Rowley went to almost exaggerated lengths to send money back to a landowner on one of the islands in enemy territory to compensate him for some cattle his men had seized and carried off.[204] He also felt himself to be honour bound to compensate Canon Doimi for any financial loss if he were not (as Rowley had promised him) able to rent some Crown land on Lissa after the British occupation.[205]

Rowley, as commodore of the Adriatic squadron in 1811, was highly critical of the extent to which some of his captains were over-zealous in the pursuit of prizes to the extent that it was complicating relations with the pashas in Albania and distracting them from their primary duties.[206] The prize system was essential in maintaining the morale of both officers and men, and both Fremantle and Rowley were implicated, as were all senior officers in the British navy, because they benefited handsomely from their share of the proceeds resulting from the captures made by their fellow or subordinate officers. But even by the standards of the time, some captains such as Hoste (or Hoste's earlier mentor in the Adriatic, Captain Patrick Campbell) could overstep the mark in their rapacity and disregard of both the legal and moral limits.

Many British naval officers resented the relative freedom enjoyed by the privateers to prey on merchant shipping, but both Fremantle and Rowley took strong action to check the abuses of the privateers, particularly their mistreatment of the local inhabitants.[207] In some cases the

---

[201] Bibliotechae Johnsoniana, 1817, BL
[202] FO 7/111 (Johnson) PRO, 7 Mar. 1812
[203] Hoste Memoirs, 31 Aug. 1810
[204] ROW 5, NMM, Dec. 1812
[205] ROW 5, NMM, 30 Sep. and 1 Oct. 1812
[206] Lowe Papers, Add. 20110, f. 151
[207] idem, f. 98. Portland Papers 2565/1, Fremantle-Bentinck. Portland Papers 4725 a and b, Robertson-Bentinck

British were prepared to send inhabitants of the smaller islands that had suffered the worst depradations to Malta to give evidence against the privateers.[208]

***

Developments as seen from the point of view of the local inhabitants were recorded by the priest, Canon Doimi, although his full original account has not been found and it has come down to us through the filters of later Dalmatian historians.

The life of the local inhabitants must have been severely disrupted. Before the regular occupation of the island by the British there was clearly, as recorded by Doimi, a degree of lawlessness caused by the absence of any strong authority and the comings and goings of the privateers, many little better than pirates. The British occupation of Lissa restored order and offered considerable protection.

Doimi clearly welcomed the British and enjoyed good relations with them. This should not be surprising, given that the French could be seen as godless revolutionaries who had humiliated the Pope and sent him into exile. Priests were frequently involved in conspiracies to stir up revolt to oust the French, for example the fathers Brunazzi and Dorotić, and it is clear from secret correspondence on the British side that the bishop of Agram (Zagreb) was sympathetic and willing to allow the network of priests to assist anti-French projects.[209] Both Bentinck in giving his orders to Colonel Robertson on how to govern Lissa, and Admiral Fremantle in the local constitution he agreed with the inhabitants of Curzola (Korčula), stressed freedom of religion and the reinstatement of the church in its traditional rights.[210] Relations with the church could produce unexpected complications. On the island of Augusta (Lastovo) the young British officer, ensign Hildebrand, who had been left in charge after its capture with a handful of soldiers, was called upon to adjudicate in a dispute between two parish priests. When news came through of Wellington's victory at Vittoria in Spain, he was persuaded against his reluctance to sit through a Te Deum, seated on the bishop's chair, on the grounds that the French and their local representatives had always expected Te Deums to be sung for their victories.[211] On Lissa, Colonel Robertson reported to Lord Bentinck on 14 May 1812, soon after the arrival of the British troops:

> 'The Head of the Church here has directed that sermons be preached next Sunday to instruct the inhabitants on their duties to the King of Great Britain'.[212]

Normal life for the long-term inhabitants of Lissa must have been disrupted not only by the arrival of the British but also by the influx of refugees and adventurers from the other islands or the mainland, attracted by the relative safety of Lissa and the economic opportunities it offered, either in the contraband trade, or in the paid service of the British.

---

[208] ROW 5, NMM, Apr. 1812
[209] Portland Papers 4227, Nugent-Bentinck. Fremantle Papers, 40/2/18/8. FO 7/111 (Johnson) PRO, 7 Mar. 1812. Maximilian Vrhovac, Bishop of Agram (Zagreb) 1787-1827
[210] Portland Papers, 3474. ADM 1/426, Fremantle-Admiralty, 13 Feb. 1813. When the Franciscans of Korčula appealed against the conversion by the British of their monastery (Badia) into a lazaretto, Fremantle decided in their favour.
[211] Hildebrand Memoirs, National Army Museum
[212] WO 1/311, p. 363

Figure 48. View of Hoste Island looking towards Lessina (Hvar) and the mainland beyond. By William Innes Pocock (National Maritime Museum).

It has been estimated that in two years the population grew from 4000 to 11,000.[213] Both for these newcomers and for the local inhabitants themselves, collaboration with the British offered rewards and brought dangers. (An outstanding example of the advantages and risks of collaboration with the British right through the period is that of the important Istrian merchant Adamić, who even though living in French-held Fiume, took extraordinary risks and was eventually arrested by the French authorities, but survived to be one of its richest men and, by appointment by Fremantle, British consul).[214]

Exploitation of the economic opportunities offered by collaboration with the British was clearly the most tempting. Some indication of the level of traffic involving Lissa is given in British reports. As early as 22 August 1811, well before the British military occupation made conditions more secure, Captain Maxwell, in a letter to Rowley, gives some idea of the level that the traffic had already reached:

> 'As a smuggling depot for the vent of Colonial produce, Lissa is invaluable. Maltese merchants are cautious but whatever coffee, sugar, pepper, bark etc as has come has been immediately sold. The number of arrivals and departures from and to the Enemy coast (notwithstanding rigorous provisions since Lissa was declared in state of blockade since the defeat of 13 March) and since I took over from Capt. Griffiths on 30 June, has been 417 arrivals and 523 departures.
>
> Importations: - grain, cattle, stock and wood
> Exportations: - wine, sugar, coffee, pepper, salt, vinegar and oil'.[215]

---

[213] Pisani, op. cit. p. 419
[214] On Adamić see, for example FO 7/111 (Johnson) PRO, 5 Oct 1813, and Fremantle Papers 38/4
[215] PEL 14, NMM

Fremantle was determined to maintain or increase the level of traffic by keeping Lissa a free port and was able to overrule the decision of the Robertson and the legislative council to introduce duties on goods to defray their costs.[216] In a letter to Admiral Pellew of 24 October 1812, he estimated that at any one time there were 80 sail of vessels in the harbour, nor including prizes or British ships.[217] Another document indicates that for the four-month period 24 October 1812 to 24 February 1813, a total of 1028 vessels left the port, while from 1 October 1812 to the end of January 1813 there were 1180 arrivals.[218] The French authorities on nearby Lessina admitted that they were unable to stop local ships visiting Lissa despite measures by their superiors to stop it. As Fremantle wrote July 1812:

> 'The French have issued a decree declaring death to any who supply Lissa with provisions. Lissa produces nothing but wine'.[219]

Although it was most probably Maltese merchants who brought British colonial produce to Lissa, it was the Dalmatians who then ensured that it reached the mainland. The merchants of Lissa itself were also involved in bringing in supplies from enemy-occupied Italy. Soon after the arrival of the British troops on Lissa, Colonel Robertson sent to Lord Bentinck notes and suggestions for trade he had received from a Stephen Scamparini, whom Robertson described as one of the principal merchants of the island.[220] Scamparini argued for freedom of imports and exports, except for naval and military stores for enemy countries. He described some of the subterfuges merchants used to avoid French restrictions:

> 'A vessel has to load in Puglia a cargo of provisions for Lissa – the master appears to load it for a French port and must give bonds to produce in a fixed time the certificate to have unloaded his cargo in the port he is bound. He therefore clears in the customs house only a small part of cargo and smuggles the rest to Lissa, sails on to the enemy port to get the certificate to cancel bonds and new clearance to come to Lissa and take a return cargo'.

While many were willing to run the risks of enriching themselves by engaging in this trade (no doubt frequently with the collusion of officials in the enemy ports), other forms of collaboration were more problematic. There must also have been local animosities and enmities that were served by the possibility of either French or British occupation, and collaboration with either might bring retribution if the situation changed again.[221]

While French edicts against supplying Lissa appear to have had little effect on the supply of provisions to Lissa, which was a profitable business, they may have influenced the local inhabitants in their lack of zeal in volunteering either for Colonel Robertson's militia on Lissa

---

[216] Portland Papers, 4725, 2565/1, 2559/1, 2555. Fremantle pointed out to Bentinck the unsatisfactory effects the duties and other limitations were having on the cost of wine and local fishermen. Fremantle complained rather too much to Bentinck about Robertson and the legislative council, given that it was Bentinck himself who had ordered Robertson to set it up (Portland Papers, 3474)
[217] PEL 16, NMM
[218] Fremantle Papers, 39/8
[219] Wynne Diaries, July 1812
[220] Portland Papers, 4723 dated 12 may 1812
[221] Lowe Papers, Add. 20110 f. 196, Rowley-Lowe. Portland Papers 2556-7. Fremantle Papers 40/2/1 include a copy of the warning of the officer commanding on Lessina (Hvar) to the inhabitants of Lissa against collaborating with the British.

or that provided for by Fremantle's convention with the inhabitants of Curzola (and it seems for the building of the tower above the town).[222] But it was perhaps soldiering which attracted them least, because in other respects the local inhabitants seem not to have been reluctant to collaborate, particularly after the British occupation of Lissa and events reduced the risk of a French return, and when it was clear that the British were prepared to protect not only the island against further French attack (and the penalties announced in French edicts) but also their economic interests. Captain Maxwell's protection of their wine and sardine exports was early evidence of this.[223] Even with these economic advantages, there must have been winners and losers, as the demand for goods and services undoubtedly led to rampant inflation and profiteering (witness the increase in the price of water).[224]

Many local inhabitants voluntarily served on the British warships, especially to avoid conscription or forced service imposed by the French,[225] and there is evidence that, even given the frequently harsh discipline and conditions for which service in the British navy at that time has become notorious (although conditions at sea may often have been preferable to those on land), they were treated with consideration. For example one captain who was taking his ship out of the Adriatic was ordered to ensure that he arranged for the return of the volunteers from Lissa who had served on gunboats and whom he was carrying to be sent back.[226]

Some of the local shipowners of Lissa took collaboration with the British to an unprecedented level. To enjoy the profits and status of privateers, and the legal protection to prevent them being treated as pirates if captured by the French, they needed letters of marque issued by the British Admiralty or one of its courts, the nearest being on Malta. However, they came to an arrangement with Admiral Fremantle that effectively attached them to the British navy by making their ships 'tenders' to his flagship MILFORD. Fremantle confirmed his agreement on 22 October 1812:

> 'Messrs Tagliafero, Tursovich, and Albanassi, merchants of Lissa having proposed to equip 4 or 6 small vessels to be armed for the protection of the trade of the island, I have no objection to them becoming tenders to Milford provided the persons who command will separately take their commissions from me and that they and their owners pledge themselves to be under my orders'.[227]

This arrangement was approved by Fremantle's superior, Admiral Pellew, who replied to an enquiry from the Admiralty (that did not approve) on 4 November 1813. He emphasised that the vessels had been fitted out by the merchants and that there was no expense to the British government, which was why he had sanctioned the arrangement. By this time, however,

[222] Fremantle Papers 38/6/31, Lowen-Fremantle. As no volunteers came forward for the agreed militia, the local authorities agreed to nominate recruits from each community.
[223] PEL 14, NMM, Maxwell-Rowley, 22 Aug. 1811
[224] PEL 16, NMM, Fremantle-Pellew 24 Oct. 1812. Water cost 1 Spanish dollar per ton. See also Pisani, op. cit. p. 419
[225] ROW 8, Leard, British consul in Durazzo, Albania to Wellesley, the Foreign Secretary, 9 Mar 1812. Leard claimed that many Dalmatian and Ragusan seamen, who were unwilling to serve in the French navy or dockyards, came to him and that he sent them on to Malta or the British-occupied Ionian Islands. Portland Papers, 4744, Robertson-Bentinck 29 Nov. 1812. 'Inhabitants from the Continent come here in numbers to avoid the French conscription'.
[226] ROW 5, NMM, 28 Apr 1812
[227] Fremantle Papers, 40/5/4. A list of prizes taken by the tenders dated 24 Feb. 1813 is given in 38/4/43

Figure 49. Port St George with the 74 gun ship-of-the-line HMS EAGLE, on which the artist, William Pocock served as Lieutenant. (National Maritime Museum).

Fremantle's squadron had moved away from Lissa to the upper Adriatic and the tenders had been discharged.[228]

The British made real efforts to involve the local inhabitants in the government of Lissa.

Although Fremantle was quite scathing about it, especially in his letters to Bentinck,[229] and although in general the British preferred the locals to govern themselves, Colonel Robertson seems positively to have enjoyed his role given to him by Bentinck as governor in charge of local administration and in working together with the local notables.[230] We have lists of the local men involved in the administration of the island and the honoraria they were paid.[231]

Whatever Fremantle thought of Colonel Robertson's efforts to introduce local self-government on Lissa, he was proud of his own efforts to do the same on Curzola after its capture in February 1813.

---

[228] ADM 1/428, No. 49. The tenders had been in action at least once. On 20 May 1813 Fremantle reported to Pellew that three of the tenders under a Capt. Colli had captured a fort at the Bocca Falsa, where they destroyed the battery, brought away all the ammunition, 45 prisoners and 5 small vessels. ADM 1/427, no. 427. Fremantle Papers also include a list of the prizes they captured (38/4/43)
[229] For example Portland Papers 2555, 2559/1
[230] On the local government see Pisani, op. cit. p. 418
[231] Fremantle Papers 40/2/11-12

'I hope all I have been doing at Curzola may be useful to our cause... The Constitution I have formed for Curzola seems to answer all the purposes and I am much pleased by the reception I always get from the inhabitants'.[232]

The repeated reports by the British commanders that the locals welcomed British occupation were perhaps exaggerated or wishful thinking. Henryson, the Royal Engineers officer wrote to Fremantle on 9 February 1813, immediately after the British capture of Curzola, enclosing a list of names and notes in Italian on the sympathies of the principal inhabitants, which had been supplied by the local priest (Canonico):

'Conte Jacomo Spanick – an agreeable man (uomo di garbo) but indifferent on account of the French or the British.
Sig. Teodoro Andrick – one who has suffered from the persecution of the Fench for saying that they were being worsted by the Russians
Sigr. Tamucle (or Samucle?) – most indifferent
Sigr Longo – French to the bones – took arms against us in this last affair'.[233]

However, it is clear that many of the local inhabitants preferred the British to the French and that some of the British were liked and respected by the local people. Captain Lowen is commemorated by an inscription at the town of Korčula (despite his best efforts on their behalf the inhabitants seem not to have taken to Fremantle).[234] On Lissa some of the names of the British officers given by the British to the forts and hills (some with a lack of modesty, given that the persons concerned were still present on the island) remained for some time after their departure. Curiously, it is the senior officers who were most concerned for the welfare of the local people, Fremantle and Rowley, who have disappeared from the local history books, while it is Hoste, who seems to have had the least sympathy with them, who remains.

***

At another level, one can be certain that the presence of a large number of soldiers and seamen meant a higher level of crime, violence, drunkenness (a particular failing of the British at that time and since), and prostitution.[235] There were over 600 troops in British pay on the island, and at any one time a considerable number of sailors with shore leave when their ships were in harbour (MILFORD 74 and EAGLE 74 had crews of 650-700 men, the frigates about 300 men, and sloops and brigs about 200), together with the seamen from the privateers and merchant ships. There are references in official correspondence to some troops behaving badly, the most unruly being the Corsicans, large numbers of whom deserted.[236] Murder was possibly much rarer than one might suppose, given that the way that the one case found in the official records was recorded suggests it was exceptional.[237] But while many soldiers and

---

[232] Wynne Diaries, 30 March 1813
[233] Fremantle Papers, 38/6/32
[234] For Fremantle' personal interest in Curzola (Korčula) see Wynne Diaries, 30 Mar. 1813
[235] Pocock: Remember Nelson, p. 184, states that there were 14 taverna and 6 billiard rooms along the half mile of waterfront to cater for some of the needs of the sailors and soldiers.
[236] Portland Papers 4725 a and b, 4744, Robertson reports to Bentinck. Fremantle Papers 38/6/22 Robertson – Fremantle on a Lt. Rigo who deserted to French after robbing a house on Lissa.
[237] ROW 6, NMM, Rowley-Laughorne 21 Feb. and 25 Apr. 1812 re marine sent to Malta for trial for murder

seamen were most certainly brutal, there is evidence of others who were decent and honest and in no way brutalised by the service. One example is that of young Robert Wilson, able seaman on UNITÉ and in the Adriatic from 1806-8. From his journal, we know that Lissa was where several sailors deserted.[238] While at Comisa (Komiža) in early 1808, he had gone for a walk on his own and climbed the hill to watch out for UNITÉ's return. On this early occasion, long before the islanders had become used to British comings and goings, when he tried to ask for water, the local people were afraid of him and closed their doors and windows. When he finally forced his way into a house and had been given water, and after his offer of payment had been declined, he gave his coin to a child.[239]

Another interesting example is that of Captain W. F. J. Matthews, a young officer of marines on Rowley's EAGLE, whose little black notebook, containing in tiny handwriting his diary in note form and detailed accounts, has survived.[240] He records that he was given a hen canary by a child at the home of Canon Doimi and in return presented the child with his silver snuff box (his accounts show the purchase of another snuff box a few days later). Whenever EAGLE returned to Lissa after being away for lengthy tours of duty, his accounts show payment of a waterman to take him to shore and then an asterisk and payment of one Spanish dollar (which he converted at a rate of exchange of 5 shillings 2 pence) for an unspecified service that can easily be guessed at. Other entries which indicate his generosity (especially after distribution of prize money) and give some idea of relative prices and values include:

(1811)

25 Oct.	pd for hire of a mule from Comisa to George town one Spanish dollar		5s 2d
5 Nov.	gave a lad who returned me my purse 2 x 15 soldi pieces		5d

(1812)

19 Mar.	pd for eggs half a dollar		
April	Gave a poor clergyman at Melada whose house was plundered by privateers	2 dollars	10s 4d
23 April	Gave a little boy at Padre Antonio's house	1 dollar	5s 2d
26 April	pd dinner ashore for a few friends	10 dollars	£2 11s 0d
	gave some privateers wine to drink on shore	1 dollar	5s 2d
27 July	pd bottle wine, lemonade, charity & waterage		3s 11d
30 Sept.	gave some grape pickers 7 1/2		
	paid waterage 7 1/2		1s 3d
7 Oct.	4 pieces silk for pantaloons	21 dollars	£5 0s 6d

There is other evidence of individual British befriending the local people. Ensign Hildebrand of the 35th Regiment of Foot, as an old man wrote down his memoirs, possibly for the

---

[238] In Thursfield, H. G. (ed.): Five Naval Journals
[239] idem, entry for 1 July 1808
[240] Journal of Capt. W. F. J. Matthews, NMM

Figure 50. Royal Marines private, 1815, aquatint by J.C. Stadler.

amusement of his grandchildren.[241] Many of his stories must be taken with a pinch of salt, some are contradicted by the facts recorded elsewhere, but they definitely relate to his experiences on Lissa, on Augusta after its capture, and in the last days of French rule in Ragusa when the inhabitants tried to anticipate the arrival of the Austrians by revolting against the French and restoring their earlier republic. Hildebrand claimed to have befriended and fought alongside the Ragusans, and there are letters of his to Jero Natali, a member of the old Ragusan aristocracy, whom the British appointed to be briefly governor of the Ragusa islands, which would seem to substantiate his claim.[242] Even Hoste, otherwise so indifferent in his letters, had a grudging respect for the Vladika of Montenegro, whom he met at the Bocca di Cattaro in 1813, and had pleasant memories of a Fiume family (possibly Flemish) who helped to nurse him back to health in 1809 and to members of which he waved as he sailed down the coast some time later.[243]

There were inevitably barriers of culture and language. Most officers, here as almost everywhere else in Europe at that time, could communicate with each other in French

[241] Hildebrand Memoirs, National Army Museum
[242] Hoste Papers, MRF 100, NMM, Hildebrand-Natali
[243] Hoste Memoirs, July 1813

(Fremantle also had good Italian with which to communicate with the Dalmatians). In a way which would be unthinkable in later wars, it was possible for British officers to send personal letters to old friends serving on the French side,[244] and there were regular official contacts, even in time of war, to negotiate the exchange of prisoners or their release on parole (neither side liked the trouble or expense of guarding and feeding large numbers of prisoners of war).[245] The conduct of war still preserved some of the chivalry that the ruthless professionalism of Napoleon's pursuit of war was rapidly undermining. This concept of what was honourable or gentlemanly must also have ameliorated the conditions of the local inhabitants. When the British fleet attacked Fiume in early 1813 the French tried to make much of alleged atrocities (Fremantle kept a collection of the various French reports in his personal archives),[246] but it is clear that, while the British did their best to disable the batteries and to burn, destroy or carry away the goods they found in the warehouses, they inflicted little hurt on the inhabitants either through bombardment or in the course of their landings.

The lingua franca used by both officers and men in almost all of their communications with the local population was Italian, or at least the vulgar, often largely ungrammatical Italian used by the Slav populatians of the islands and by the Maltese and even Greek seamen. A good example is in the communications of Lancelot Cooper, the British consul in Ragusa in 1813-15. Appointed because he was an ex-sailor who could collect and report intelligence on shipping, he was at a loss to understand the last minute diplomatic manoeuvring before the Austrians smothered the last embers of Ragusan republicanism. His poor ungrammatical Italian has caused perplexity or derision among Dalmatian historians.[247] How other British sailors coped with the language, especially those who jumped ship and deserted and then had to evade detection and arrest by the French, is unrecorded. However, seamen everywhere, and especially in this period, were such a mixed bunch, that the occasional Englishman with little knowledge of the language was probably unexceptional. By the same token, although the officers in the British navy were predominantly British (and less mixed than in the continental navies), the crews of British warships had such a high percentage of non-British sailors that racial or national discrimination was probably minimal. It would have been relatively easy for a Dalmatian sailor, fleeing compulsory service in the French services, to have found his place in the crew of a British warship.

The other important function of Lissa was to provide a place from which to organise communications between Austria and Lord Bentinck in Sicily. This fell largely to the spy-master Johnson, although he needed the agreement of Fremantle in making available the warships or special passes for other ships to go to the mainland to meet the many Austrian officers (the most important being General Nugent) and other agents. Because the French held Trieste, the route they took was from Brod on the Sava frontier of Austria with the Ottoman Empire down via Bosna Serai (Sarajevo) to Scutari (Skadar) and then to the coast at the mouth of the Buna or Bojna river in the Bay of Drin or Ludrin. Johnson's functions were meant to be secret, but the fact that strangers were constantly coming and going and that he disbursed large sums of money did not escape notice. Doimi wrote in his memoirs about 'Lord Jonson' the authority or commisary for 'business' in the Adriatic, who lived incognito on Lissa

---

[244] ROW 5, NMM, 14 May 1813
[245] See for example ROW 5, NMM, 25 July 1812 and 15 Jan. 1813
[246] Fremantle Papers 39/14
[247] For example Pisani, op. cit., p. 475

Figure 51A. Graf Laval Nugent in 1837, watercolour by Moritz Michael Daffinger.

Figure 51B. Francis Archduke of Austria-Este (1779–1846) visited Lissa in September 1813. Portrait by Adeodato Malatesta (Palazzo Ducale, Modena).

with his team, with a war-chest administered by a treasurer called Pemberton and his two assistants.[248]

Among all the arrivals and departures in 1813 as the British stepped up their attacks on the mainland, Lissa saw some distinguished visitors. The Austrian Archduke Francis and his wife, a princess of the royal house of Sardinia, were brought to Lissa from Sardinia to await the opportunity for a joint Austrian and British invasion of French-held north Italy. Rowley brought Archduke Francis to Lissa on EAGLE on 23 September 1813. The royal couple stayed on Lissa until Rowley returned to take them to Fiume on 11 October.[249] There is no indication of where they stayed. Although one warship was left to protect the island, most of the rest of the squadron was away to the north, involved in the liberation of Istria and the siege of Trieste. Archduke Francis was to become the unpopular ruler of Modena after the peace settlements of 1814-15.

Lissa almost also saw Queen Maria Carolina of Naples, a daughter of the Empress Maria Theresia of Austria and sister of the executed Marie Antoinette, Queen of France. An intriguer and no friend of the British or Lord Bentinck, she was finally forced to decide to return to Vienna. On 28 July 1813 she was at the Ionian island of Zante and expected to sail from there to Lissa.[250] She decided, however, to take the long overland route over the Turkish Balkans, arriving at Vienna only in February 1814.

---

[248] Foretic, op. cit., p. 706
[249] ROW 5, NMM, 25 Sept. 1813
[250] ADM 12/161 and ADM 1/427, no. 264, Admiral Pellew to Admiralty, 6 Sept. 1813

Figure 52. Grenzer Uniforms. By late 1813, Italian and Grenzer
troops made up the majority of Napoleon's forces in Illyria.

Whatever effects the presence of the British may have had on the life of Lissa, their withdrawal in 1813-14 must have even more drastic. With the recapture and reopening of Trieste and Fiume in 1813, the merchantmen deserted Lissa and its economic importance collapsed. Even before peace was made, most of the British soldiers and warships had left Lissa. But the strategic importance of Lissa was not lost on its new Austrian owners who continued to man its defences. Nevertheless, whether it had been a comfortable experience or not, Lissa would never relive its experiences or again achieve the importance it enjoyed in 1809-13.

***

The British leave Lissa

There was a last flurry of activity at Lissa in the second half of 1813. Austria entered the war against France on 12 August. General Laval Nugent, funded by the British to raise two regiments of Croatian soldiers, crossed the Sava to drive the French from the Illyrian Provinces. Most of the British squadron left Lissa under Admiral Fremantle to help him attack Fiume and the towns around the coast of Istria to Trieste, which surrendered after a siege on 30 October. After this Fremantle made Trieste his base and was not to return to Lissa before giving up his command and returning to England in March 1814. In the meantime other warships of his squadron were involved in forcing the surrender of Napoleon's garrisons (by now almost all Italian or Grenzer 'Croatian') in the Bocca, Ragusa, Lesina, Spalato, and Zara, and in ferrying the Grenzer soldiers, who now returned into Austrian service, first to Lissa and then on to join the other Austrian forces in Istria, and after the fall of Trieste, in the invasion of northern Italy. Almost all of the British garrison of Lissa left as well. Robertson and the 35th Foot with most of the Calabrians and Corsicans left Lissa on 10 October for Trieste, after which they fought ther way across northern Italy with the Austrians and joined up with other British forces at Genoa, which was attacked and captured in early 1814 by Bentinck with forces from Sicily. Venice finally fell to the Austrians in April 1814, and by the end of that month all of Napoleon's kingdom of Italy was in their hands. Joachim Murat, King of Naples, betrayed Napoleon and joined the allies and his army besieged and captured the port and citadel of Ancona. In the meantime, Paris fell to the allied armies on 30 March and Napoleon abdicated on 6 April and 11 April 1814.

Throughout most of this, Lissa, with a much-depleted garrison and reduced stores, was left under the command of Captain Barbier of the Swiss Roll's regiment. Fremantle was anxious to move as many troops and as much material as possible to Trieste. When he heard that the the Grenzer garrison on Lesina had mutinied against their officers and surrendered the town of Lesina and Fort Napoleon on 14 November 1813, he wrote on 7 December to Barbier:

> 'The surrender of Lessina makes Lissa secure. Embark the number of men specified on the enclosed list written by Major Slessor on Elizabeth that they may be employed by Robertson at the mouth of the Po'.[251]

On that same day 7 Dec. 1813 he ordered Captain Gower of ELISABETH 74 to go to Lissa and bring back the stores and provisions that remained. He was to put the dockyard at Port St George in the charge of the officer commanding the remaing troops there. He repeated these orders on 2 Jan. 1814 to Lt. Willison of his flagship MILFORD 74. Willison was to take the transport ship ALEXANDER to Lissa and take on board all the remaining provisions, leaving the Arsenal in the charge of the officer commanding King's troops.[252]

It was, however, to be some time before the British were to finally leave Lissa and the process was almost as protracted and uncertain as that which had attended their occupation of the island. The Austrians, having occupied mainland Dalmatia, were anxious to take over Lissa and the other islands held by the British. Colonel Danese, the Dalmatian officer who had been helping the British as a secret agent, was now again in the Austrian army, promoted to Major-General, and he was ordered by Lt. Gen. Tomassich, the new Governor of Dalmatia in command at Zara, to try to persuade the British to leave. He wrote from Macarsca on 22 January 1814 to Captain Barbier on Lissa:

> 'The General in Chief of Dalmatia the Baron Tomassich desires me to send an Austrian garrison to Lissa passing intelligence with you to receive that island as belonging to Dalmatia – I therefore send an Officer expressly, to know and to concert the measures, that according to his instructions, you will think proper to participate to me, having given directions. The garrison at Lessina should be transferred to Lissa and the officer I have sent who commands it will receive stores and sign the inventory for reciprocal caution of the items given up. The bearer is Capt. Zupan of the 6th Conale Company'.[253]

Barbier declined to hand over the island, on the simple grounds that he had no orders or instructions. But some time after this, Lt. Gen. Milutinovich, commanding in Ragusa, sent his aide-de-camp to request Barbier to inform him what islands belonging before to Dalmatia and Ragusa were still occupied by the English. Barbier told him that while Lissa, Curzola and

---

[251] Fremantle letter book, NRA 20664, NMM
[252] idem
[253] Aberdeen Papers, Add. 43077, BM

Figure 53A. Baron Franjo Tomassich (1761–1831), Governor of Dalmatia from 1814.

Figure 53B. Sir John Gore (1772–1836) (Unknown artist, National Maritime Museum).

Augusta had been taken by the British navy and army, the islands of Mezzo, Giupanna etc. (those near Ragusa, formerly belonging to the republic of Ragusa) had been taken by the navy only. In Barbier's opinion, 'the Colours should remain as they are at present until the decision of the courts'. But Barbier was worried. He wrote on 16 March 1814 to Admiral Gore, who had taken over command of the British squadron now based at Trieste, enclosing Danese's letter and reporting all these developments, and asking for advice and instructions. There is a suggestion that he thought the Austrians might try to cut off Lissa's supplies, using the health risk as an excuse:

> 'I take every measure to prevent Lissa being separated from Dalmatia, Spalato being principally necessary for supplies for the Islands garrison by the English, but the Health Offices there are very punctilious and perhaps I shall not succeed in my wishes...A public building was occupied here, for an Arsenal, which is at present empty. I shall take the liberty to request you will have the goodness to let me know if it can be disposed of or still to continue for Public use'.[254]

Gore at Trieste replied to Barbier on 23 March. A similar approach had been made by the Austrians to him. He had told them that the islands could not be surrendered without a formal act and instructions from their respective governments. Gore had sent letters asking for full instructions both to the British Government in London and the British ambassador to Austria. As far as the arsenal on Lissa was concerned, 'it should remain as it is, for we cannot

---

[254] idem

at the moment judge of the necessity which may require its re-occupation, but as I am totally unacquainted with the localities at Lissa, you must be better able to decide for yourself'.[255]

The approach to which Admiral Gore referred was a letter in German, addressed to his predecessor, Fremantle, from General Baron Franjo Tomassich in Zara dated 4 March 1814. By way of a farewell present, and perhaps as an added hint that it was time for the British to leave, the Austrians were showering orders and decorations on the British officers. Together with his congratulations and a further clutch of medals, Tomassich wrote (as crudely translated for Gore):

> 'General Baron Tommassich ...begs further You may let him know if You did not find it necessar to keep an English garrison at Lissa Augusta and Curzola, in order to be in time to send an Austrian garrison to take possession of it, and expects Your Kind answer'.[256]

Gore replied to Tomassich on 21 March to say that it was not in his power to give him a reply but that he had transmitted the general's letter to His Majesty's Government in London. He therefore requested that the islands be allowed to continue as they were until its decision had been received. Gore wrote that same day to the Admiralty in London asking for instructions:

> 'Having received the enclosed letter from His Excellency General Baron Tomassich, Governor of Dalmatia, requesting an Austrian Garrison may be allowed to take possession of the islands of Lissa, Augusta and Curzola, I request You will be pleased to lay the same with my reply thereto, before their Lordships.
>
> I have received no Official documents from Rear Admiral Fremantle on his departure respecting any of these Islands, he having merely stated that Curzola and Augusta were subject to the British Government, and as Lissa was captured by His Majesty's Arms previous to our Alliance with Austria, I am anxious to receive their Lordships instructions for my further guidance on this subject'.[257]

Not everybody wanted the Austrians to return. The British (in the person of Captain Hoste) had allowed the Montenegrins to occupy the Bocca di Cattaro, before the arrival of the Austrian army that was advancing down the coast of Dalmatia, and they had also raised the hopes of the Ragusans by helping a last minute insurrection against the French. When the British navy took over the Ragusan islands (Giupanna, Mezzo, and Calamotta), they had appointed a Ragusan noble, Count Girolamo di Natali, as governor. Fremantle had taken Curzola under his personal protection. None of these were happy to be handed over to the Austrians. Nor were the Austrians happy to be left with these problems to resolve.

The day after he had written to the Admiralty, Gore decided to write direct to Lord Aberdeen, the British ambassador to the Emperor of Austria,[258] who was then in France, accompanying

---

[255] idem
[256] The original letter in German and translation are in ADM 1/428, no. 140, PRO
[257] idem. Gore's letter was endorsed as received 17 May and copied that day to the Secretary of State for Foreign Affairs (Lord Castlereagh).
[258] George Hamilton 1784-1860, Earl Aberdeen, was sent on a special mission to Austria on 11 August 1813 (the day before Austria declared war on France), appointed ambassador to Austria on 28 September and accompanied Emperor

Figure 54. Lord Aberdeen (1784–1860), British
ambassador to the Emperor of Austria in 1814.
Portrait by Thomas Lawrence.

the advance of the allies. This letter was less restrained and formal than Gore's letter to the Admiralty. He explained that Tomassich had asked him to hand over Lissa, Augusta and Curzola, but that Lissa had been taken from the French by force of arms while Britain had been at war with Austria. As far as Augusta and Curzola were concerned, Gore had been told in conversation with his predecessor that he (Fremantle) had guaranteed the independence of those islands in the name and on behalf of HBM (His Britannic Majesty) on condition that they should keep up a certain force at their own expense for the defence of the island, which they had done, as well as building towers and batteries and fitting gunboats etc.

> 'As I have no sort of official document to guide my judgement, and as in conversation with Lt. Gen. Count L'Espine, Gov. of this place (Trieste), I can perceive that the Austrian Government entertain a lively jealousy on this subject, I am most anxious to avoid giving cause for that jealousy, or to occasion any misunderstanding'.[259]

On 23 March 1814 Gore wrote another letter to Aberdeen to say that, after closing his letter of 22 March, he had received one from Captain Barbier, which he enclosed to show the urgency with which the Austrian government was pressing for the cession of the islands.[260]

Aberdeen replied to Gore on 8 April 1814 from Dijon in France. He acknowledged Gore's letters of 22 and 23 March with their enclosures and declared himself happy to give instructions. All those possessions of the Venetian State taken by the British since the treaty that Aberdeen

---

Francis throughout the advance into France.
[259] Aberdeen Papers, Gore-Aberdeen, dated Trieste 22 March 1814, Add. 43077, f. 266, BM
[260] idem

had signed with the Austrians on 3 Oct 1813[261] should be restored to the Austrian Emperor. Those conquests of ex-Venetian possessions made previously to Britain's alliance with Austria were not to be surrendered by one officer to another but were to be left for arrangements to be made by the governments.[262]

> 'It is wished however that you should give the assurance of this arrangement being completed in the most speedy manner, and most calculated to give satisfaction to His Imperial Majesty.

> You will of course understand that the restitution of the Ex-Venetian territories to the house of Austria does not extend to those which formed the Septinsular Republic (the Ionian Islands) but to such only as were in the possession of Austria before the war of 1805'.

Aberdeen's answer was not as helpful as it might seem. All of the Dalmatian islands held by the British had been taken before 3 Oct.1813. The Ragusan islands had not been Venetian possessions (although Ragusa and its territories had been held by Austria before the war of 1805), and all of the earlier possessions of the Venetian state taken after that date were in mainland Dalmatia and had already been re-occupied by the Austrian forces.

But Aberdeen's letter did indicate what was the real bone of contention. It was the Ionian Islands, controlling the entrance to the Adriatic and the crossing from Italy to Greece. While with the re-occupation by the allies of Trieste, Venice, Ancona and other Adriatic ports, Lissa had become much less important, it was still a pawn in the negotiations concerning the Ionian Islands.

News of the fall of Paris and of Napoleon's abdication had still not reached Trieste by 26 April, when Gore wrote to the Admiralty to report that Venice had surrendered to the Austrians. He was proceeding against Corfu (which was still held by the French), after which he would return to Trieste 'to await their Lordships instructions respecting the further destination of the Squadron, as well as the Islands subject to the protection of the British Government in the Adriatic'.[263]

Gore was at Corfu on 11 May 1814, when he wrote to the Admiralty that it was expected that Corfu would soon surrender (without the need for an attack). He added as a postscript that news had only just been received of the cessation of hostilities (one month after Napoleon's abdication).[264] Gore returned to Trieste, where he found Aberdeen's letter of 8 April waiting for him and wrote on 24 May to Captain Barbier or whoever was now commandant on Lissa:

> 'Having referred to the Earl of Aberdeen your letter respecting the islands in the Adriatic, which have been taken under the protection of Great Britain, I now enclose the copy of His Lordship's reply for your further information and guidance on the subject. You will observe that the Islands are not to be surrendered by one Officer to

---

[261] The preliminary treaty of alliance between Britain and Austria signed at Toplitz.
[262] Aberdeen Papers, Add. 43077, f. 281, BM, and ADM/1/428, no. 160, PRO
[263] ADM 1/428, no. 160
[264] ADM 1/429, no. 213

Figure 55A. François-Xavier Donzelot (1762–1843), commander of the French forces in Corfu. Portrait by Charles Mullié.

Figure 55B. Lord Castlereagh (1769–1822). Portrait by Thomas Lawrence (National Portrait Gallery).

> another and they must therefore continue under the protection of Great Britain until the final arrangements of His Majesty's Government respecting them, shall be made known'.[265]

But there were further complications. General Donzelot, commanding the French forces on Corfu, refused to hand over the island to the British, on the grounds that he had not surrendered before news had arrived of cessation of hostilities and must await instructions from whatever authorities in France to whom he was now responsible. On 2 June 1814 Admiral Gore received instructions from Lord Castlereagh, the Foreign Secretary himself, to go back to Corfu to give instructions and assistance to General Campbell to force the surrender of Corfu. Gore took the opportunity to write back direct to Castlereagh to point out that he had still not received final instructions respecting the evacuation of the Adriatic islands[266] (although it is clear from the date of his letter to Barbier that he had received Aberdeen's letter only a few days before). Gore now took it upon himself (having discussed it with Campbell when he was at Corfu in early May) to send one of the ships of his squadron to Lissa to ask Colonel Robertson, who had by now returned there from Italy, to send 100 men of the 35th Foot to reinforce Campbell. Interpreting the spirit rather than the letter of Lord Aberdeen's communication, Gore sent a copy to Robertson, adding:

---

[265] ADM 1/429, no. 215. Weil, Maurice H: Le Prince Eugène et Murat 1813-14, 1902, p. 595 says that Sir John Gore received orders on 8 June 1814 to give Austria all the islands occupied since 3 Oct. 1813, but this seems to be a mistake.
[266] Gore on REVENGE, Trieste 2 June 1814 to Viscount Castlereagh, FO 42/15, PRO

'... you will perceive that the Islands are soon to be ceded to the Austrian Government. Under <u>existing circumstances</u> I strongly recommend to you to withdraw the troops from the island of Curzola and l'Augusta and keep only such a force at Lissa as may be barely sufficient to guard the Stores on that Island and send all the others to General Campbell. This will not only very materially assist present exigence but also facilitate the ultimate evacuation of Lissa. Captain Campbell (of TREMENDOUS) has my directions to receive on board such troops as you may please to send to Corfu, whither I am proceeding with my squadron and I earnestly recommend as much dispatch as possible'.[267]

Gore was mistaken in his interpretation of the situation. In a letter to the Admiralty of 18 June 1814 he explained the situation that had arisen and his decision to ask Robertson for help but added:

'I have subsequently been directed by the Commander in Chief (presumably Admiral Pellew) not to withdraw the Garrison of Lissa Augusta & Curzola without Instructions from England or Lord William Bentinck for that purpose, and recommending a Sloop of War to attend to be stationed off these Islands; I will therefore communicate the same for the further guidance of Colonel Robertson, and as soon as any Sloop joins me, I will appropriate her to that Service until Instructions are received from His Majesty's Government respecting the future disposal of the said Islands'.[268]

With no apparent threat from the French, it is possible that the garrison and the sloop were intended to prevent the Austrians from taking over Lissa before agreement had been reached. As Gore reported to the Admiralty on 30 June 1814, General Donzelot at Corfu had been persuaded to cede this last French fortress in the Adriatic to the British.[269] Gore himself was recalled to England, where he arrived on 17 August.[270]

The question of whether and when the British would evacuate the Adriatic islands they had occupied was to drag on for another year. It has been suggested that in June 1814 the Austrians tried to use Archduke Francis d'Este, who like Danese had enjoyed close relations with the British in 1813, to secure the Adriatic islands for them. On 28 June it was believed that agreement had been reached and that the English were prepared to leave. The Austrians were again preparing to take over when orders came from Vienna to suspend preparations for the takeover.[271]The allied powers were sending their representatives to the Congress of Vienna that convened in September 1814 and was to last until 9 June 1815. There were many problems to be resolved and much hard bargaining. The future of the Ionian Islands, with which that of Lissa had become linked, became a particularly difficult problem to resolve, given the interest of Russia which had been guarantor and protector of the earlier Septinsular Republic of the Ionian Islands before surrendering it to France at Tilsit in 1807, and the fact that Count Capo d'Istria, the Tsar's foreign minister, was a Greek native of the islands.

---

[267] ADM 1/429, no. 238, PRO marked received 15 July.
[268] idem
[269] ADM 1/429, no. 268, PRO
[270] ADM 1/429, no. 270, PRO
[271] Pisani, op. cit. p. 475. Nothing has been found in British records to substantiate this.

The proceedings of the Congress were rudely interrupted when, on 1 March 1815, Napoleon returned to France. Joachim Murat, King of Naples, who had betrayed Napoleon in 1814, now declared for Napoleon, causing Austria to declare war on him on 12 April and to invade his territories. Murat had been defeated by 20 May and fled to France. British warships again entered the Adriatic, this time to bottle up the Neapolitan frigates in Brindisi. The Neapolitan captains had no stomach for a fight and quickly abandoned Murat, declaring allegiance to the Bourbon King Ferdinand, whom the allies now restored to the throne of Naples. There is one last mention of Lissa being used by the British navy. Captain Heywood of MONTAGU off Brindisi wrote to Admiral Pellew on 12 June 1815:[272]

> 'Met UNDAUNTED off Tremiti Islands which had just surrendered to it. Left UNDAUNTED there with orders to collect his people and settle his prize concerns at Lissa and then join me off Brindisi'.

Castlereagh had proposed that the Ionian Islands might be given to Ferdinand of Sicily to compensate him for the loss of the kingdom of Naples, which the allies had allowed Murat to keep. The fall of Murat changed the situation and pointed to the danger of the same power controlling both sides of the entrance to the Adriatic and made such a solution unacceptable to Austria. It was no longer possible, with Ferdinand restored to Naples, to allow him to have the Ionian Islands. Alternatives were to restore the Septinsular Republic or to give them to Austria (favoured by Britain but opposed by Russia). The problem had not been resolved before the Congress of Vienna closed on 9 June 1815. The solution, only finally agreed in the Second Peace of Paris of 20 November 1815, was to leave the Ionian Islands as a British protectorate and occupied by the British (they were not to be handed over to the kingdom of Greece until 1863).[273]

In the meantime and at the local level, the situation concerning Lissa and the other islands held by the British declined almost to farce. The British consul in Ragusa, Lancelot Cooper, was a sailor, useful for collecting intelligence about enemy ships, but with no diplomatic training and little knowledge of languages. His communications of June 1815 in Italian to the Austrian commander in Ragusa, General Todor Milutinovich, and to Count Natali, the Ragusan nobleman appointed governor of the Ragusan islands held by the British, have bewildered at least one historian of Dalmatia, and are still, even with benefit of hindsight, difficult to decipher.[274] In his first letter of 13 June to Milutinovich, and possibly in an identical letter of 14 June to Natali, he wrote that in his opinion it was not possible to hand over the Ragusan islands without orders from General Campbell on Corfu or Lord Clancarty[275] and Lord Stewart at Vienna. A letter from Cooper of 16 June informed Natali that Milutinovich would leave the next day with an Austrian goletta (a type of ship) for Lissa. A letter from Cooper of 19 June appears to be another to General Milutinovich (but is possibly to Natali) saying that he will soon have to return from Lissa without being able to take it. A further letter from Cooper to Natali of 24 June tells him that General Milutinovic returns 'quanto prima da Lissa'. It is only

---

[272] PEL 16, NMM

[273] C. K. Webster: The Congress of Vienna 1814-15, 1963

[274] Pisani, op. cit., p. 475 quotes Cooper's letters of 13 June and 19 June as being addressed to Milutinovich; Cooper's letters to Natali, which appear to be copies from originals in the Dubrovnik archives, are in the Hoste Papers, MRF 100, NMM.

[275] He evidently meant Lord Cathcart, the British ambassador to Russia, who had assisted Lord Aberdeen at the Congress of Châtillon in Feb-March 1814 and would have been at the Congress of Vienna.

Figure 56. Henry Bathurst (1762–1834). Engraving
by Henry Meyer after Thomas Phillips (National
Portrait Gallery).

with reference to Canon Doimi's journal that this becomes clear. Disregarding Cooper's advice, Milutinovich had sailed to Lissa to try to take possession of it, in the belief, most probably based on information that he had received, that it had been agreed at Vienna that Austria should have it, but Colonel Robertson had refused to let him land on the grounds that he had received no orders.[276]

Orders were in fact already on their way, with the usual disadvantage of the length of time that it took communications from London to reach the Adriatic. On 8 May 1815 Henry Goulburn of the War Department wrote to the Admiralty:

> 'I am directed by Lord Bathurst to acquaint you for the information of the Lords Commissioners of the Admiralty that instructions have been sent to the Officer commanding His Majesty's Forces in the Mediterranean to cause the Island of Lissa to be evacuated and delivered up to the Austrian Authorities'.[277]

On the same day H. E. Bunbury of the War Department wrote a similar letter to the Foreign Office:

---

[276] Pisani, op. cit., p. 476. Pisani, quoting Doimi, says that the decision of the powers was made in spring and this abortive attempt took place in March 1815. Pisani also believed that the English, having been given the Ionian Islands wanted Lissa at least as a dependence of Corfu, but this is not supported by the evidence on the British side, nor by the dates.
[277] WO 6/154, p. 40, PRO

'I am directed by Lord Bathurst to transmit to You for the information of Viscount Castlereagh copies of dispatches which his Lordship has addressed to Lord Wm Bentinck and Lt Gen. Campbell on the subject of delivering the Island of Lissa to the Austrian Authorities'.[278]

The instructions from Lord Bathurst to Bentinck, also dated 8 May 1815, were:

'I am to desire that on the Receipt of this Dispatch, Your Lordship will give orders for withdrawing from Lissa the Troops composing the Garrison of that island and for sending them back to Corfu delivering over the island of Lissa to the Authorities who may be empowered by the Govt. of Austria to receive possession of the same'.[279]

The Admiralty sent a letter to inform Admiral Pellew (now Lord Exmouth) on 9 May, of which he acknowledged receipt on 7 June. He in turn informed Captain Vincent on TRIDENT at Malta. There were still doubts as to whether Lissa was plague-free and whether this would affect its evacuation, until Robertson's assurances of 12 June that there no health problems had been received at Malta.[280] The British evacuated the Ragusan islands on 16 July, Curzola on 20 July, and Lissa on 27 July.[281] In the meantime, on 18 June 1815, other officers and soldiers of the 35th Foot who had served on Lissa faced the onslaught of the French at Waterloo.

The Austrians may have regretted the departure of the British navy from the Adriatic. The vacuum was filled by the Barbary pirates of Algiers and Tripoli who became another kind of plague in the Adriatic from 1814 and until Lord Exmouth attacked Algiers in August 1816.

***

Given its strategic importance, the island of Lissa or Vis was to serve the British as a base for attacking the enemy in Yugoslavia in much the same way towards the end of the Second World War.

Thanks to having been until recently a place of military importance, the island of Vis was not open to foreigners and has so far been spared major development for tourism. The harbour of St George is little changed. Although in the nineteenth century the Austrian military authorities altered and partially dismantled them, some of the British fortifications remain today although through time the names which commemorated British army and naval officers involved in its defence so long ago have faded away and been replaced, except ironically for Velintun (Wellington), the famous British general who had nothing to do with Lissa.[282]

---

[278] WO 6/167, p. 29, PRO
[279] WO 6/57, PRO
[280] See above, letter Grimes-Vincent of 28 June and note 181.
[281] Pisani, op. cit., p. 476, bases these dates in a proclamation of Milutinovich and includes Lesina on 15 July, although the British did not have any forces there (nor is there any evidence that there were any on the Ragusan islands, although they could have been considered under British protection). Other sources give 19 July as the date of British evacuation of all the islands.
[282] See Appendix 5: Remains

Figure 57A & B. Fort George Gate and Inscription to George III 195

Appendix 1: Sources

1 Primary Sources

<u>Public Record Office</u> (PRO), now National Archives, Kew, London
All British Government papers including:
    <u>War Office</u> (WO)
        WO 1 Correspondence received by War Office
            WO1/310-315 Despatches from Mediterranean
        WO 6 Correspondence sent by War Office
            WO 6/57 Letters sent to Mediterranean
    <u>Admiralty</u> (ADM)
        ADM 1 Correspondence received by Admiralty
            ADM 1/413-431 from Admiral commanding Mediterranean
1807-15
            ADM 1/4366-5113 Promiscuous (miscellaneous, including
            correspondence with merchants)
        ADM 2 Letters sent out by Admiralty
        ADM 12 Indexes and digests of Admiralty correspondence in ADM 1
            ADM 12/134-174 1807-15
        ADM 37 Muster lists (monthly lists of all members of crew and persons
            carried on Royal Navy ships)
        ADM 51 Captains logbooks (giving detailed daily movements of
            Royal Navy ships)

    <u>Foreign Office</u> (FO)
        FO 7 Austria
        FO 42 Ionian Islands
        FO 70 Naples and Sicily
        FO 78 Turkey

<u>British Library</u> (BL), London
Special collections in Additional Manuscripts (Add Mss):
    <u>Lowe Papers</u> (Add Mss 20110) Official and private correspondence of Colonel
Hudson Lowe, serving in Ionian Islands, including letters to Captain Charles Rowley.

    <u>Collingwood Papers</u> (Add Mss 14273-80) Letter and order books and journal
            1807-08
            (Add MSS 40096-8) Letters and reports received 1805-09

    <u>Aberdeen Papers</u> (Add Mss 43073-77) Letters to and from Lord Aberdeen as
                   Ambassador to Austria

<u>National Maritime Museum</u> (NMM), Greenwich, London
Special collections:
    <u>Hoste Papers</u> Private papers of Captain William Hoste concerning principally
    correspondence and notes on prize money; his widows correspondence

with other Royal Naval officers concerning material for his biography; but also including papers concerning his disputes on Vis with Admiral Fremantle.
<u>Collingwood Papers</u> Copy books of official correspondence (in-books and out-books) of Admiral Lord Collingwood in command of the Royal Navy in the Mediterranean 1805-10.
    <u>Cotton Papers</u> Correspondence Admiral Cotton in command of Royal Navy in Mediterranean 1810-1811
          <u>Fremantle Letter Book</u> 1813-14 and other papers of Admiral Thomas Fremantle
<u>Pellew Papers</u> Official correspondence (in-books and out-books) and order books of Admiral Sir Edward Pellew in command Royal Navy in Mediterranean 1811-14.
    <u>Rowley Papers</u> Letter books of official and private correspondence of Captain Charles Rowley commanding H.M.S. Eagle and Royal Navy squadron in the Adriatic.
    <u>Matthews Journal</u> Journal of Captain W. F. J. Matthews, Royal Marines, serving on H.M.S. Eagle in Adriatic.

<u>National Army Museum</u>
    <u>Hildebrandt Memoirs</u> Typescript copy of memoirs 1809-15 of Lieutenant Hildebrandt serving with British army on Vis.

<u>University of Nottingham</u>
    <u>Portland Papers</u> Copy books of correspondence of General Lord William Bentinck, commander-in-chief of the British army in the Mediterranean 1811-14

<u>Buckinghamshire County Record Office</u>, Aylesbury
<u>Cottesloe/Fremantle Papers</u> Copies of official correspondence and other papers of Thomas Fremantle in command of Royal Navy squadron in the Adriatic.

2 Published Sources: Select Bibliography

Anderson, R. C.: Naval Wars in the Levant, Liverpool 1952
Brenton, Capt. Edward Pelham: Brenton's Naval History, 1837
Colledge, J. J.: Ships of the Royal Navy - An Historical Index, 1969
Erber, Tullio: Storia della Dalmazia, Zadar 1886-92
Fisković, Cvito: Spomenici otoka Visa od IX do XIX stoljeca, Prilozi povijesti umjetnosti u Dalmaciji, no. 17, Split 1968
Fisković, Cvito: English Monuments in Dalmatia (paper for 1976 symposium on Dubrovnik's relations with England), Zagreb 1977, republished as Engleski spomenici i umjetnine u Dalmaciji, Zagreb 1979
Foretić, D: Vis u medjunrarodnom zbivanju na pocetkom XIX st., Mogucnosti III, nos. 7-8, Split 1956 (based largely on now lost memoirs of Canon Doimi, original manuscript of which was in library of Zadar Gymnasium in 1894, published in Dalmata, Zadar, Sept/Oct. 1886)
Gardiner, Robert ed.: Fleet Battle and Blockade, 1996
Gay, Franco: Le Costruzioni navali nell'Arsenale di Venezia, Rivista Marittima, 1989
Fremantle, Anne Marie Huth: The Wynne Diaries 1789-1820, Oxford 1935, abridged

edition 1952 (includes letters from Admiral Fremantle to his wife and extracts from his now lost diaries while in the Adriatic)

Horward, Donald D. (ed.): Napoleonic Military History - A Bibliography, New York 1986, Chapter XIX, Illyria and Dalmatia

Hoste, S. H: Service Afloat: or the naval career of Sir William Hoste, London 1887

Hoste, William: Memoirs and Letters of Capt. Sir Wm. Hoste, 1833
        NB This publication edited by his widow includes much
        material not written by Hoste but by his naval chaplain Rev. Yonge.

James, William: The Naval History of Great Britain, first publ.1837 (based on official reports issued by Admiralty)

King, D. W: A British Officer in the Eastern Adriatic 1812-15 - The Story of Captain Pearce Lowen of Korčula, Journal of the Socirty of Army Historical Research, Vol. 58, no. 223, Spring 1980

Laverty, Bernard: Nelson's Navy, 1989
        The Arming and Fitting of English Ships of War, 1987

Leckey, H. S.: The King's Ships, London 1913-14 (histories of ships of Royal Navy)

Levi, Cesare Augusto: Navi di Guerra costruite nell'Arsenale di Venezia, 1896

Lyon, David J.: The Sailing Navy List 1688-1860, London 1993 (notes on all ships of the Royal Navy)

Mackesy, Piers: War in the Mediterranean 1803-1810, London 1957

Marshall, John: Naval Biography, London 1823-30 (uses reports issued by Admiralty)

Masson, Philippe: Histoire de la Marine, Paris 1981

Napoleon I: Correspondance de Napoleon Ier, Paris 1858-69

Novak, Grga: Vis u doba Francuskog gospodstva u Dalmaciji, Zagreb 1961

O'Bryne, W: A Naval Biographical Dictionary, London 1849 (republ.1994)

Parry, Ann: The Admirals Fremantle, London 1971

Pisani, Paul: La Dalmatie de 1797 à 1815, Paris 1893
        (based largely on French official records and archives in Dalmatia and Paris)

Pivec-Stelè, Melitta: La Vie Économique des Provinces Illyriennes 1809-1813, Paris 1930 (covers British naval activity and its effects)

Pocock, T: Remember Nelson, London 1977 (biography of Captain William Hoste)

Ralfe, J: The Naval Biography of Great Britain, London 1828

Safanof, Nikola: Ratovi na Jadranu 1797-1815, Belgrade 1988

Thursfield, H. G. (ed.): Five Naval Journals 1789-1817, Greenwich Navy Records Society1951 (includes journal of Robert Mercer Wilson, seaman who served in Royal Navy in Adriatic 1805)

Stewart, Robert ed. Vane, C. W.: Memoirs and Correspondence of Viscount Castlereagh, London1848-53

Webster, C. K.: The Congress of Vienna 1814-15, London 1963

Weil, Maurice H: Le Prince Eugene et Murat 1813-14, 1902

Woodman, Richard (and Gardiner, Robert): The Victory of Seapower, 1998

Appendix 2: Names

Because of the importance given to quoting original documents the spelling of names is transcribed and used in the text irrespective of the modern names of places in the Slav or other languages of the countries in which they are to be found today. The same name could also be spelt differently in different documents. The following concerns the period 1805-15 in the Adriatic area in general and not only the names appearing in the main text.

Place-names

The British navy usually used the Italian names of places around the Adriatic. These were either taken from charts (see below Maps and Charts) or phonetic transcriptions of the names as they were heard. More rarely they attempted translation of the meanings of place-names into English. Thus what is now called in Croatian and Serbian Boka Kotorska was called Bocca di Cattaro or Bocche di Cattaro or the Mouth/s of Cattaro or (with the risk of confusing the inlet of the sea and the town) simply Cattaro (and its people Bocchesi). Similarly French texts could refer to Bouche/s de Cattaro.

Places in the Istrian and Croatian or other provinces of the Austrian Empire could also have German names in addition to their Slav and Latin/Italian names eg Pressburg = Pozun = Pozony (Hungarian) = Bratislava, Mittelburg = Pazin = Pisino in Istria, and Agram = Zagreb, and Karlstadt = Karlovac in Croatia.

In much the same way as English seamen could produce Leghorn out of Livorno, a relatively easy name such as Umag (Croatian), Umago (Italian) could become Margo. Split, in Italian Spalato, was commonly rendered as Spalatro in Italian, French and English.

The names used for countries and geographical areas were more loosely applied and often different from their more precise application today. Thus Albania (sometimes anglicized as Albany) included Venetian Albania i.e. the area formerly held by the Venetians around and to the south of the Boka Kotorska, as well as Montenegro and the Epirus area of modern Greece.

Some traditions derived from classical geography. Geographical concepts such as Macedonia survived despite the disappearance of an administrative district or specific language and culture. Similarly the French revived the classical term Illyria. The British preferred to use the Latin name Apulia instead of the Italian Puglia, although the Venetian name Morea was always used for the Peleponnese.

The Adriatic itself was often taken to include part of the Ionian Sea outside the Strait of Otranto. The term Gulf of Venice could be applied to the entire Adriatic north of Otranto as well as in its more limited sense meaning the area between Venice and Istria. Barbary was the berber Mediterranean coast of Africa.

Peoples

There was relative ignorance of racial or ethnic distinctions in the modern sense. The Slav peoples of the Balkans might be referred to as Sclavonians but more commonly according to the powers to which they were subject e.g. as Austrians or Turks or to the geographical areas they inhabited. The Croats or Croatians of the various regiments of the military frontier areas of Croatia were largely Serbian and Orthodox. Turks were subjects of the Sultan or the Supreme Porte of the Ottoman Empire irrespective of race, language or religion, although within this category there were the inhabitants of the different regions or provinces, Albanians, Montenegrins, Serbs. On the other hand Greek could mean anyone who was Orthodox by religion and was for example applied to the Orthodox inhabitants of the Boka Kotorska; and Croates ottomanes in French was applied to inhabitants of north-west Bosnia although it not entirely clear that this term was limited to the Catholic subjects of the Ottoman Empire in that area.

'The French' was interchangeable with the term 'the enemy' irrespective of whether the soldiers or seamen involved were in point of fact Italian subjects of Napoleon in his capacity as King of Italy, southern Italians in the kingdom of Naples, or Istrians, Croats and Dalmatians in the Illyrian Provinces. Enemy ships in the Adriatic usually flew the colours of the kingdom of Italy and as their main base was Venice were frequently described as Venetian. Some French warships that entered the Adriatic from bases in France proper might more correctly be described as being French.

The British never recognized the French Empire. For them the terms Imperial or Imperialist in the context of the Adriatic always meant Austrian.

Individuals

As the British did not recognize his imperial title they never referred to Napoleon but always to Bonaparte.

On the British side, ennobled individuals were always referred to by their title rather than their family name but the titles could and did change e.g. Lord Hawkesbury became Lord Liverpool. French generals were also ennobled by Napoleon, although history has persisted in recognizing them by their family names rather than by their titles e.g. the title Duke of Ragusa has not concealed Marmont, and the official title of Duke of Otranto has not substituted for Fouché, or d'Abrantès for Junot.

Some common English family names could be spelt inconsistently e.g. Harvey or Hervey, Mowbray or Moubray. Fremantle could write of his military colleague on Vis as 'Robinson' instead of Robertson. In French also there were variations in spelling: L'Espine could be written L'Épine or Lépine, or Danthouars could be used instead of d'Anthouars.

Some foreign names gave particular difficulty to English writers. Whereas the average officer would be familiar with French and possibly Italian, few were familiar with Russian or the Cyrillic alphabet (except perhaps insofar as they might have learnt Greek), and their communications with the officers of the Russian navy (when both navies were acting against the French in the Adriatic before 1807) were most likely to have been in French or in English, especially given that many British officers were recruited into the Russian service. It is curious that the name of one of these, Bailey, has been retranscribed into the Latin alphabet from its phonetic Cyrillic form in Russian documents as Belli. The Greek Foresti at Corfu (a

British consular official) had difficulty with the Russian names of ships and is not consistent in his spelling of the names when he transcribes them into the Latin alphabet. He also tried to translate their names according to their meaning into Italian or English. Communications between the British and the Prince-Bishop (Vladika) of Montenegro were invariably in Italian, which served as the lingua franca of the entire Adriatic littoral.

Historians in other languages have also had problems with their rendering of British names. The ship's name ACORN has been passed down by Dalmatian historians in a germanicized form AICHORN.

Naval and military designations

The British navy has been called the Royal Navy since the reign of Charles II in the second half of the seventeenth century, but with international readership in mind, and because of the existence at the beginning of the nineteenth century of other royal navies, the term British navy has been used throughout the main text.

The commander of any ship of the British navy could be called captain although the actual rank of those in command of smaller vessels might be that of commander or lieutenant i.e. below that of captain (or post-captain). The term commodore was not a rank but was applied to a captain placed in command of two or more warships only for the period during which he commanded them. The person in command of a merchant vessel might be addressed as captain but was usually described as being the master of his vessel. The person called master on a British warship was the sailing master who assisted the captain in the handling of the ship, navigation and chart-making.

French naval ranks of capitaine, lieutenant and enseigne were qualified by de corvette, de frégat, de vaisseau (i.e. ship-of-the-line) with seniority according to the size and importance of the category of warship.

In the French army after maréchal followed général de division, général be brigade, colonel, commandant chef-de-bataillon. Headquarters were état-major to which were attached a chef d'état-major and officiers d'état-major (although Napoleon's own chief of staff, Marshal Berthiér, was referred to as major-général). Artillerymen were artilleurs. Officers with skills in engineering were described as being of (the) 'génie' ie 'ingénieurs', and their troops were 'sapeurs'. Other French military expressions that present some difficulty in translation into English are 'chasseurs' (literally 'hunters' but meaning light infantry or cavalry), 'voltigeurs' (literally 'acrobats' but élite companies of short men used as skirmishers or flank companies, balancing the élite companies of 'grenadiers' or tall men). The ordinary companies of 'ligne'(line) infantry regiments consisted of 'fusiliers' meaning simply men you carried 'fusils' (the standard flintlock muskets). The ordinary companies of the 'léger' (light) infantry or 'chasseur à pied' regiments consisted of 'chasseurs' with élite companies of 'carabiniers' (armed with the lighter and shorter carbine). Titles of infantry regiments were usually abbreviated e.g. 60e ligne, or 18e léger.

Maps and charts

The maps available to the British in the period 1805-10 are important in helping to identify the places they referred to. Those now in British official collections were usually bound into atlases for the libraries of the Admiralty, War Office, Foreign Office or Board of Trade. The individual maps in such atlases were made and corrected at different dates before being put together (map collection catalogues now usually give the approximate date that the atlas was compiled). Even though the compilation date is often later than the period of interest, and the individual maps were reprinted with later corrections, it is possible to identify those that were probably used by the British in the Adriatic, not only because each map gives the original date that it was published, but also because of the idiosyncracies of particular names and spellings.

The Hydrography Office of the Admiralty was established in 1795 with responsibility for commissioning and purchasing maps and charts and distributing them to British warships. Such maps were published by a number of mapmakers in London. When commissioned or issued by the Hydrography Office these carried its seal or stamp. The publishers were also required by law to identify themselves and had an interest in declaring royal or Hydrography Office patronage. The following items in the collection of the National Maritime Museum in Greenwich are of particular interest.

Board of Trade Atlas of Europe 1821 (NMM, C5371)
This includes:

Map 38: North end Gulf of Venice
Published London, 11 June 1804 (with additions to 1819), by A. Arrowsmith, Hydrographer to His Majesty, No. 10, Soho Sq.

Maps 43-44: Dalmatia (from T***X)
Published London, 3 April 1812, by A. Arrowsmith, Hydrographer to HRH the Prince of Wales, 10 Soho Square
Because of the use of both Italian and German names these can be related to maps in the atlas of the War Office library, now in the Public Record Office, Kew, WO 78/5775 Trau 1810:
Maximilien de Traux: Carte von Dalmatien (8 Quellen), Vienna, 1810

Admiralty Atlas 1827 (NMM, PBD8481)
This includes:

Chart of the Adriatic or Gulf of Venice
Constructed from the Venetian, Neapolitan and French observations
by J. F. Dessiou, Master of the R.N.
published London by W. Faden, Geographer to His Majesty and to HRH the Prince of Wales, Charing Cross, 12 August 1806
(the map is overstamped 'Hydrographical Office')

Glossary of place-names

A

Abbruzzo/Abbruzzi = northern region of Kingdom of Naples on Adriatic coast of Italy

Agram = Zagreb capital city of Croatia

Albania = Balkan region with Adriatic seaboard then extending from Bocca di Cattaro (Boka Kotorska) in the north to and including Epirus in the south

Almissa/Almizza = the Dalmatian town of Omiš

Amontre/Friar's Island = island off coast of Istria near Parenzo (Poreč) = Sv. Nikola?

Ancona = town and harbour of the Papal States held by the French

Antivari = the town of Bar now in Montenegro

Apulia = region of south-east heel of Italy = Puglia

Arbe/Arbora = the island of Rab

Arcangelo = the island of Arkanđel between Trogir and Šibenik

The Arsenal = the naval dockyard of Venice

Augusta/Lagosta = island of Ragusan republic = Lastovo

B

Barletta = port of Kingdom of Naples on Adriatic coast of Puglia

Blata = village on west end of island Curzola (Korčula) = Blato

Bocca/Bocche (di Cattaro) = the Mouth/s (an inlet of the sea) of Cattaro = Boka Kotorska

Bocca Falsa = channel between islands of Olipa and Jakljan east of Pelješac

Bosnia = province of the Ottoman Empire with seat of the pasha at Travnik

Brazza = the Dalmatian island of Brač

Brenn/Breno = locality to south-east of Ragusa (Dubrovnik) = Srebreno

Brindisi = port of Kingdom of Naples on Adriatic coast of heel of Italy in Puglia

Bukari = town on Croatian coast east of Fiume (Rijeka) = Bakar

Burat = inland town of Albania = Berat

Busa = locality on island Lissa (Vis) =?

Butrinto = town on coast of Albania opposite Corfu = Butrint

C

Calabria = southernmost region of mainland Italy opposite Sicily

Capodistria = town on northern coast of Istria = Koper

Castel Nuovo/Castelnuovo = the town of Herceg-Novi

Chiozza = Chioggia

Cattaro = the town (or gulf) of Kotor

Cazza = island of Sušac

Cefalonia/Cephalonia = the Ionian island of Kefalloni

Cetina = river of Dalmatia reaching sea at Almissa (Omiš)

Cherso = the island of Cres

Citta Vecchia = Stari Grad on island Lessina (Hvar)

Comisa/Comissa = town on west coast of the island of Lissa (Vis) = Komiža

Constantinople = capital of the Ottoman (Turkish) Empire, seat of the Sultan (Grand Signore/Grand Seigneur) and his court and government (SublimePorte/Porte/Divan/Diwan) = Istanbul

Corfu = Ionian island and town, capital of Septinsular/Seven Island/Ionian Republic = Kërkyra

Cotrana = town on eastern seabord of Calabria in Italy = Crotone

Croatia = province of the Austrian Empire divided into civil and military Croatia (the Military Frontier or Militär-grenz settled by the soldier-farming families of the Croatian or Grenzer regiments)

Curzola = the Dalmatian island of Korčula

D

Dalmatia = the coastal and island province then extending from the capital town of Zara (Zadar) and the nearby islands in the west to the River Narenta (Neretva) and island of Curzola (Korčula) in the east

Drin/Ludrin = gulf of Drinit in northern Albania

Dulcigno = the town of Ulcinj

Durazzo = town on coast of Albania = Durrës

E

Egnatia, Via = road from Durazzo-Elbasan-Ohrid-Salonika

Elbasan = town of central Albania inland from Durazzo on road to Ohrid

F

Fano = small island just north-west of Corfu = Othoni

Faro = originally lighthouse on Sicilian side of Strait of Messina (classical Carybdis) but used for the strait itself

Fiume = the Croatian town of Rijeka

G

Giuppana/Zupanio = island west of Ragusa (Dubrovnik) = Šipan

Gospic = town of inland Croatia on road Karlstadt (Karlovac) - Zara (Zadar) in Dalmatia

Grao/Grado = Italian town on northern side of the Bay of Trieste

Gravosa/Santa Croce/St.Croix = harbour on north side of Ragusa (Dubrovnik) = Gruž

H

Herzegovina = province of Ottoman Empire to south-west of Bosnia = Hercegovina

I

Illyrian Provinces = region of the French Empire established by Napoleon to include Slovenia, Istria, Croatia west of the River Sava, and Dalmatia

Istria = peninsula and province at north-east end of Adriatic

Isola Lunga = the island of Dugi Otok

Italy = Napoleon's Kingdom of Italy initially comprised the regions of Lombardy and Venice

J

Joannina/Yannina = town of Albania and capital of pashalik = Ioannina in Epirus province of Greece

K

Karlstadt = fortress town of inland Croatia = Karlovac

Kastela = villages to west of Spalato (Split)

Klobuk = locality in Herzegovina east of Trebinje on the present border with Montenegro, which, since the decline of inland trade routes from Ragusa (Dubrovnik) has now disappeared

L

Ladri, Porto or Golfo dei = behind southern end of Sabioncello (Pelješac) peninsula

Les Essara = locality on island of Veglia (Krk)? = ?

Linguetta = cape of southern Albania near Valona (Vlore) = Kep I Gjuhëzës

Lagosta/Augusta = the Dalmatian island of Lastovo

Legnian, Point = cape of Istria seven miles north-west of Pola (Pula)

Lemo = a creek or inlet of the sea on the west coast of Istria = Limski Kanal

Lessina/Lesina/Liesina = the Dalmatian island and town of Hvar

Linguetta, Punto = small peninsula on Albanian/Epirus side of Strait of Otranto

Lissa = the Dalmatian island of Vis

Ludrin/Drin = gulf of Drinit in northern Albania

Lussin/Lussino = the island of Lošinj

Lussin/Lussino Piccolo = the town and harbour of Mali Lošinj

Lussin/Lussino Grande = town of Veli Lošinj

M

Macarsca = town on coast of Dalmatia = Makarska

Malamocca/o = the channel from the Venice lagoon to the Adriatic

Malta = main British naval base in Mediterranean

Manfredonia = Adriatic port of Kingdom of Naples on south side of Gargano promontory

Margo/Umago = the Istrian town of Umag

Mataban/Matapan = cape at southernmost tip of mainland Greece

Messina = town of north-east Sicily and strait between Sicily and mainland Italy (see Faro)

Milna = town on west side of island Brazza (Brač)

Mittelburg = the Istrian town of Pisino = Pazin

Monaco = small port in gulf of Fiume (Rijeka) =?

Montenegro/Mte.Negro = the Black Mountain = mountainous independent area of northern Albania under a vladika or prince-bishop = Crna Gora

Morea = the Peleponnese peninsula of Greece

Mosco/Mous/Muschio = locality on island of Veglia (Krk) = Omišalj

Mutograsso = locality on Dalmatia coast to east of Spalato (Split)

N

Naples = city and kingdom (with that of Sicily) comprising all southern Italy

Narenta = the river Neretva

O

Ogulin = town of Croatia to south-west Karlstadt (Karlovac)

Ombla = deep inlet of the sea/river behind (north of) Ragusa/Dubrovnik

Opus, Fort = fort guarding northern (Dalmatian) side of entrance to Narenta (Neretva) river = Opuzen

Orsera = town of Vrsar in Istria

Ostro = cape on west side of entrance to Bocca di Cattaro = Oštri rt

Otranto = port on Italian coast of Puglia and strait at entrance to Adriatic Sea
Ottoschatz = town in south-west Croatia in military frontier; centre of regiment; on road
    Karlstadt (Karlovac) - Zara (Zadar) in Dalmatia

P
Palermo = town on north-west coast and capital of Sicily
Panormo/Panormus/Palermo = town on coast of southern Albania just north of Corfu
    = Piqueras
Papal States = in central Italy with Adriatic seaboard from mouth of River Po and Kingdom
        of Italy in north to Kingdom of Naples in south
Parenzo/Parenso = the Istrian town of Poreč
Pelagosa = the island of Palagruža (see S. Andrea)
Perato = shipping town in Bocca di Cattaro = Perast
Permite = town to south-east of Berat in Albania = Permet
Pesaro = Adriatic port of Papal States
Pille = part of Ragusa (Dubrovnik)
Pirano = town on north-west corner of Istria = Piran
Pisino = Mittelburg in Istria = Pazin
Podgora = village on coast of south Dalmatia
Poglizza = area on Dalmatian coast to south-east of Spalato (Split)
Pola/Paulo = the Istrian town of Pula
Port St George = the main harbour of Lissa (Vis)
Promontore/Promontorio = the Istrian cape Rt Kamenjak with the village Premantura

Q
Quarnaro = gulf to east of Istria = Kvarner

R
Ragosniza/Rogosnizza = Rogožnica on Dalmatian coast
Ragusa = the town, republic and territory of Dubrovnik
Ragusa Nuova = locality to east of Ragusa (Dubrovnik)
Ragusa Vecchia/Old Ragusa = the town of Cavtat
Rebich or Orebich = town of Orebić
Rimini = Adriatic port of Papal States
Risano/Rissano = town in Bocca di Cattaro = Risan
Rosas/Porto-Rosso = point on eastern side of entrance to the Bocca di Cattaro = Rose
Rovigno = the Istrian town of Rovinj

S
Sabbioncello = the Dalmatian peninsula of Pelješac
Salonika = principal town and port in north of Aegean Sea = Thessalonika = Thessaloníki
S. Biagio/St.Blaize = fortified hill above Curzola (Korčula) = Sv.Vlaho
Santa Croce/St.Croix/Gravosa = the harbour on the north side of Ragusa (Dubrovnik) = Gruž
San Marco or Croma = island on south side of Ragusa (Dubrovnik) = Lokrum
Sta. Maria = locality on Croatian coast east of Fiume (Rijeka) =?
St. Marie's = cape on Italian side at entrance to Strait of Otranto and Adriatic Sea = Capo
    S.Maria di Leuca

Santa Maura = the Ionian island of Leucade = Lefkada

S. Andrea (on maps named S. Andrea in Pelago or Pelagosa) = island of Svetac

S. Nicolo = island fort off Šibenik

S. Pietro de Nimbo/de Nembi = small island near and to south-east of Lussino (Lošinj) off Ilovik

St. Sergius/S. Sergio = hill behind Ragusa (Dubrovnik = Sv. Srđ)

Salvore = cape at north-west corner of Istria = Rt Savudrija

Sansego = island to south of Istria = Sušak

Sclavonia = lands of the Slavs

Scutari = the town and pashalik of Skadar/Shkodër in north Albania

Scylla = fortress on coast of Calabria opposite Sicily = Scilla

Segallo = small port in gulf of Fiume (Rijeka) =?

Segna = town on coast of Croatia = Senj

Septinsular Republic = the Seven Island Republic = Ionian Islands including Corfu, Santa Maura (Leucade), Ithaca/Itaca, Cefalonia/Cephalonia, Zante.

Sicily = used both for the island and the kingdom of the Two Sicilies (Naples)

Sebenico = town on coast of Dalmatia = Šibenik

Slano = town on coast to north-west of Ragusa (Dubrovnik) in Ragusan territory

Socoliz/Sokolica = locality at north-west end of island Lesina (Hvar)

Solta = the Dalmatian island of Šolta

Spalato/Spalatro = the Dalmatian town of Split

Spartivento = cape at southernmost end of Calabria and Italian mainland

Stagno = town on neck of Sabioncello (Pelješac) peninsula in territory of Ragusa (Dubrovnik) = Ston

Stanjevic = monastery in Montenegro just to north of Budva = Stanjevici

Stobrec = bay and river just to east of Spalato (Split)

Strosanac = locality just east of Stobrec river east of Spalato (Split)

T

Taranto = port of Kingdom of Naples on south side of Puglia

Tenedos = island in Aegean Sea near entrance to Dardanelles = Bozca Adasi

Trau = the Dalmatian town of Trogir

Travnik = seat of the Pasha of Bosnia

Trebinje = town of Ottoman Empire inland from Ragusa (Dubrovnik)

Tremiti/Tremitti = group of small islands off Italian coast of Adriatic to north of Gargano promontory including S.Nicola and S.Dominico

Trieste = port in north-east corner of Adriatic, developed by Austria

U

Umago/Margo = the Istrian town of Umag

V

Valletta = principal harbour and fortress-town of Malta

Valona = town on coast of southern Albania = Vlorë

Veglia = the island of Krk

Venice = city and region of Italy and republic with territories down eastern seaboard of Adriatic, Albania and Greece suppressed by the French

Venice, Gulf of = between Venice and Istria but sometimes used for whole of Adriatic Sea

X
Xupra = area to south-east of Ragusa (Dubrovnik) = Župa on bay of Župa (Župski zaljev)

Y
Yanina = Joannina = Ioannina in southern Albania (Epirus province of modern Greece)

Z
Zante = the Ionian island of Zkynthos
Zara = town in north-west Dalmatia and administrative capital = Zadar
Zupanio/Giuppana = small island west of Ragusa (Dubrovnik) = Šipan

Appendix 3: Biographical notes

The short periods they spent on Lissa or in the Adriatic were for most of the protagonists only parts of longer careers. Most were young and many went on to distinguished careers, others disappeared from public view and the official records. The following notes place the Lissa or Adriatic episode in the larger context of the lives and careers of selected individuals. Some of the more important French individuals responsible for the area are also included, together with the closest Austrian and Croatian collaborators with the British.

British

Naval ranks. In the Royal Navy the first commissioned rank is Lieutenant (usually after service as Midshipman), after which comes Commander, (Post) Captain (i.e. of rated post ships of 20 or more guns), Rear Admirals, Vice Admirals and full Admirals. In each category of admiral there are admirals of the Blue, White and Red. Finally there is Admiral of the Fleet.

Army ranks. In the annual Army List, an officer's rank is given both within the army and within a regiment, and the two can be different. Officers could also serve outside the regiment in which they held their commission. In times of peace, officers of both the army and navy were placed on half pay, held no commands, but could be recalled to service. As such they could remain in the Army List long after they had seen active service. Some ranks, such as Colonel (as opposed to Lieutenant Colonel) are honorary and reserved for the 'colonels' of regiments (who often hold higher military rank).

BENNETT, William -1821 Gosport
British Army, Royal Engineers: Second Lieut. 1798, Capt.1809, served Sicily 1810 and 1812-15, Major 1819.

BENTINCK, William Cavendish (Lord) 1774-1839 Paris.
British soldier, diplomat and administrator. Second son Duke of Portland. Capt. 1792, Lieut.-Colonel 1794. Attached to staff of Russian General Suvorov in North Italy 1799 and Austrians 1801. Governor of Madras, India 1803. Major-General 1807. In 1811 made Lieut.-General and commander-in-chief of British army in Mediterranean as well as minister to court of King Ferdinand of Naples (on Sicily). From May–Sept.1813 absent from Sicily on campaign in Catalonia, Spain. Commanded expedition to Genoa 1814. Left Sicily July 1814. As a liberal, opposed to restoration ancien régimes and favoured unification Italy. Governor-General of Bengal 1827 and first Governor-General of India 1833-35 (remembered for his reforms and the suppression of suttee and thugee). Liberal Party MP for Glasgow 1837.

CAMPBELL, Patrick 1773-1841
Royal Navy: Lieut. 1794, Capt. 1800, commanded UNITÉ frigate from 1806, Knight 1836, rose to Vice Admiral 1838.

COLLINGWOOD, Cuthbert (Lord) 1750 Newcastle-Mar. 1810 at sea
Commanded ROYAL SOVEREIGN as second-in-command to Nelson at Battle of Trafalgar 1805. Succeeded Nelson as admiral of Mediterranean fleet and made peer 1805.

COTTON, Charles 1753-1812
Royal Navy: Entered 1772, active service 1772-83 in War of American Independence, 1793-1801 in French Revolutionary War, Rear Admiral 1797, Vice Admiral 1797. Succeeded Collingwood as commander-in-chief Mediterranean fleet March 1810. Recalled May 1811.

FREMANTLE, Thomas Francis 1765-1819 Naples
Royal Navy: Lieut. 1782, Capt. 1793. Friend of Nelson who was witness at his marriage in 1797 to Elisabeth Wynne. Fought in Battle of Copenhagen. Commanded NEPTUNE 90 in Battle of Trafalgar 1805. Rear Admiral of Blue 1810, Rear Admiral of White 1812, Rear Admiral of Red 1814. Baron of Austrian Empire 1815. Appointed commander-in-chief of the Royal Navy in the Mediterranean Jan. 1819 and promoted Vice Admiral of Blue Aug. 1819 but died soon afterwards in Dec. 1819 in Naples (General Nugent was in Naples at same time).

Family home at Swanbourne, Buckinghamshire. Descendants included two other admirals and Barons Cottesloe.

GORDON, James Alex 1782 -1869
Royal Navy: Entered 1793, Lieut. 1800, Capt. 1805, commanded ACTIVE frigate 1808-1812, in Battle of Lissa March 1811, battle off Augusta (Lastovo) Nov. 1811 (lost leg), Knight 1815, Rear Admiral 1837, Vice Admiral 1848, Admiral of Blue 1854. Retired as Admiral of the Fleet 1868.

GOWER, Edward Leveson
Royal Navy: Lieut. 1793, Capt. 1795, commanded ELISABETH 74 from 1813, Rear Admiral of Blue June 1814 (succeeding Fremantle in command Adriatic squadron), Rear Admiral of White 1819, resigned 1821.

HENRYSON, John -1841 Exeter
British Army, Royal Engineers: Second Lieut. 1806, Second Capt. May 1811, Capt. Dec. 1814, served Sicily 1810-15 with period on Lissa 1812-13. Before leaving Sicily in 1813 accompanied William Henry Smyth, the important hydrographer, on a survey of the coast of Sicily. (Smyth, later Admiral Sir W. H. Smyth 1788-1865 was commissioned by Austria in 1818-19 to undertake surveys in the Adriatic). Henryson retired 1830.

HORNBY, Phipps 1785-1867

Royal Navy: Entered 1797, Lieut. 1804, Capt. 1810, commanded VOLAGE corvette from 1810, Battle of Lissa March 1811, Knight 1852, rose to Admiral of Red 1863

HOSTE, William 1780 Norfolk-1828
Family originally from Bruges, Flanders. Son (like Nelson) of Church of England vicar in Norfolk. Knight 1814. Entered Royal Navy 1793 serving five years on ships commanded by Nelson. Commanded AMPHION frigate from 1805, Battle of Lissa March 1811, BACCHANTE frigate from 1812. Left Royal Navy in 1815 (a rich man from prize money, although much spent on his father's debts) and married Lady Harriet Walpole, dau. of Earl of Orford. After his death, she commissioned his memoirs and his tomb (near that of Nelson) in the crypt of St. Paul's Cathedral, London.

JOHNSON, John Mordaunt   1776? Dublin-1815 Florence
British secret agent. Junior officer in British army 1798-1800. Sold commission and went to Germany. An excellent linguist, he learned several languages. He was working as a British secret agent from about 1804, mainly in Vienna and the Austrian Empire, including Hungary and Croatia, and with missions into European Turkey. He was transferred from Vienna to Lissa in March 1812. In late 1813 he was in Vienna, Prague, and Holland. In 1814 he was appointed British chargé d'affaires in Brussels but soon transferred to be British consul in Genova. A well-educated man, he had a good collection of books that was sold after his death (diaries in Yale University).

LOWE, Hudson 1769-1844 London
British Army: Son of army surgeon, Ensign 1787, Capt. 1795. Served Toulon and capture Corsica, where 2 years in garrison Ajaccio, Elba, Portugal, Minorca. Put in charge 200 Corsican emigrés on Minorca 1799 and served with them in Egypt 1801. Corsicans disbanded at Peace of Amiens 1802. As Major empowered to raise new regiment of Royal Corsican Rangers on Malta 1803, Lieut.-Colonel 1804. Served in Italy (defence of Capri 1808), in capture 1809-10 and garrisoning (1810-16) Ionian Islands. On military missions in Germany and to Sweden and attached to Prussian army of General Blücher 1813-14. Knight and Major-General 1814. In Hundred Days to Genoa to invade southern France (with Austrian General Nugent). Governor of St. Helena during captivity Napoleon until 1821. Governor Antigua, West Indies 1823, second-in-command Ceylon 1825-30. Lieut.-General 1830. Excellent linguist.

LOWEN, Pearce 1773 Dover-1846 Grahamstown, South Africa
British Army: Entered aged 26, Ensign 1799 in Albanian Regiment raised on Corfu, joined Royal Corsican Rangers as Lieut.1805. Served in British capture Ionian Islands 1809, Capt. 1811. Married on Cephalonia, Ionian Islands Feb. 1810. Children born Cephalonia Nov. 1810, Lissa Aug. 1812 (named Wellington) and Corfu Sept. 1816. Left in command on Curzola (Korčula) after its capture in February 1813. Went to South Africa in 1820 to serve as Capt. later Major (1830) in Cape Corps (later Cape Mounted Riflemen). Involved in early British wars against Zulus. Retired 1841. Commemorated in inscription on monument in Korčula.

MAITLAND, Frederick   1763-1848 Tunbridge Wells
British Army. In Jan. 1812 as Lieut.-General made second-in-command British army in the Mediterranean to Lord Bentinck based in Sicily. Sent on campaign to Spain July 1812 but fell sick, resigned command and returned to England Oct. 1812. Lieut. Governor of island of Dominica, British West Indies 1813. Promoted to full General 1825.

MAXWELL, Murray 1775-1831
Royal Navy: Entered 1790, Lieut. 1796, Capt. 1803, commanded ALCESTE frigate from 1807, in Adriatic from spring 1811, battle off Augusta (Lastovo) Nov. 1811, sailed to India (wrecked off Ceylon/Sri Lanka 1813), took British ambassador to China 1816, Knight 1818

PELLEW, Eduard (Lord EXMOUTH)
Royal Navy: famous for exploits as a frigate captain. Knight 1783. Succeeded Collingwood as Commander-in-Chief of Royal Navy in Mediterranean. Commanded British attack on Algiers 1816.

ROBERTSON, George Duncan 1766-1842
British army: Entered in 1782 aged 16 as Ensign. Promoted from15th Regiment Foot to 35th Regiment Foot as Capt. 1794. Served Guadaloupe, West Indies and campaign in Holland 1799. Served in 1st Guards and 30th Foot before being promoted back into 35th Foot as Major 1805. Promoted to Lieut.-Colonel in Sicilian Regiment of Foot 1807. Defended fortress of Scilla on Straits of Messina 1808. To Ionian Islands. On suppression Sicilian Regiment transferred to 89th Foot on half pay. Promoted to Major-General on half pay 1821. Became Colonel of 89th Foot 1837. Succeeded as chieftain (laird) of a Scottish clan in 1830.

ROWLEY, Charles 1770-1847 Brighton
Royal Navy: Lieut. 1789, Capt. 1795, commanded EAGLE 74 from 1806, to Adriatic April 1811, Knight 1814, Rear Admiral 1814, Commissioner of the Admiralty 1834-35, Governor of the Royal Hospital Greenwich 1836, Admiral of the White 1841, died Brighton 1847

SMITH, John Mark Frederick 1790 London-1874 London
British Army, Royal Engineers: Second Lieut. 1805, Second Capt. 1811, Capt. 1814, served Sicily from 1807-11 (there was another officer RE serving in Sicily 1811-13 called Henry Nelson Smith but only as Lieut.). Knight. Rose to army rank of full General 1863 and colonel commanding RE 1860.

TALBOT, John 1769-1851
Royal Navy: Entered 1784, Lieut. 1790, Capt. 1807, commanded VICTORIOUS 74 1809-14, battle with RIVOLI Feb. 1812 (wounded), Knight 1815, Admiral of White 1846.

TAYLOR, Bridges Watkinson -1814
Royal Navy: Lieut. 1799, Capt. 1802, commanded APOLLO frigate 1808-14, captured Augusta (Lastovo) and Curzola (Korčula) Feb. 1813, drowned at Brindisi 1814.

WHITBY, Henry - May 1812
Royal Navy: Lieut. 1799, Capt. 1804, commanded CERBERUS frigate 1809-12, Battle of Lissa March 1811. British named hill on Lissa after him.

French

BEAUHARNAIS, Eugène 1781 Paris –1824 Munich
Step-son of Napoleon, son by first marriage of Josephine. Accompanied Bonaparte on campaigns in Italy and Egypt. Made Viceroy of Napoleon's Kingdom of Italy 1805. Accompanied Napoleon on 1812-13 campaigns in Russia and Germany. Defended Kingdom of Italy against Austrians and British in 1813-14, after which he found refuge in Bavaria.

BERTRAND, Henri Gratien (Count) 1773-1844
French soldier. Fought in battles Iena 1806 (Gen.of division May 1807), Friedland 1807, and Wagram 1809. In April 1811 succeeded Marmont as Governor-General of Illyrian Provinces (until Jan. 1813). Fought at Lutzen and Leipzig. Accompanied Napoleon to Elba and St. Helena. Brought ashes of Napoleon back to France 1840. Buried alongside Napoleon in Les Invalides.

DUBOURDIEU, Bernard 1787-1811

French naval officer. Commanded 1810 French raid on Lissa and in Battle of Lissa March 1811. Died of wounds. His son was the French admiral at the Battle of Navarino 1827.

FOUCHÉ, Joseph (Duc d'Otrante) 1759-1820 Trieste

French politician. In French Revolution involved in execution Louis XVI and organisation of Terror. Minister of Police 1799-1809. Became Duc d'Otrante 1809. Succeeded Junot as Governor-General of Illyrian Provinces July 1813. During the Hundred Days was again Napoleon's chief of police. Assisted the Bourbon restoration, but as a regicide was obliged to leave France. Took Austrian citizenship.

JUNOT, Androche (Duc d'Abrantes) 1771-1813

French soldier. Sergeant secretary to Bonaparte at Toulon 1793, then aide de camp 1794. Accompanied Bonaparte to Egypt. General of division 1801. Fought Austerlitz 1805. Commanded French army in Portugal 1807-8. Went on Russian campaign 1812. Succeeded Bertrand as Governor-General of Illyrian Provinces May 1813 but became mentally ill, returned to France and committed suicide July 1813.

MARMONT, Auguste Frédéric Louis VIESSE de (Duc de Raguse)
1774 Châtillon-sur-Seine–1852 Venice

French soldier. Associate of Bonaparte from Toulon 1793, accompanying him on campaigns in Italy and Egypt. Became Governor of Dalmatia 1806 and Illyrian Provinces from 1809, and Duc de Raguse 1808. Promoted to Maréchal after Battle of Wagram 1809. Left Illyrian Provices for Spain Jan. 1811. After 1814 he was made a peer of France by Louis XVIII. Tried unsuccessfully to suppress Paris Revolution of 1830 and went into exile.

Austrian (and Croatian)

ADAMIĆ, Andrija Ljudevit 1769-1828

Important merchant of Fiume (Rijeka) who supplied British Navy, and even after 1809 and the establishment of the Illyrian Provinces went to Sicily and London for discussions at the Admiralty concerning a large contract to supply Croatian timber. Assisted agents and communications passing through Rijeka. Possibly also involved in conspiracies against French. After French expelled from Istria in autumn 1813, Admiral Fremantle appointed Adamić British consul in Fiume. Became important benefactor of his home town, where a central street is named after him.

DANESE, Francesco Vincenzo 1759-1844

A Dalmatian from Zadar, originally in Venetian service, entered Austrian army as Colonel after Austria acquired Dalmatia in 1797. Stayed in Dalmatia after it was acquired by the French in 1805 and was involved in the unsuccessful uprising in 1806, after which he fled via Bosnia to Austria. Came back to Dalmatia in war of 1809 but left again after Austrian defeat. Sent by Bentinck from Sicily to Lissa in June 1812 to assist Fremantle in a British expedition to support a Montenegrin attack on the French. Sent by Fremantle to negotiate with the Bishop (Vladika) of Montenegro. Re-entered Austrian army service when Austria went to war with France in

August 1813, and assisted in Austrian military occupation of Dalmatia. Married a daughter of A. L. Adamić.

NUGENT, Laval   1777-1862

Austrian and later Croatian soldier of Irish birth. After Austria's defeat at Wagram in 1809, became principal intermediary between the British and the Austrian court to try to bring Austria into war against France again, and the main agent, using Austrian archdukes, other foreign officers whom the French had forced the Austrians to dismiss, and other disaffected persons, to raise insurrections against the French, particularly in the Illyrian Provinces. British gave him subsidy to raise two regiments of Croatian soldiers with which to invade the Illyrian Provinces after Austria entered the war in August 1813. Liberated Istria and besieged and captured Trieste in close cooperation with Admiral Fremantle and the British fleet and other forces from Lissa. With British help, invaded Italy from mouth of Po, defeating French in North Italy in 1814. In Hundred Days invaded southern France. Commanded Austrian troops in Naples 1815 and the Neapolitan army 1817-20 (present at funeral Admiral Fremantle). Commanded Austrian division at Venice and supervised the fortification of Trieste and coast Istria 1828. Involved in suppression revolution of 1848 in Hungary (captured Osijek March 1849). Became Field Marshal Nov. 1849. Count and Prince of the Holy Roman Empire. Present at Battle of Solferino 1859. Acquired and restored Croatian castles of Trsat (Rijeka) and Dubovac (near Karlovac) and built Bosiljevo where he died 1862. Married dau. of Duke of Riario-Sforza. Also collector of art and antiquities (the latter now in Archeological Museum Zagreb).

Appendix 4: Ships and soldiers

Warships

Guns

British warships carried a range of different types of guns categorised by the weight of the solid metal ball shot they fired (exploding balls were considered too dangerous as ammunition on warships). They ranged from 32 to 24, 18, 12, 9 and 6 pounds (the standard size of a field gun used by the armies of the time on land). The heavier the shot and the weight of the gun, the slower the rate of fire, and the more men required to serve the gun. A 35 pounder long gun or demi-cannon consisted of 2 ½ tons of metal on a timber carriage (about 3 tons in all) and needed 10-12 men (increased to 14 to improve the speed of fire). Broadsides were sometimes described by the weight of shot that could be fired in one discharge of all the guns on one side of the ship. Such broadsides usually exceeded by far the capacity of coastal batteries (the main danger from which was heated shot which could start fires on the wooden ships, so they were often attacked on land by sailors landed from the warship's boats). Rate of fire and accuracy at longer range were often preferred to weight of broadside, especially for the lighter, faster vessels such as frigates and brigs. (Nelson's CAPTAIN 74 could fire three broadsides in two minutes).

Most guns were long guns (going up to over 9 feet or 3 metres), which had a longer range and were relatively more accurate. Maximum range was up to two miles (with the maximum elevation of the gun of about 10 degrees), but the optimum range was reckoned as only half the effective killing range of 200 yards of a musket shot i.e. 100 yards. A newer kind of gun, the carronade, came into use from the late 1770s and often replaced some of the long guns or supplemented them in a ship's armament (making it difficult to add up the number of guns to the official rating of the number of long guns). The carronade was lighter and shorter (one quarter of the weight of a long gun of the same calibre and between 3-4 feet or about one metre long), fired heavy shot of 32, 24 or 18 pounds, and could be worked faster by fewer men (three or four although as few as two men could fire it). Although it had a shorter range, within that range it packed a high timber-shattering impact.

It is sometimes difficult to establish the armament of warships given that it was often changed during their long periods of service.

The total weight of the guns, and of the ball shot which had to be carried for them, was very considerable and had to be distributed about the vessel with care.

Ships-of-the-Line

So-called because they formed a line in battles between fleets. They had two to three covered gun-decks. The largest had 120 guns on three covered gundecks. In the Adriatic in the period under review, the British ships-of-the-line were so-called 3rd rate ships of two gun-decks and 74 guns, which became standard in the later period of the war. (By 1814 out of a total of 99 ships-of-the-line in the British navy in service at sea, 85 were 74s). They weighed between 1600-2000 tons (calculations of tonnage and draught were arbitrary and could vary). They had crews of more than 600 sailors and marines, a large number being required to man the range of heavy guns in rapid broadsides. Marines, as well as serving as marksmen in close engagements, also helped to serve the guns, and were meant to help police the vessel and support the officers in the event of indiscipline or mutiny by sailors. From 1808 the number of marines was set at one fifth of the ship's complement (one sixth on smaller ships) .

An example of a ship-of-the-line in Admiral Fremantle's squadron in the Adriatic is:

MILFORD, 3rd Rate Ship-of-the-Line 74
Fremantle's flagship, commanded by Capt. John Duff Markland
Built Milford Haven, Wales. Launched and went into service 1809
1919 tons
181 ft x 50 ft x 21 ft(hold)
Crew of 640 men
28 x 32 pdrs on lower gundeck
30 x 18 pdrs on upper gundeck
14 x 32 pdr carronades on quarterdeck
4 x 32 pdr carronades on forecastle
6 x 18 pdr carronades in the roundhouse/poop
MILFORD went into harbour service and was broken up in 1846

Frigates

Smaller than ships-of-the-line, frigates (with three masts) and brigs or sloops (with two masts), were often collectively described as cruisers. They were lighter and faster and with less draught could move in shallower waters. With favourable weather a frigate could achieve a speed of 14 knots or 14 sea miles (about 26 kilometers) per hour, but its average speed was much less. Cruisers were used for patrolling (the eyes of the fleet), commerce-raiding, carrying messages and passengers. They were the normal vessels making up the Adriatic squadron, supplemented by one or more ships-of-the-line whenever there was the danger of a French ship-of-the-line coming out of Venice.

The armament of a frigate was variable (it is difficult to reconcile the data in different sources) and never seems to have been as standardised as their ratings by long guns would suggest.

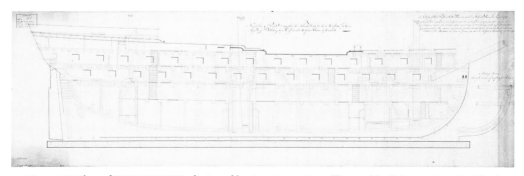

Figure 58. Plan of HMS MILFORD, designed by Jean-Louis Barrallier and built by Jacobs of Milford Haven, 74-gun 3rd rate ship-of-the-line (National Maritime Museum).

It would seem that it was possible to replace long guns with a greater number of carronades, irrespective of the limited number of gunports on the single largely covered gundeck, by placing them on the surface decks (quarterdeck and forecastle). Their main weapon on the gundeck was the 18 pounder long gun or culverin. The 9 pounder long gun or demi-culverin on the suface decks was progressively replaced by the carronade.

Of the 121 x 5th rate frigates of between 32-44 guns of the British Navy that were in full commission for service at sea in 1814, 51 were classed as having 38 guns and 48 as having 36 guns (but these figures are deceptive given the addition of carronades). Their tonnage ranged from 900-1100 and they carried crews of 200-300 men. A good example of a frigate serving in the Adriatic is:

APOLLO 5th Rate Frigate 38
Launched 1805 Burlesdon
1086 tons
154 ft x 40 ft x 15 ft (draught)
Crew of 284 men
28 x 18 pdrs on gundeck
2 x 9 pdrs + 12 x 32 pdr carronades on quarterdeck
2 x 9pdrs + 2 x 32 pdr carronades on forecastle

APOLLO was commanded from 1808 by Captain B. Wilkinson Taylor. It supported the capture of the islands of Augusta (Lastovo) and Curzola (Korčula) in February 1813. Captain Taylor was drowned at Brindisi in 1814.

APOLLO stayed in service until the Crimean War of 1854-56 and was broken up in 1856. Other frigates that saw service in the Adriatic met worse fates. Hoste's AMPHION, that he commanded in the March 1811 Battle of Lissa, was deliberately sunk at Greenwich in 1820 to serve as a breakwater. The older UNITÉ, originally a French vessel but captured by the British, which was first in the Adriatic from 1806-9 under Captain Patrick Campbell and from Sept.1811 under Captain Edwin Henry Chamberlayne, had the dubious distinction of being one of the last of the notorious prison hulks, moored in the Thames at Woolwich before being broken up in 1858.

Brigs and Sloops

This category is more difficult to characterise as the same vessels are sometimes described both as brigs and sloops. Sloop was a general term for warships of under 20 guns. Contemporary listings distinguished between ship-sloops and brig-sloops. Essentially they were smaller than frigates, had two masts and a single gundeck. As 6th Rate vessels they ranged from 270-400 tons. Of the 207 brigs/sloops of the British navy at sea in 1814, 121 carried 18 guns and 42 carried 16 guns. Their main armament was the 24 pounder carronade. They had crews of 90-120 men (a commercial brig of equivalent tonnage but without guns could be sailed by a crew of 10-12 men). Those that served in the Adriatic included:

WEAZLE Brig-Sloop 18 of 'Cruizer' class
Launched 1805, Topsham (nr Exeter, Devon)

Figure 59. Frigate of 38 guns, built 1805 (National Maritime Museum).

388 tons
100 ft x 31ft x 12 ¾ ft (hold)
Crew of 121 men
16 x 32 pdr carronades
2 x 6 pdrs
WEAZLE was in the Adriatic 1806-7, 1809, 1810-14

Captains included Commander promoted Capt. John CLAVELL Oct-1807-June 1811, Commander J. W. ANDREW (battle with RIVOLI Feb. 1812), Commander James BLACK 1813.

Fremantle's squadron reached its maximum strength in January-February 1814 with four ships-of –the-line (74s), four frigates, and five sloops.

Boats

All British warships of the categories described above carried boats. These played an important part in their activity in coastal waters and among the Dalmatian islands, particulary in attacks on coastal batteries and fortifications, or in 'cutting-out' actions to capture vessels in harbours. The largest was the **launch** of variable lengths between 18 feet (about 6 metres) and 34 feet (10 metres) according to the size of warship carrying it, armed with a carronade

Figure 60. HMS REINDEER, 18-gun Cruizer-class brig, built 1804.

on a slide, with 14-16 oars and rigged as a sailing vessel. **Barges** and **pinnaces** were between 28-32 feet (8 ½ -9 ¾ metres) and had between 8-16 oars, and were fitted with masts. **Cutters** of 25 feet (about 7 ½ metres) had 8 oars and were also fitted with masts. Finally there was the **jolly-boat**, a smaller cutter of 18 feet (5 ½ metres). Ships-of –the-line carried six boats (launch, barge, pinnace, two cutters, and jolly-boat); frigates five (barge, launch, two cutters, jolly-boat); brig/sloops two-three. All these boats were fitted into the waist of the ship between the forecastle and quarterdeck with their masts taken down, except for the jolly-boat which was dragged astern. They could take considerable numbers of men (a cutter could take 30-40) for the kinds of attacks described.

Gunboats

The gunboats, brought to Lissa with the British army force in 1812, officially belonged to the navy of Sicily, where the flotilla was commanded by a British naval captain (Captain Robert Hall, who was seconded to the Sicilian navy with a special rank and wore Sicilian uniform). It was placed at the disposal of the British army (and was hence often described as the army flotilla of gunboats, even though they continued to fly Sicilian colours). The gunboats were commanded by British army officers and crewed by Sicilian or other local sailors, with some soldiers seconded to them.The gunboats which came to Lissa had been sent first to the Ionian Islands for use by the British army garrison there, after the islands (except Corfu) were captured from the French in 1809-10. Such gunboats (and those built and used by the French for the defence of the Adriatic coasts) were usually no larger than ship's boats, had both oars and sails, and were armed with one or two guns, either long guns or more probably carronades mounted on slides, which pointed fore and aft (so that the direction of the boat had to be changed to aim them). The gunboat flotilla was given back to the Sicilian government in 1814.

Supplies

In the Adriatic, where so much of the coast was under enemy control, the supply of food and drink for the large crews of the British warships was a problem. A ship-of-the-line with a crew of 600 men often needed to be 'completed' with enough food, drink (and ammunition) for six months. Very large quantities were needed, posing problems of safe storage and conservation on board ship. In times before refrigeration, on both land and sea, food was preserved by salting, smoking and pickling. In the Adriatic, the supplies to British warships included vinegar and currants. Drink, especially safe fresh water, was a particular problem. The abundant fresh water spring near the shore at Comisa/Comissa (Komiža) on the south-west coast of Lissa (Vis) was particularly important. Otherwise, besides rum (for mixing with water to make grog), British warships in the Adriatic carried large amounts of wine, and lemon juice (with

Figure 61. British Army Gunboat, 1800.

220

sugar to mix with it). More surprisingly, they also carried large quantities of cocoa. Whenever possible, supplies were bought from the inhabitants of the islands and coastal communities, with even live cattle being taken on board. Otherwise the British squadron was supplied by transport ships, usually from Malta. Everything had to be accounted for. The records of a warship included monthly registers giving not only the number and names of the crew, but also of all passengers (including prisoners of war) and whether given full or half rations.

Visibility at Sea

In good weather, the sail of another vessel (hull-down) could be seen on the horizon, from the mast-head, at a distance of about 12 miles (19 kilometetres), giving all-round visibility of about 24 miles (38 kilometres). The narrowest part of the Adriatic, at its entrance in the Strait of Otranto, is about 45 miles or 75 kilometers. Similarly the distance from the north-west corner of Istria to Venice is about 55 miles or 90 kilometers. These are important considerations in assessing the ability of the British cruisers to detect the movement of enemy ships.

The entrance to Port St George on Lissa (Vis) was only about 14 miles or 22 kilometers from the town of Lessina (Hvar) behind which the hills rose to between 300 feet or 100 metres and about 800 feet or 240 metres (where the French built Fort Napoleon). In all but the worst daytime weather conditions, Lissa was clearly visible from Lessina, and vice versa. Similarly the hills around Port St George rise to about the same height (which considerably increases the view to the horizon). The distance from there to the channels between the islands (between the mainland and the western end of the Island of Brac), through which all coastal shipping had to pass to move up the Dalmatian coast, was between about 20 miles or 32 kilometers and 28 miles or 45 kilometers. The British could have seen almost all daytime movement of shipping.

Sources

Archibald, E. H. H.: The Fighting Ship in the Royal Navy
Colledge: Ships of the Royal Navy – An Historical Index, 1969
Gardiner, Robert ed.: Fleet Battle and Blockade, 1966
Lavery, Bernard: Nelson's Navy, 1989. The Arming and Fitting of English Ships of War, 1987
Leckey, H. S.: The King's Ships, London 1913-14
Lyon, David J.: The Sailing Navy List 1688-1860, London 1993
Woodman, Richard (and Gardiner, Robert): The Victory of Seapower, 1998

Soldiers

Regiments of the British army usually had two battalions each of 1000 or more men, and each divided into ten companies of about 100 or more men. Except for sharing the same depot in Britain, wearing the same uniform, and sharing the same honorary colonel, regimental standard and battle honours, the two battalions could follow very different paths. Companies or smaller units or even individual officers, could be detached to serve elsewhere. Officers could be promoted into (or purchase commissions in) a series of regiments. English infantry regiments, while sometimes already strongly associated with counties in England (that were later to be recognised in their names), were known by their number, e.g. 35th Foot

Most armies during the Napoleonic period had foreign officers and recruited their troops from a variety of non-national sources. There was a long tradition of Irish military families serving in the Austrian army, which also had many French or Savoyard officers, as well as Croatian and Serbian soldiers in the Grenzer regiments of the military borderland. (The Russian army and navy also had numerous foreign officers, its navy being particularly dependent on British officers who had permission to join it, especially in time of peace when the British navy could not employ all its officers and put many on to half pay).

Throughout the nineteenth century the British army depended heavily on Ireland as its principal area of recruitment, even for its nominally English regiments. (There were also large numbers of Irish in the Royal Navy). From the second half of the eighteenth century and during the Napoleonic wars, Scottish regiments (recruited with the help of Highland clan chieftains) were important, and a large numbers of officers throughout the British army were Scots. By the middle of the nineteenth century, the depopulation and resentments brought about by the Highland clearances, and the decline of the clan system, reduced the numbers of Scottish recruits. On the other hand, the great famine in Ireland drove even more Irish to join the British army for service throughout the growing British Empire. It has been estimated than a half to two-thirds of recruits to the British army at the middle of the nineteenth century were Irish.

The constant need for men for the increasing large armies of the later Napoleonic wars meant that the British army also raised formations of foreign troops, either of emigrés or in the areas in which it was engaged.

The British Garrison on Lissa

Canon Doimi gives a detailed description of the arrival of the British garrison, but much of the detail can be improved or corrected by reference to the official British records.

The commander of the garrison on Lissa, Lieut.-Colonel Robertson (see Appendix 3: Biographical Notes) held his commission in the **Sicilian Regiment of Foot**, a regiment which had been raised in Sicily in 1806 and sent to Malta in 1807 (and was to be disbanded in 1816). Although no other officers or men of this regiment were posted to Lissa. Robertson had, however, held two commissions in his earlier military career in the 35th Regiment of Foot that formed the main part of the Lissa garrison.

The details of the troops under Robertson's command can be found in the records of the individual records. Robertson summarised the situation in a list of the units and their numbers dated 16 August 1813.[1]

35th Regiment of Foot

Also called the Sussex Regiment (1805), Royal Sussex Regiment (1832) merged with other regiments to form the third battalion of the present Queen's Regiment.

Regimental museum is in the Redoubt Fortress, Eastbourne, Sussex

---

[1] Fremantle Papers, 38/6/7

In 1812 the 1st battalion of the regiment was stationed in the Ionian Islands with its headquarters on Zante. In the regimental monthly returns for March,[2] the following data is given about the forces sent to Lissa:

1 Major: John Herries
2 Captains: Francis May, Thomas King
2 Lieutenants: Archibald McDonald, Richard Webb
1 Ensign: J. B. Hildebrand
1 Asst. Surgeon: J. H. Ludlow
8 sergeants
3 drummers
200 rank and file (i.e. 2 companies each commanded by a captain)

An additional note indicated that Lieut. McDonald and 27 men were attached to the army flotilla. (Doimi calls him Henry and says there were 6 gunboats, whereas it seems only 3 plus a bow-boat were sent to Lissa).[3]

There were minor changes in the monthly returns for the next 3 years. Captain King and then Major Herries were replaced by Captain (promoted Major) John Slessor by January 1815 (Doimi has Slessor in the first parade immediately after the arrival of the garrison),[4] and additional lieutenants, Richard E. Butler and Phineas Ellis arrived in July 1812 and Sept. 1813 respectively. McDonald had been promoted to captain and Hildebrand to lieutenant by Dec. 1813.[5]

Of these officers three, Slessor, McDonald, and Hildebrand, fought at and survived Waterloo (although McDonald was severely wounded).[6]

The regiments wore a scarlet uniform with yellow facings.

Royal Corsican Rangers

Raised from 1803 in Minorca (Balearic Islands) by Hudson Lowe (see Appendix 3: Biographical Notes) from Corsican emigrés. They fought at Maida in Italy (1806) and in the capture of the Ionian Islands (1809-10) where they subsequently formed part of the garrison until disbanded at the end of the war. In 1809 the regiment had 1368 men in 12 companies. Some were detached to Sicily and Malta. 200 (two companies) were sent to Lissa. Their officers were:[7]

Captains: P. A. Gerolamé or Girolamia, Pearce Lowen (See Appendix 3: Biographical Notes)
Lieut.: Cosmo Pagliano
Ensigns: D. A. Peretté, Luigi Rigo
(Doimi names the officers as Girolimi, Paretti, and Rigo and Giammeria).[8]

2   PRO, WO 17/145
3   Foretic, op. cit. and Novak, op. cit.
4   idem
5   PRO, WO 17/262
6   Trimen, Richard: A Historical Memoir of the 35th Royal Sussex Regimet of Foot, Southampton 1873
7   Army Lists. PRO, WO 380/5
8   Foretic, op. cit., p. 630, rendered somewhat differently in Novak, op. cit., p. 211

Robertson frequently complained about the indiscipline and desertions of the Corsicans. Even an officer, Rigo, promoted lieutenant, deserted after robbing a house.[9]

The Corsicans wore green uniforms with scarlet facings.

De Rolls Regiment

Named after Louis-Robert-Francis-Joseph, baron de Roll d'Emenholz de Soleure, captain of the French king's Garde Suisse before the Revolution, who died in England, near Tonbridge, Kent in 1813. He raised the regiment in 1794 to serve in the British army, recruiting it mainly from emigré Swiss members of the former Garde Suisse. It served in Egypt in 1801 and 1807. In 1812, out of its 12 companies, four were in Sicily, three in Malta, three on campaign in Spain, and two in the Ionian Islands, one of which was sent to Lissa under the command of:

Captain Joseph Barbier
Lieut. Otto Salinger

(Doimi remembered/invented a Major Roll, not found in any British records and whose name clearly reflects that of the De Rolls Regiment).

The regiment was disbanded in 1816.[10]

Calabrian Free Corps

Raised in 1809 as sharp-shooters and recruited from the Calabrian insurgents against the French who fled to Sicily. The company of 100 men that was sent to Lissa was commanded by Captain Roncus (Doimi's Ronca or Rocca). Their officers wore scarlet jackets and light blue pantaloons, the men blue-green jackets and light grey pantaloons, facings of light yellow.[11]

Royal Artillery

A small detachment of one lieutenant, one sergeant, 2 bombardiers (i.e. corporals) and 10 gunners accompanied Robertson's force. These were involved in the British attack on Augusta (Lastovo) and Curzola (Korčula) in Feb. 1813. The lieutenant was W. K. Rains whom Doimi called Capt. Rens and described as an excellent soldier and a coin collector.[12]

Colonel Robertson's list of the garrison of Lissa in August shows two significant additions, bringing the total size of his force from 600 to 820 (of which about 100 were by now detached to Augusta and Curzola and which, as the list notes, included only 160 British nationals). The two new formations were:

Italian Levy

---

9   Fremantle Papers, 38/6/22
10   Grouvel, Vicomte: Les Corps de Troupes de L'Emigration Française 1789-1815, 1957. PRO, WO 17/298
11   Foretic and Novak, op. cit. Journal of the Society of Army Historical Research, no. 50 (1972): The Auxiliaries: Foreigners and Miscellaneous Regiments 1802-17
12   Laws: Battery Records, pp. 154 and 157, Foretic, op. cit., p. 631

This was the result of a project favoured by Lord Bentinck (who sympathised with Italian nationalists who sought the unification of Italy). It was raised in 1812 from Italian prisoners-of-war in England, in Sicily, and from various other Italians and non-Italians who were disaffected with French rule. The Austrian general, Laval Nugent, proposed to Bentinck that it could absorb some of the many Austrian officers who had been discharged under French pressure from the Austrian army or who otherwise wanted to join the British to fight the French. Nugent hoped that the Italian Levy could give him substantial support in his plans to raise insurrection against the French in the Illyrian Provinces. In August 1813 there were only 91 soldiers of the Italian Levy on Lissa, and they did go, together with most of the other troops on Lissa, to fight alongside the Austrians under Nugent in north Italy. Bentinck himself used the bulk of the Italian Levy (two battalions) for his march on Genoa in April 1814.

Illyrian Light Infantry

Robertson had proposed to Bentinck (and Bentinck had sought and obtained approval from the War Office in London) that he raise a force of Croatians, soldiers of the Grenzer regiments and others who were deserting from the French in increasing numbers (see Defence of Lissa). In August 1813 it appears in Robertson's list with the name Illyrian Light Infantry. It had only 50 men, but by this stage, as Austria had entered the war, the Grenzer soldiers, who were deserting the French in large numbers, were transferred either directly to Nugent's forces in Istria, or joined the other Austrian forces which advanced south into Dalmatia.

Appendix 5: Remains

The following account of what has become of the forts and other British sites on Vis and Korčula is extracted (with some editing and updating) from the paper on English Monuments in Dalmatia by Cvito Fiskovic at the 1977 symposium on Dubrovnik's Relations with England organised by the University of Zagreb.

Vis (Lissa)

The main British fortress was low and long, with sloping walls, surrounded by a ditch. Originally named as Fort George after the then king George III, it is now called Fortica. Substantial remains (mainly built of rough-hewn stone) have survived. There are signs that the entrance was approached by a wooden drawbridge. The key-stone to the arch of this gate is carved with a Union Jack. There are flower-reliefs on bosses above and on each side of the arch, above which there is the inscription (now partly missing):

GEORGE THE THIRD
By the Grace of God King of Great Britain and Ireland etc.
1813

Inside the fort there are two courtyards surrounded by ditches. In the north courtyard there is a well. On the terraces of the internal fortifications there are platforms for cannon with semi-circle apertures in the walls that are also loop-holed for muskets. The arches of doors and other apertures are built of brick. Some parts of the interior were changed during the Austrian period, when the present barracks building was added. Fort George was used as a barracks by the Yugoslav army, after which it has been abandoned and become derelict.

South of Fort George, above the cove of Svitnja, but not vible from the harbour or its approaches, there are the remains of the British three-storey circular tower, with a roof terrace above the strong vault, which was named after Bentinck. The first Austrian maps continued to use this name, but it is now long-since forgotten and the tower is popularly called Terjun. The base of the tower is surrounded by the substantial remains of a star-shaped rampart. It would appear from debris around the tower that attempts were made to blow it up.

Of the third fort named after Robertson, a small part of the wall remains, clearly visible on the top of its hill from the harbour. The fourth, Wellington was on Juraj Hill (the British called it Whitby Hill) on the east side of the entrance to the harbour. It had circular walls, thinner than those at Fort Bentinck, which were loop-holed. Internally it was strengthened with two cross-walls, between which there was the circular support for the brick-built vault, which has now disappeared. Some ruins remain but are not visible from the harbour.

On the eastern side of the little island in front of the entrance to Vis harbour, the English built a low battery the ruins of which can still be seen. The British named the island after Hoste. The Austrians continued to call it Hoste Island, but since the construction of the lighthouse it has been called Mala Lanterna.

After the departure of the British, the Austrians strengthened the forts, until they suddenly decided to evacuate and disarm Vis, partially demolishing the forts. (There had been yet another Battle of Lissa/Vis in 1866 when the Austrian navy, largely crewed by Croatian and Dalmatian sailors, decisively defeated the Italian navy).

A lonely cemetery for British seamen remains beside the sea on the Sveti Juraj peninsula (on the eastern side of the entrance to Vis harbour), although the bones of the seamen were removed after the Second World War to the British military cemetery in Belgrade. The cemetery is encircled by a stone wall, which is entered through a small gate or 'bugnato' (between rusticated square pillars). On the wall there was the inscription:

HERE
LIE INCLOSED HTEREI MAIN
OF BRITISH SEAMAN WHO
LOST THEIR LIVES IN
DEFENCE OF THEIR KING
AND COUNTRY
A. D. MDCCCXV

The mistakes in the second line are ascribed to the lack of knowledge of English of the stonemason.

In the middle of the cemetery there was a three-sided stone prism with stone vase above it. The inscription on a marble tablet read:

THIS
MONUMENT WAS ERECTED
BY THE CAPTAIN AND OFFICERS
OF
THE BRITISH LINE OF BATTLE SHIP
'VICTORIOUS'
IN MEMORY OF
ELEVEN BRAVE ENGLISHMEN
INTERRED NEAR THIS SPOT
WHO DIED OF THE WOUNDS THEY RECEIVED
ON THE 22 OF FEBRUARY 1812
IN ACTION WITH THE FRENCH SHIP
'RIVOLI'
OF 74 GUNS
ON THE COAST OF VENICE
AS
A TRIBUTE DUE TO THEM
AND THE MANY GALLANT FELLOWS
WHO LOST THEIR LIVES ON THAT DAY
IN THEIR COUNTRY'S CAUSE

In 1963 this was replaced by a new inscription, now on the inside wall of the cemetery (together with two others dedicated to the British dead in the Second Wold War), with the additional words:

THE ABOVE WAS INSCRIBED ON A MONUMENT FORMERLY
STANDING IN THIS CEMETERY WHICH

WAS DESTROYED DURING WORLD WAR II
APRIL 1963

During the Italian occupation at the beginning of the Second World War, a four-sided stone pillar disappeared from the cemetery. (A lion monument to the Austrian victory over Italy in the battle of Lissa of 1866 was also removed but a copy has been installed with other recent memorials in the main graveyard closer to the town). An inscription on the pillar read:

ERECTED TO THE MEMORY
OF BRITISH OFFICERS AND
MEN KILLED IN THE BATTLE
OF LISSA ON 13TH MARCH 1811

On the ground there is still a low tomb covered with the original slab on which is inscribed:

HON CHARLES ANSON
A. D. 1812

This was the unfortunate midshipman killed by the accidental and never-explained discharge of one of BACCHANTE's guns.

Korčula

The round tower on the hill of Sveto Vlaho (S. Biaggo or St. Blaize) above the town of Korčula (Curzola) still remains intact, although restored and remodelled, and used for various purposes since it was built in 1813. It was built after the capture of Korčula by the British in February 1813 and according to the agreement Admiral Fremantle had made with the inhabitants. It was designed by Captain Taylor of the Frigate APOLLO and a Lieut. Cole of the 81st. Regt., and built with the help of the crews of various ships of the British squadron which made detours to Korčula for this purpose. It was built within earlier Venetian fortifications, but nothing remains either of these or of any other structures or subsidiary ramparts the British might have erected. At some stage there seems also to have been a small battlemented watch-tower which stood on top of the tower but this also disappeared (it is not shown on the original British plans and was probably a later decorative addition).

The British also paid the local stonemasons and builders to build roads, particularly one from Korčula to Lumbarda.

On the promenade beside the sea on the south side of the town, there is a semi-circular enwalled space lined with a stone bench. At each end of the wall there are stone spheres on pillars, and next to the low gate that opens towards the seat and on the stone pavement, there are two obelisks (which had stone balls on top which have disappeared). Two latin inscriptions are cut into the pedestals of the obelisks, in honour of Captain Lowen (see Appendix 3: Biographical Notes), the army officer seconded to Korčula from Vis. These were placed there by the inhabitants after his departure, and record their gratitude to him and the freedom they had enjoyed under him.

Part 3:
A Diversionary Attack in the Adriatic 1812

The British, Montenegro and Russia 1812

The present study is part of a larger project concerning the activities of the British in the Adriatic during the Napoleonic wars, particularly their occupation of the island of Lissa (Vis).[1] Throughout this period, the officers of the British Royal Navy had close links with those of Tsarist Russia, a number of the latter being British by birth who had transferred to the Russian service during the reign of Catherine the Great. This facilitated cooperation in the Adriatic in the earlier stages of the wars against the French. Although broken by Tsar Alexander's agreement with Napoleon at Tilsit in 1807 and the subsequent loss of the Russian Mediterranean fleet, they were to be restored in 1812 with Napoleon's invasion of Russia. This is the story of proposals for collaboration in the Adriatic between Britain and Russia, also involving the people of Montenego. They represent an alternative scenario that was never realised, except insofar as the British did go on in 1813 to liberate the eastern cost of the Adriatic, but in collaboration with the Austrians, and the Montenegrins took action against the French in 1813-14.

The People of Montenegro, being Greek Orthodox, had enjoyed a long relationship with Russia, dating back to the time of Peter the Great. As recently as 1806-07 they had assisted the Russian fleet, based in the Bocca of Cattaro (Boka Kotorska now in Montenegro), to attack French-held Dubrovnik. However, the agreement reached by Napoleon and Tsar Alexander at Tilsit in June 1807, guaranteed the French in their possession of Dubrovnik, the Bocca, and

Figure 1. Peter Petrovich Njegos (1748–1830), Serbian Orthodox Prince-Bishop of Montenegro.

---

[1] NB The British used Italian place names and not the Slav names used today. In transcribing and summarising documents in reported speech, the author has tried to use the language and names of people and places as given in the text.

Figure 2. French power in the Adriatic before Napoleon's attack on Russia in 1812.

the coast as far south as Budva. The Prince-Bishop, or Vladika of Montenegro, Peter Petrovich Njegos, was sworn to desist from further attacks on the French.

The steady deterioration in relations between France and Russia meant that by late 1811 war between them seemed inevitable. Although, since Tilsit, Britain had been technically at war with Russia as an ally of France, it could look forward with satisfaction to again having Russia as an ally against France. This added a new dimension to the British objective of stirring up revolts against the French in the Adriatic. British plans had relied on Austrian involvement or compliance in coordinated risings against the French in the Illyrian Provinces,[2] North Italy, Vorarlberg and Tirol. However, on March 1812, Austria was forced into an alliance with Napoleon to support him in his attack on Russia. (The Austrians subsequently tried to reassure both the British and the Russians that they were reluctant allies and that their forces would endeavour to avoid major military confrontations with the Russians). The question that arose from late 1811 was how, when Napoleon attacked Russia, the British could help the Russians by involving themselves in a diversion in the Mediterranean.

But first, the Russians would have to extricate themselves from their war on the Danube with the Ottoman Empire, begun in 1806 and renewed in December 1809 after a two-year truce mediated by Napoleon after Tilsit. A Russian army had occupied the principalities of Wallachia and Moldavia to the north of the Danube. Peace talks with the Turks were begun in October 1811. The young Stratford Canning, British ambassador in Constantinople, was able to facilitate the lengthy and problematic negotiations, despite the contrary efforts of the French ambassador to keep the Turks at war with the Russians. The Treaty of Bucharest was finally agreed, signed for the Russians by General Kutuzov, on 25 May 1812.

---

[2] Created by Napoleon after acquiring from Austria by the war of 1809 Croatia west of the Sava, which was joined to Dalmatia to the south, and Istria and parts of what is now Slovenia and Italy to the north.

Figure 3A. Stratford Canning, 1st Viscount Stratford de Redcliffe (1786–1880), British Ambassador to Constantinople. Portrait, aged 29, from biography by Stanley Lane-Poole, 1888.

Figure 3B. General Mikhail Kutuzov (1745–1813), supreme commander of the Russian forces, 1812, portrait by R.M. Volkov, 1850.

In the meantime, Tsar Alexander had been advised, in a memorandum of 3 February 1812 from his war minister, Barclay de Tolly, that, after peace was made with the Turks, there should be a diversionary attack on the French in the Mediterranean.[3] Alexander welcomed the idea. The Tsar was also excited by the possibility of rousing the Orthodox Slav peoples of the Balkans in support. Alexander's grandmother, Catherine the Great had nurtured the ambition of extending Russian protection to the Orthodox and Slav subjects of the Ottoman Empire, particularly in the Balkans. (The policy was to be pursued throughout the nineteenth century, and it persists to this day in Russian relations with Serbia and Montenegro). On 9 April 1812, Alexander, in an audience with his former minister for the navy, Admiral Pavel Chichagov (or Tchitchagoff), ordered him to develop plans for such a diversionary counterattack against the French. He was to proceed to Bucharest to replace General Kutuzov as commander of the Russian army on the Danube, speed up the conclusion of peace with the Turks and even endeavour to persuade them to join an alliance with Russia.[4]

Chichagov only arrived at Bucharest on 27 May, two days after the Treaty of Bucharest had already been signed by Kutuzov. However, it had still to be ratified by the Sultan and the Tsar. From the point of view of using the Danube army for a diversionary attack on the French, the treaty was problematic. While it gave Russia Bessarabia (present-day Moldova), it confirmed Wallachia and Moldavia as being subject to the Sultan. This implied that the Russian army

[3]   Alan Palmer: Alexander I (London 1974) p. 209
[4]   ibid p. 214 and Joanna Wood: The Commissioner's Daughter: The Story of Elizabeth Proby and Admiral Chichagov (Witney, Oxon 2000) p. 205 & note. Like other officers of the Russian navy he had trained in England where he married the daughter of the RN commissioner at Chatham.

Figure 4A. Tsar Alexander I (1771–1825), oil painting by Stepan Shchukin, 1809 (Regional Art Museum, Tver).

Figure 4B. Prince Michael Andreas Barclay de Tolly (1761–1818), detail of portrait by George Dawe, 1829 (Military Gallery of the Winter Palace, Saint Petersburg).

Figure 5. Admiral Pavel Vasilyevich Chichagov (1767–1849), portrait by James Saxon, 1824 (State Hermitage Museum copy from Saxon portrait).

would have to evacuate them by withdrawing to the east. On the other hand, Serbia was given a limited measure of autonomy. To reach the Mediterranean on the Adriatic coast, the Russians would have to move west from Bucharest and Wallachia, cross Serbia and the Turkish Sandjak of Novi Pazar to reach Montenegro, or cross Serbia and Bosnia to reach the Adriatic coast further north. This would clearly need the agreement of the Sultan. The Austrians, whose territories reached the Danube north of Serbia and who were already unwilling allies of the French, were clearly also going to be hostile.

Admiral Fremantle goes to Lissa

On 5 April 1812 a British garrison had finally arrived on the island of Lissa (Vis) in the Adriatic, long used as a base for ships of the Royal Navy. Lissa now became a base for any operations against the French. Premature rumours of movements by the Serbians and Montenegrins were reaching Lissa by May, when Captain Taylor of the frigate 'APOLLO' reported this to his superiors.[5] Colonel Robertson, the commander of the garrison was soon after (14 May) to report further developments to general Lord William Bentinck, the commander-in-chief of the British armies in the Mediterranean, who was based in Sicily. He had just received news of a battle between the French and the Montenegrins at the Bocca, in which the French had suffered many casualties. The Montenegrins had 20,000 men at the Bocca and its vicinity, as against 4000 French, and a further attack was to be made on 25 May. Furthermore the Montenegrins had a Russian general, two colonels and many other Russian officers with them.[6]

Figure 6. Colonel George Duncan Robertson of Strown (d. 1842), commander of the garrison of Lissa (Vis) 1812 (artist unknown).

---

[5] Copy of text not found although enclosed Rowley at Messina to Fremantle 3 Jun 1812 (National Maritime Musem, Rowley papers)
[6] National Archives WO 1/311

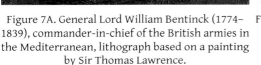

Figure 7A. General Lord William Bentinck (1774–1839), commander-in-chief of the British armies in the Mediterranean, lithograph based on a painting by Sir Thomas Lawrence.

Figure 7B. Admiral Thomas Fremantle (1765–1819), in command of the British navy in the eastern Mediterranean, artist unknown.

No evidence has been found of any attack by the Montenegrins on the French in May 1812 or that numerous Russian officers had arrived at the Bocca . The Vladika was biding his time. But when Bentinck received Robertson's letter, he had to take it seriously and took immediate action. He immediately solicited the assistance of Admiral Thomas Fremantle, then stationed in Sicily and in command of the British navy in the eastern Mediterranean, including the Ionian and Adriatic seas. He asked Fremantle to sail to Lissa, stopping at Zante in the Ionian Islands to pick up British troops, and to support the Montenegrin attack on the French. In his letter to Fremantle of 8 June, Bentinck wrote that he had hoped that any partial uprising against the French on the eastern side of the Adriatic might have waited until an uprising he was hoping for took place in Italy.

> 'But as this insurrection has unfortunately broken out; and the apparently certain occurrence of War between Russia and France, may probably produce a similar effect in Italy, and thus give accidentally to this transaction the desired coincidence, I have determined to give to the Montenegrins every assistance that the limited Force in the Ionian Islands will afford. If the Dalmatians should be successful, it is impossible to calculate the extent to which this insurrection may go, or the important diversion that may be made in favour of Russia and Spain'.[7]

On 10 June, Fremantle wrote to his superior, Admiral Pellew, commanding the British fleet in the Mediterranean, to explain why he had agreed to Bentinck's proposal without waiting for

---

[7]   quoted Ann Parry: The Admirals Fremantle (London 1971) p. 101-02

Figure 8. Admiral Edward Pellew, 1st Viscount Exmouth
(1757–1833), commander of the British fleet in the
Mediterranean, portrait by James Northcote, 1804
(National Portrait Gallery).

Pellew's approval. He left Palermo on 13 June, taking with him a number of persons whom Bentinck thought would be useful,[8] including Colonel Francesco Danese, a Dalmatian, who had served both Venice and Austria and had been involved in failed uprisings against the French in 1806 and 1809 before taking refuge in Vienna. The previous summer, as one of a number of officers and agents in a network being established by the Austrian general Laval Nugent and the chief 'confidential agent' in Vienna, John Mordaunt Johnson, he had left Vienna and proceeded via Brood (Slavonski Brod on the river Sava), and Sarajevo to Scutari (now Shkoder in northern Albania), which neighboured Montenegro, and where there was another member of the network, the Austrian consul, Somma. Danese had established good relations with the local Turkish pasha.[9]

Fremantle picked up the first 400 of the 1200 British troops that Bentinck had provided him at Zante on 28 June and proceeded to Lissa, where he arrived on 4 July. In a letter to his brother of 17 June at sea after leaving Palermo he had written that he was 'quite undecided as to the steps I shall pursue, all depends upon the information I obtain at Lissa'.[10] Before reaching Lissa, on

---

[8] Buckinghamshire County Archives,Fremantle Papers D/FR 39/3/9 Bentinck-Fremantle 10 June 1812
[9] Universtity of Nottingham, Portland Papers 1880 and 1881 Danese to Bentinck and Fremantle Papers D/FR 10/2/18 Danese Scutari 10 Dec 1811 to Johnson
[10] quoted Parry op.cit.. p. 102-03

2 July he had already written detailed instructions for Danese,[11] who was to go immediately to Scutari and make contact with the Montenegrins. To make him even more acceptable to the local pasha, Fremantle gave him credentials and sent the pasha a promise of action against privateers about whom he had complained to Danese the previous December.[12] Danese left Lissa on his mission on 6 July. He was to discover if hostilities had commenced at the Bocca between the Montenegrins and the French, if the Montenegrins wanted the assistance of the British ships and troops, and if so where the British should join them. Danese was also to find out how many men the Vladika disposed of and how many he had in the Bocca, if he had a plan of action, and to assess the feelings of the people of the Bocca itself, whether favourable to the French or to 'the good cause'.

Fremantle was, however, to decide that it would be inadvisable to support an attack by the Montenegrins on the French before he received any news from Danese about the situation in the Bocca and Montenegro. This was because, shortly after Danese's departure, he had been able to discuss the situation with Johnson, the British agent who from Vienna had been developing elaborate intrigues and a network of agents to provoke and support uprisings in northern Italy, the Tirol and the Illyrian provinces. These had also involved the Roman Catholic inhabitants of the Bocca. In 1811 one of his agents, the priest Brunazzi, had been active there, but he had been betrayed and his efforts undone by Breyer, the French consul at Scutari.[13]

Figure 9A & B. Field Marshal Laval Nugent von Westmeath (1777–1862), commander of Austrian actions against the French in the Adriatic area. A: original lithograph 1848; B: oil painting by Friedrich Ritter von Amerling (undated).

---

[11] WO/731 p. 319

[12] Fremantle Papers D/FR 40/2/13 Johnson Vienna 19 Aug 1811 recommending Danese to Bentinck and suggesting Danese should go to Lissa. and 40/2/18 Danese 25 Dec. 1811 Scutari to Johnson in Vienna enclosed D/FR 40/2/18/8 Danese in Malta 6 Apr 1812 to Bentinck

[13] same as footnote 12 on page 239

Figure 10. Bishop Maksimiljan Vrhovac of Zagreb
(1752–1827), portrait by unknown artist.

Any premature attack by the Orthodox Montenegrins, though there had been suggestions in earlier correspondence that he would try to involve, would probably have been unwelcome to Johnson. Before Fremantle had left Sicily, Bentinck had indeed told Fremantle that, before he had decided to support the Montenegrins, he had written to Johnson, whom he supposed to be at Durazzo (Durrës on the coast of northern Albania), to ask him to try to prevent any premature action against the French.[14] Bentinck had also given Fremantle abstracts of letters from Johnson and General Laval Nugent, his primary Austrian collaborator, to explain their objectives and activity. Johnson writing from Vienna on 24 January had told Bentinck that he would be leaving Vienna but not before mid-February to go to the coast of the Adriatic, and asked that he be met at Durazzo by one of his agents, a Captain Frizzi. Nugent had also written to Bentinck on 24 January from Vienna to say that he also intended to leave Vienna at the beginning of March and would come to Durazzo.[15]

In early June, a report had been submitted to Bentinck by the Whig politician, Lucius Concannon, who had arrived in Sicily from Vienna at the end of May, having left Vienna in February on a long journey through the Illyrian Provinces, Italy and Napes.[16] He carried news from Johnson and Nugent that it had been certain that France would go to war with Russia,

---

[14] WO 1/311 p. 363 Bentinck to Fremantle 8 Jun 1812 encl. Bentinck to Liverpool 9 Jun 1812
[15] Fremantle Papers D/FR 39/3/3 abstracts for Fremantle from Bentinck Jun 1812. Both Johnson and Nugent came to Scutari and seem not to have reached Durazzo some distance to the south. There are several instances when Durazzo is named instead of Scutari.
[16] FO 70/51 Bentinck to Foreign Office 25 June 1812 encl. Concannon to Bentinck of 26 May and 9 June

probably in April. Johnson had intended to leave Vienna at about the end of February to put himself in contact with the Croatian and Dalmatian chiefs and also the Montenegrins. He was to have been accompanied by some officers of those countries where he thought he could raise 7-8,000 men. The Bishop of Agram (Zagreb) was very influential with the clergy in Croatia and Dalmatia, and was an intimate fried of Nugent and Johnson. He had offered his services on a most extended scale without fear of how his conduct would be viewed by the Emperor of Austria. Nugent's presence in Vienna would be essential after the departure of Johnson, but as soon as he had put things in order he would come to Sicily.

Johnson's progress to the Adriatic coast was slow and difficult. Indeed the final stages of his journey over the mountains to reach Scutari were to seriously damage his health.[17] In a letter addressed to the Foreign Office dated 7 March he was still in Vienna. He had decided to go without delay to the frontier of Dalmatia, accompanied by a Colonel Raamowsky (possibly Hrabowsky or Rabowsky mentioned to other correspondence), who had been at the head of the insurrection against the French in the previous war (1809). He hoped to have the cooperation of the bishops of Agram and Montenegro, and he was confident that he could promote the success of any operation that British forces might undertake on the coast of the Adriatic. In a further letter of 20 March he had fixed his departure for 23 March.[18] On 3 April he had been at Pressburg (now Bratislava), and by 14 June he was at Sarajevo, from where he had written to Bentinck that, although Napoleon had not declared war on Russia, French troops were assembling on the Vistula. Later in June he was at Scutari, where he also had discussions with the pasha concerning the possibility of using routes through Scutari for the passage of British goods through to the Austrian Empire. But there is no evidence that he made contact with the Montenegrins.

On 29 June Captain Rowley, in command of the British ships in the Adriatic pending the arrival of Fremantle, was off Fano near Corfu. He ordered Captain Chamberlayne of the frigate UNITE to take Captain Frizzi from his own ship EAGLE and land him at the Bojana river (near Scutari), where he was to wait until Frizzi returned with Johnson with dispatches for Bentinck and to bring them both back to Rowley off Fano. However, on 7 July, Rowley, still off Fano, gave orders to Captain Tritton of KINGFISHER to take Frizzi with dispatches to Messina. So where was Johnson? On 7 July, still on UNITE, which had picked him up near Scutari on 3 July, wrote to Bentinck that he had just been given a letter from Bentinck dated 13 June. He had intended to proceed to Sicily, but now that he had learned that Fremantle had gone with British forces to Lissa, he had decided that he had to go there to give Fremantle details of what he had learned about the situation on the Adriatic coast while he had been at Scutari.[19] Johnson was then taken on board Rowley's EAGLE and delivered to Lissa on 16 July. He immediately reported to Fremantle, but, having himself left Scutari on 3 July, he had missed Danese, who had left Lissa to go there on 6 July.

Johnson quickly persuaded Fremantle that Danese's mission was in vain. On 18 July, the day after Johnson's arrival at Lissa, Fremantle wrote to Bentinck:

---

[17] Johnson's Journal of Mission to British Fleet in Adriatic is now in the Yale University Library
[18] National Archives FO 7/111 nos. 1 and 5
[19] Portland Papers 2951

'We have little prospect of doing anything in this quarter, but this can all be explained to you by Mr Johnson'[20]

Having put Fremantle in the picture from his own point of view, Johnson sailed to Sicily.

In his letter to Bentinck of 7 July, saying that he was going to Lissa to meet Fremantle, Johnson had added that General Nugent would have explained to Bentinck the delays in his own progress through Hungary and the Turkish provinces. By yet another of the accidents and delays that would bedevil the British communications, on his way to Lissa, Fremantle had passed, going in the opposite direction to Sicily, General Laval Nugent. Nugent had left Vienna on 21 April bearing a letter for delivery to the Prince Regent in England to explain why the Austrians had felt obliged to sign the treaty of alliance of 14 March with Napoleon.[21] Nugent had been expected at Scutari by mid-June after travelling via Brood on the Sava (now Slavonski Brod in Croatia), and Bosna Seraj (now Sarajevo). Nugent had been met on the coast near Scutari by the British brig KINGFISHER and taken south, meeting Rowley off Corfu on 12 June, and arriving in Sicily before the end of June. He, like Johnson, must have been shocked to hear from Bentinck that Fremantle had gone to Lissa to support a Montenegrin attack on the French. Not only had Nugent been elaborating proposals with the British for liberating the Illyrian Provinces from the French and installing an Austrian archduke to rule them, but he was able to inform Bentinck of the Austrian alliance with French. One consequence of this was that, in the event of the British supporting an uprising in the Illyrian provinces, the Austrians would be obliged to go to war with Britain.

Bentinck immediately wrote to Fremantle on 1 July 1812 to abort the expedition and return the troops he had taken to Lissa to Zante:[22]

> '...General Nugent arrived from Vienna, and brought me a copy of the alliance made between France and Austria. By this both parties have engaged to guarantee the possessions of the other...The Emperor was of course forced into this measure.... Nugent ascertained that if the Illyrian Provinces were attacked, the Emperor would feel himself obliged to act against us... The same reasons are still more powerful against the plan which you were to execute. We must therefore abandon it for the present....'

Bentinck had also immediately prevented the remainder of the troops he had promised Fremantle from leaving Zante. They would be instead sent to Spain (where the British were fighting the Peninsular War against the French).

Fremantle at Lissa replied to Bentinck in two letters dated 24 July.[23] In the less formal and more personal of these, Fremantle told Bentinck that his letter had relieved him from much anxiety as he was fully persuaded that it would be imprudent to press the inhabitants of that county into hostilities without adequate means of supplying them. Indeed from what he had gained from Johnson it would be best to send small vessels and gunboats among the islands to empty the people and show some ostensible reason for bringing the troops without

---

[20] Portland Papers 2555
[21] Alan Palmer: Metternich, London 1982 p. 89
[22] Fremantle Papers D/FR 29/3/11 quoted Ann Parry op. cit. p. 104
[23] Portland Papers 2556 and 2557

committing their friends. Fremantle undertook to immediately send back the 400 troops he had been given to Zante. Colonel Robertson (whose initial report that the Montenegrins had attacked the French had caused Bentinck to send Fremantle to Lissa) had been with him that morning and shown him a letter (in English) from the Bocca. 'I am afraid he is much mislead in his information by a Man here who furnishes him with document, be quite assured that the whole of this country is completely subdued...without 10,000 men we can at the present moment have no reasonable hope of carrying the Natives with us'. There were as many as 700 Croats at Lessina (Hvar) and 1000 at Spalato (Split) serving the French. The only native French troops, of the 23rd Regiment of Infantry, together with Italian troops, were at Ragusa (Dubrovnik) and the Bocca, numbering not over 4000 men.[24]

In the more formal letter that he sent Bentinck on 24 July he said:

> 'Before you receive this, Mr Johnson will have informed you of my sentiments re any offensive operations which are in perfect unison with those conveyed in your letter'.

Robertson had already sent a copy of the letter he showed to Fremantle on 24 July to Bentinck on 22 July. In the covering letter to Bentinck, he stated that he had reason to believe that the inhabitants of the Bocca were ripe for revolt. He described the enclosed letter as being from a person of considerable interest in the Bocca to his brother at Lissa. The letter itself purported to be from Brother Avise at Perasto in the Bocca to Brother Anton on Lissa and was dated 19 July. The date is suspect as it is unlikely it could have reached Lissa by 24 July, but otherwise and in retrospect, the letter does not seem as preposterous as Fremantle attempted to present it. How it came to be in English is a mystery (unless it was a translated copy made for Robertson). It claimed that the French forces in the Bocca, consisting of French, Italian and Croatian troops were at loggerheads. It described the batteries guarding the entrance to the Bocca. The Catholic communities of the Bocca would collaborate with the British if ships were sent.[25]

(On this, as on future occasions, there was an almost childish competition between Fremantle and Robertson, and later Johnson, to impress Bentinck with information that they reported to him direct, together with a growing disinclination to share the intelligence they received).

So by 26 July, when Colonel Danese returned to Lissa from the Bocca, Fremantle was convinced that nothing could be done. On 3 August 1812, from his ship MILFORD in St George's Harbour Lissa, he wrote his report, enclosing all the relevant correspondence, to Admiral Pellew.[26] It was received by Pellew more than a month later on 11 September, forwarded by him on 29 September to the Admiralty in London, which copied it to the War Office where it was received on 14 November, almost 3 ½ months after Fremantle wrote it.

Fremantle wrote that on 6 July 1812 Colonel Danese left Lissa to visit the Pascia of Scutari to explain the steps taken to suppress the outrages of the Maltese and Sicilian privateers that had been the subject of a complaint to Bentinck. It was desirable to ascertain the real state of the Montenegrins. Danese was given credentials and other papers (copies enclosed) to visit the

---

[24] This information is almost the same as that given in the letter from Colonel Robertson to Bentinck of 22 July.
[25] Portland Papers 4839 Robertson to Bentinck 22 July encl. 4740
[26] National Maritime Museum Pellew Papers PEL/16 and WO 1/731 Croker Admiralty to Col. Bunbury War Office

Metropolitan and Primate of Montenegro. Danese returned on 26 July with papers from the Pascia of Scuttary and the Metropolitan of Montenegro, the former only an acknowledgement of his letter but the later contained answers to the questions of Danese. From these papers as well as the information from other sources 'I am of opinion there is no prospect of my being further useful at the present moment in the Adriatic, the purport of my Mission being entirely done away'.

The letter from Mustafa Pasha of Scutari written in Italian and dated Dulcigno (Ulcinj) 11 July 1812 was rather fuller than Fremantle suggested. The Pasha had received Fremantle's letter and seen the person sent by him (Danese) with pleasure because he knew him well. Danese had told him of all the admiral's concerns, and he would do everything in his power to be of assistance.

The written replies of the Vladika (in Italian but translated in the copy sent to Pellew) were dated Zernizza (?) 7/20 July and he styled himself 'Metropolitan Primate of Montenegro and knight of the Russian Empire of the order of Alexander Nevski'. He had been shown Fremantle's instructions to Danese by his counsellor Saverio Plamenaz. His answers were full and carefully reasoned:

It would be difficult for him to order his people to rise against the formidable power of France without knowing what advantages were to be given by the British. He had induced the whole population of the Bocche to participate with the Russians in the last war between Russia and France (in 1806-07) to prevent the Bocche falling into the hands of the French but the result had been French occupation and greater oppression. He now had no connection with the Bocchese (the Roman Catholic communities of the Bocca). He believed they would again join him but he was not willing to stir them up without an agreement with the British, the proposed terms of which he enclosed. There then followed a list of points that more or less answered the questions Fremantle had listed for Danese:

1. The Montenegrins were not then at war with French who were endeavouring to live in a good understanding with the Montenegrins and between whom there was reciprocated commerce.
2. The Montenegrin nation had no regular troops or artillery and could not fight the French without the aid of some foreign power. If this was to be Britain they would need support by sea and by land, ammunition and 'other disbursements'.
3. The Montenegrins could not absent themselves for long from their country. They would wish to know which communes in the Bocca would side with the French and which with the British.
4. The number of inhabitants who could fight could not be given as many worked in neighbouring provinces.
5. The garrisons of the Bocca were variable and composed of French, Italians and Sclavonians without any local inhabitants. There were 4000 soldiers doing garrison duty in Cattaro (Kotor). Castel Nuovo (Herceg Novi), and Budva and in the interior commune of Risana (Risan).
6. The Montenegrins were under the protection of Russia to whom they owed allegiance. They would want to know if Britain was allied with Russia. Otherwise there was no pretext for war against the French.

7. The British would have to give an assurance that, after the French were expelled from the Bocca and the coast, the Canoale (?) of Ragusa (the Konavlje area south-east of Dubrovnik) should be recognised by Britain and Russia as a small republic.
8. Montenegro needed the continued protection of Britain.
9. If the French returned in strength, the British fleet should take the Montenegrins and their families to a dependency of Britain or Russia, and if in England they should enjoy the freedom to practice the Orthodox religion and to build churches.[27]

There followed a detailed plan of action. The British should land troops to join the Montenegrins to take possession of Budva and then to attack Fort Trinita between there and Cattaro and overrun the Bocchese province. British ships should force the entrance to the Bocca and blockade Cattaro. Many more details and names of localities followed. It was estimated that at least 10-20,000 soldiers would be needed to place all the French fortresses in a state of blockade. The British should also provoke an insurrection in Ragusa and Dalmatia. The British should also supply muskets for the Montenegrins and Bocchese (size of flints and balls to be specified)

Fremantle's dismay when he received all of the above, coming on top of all the other discouragements, can be imagined. However, having prepared himself to leave Lissa and hand over command of the Adriatic squadron to Rowley, on 17 August he received orders from Admiral Pellew dated 14 July that he was to use his own discretion as to whether to stay in the Adriatic. Fremantle answered on 21 August that there were other important reasons for him to remain, particularly the danger of French ships-of-the-line being built and put to sea from the Venice Arsenal, and blockading the French on Corfu, the last remaining Ionian island remaining in their hands.[28] But as we shall see, whether he liked it or not, Fremantle was not able to wash his hands of further involvement with the Montenegrins.

What neither Nugent nor Bentinck nor Fremantle knew, and were not to know for some time, was that on 24 June Napoleon had crossed the river Niemen and begun the long-expected invasion of Russia.

News of Chichagov

Fremantle had left Sicily for Lissa on 13 June almost exactly at the time that Stratford Canning, the British ambassador in Constantinople, received communications from Chichagov at Bucharest. There is a problem with these, and with subsequent letters, because of the dates, which gave both the Russian date and the western date 12 days later. Chichagov's letters to Canning are dated Bucarest 7/19 May and 20 May, although various other sources say that he only arrived a Bucarest on 27 May. The letters were brought to Constantinople by Admiral Aleksey Grieg. He had no doubt been chosen because, born in Scotland, he was the son of Admiral Samuel Grieg, the architect of Catherine the Great's navy. He had already also served in the Adriatic in collaboration with the British navy.

---

[27] Quoted in fuller version Parry op cit. p. 109-10
[28] Quoted Parry op. cit. p. 110

Figure 11A & B. Admiral Aleksey Greig (1775–1845), admiral of Scottish extraction in the Russian navy. A: portrait by Georg von Bothmann, 1877 (Hermitage Museum); B: lithograph by unknown artist.

Canning immediately wrote to the Foreign Office in London on 15 June[29] to report that Grieg had arrived in Constantinople on 14 June, carrying the letters from Chichagov. Grieg was also ordered to proceed to Sicily to make proposals to Bentinck for joint operations in the Adriatic. In his letters to Canning, Chichagov solicited the assistance of Canning in gaining the Sultan's consent for the project and even for a formal alliance against the French of Britain, Russia and Turkey:

> 'Il s'agit donc d'obtenir pour le moment de la Porte un consentement tacite pour le passage de notre Armee en Dalmatie'.

Canning also pointed out to the Foreign Office that the Tsar had declared his intention of making peace with Britain. Grieg had brought the news that peace negotiations were being conducted in Stockholm with the mediation of Sweden (concluded on 18 July, it restored to Russia the ships of Admiral Seniavin's Mediterranean fleet which the British had seized after Tilsit). It was Canning's opinion that any proposals for an alliance of Russia and the Turks would have to wait for the ratification of the peace treaty made at Bucharest. A positive sign was that the Porte had agreed to the return to Constantinople of Italinsky (the former Russian ambassador). On the other hand, Chichagov had proposed to march to Dalmatia with 40,000 men, even without the permission of the Porte. As Canning was to be replaced by a new British ambassador, Robert Liston, he had referred Grieg to him for further discussion of the project.

On 17 June Canning sent a further message to the Foreign Office, in cipher and via St. Petersburg, to say that the previous day he had sent a copy by sea of the treaty between Russia

---

[29]   FO 78/77 p. 295

Figure 12A. Andrey Yakovlevich Italinsky, Russian ambassador to Constantinople, portrait by Orest Kiprensky.

Figure 12B. Sir Robert Liston (1742–1836), ambassador to Constantinople, oil painting by David Wilkie, 1811 (National Galleries of Scotland).

and Turkey, but also that the Sultan had signed the ratification which would be sent the next day to the Russians at Bucharest.[30]

Liston did not arrive in Constantinople until 28 June. In a letter to the Foreign Office reporting this and his handover, Canning noted that on 17 June he had sent a 'Person of trust' to inform Bentinck in Sicily of the Peace of Bucharest and of the diversion proposed by the Russians. He had also written to Admiral Pellew enclosing letters from Chichagov and Grieg. The Sultan's ratification of the treaty had been sent to Bucharest on 20 June, despite efforts by both the French and Austrian ambassadors to dissuade him. Canning also enclosed a copy of a letter of 15 June sent by Grieg from Constantinople to Bentinck concerning the Russian proposals, as well as his reply dated 17 June to Chichagov's letter of 7/19 May. Canning told Chichagov that while he was in general agreement with the need for concerted action by the English, Russians and Turkey, Turkey was unlikely to enter an alliance unless provoked by France, and the Porte would not allow the passage of troops across its territories.[31]

On taking over from Canning, Liston immediately wrote to Castlereagh, the British Foreign Secretary on 11 July to tell him that the Turkish ministers were still waiting for news of the (Russian) ratification of the treaty. There had been particular difficulty over the seventh article giving Serbia exemptions and rights amounting nearly to independence.[32] Liston again wrote to Castlereagh, and to Bentinck on 18 July.[33] Canning had already acquainted them with the nature of a plan formed by Admiral Tchitchagoff (Chichagov), invested by the Emperor

---

[30] FO 78/77 p. 300
[31] FO 78/77 p. 302
[32] FO 78/79 no. 1
[33] FO 78/79 no. 3 and encl. National Archives ADM 1/424 Pellew to Admiralty 14 Sep 1812

Figure 13. Sir Robert Wilson (1777–1849),
engraving by Roberts from an original
picture for C. H. Gifford's History of the Wars
Occasioned by the French Revolution, 1827.

of Russia with the chief military and political power in Wallachia, for an expedition into the French possessions in Dalmatia and Croatia for a diversion in the event of war between the Emperor and Bonaparte. The proposal had been premature because the Porte had not made peace and would not have consented. However, circumstances were changing. Hostilities began between Bonaparte[34] and Alexander on 24 June. The treaty between Turkey and Russia was ratified on 13 July. (This presumably meant that the Turks had received news of the Russian ratification on that date). More strangely, Liston claimed that Turkey also felt threatened by France and Austria (explained in his subsequent letter of 11 August). While it was possible that Tchitchagoff's (Chichagov) troops might be given another destination, Liston had not hesitated to sanction the mission of Admiral Grieg.

But by the end of July, there were more worrying signs that the Turks were more reluctant to tolerate the violation of their territory and the recent treaty by the Chichagov project. On 27 July Liston wrote that the Russian commander-in-chief continued to press for measures that could tend to endanger the neutrality of the Ottoman Government. Liston had directed Sir Robert Wilson, who was well acquainted with the then state of affairs at the Porte, to repair to Bucharest and to discourage the Admiral and then to go on to the HQ of the Emperor of Russia.[35]

---

[34] The British never called him Napoleon or 'Emperor', reserved for either the Emperor of Austria or the Emperor of Russia.
[35] FO 78/79 no. 6 Liston to Foreign Office

In a letter of 11 August to the Foreign Office,[36] Liston first summarised what had happened earlier together with the more recent developments. The Turks had wanted armed neutrality but Tchitchagoff (Chichagov) had been impatient. He had sent Chevalier d'Italinsky (the Russian ambassador) from Bucharest to Constantinople to negotiate a Quadruple Alliance between Turkey, England, Sweden and Russia. He had written to Canning to facilitate the speedy conclusion of the treaty. He had resolved on an expedition through Turkish territory to Dalmatia, and marched Russian troops into Servia without the permission of the Turks. This had caused alarm in Constantinople, where it was expected there might be an invasion of the Turkish provinces by Austria and France to counter it. There had even been talk of the recommencement of hostilities with Russia. Liston had tried to persuade d'Italinsky of the danger. With his help, Liston had sent a letter to the Court of St. Petersburg. Sir Robert Wilson had met Tchitchagoff (Chichagov). The Admiral had told him that he was bound to hazard a diversion on the orders of the Emperor. However, after a short delay, the Admiral had received counter-orders. The expedition was laid aside and the Russian army had started to evacuate Wallachia and Moldavia.

It seems probable that Chichagov received orders to abandon the project for a diversion either at the end of July or the first days of August, and to march his army far to the north where it was needed to control the movement of the Austrian army, under Schwarzenburg, that was marching east into Russia on the southern flank of Napoleon's main force. However, it was to be some time before this was known in Sicily or in the Adriatic, where the delays in communications meant that Bentinck and Fremantle only knew of Chichagov's expedition after it had already been abandoned. For long after they were taking preparatory measures to assist it, if and when it arrived on the Adriatic coast.

Admiral Grieg arrives in Sicily

Admiral Grieg arrived in Sicily on 18 August 1812. Bentinck in Palermo reported this to Lord Bathurst, the War Minister in London, on 30 August, enclosing copies of the letters that he and Grieg had exchanged.[37]

Bentinck confirmed that he had received a letter from Liston in Constantinople (that of 18 July?) to advise him that Grieg had been about to leave for Sicily on behalf of Chichagoff (Chichagov) on the Danube to concert a plan of operations to be directed against the southern provinces of France. The letter that Grieg brought from Chichagov dated Bucharest 15/27 May was little more than a letter of introduction, and it implied that Bentinck and Chichagov already knew each other:

> 'The Bearer of this expects to see you (he is my best friend). He will be able to give you a detailed account of what has passed since the interruption of our intercourse... I am appointed by the Emperor Commander-in-Chief of the army on the Danube and of the Black Sea fleet'.

Bentinck had asked Grieg to put in writing the substance of the communication that he had been directed to make to him. Grieg put the proposals in a letter to Bentinck dated Palermo 23

---

[36] FO 78/78 no. 7 Liston to Foreign Office
[37] WO1/312 p. 145

Aug 1812.[38] Chichagoff (Chichagov) had sent Grieg (appointed in this service by the Emperor himself) to confer with Bentinck on concerting measures for acting in unison against the French forces in Dalmatia, to relieve the oppressed people of the Bocca, and in the hope of a general insurrection. The Russian force proposed was 40,000 men, liberated by the treaty with the Porte. Chichagov would march from Bucharest to the Adriatic and on arrival would communicate with the British ships of war 'for his maintenance and the execution of the great object in view'. It was Grieg's duty to state that the Emperor of Russia expected as great as possible a British, Sicilian and Sardinian force, not less than 20,000 men.

Bentinck replied to Grieg on 27 August. He agreed that a Russian army of 40.000 would cause a serious diversion to the French if it could reach Italy. Part of the British army under Bentinck's command was already in Spain and he could make no further detachments from the British forces left in Sicily. The Sicilian army was weak and the Sardinian army hardly existed. However, if the Russian army reached the Adriatic, and if his forces returned from Spain, he could give 10, 000, if they did not, only half that number. If the Russian army reached Italy, he could offer 14-15,000 men (10,000 without forces from Spain). But Bentinck considered it impracticable for the Russians to march from Wallachia to Dalmatia and almost impossible when they arrived to supply such a large force by sea. It would be better if the Russian army came by sea, half to Malta and half to Messina. It could then be agreed where to attack. Bentinck asked Grieg by whom the Russian corps was to be paid and equipped and supplied. Would it treat the territories it took as conquest or restore the former rulers? Would it support the liberty of Italy to adopt constitutions and choose its own leaders (a cause to which Bentinck was personally committed), as success would depend upon the adoption of this latter principle.

Grieg answered Bentinck's questions on 29 August. Taking the lead Bentinck had given him, the objectives of the expedition were widened. The Russian army would liberate Italy and even the south of Germany. The Emperor wanted no conquests. The people were to be enabled to establish their independence. Grieg would send Chichagov the proposal for movement by sea, but (of course) provisions and equipment would be at the expense of Britain.

In a final letter to Grieg of 30 August, before he submitted the proposals to the British government, Bentinck endeavoured to deflate Russian expectations. He would not be able to undertake the payment and equipment of the Russian corps. If the march to Dalmatia had begun, he would do his best to help but he was under no commitment. If Chichagov did come by sea to Malta and Messina, he must bring corn for 3 months. As far as other British provision was concerned, Bentinck would have to wait for instructions from the British government. In the meantime, Chichagov would undertake the expedition at is own risk.

In the covering letter of 30 August, enclosing this correspondence, Bentinck pointed out that he could not receive Grieg's reply to his last letter in time for that day's despatch to London. He expected it the next day. He had found Grieg most reasonable, but he had been embarrassed, knowing as he did that HMG would not be disposed to give a subsidy Russia, and that what was being asked was tantamount to a subsidy. But he had not wanted to be too negative on the proposal that agreed with HMG's views on Italy (although it had been Bentinck himself

---

[38] do. also encl. ADM 1/424 Pellew to Admiralty of 14 Sep. 1812

who had suggested to Grieg that an emphasis be placed on the liberation of Italy). Bentinck proposed, for the Prince Regent's agreement, that it would be a lesser sacrifice of public money if Britain could provide for the eventual return of Chichagov's corps to Russia.

It appeared strange to Bentinck that it was proposed to take such a large corps 'through wild uncivilized and uncultivated country without roads as are the provinces of Servia and Bosnia'. There was the danger of it being starved or destroyed. Chichagov's idea that he could march quietly through Transylvania and Hungary, that were equally wild, relied on the disaffection of these parts of the Austrian dominions. (There had been nothing in the previous correspondence that Chichagov had proposed this as an alternative route towards Croatia and Italy). Chichagov was aware that on arrival on the coast of Dalmatia he could not proceed without British assistance with supplies. Yet he was ready to begin the march without the agreement of the Turkish government and without a British answer. Grieg had said that the Russian army was well-equipped, but the recent appointment of Chichagov and the shortness of his own stay might account for his not being well acquainted with the state of the army. Bentinck had learnt from Johnson, who had arrived in Sicily from Vienna, that he had seen correspondence from the second in command of the Russian Danube army to a general resident in Vienna in which it was admitted that it was in want of everything. Grieg had expected that Bentinck would have already received instructions from London, as he believed that the Emperor had written to HMG.

Bentinck next sent a letter to Chichagov dated Palermo 6 September 1812[39] that was to be delivered by Grieg, little suspecting that Chichagov had been told to abandon the project at least two months before, and had withdrawn the Russian army from the Danube and Wallachia and Moldavia by the end of August.[40]

However sceptical he was about the likelihood of the Russians reaching the Adriatic, Bentinck also had to alert the navy. He sent two letters, enclosing Grieg's letter of 23 August, to Admiral Pellew in the western Mediterranean that arrived on 13 September. Pellew forwarded them to the Admiralty on 14 September and they were received on 5 October. In his covering letter, Pellew wrote that Bentinck was of the opinion that the difficulties are extremely great and that the expedition was unlikely to be realised.[41]

Bentinck wrote two letters to Fremantle dated 6 September and 7 September,[42] one official and the other more personal addressed 'My dear Admiral', received by Fremantle only one month later on 10 October. The official letter of 7 September informed Fremantle that it was probable that the Russian army on the Danube was marching to the Adriatic. Admiral Chichagoff (Chichagov), who was in command, would hoist a yellow flag with a black eagle on his arrival upon the coast to make himself known to the British cruisers. However, Bentinck had no official information about the march or of the route to be taken. Dalmatia or the Bocca were the most likely destinations. Chichagov had sent Grieg to Sicily to urge him to act in concert with him and to ask for the pay, equipment and the maintenance of the army by Great Britain. Bentinck had answered Grieg that his troops were employed elsewhere and that he

---

[39] Portland Papers 6248 Secret Letters
[40] Woods op cit. p. 208 says that Chichagov left Bucharest as late as 25 August.
[41] ADM 1/434
[42] Fremantle Papers D/FR 39/3/13 and D/FR 40/9/3

had no instructions or authority to take the large army into British pay. If the army came by land it would have to live on it, as he had no transports and no magazines to supply its wants. The first question that Chichagoff (Chichagov) would ask Fremantle would be for assistance of all kinds. Bentinck could only offer ammunition, which he would send to Lissa as soon as he knew the actual march of the army and that transports and a convoy could be prepared. He would also send medicines if they could be spared.

In the more personal letter, Bentinck referred to the official letter he was sending separately. The Russian proposal had embarrassed him very much. When Admiral Grieg had first come to him, it had been understood that he could give Cichagov an answer. He had strongly advised that the Russians should not come by land. He had never believed that the Turks would agree. If they had come by sea, Bentinck had undertaken to feed them and to provide for their return in the event of Government being unwilling to take this charge. Bentinck had unfortunately heard from Yannina (the chief city of the Turkish pasha in southern Albania now Ioannina in north-west Greece) that the army had actually begun its march and had crossed the Danube at Widdin (now Vidin north-west Bulgaria on Danube). He had delayed giving a reply to Grieg until the packet (the post ship) arrived on 3 September. The Government had given their opinion on his proposed expedition (another earlier and quite different proposal to that concerning the Russians?) and expressed the greatest disappointment on the assumption that Bentinck's force might have been diverted to that object instead of to Spain. He had therefore decided not to cooperate.

This second letter appeared to contradict the first. What was Fremantle supposed to do if the Russians arrived? Whatever the level of cooperation he might be called upon to give the Russians, the other schemes for an uprising against the French in Dalmatia had not been abandoned. In yet another letter dated 7 September, also received on 10 October, Bentinck informed Fremantle that he had on that day instructed Johnson to go to Lissa (he presumably arrived with the letter) to establish connections and points of communication with the surrounding coasts of the enemy. In the execution of this service, the local knowledge of Colonel 52.11.17.33.39.13 (although given in code this was clearly Danese) would be imminently useful and Fremantle should direct that officer to place himself entirely at the disposal of Johnson. The success of the mission would depend on the facility provided Johnson of communication with the enemy's coast and the assistance of HM Navy. Bentinck suggested a gunboat or other armed vessel be constantly appropriated to that service.

Back in July after General Nugent had arrived in Sicily, he had submitted several memoranda to Bentinck concerning his proposals for insurrections against the French. In one of these dated 15 July,[43] he had maintained that Johnson was the only person who could direct the whole and proposed that Johnson be entrusted with all political affairs in the Adriatic. He should establish a secure and permanent communication with Austria and have persons at Scutari and Brod (at the latter there was already a person who could remain). He should change his place of residence according to the circumstances, treat with the adjoining Turkish governments, and be in correspondence with the British commanders at Zante and Lissa and the admiral of the fleet who were to be informed of his situation. In another letter dated 25

---

[43] Portland Papers 4220 encl. 4219

July,[44] Nugent mentioned Danese again as being most useful and suggested he could be used by Johnson.

Between Nugent's proposals in July and Johnson's arrival at Lissa in early October, Fremantle had decided to send Danese back to the Adriatic coast of northern Albania. In a 'private' letter from Lissa dated 22 August to Bentinck,[45] Fremantle told him that he was sending Danese to remain at Durazzo (?) for the time being as the poor man found no employment at Palermo and might be useful in giving Bentinck information from there.

Only a few days later, there was to be a surprising development, drawing Fremantle and Danese yet again into dealings with the Vladika of Montenegro, before any intelligence about Chichagov had reached them via Constantinople and Sicily.

Fremantle and Montenegro: Second Phase

On 26 August 1812 and 2 September,[46] Fremantle wrote to report to Bentinck some extraordinary intelligence he had received. Because of its urgency, the first message was sent, with all the proper names in cipher, not on a ship of his squadron but on an unnamed Sicilian vessel, arriving only on 27 September. The second fuller message sent on 2 September overtook the first and was received by Bentinck on 18 September. Both had crossed with Bentinck's letters to Fremantle of 6 and 7 September. Fremantle also wrote on 11 September to give the same news to Admiral Pellew (only received at Mahon in the Balearic Islands on 24 November).[47]

The information provided these letters was that on 25 August a man called Veijo (?) Pavassovich had arrived at Lissa who had been sent by Admiral Chichagoff (Chichagov) at Bucharest 41 days earlier (about 7 July) to take dispatches to the Bishop of Montenegro. He had delivered them 18 days later (about 25 July) and had been sent on by the Bishop to Lissa to bring the news to Fremantle. The dispatches informed the Bishop that an army of 40,000 men was on the march from Moldavia, Vallachia and Servia to take Dalmatia, Istria etc. and called on him to unite with the Russians in common cause against the French. Pavassovich had travelled from Bucharest as far as Belgrade in company with Count Orok, who commanded the advance guard of 17 battalians. Fremantle had carefully examined the messenger who was an emigrant from Dalmatia and well known to several friends, including Colonel Danese. He had left Lissa to go to Dalmatia and advise his family to come to Lissa.

Fremantle added various other items of information that complement that given above in the various letter from Constantinople and the interchanges between Admiral Grieg and Bentinck. Surprising, Fremantle wrote that Chichakov (Chichagov) had permission (from the Turks) to pass through the Dardanelles with the Russian Black Sea fleet under his command, and Fremantle claimed that it was coming 'here' (to Lissa?)

Italinski, the former Russian ambassador in Constantinople, had been at Bucharest as a plenipotentiary before Pavassovich had left. He had gone to Shumla (south of the Danube in

---

[44] Portland Papers 4221a
[45] Portland Papers 2559/1
[46] Portland Papers 2560, 2561, 2562
[47] Pellew Papers PEL 16

Bulgaria) where the Turkish army under the Vizier was encamped. After staying there three days, he had gone on to Constantinople with a Turkish escort of 400 troops to take possession of the house he had previously occupied.

Pavassovich had also told Fremantle that the Pasha of Scutari had received official notification of the ratification of peace between the Turks and the Russians. However, (not having heard of the peace between Britain and Russia made in Stockholm on 18 July), Fremantle understood that the British were officially to consider the Russians as enemies and asked Bentinck for authority to seize any occasion provided by the development of the situation.

In his second letter to Bentinck, Fremantle added a personal detail. He knew Chichagoff (Chichagov), who had married the English daughter of Commissioner Proby in charge of the Royal Navy dockyards at Chatham.[48]

It difficult to put together the subsequent developments in this story, because of uncertainty over the dating, whether in the Russian or western calendars. In his letter to Admiral Pellew of 11 September, Fremantle had enclosed a copy of a letter dated 1 September[49] that he had sent to the Bishop of Montenego in which he acknowledged receipt of a note brought by Pavassovich and saying that he would not be wanting if the opportunity offered itself. Danese was still at Scutari (or Antivari/Bar on the coast of the territory of the Pasha of Scutari) and could have arranged delivery of Fremantle's letter to the Bishop. It is strange that in a letter from the Bishop, signed Pietro Petrovic dated Zetignie (Cetinje) 3 (5?)/17 September and written in Italian,[50] the Bishop acknowledged receipt of a letter dated 1 September but he had not fully discovered Fremantle's sentiments because the letter was written in English!

The Bishop told Fremantle that, after receiving the message brought by Pavassovich from Chichagov, he had sent his nephew into Serbia to try to reach Chichagov and to deliver letters asking for more precision on the proposals. Some of his people, who had accompanied the nephew as far as the border with Serbia on the river Lim, had come back bringing the news that he had entered Serbia. The nephew (or they?) had heard that Chichagov was still at Bucharest and had gathered together 'il sig. commandante Giorgio' (Karadjordevic) with all the chiefs of Serbia to treat on present affairs. A column of Serbians with some Russian troops were to have passed into Dalmatia and 'into these parts' (i.e. Montenegro), but the project was suspended because the Emperor of Austria had declared war on Russia in alliance with Napoleon.

Even more seriously, and demonstrating how much better and faster French communications were compared with the painfully slow passage of information between the British, the Bishop told Fremantle that he had been sent news by the French general commanding in the Bocca that the French army had in the first days of August been between the borders of Poland and Russia in the places indicated in an enclosed letter and bulletin of which the Bishop was sending Fremantle a copy. The enclosure, from General of Brigade Gauthier, dated Cattaro 30 August 1812 addressed to the Bishop and written in Italian, described the victorious advance

---

[48] The extraordinary love story of Chigagov and Elisabeth Proby, and of their marriage, opposed by Commissioner Proby and the Emperor Paul, is told by Joanna Woods op cit.

[49] Portland Papers 2563

[50] Fremantle Papers D/FR 40/9/1/1

Figure 14. General Jean-Joseph Gauthier (1765–
1815), général de brigade in the French Illyrian
provinces (Jura Musées).

of the French army in Poland and Russia as given in a handwritten copy of bulletin 69 of
the Grande Armée. Worse still Gauthier wrote that the six thousand Russians who were in
Serbia commanded by Admiral Chichacov (Chichagov) destined to act against those parts had
received orders to rejoin in haste the main army of the Emperor Alexander, the same order
being given to the army of Valachia and Moldavia.[51]

Relations between the Montenegrins and the Pasha of Scutari had deteriorated, thanks to the
intrigues of Bruere, the French consul at Scutari, and the Bishop asked Fremantle to try to
intervene.

The mystery in what ensued is why Fremantle and Danese seem not to have accepted the
information sent by Gauthier to the Bishop. Did they think that it was lies deliberately
fabricated to discourage the Bishop from taking hostile action against the French in the Bocca?
Did they prefer to believe the other information received from the Bishop that Chichagov was
still at Bucharest?

On 27 September, Fremantle wrote to Admiral Pellew[52] that he had sent KINGFISHER to
Durazzo (another example of it being confused with places further north on the Albanian

---

[51] do. D/FR 40/9/1/2
[52] Portland Papers 2564

coast?) on 11 September. It had returned on 26 September with a report from Danese (possibly at Antivari now Bar on the present coast of Montenegro). Danese had reported that Chichagoff (Chichagov) remained at Bucharest and was possibly not advancing because Austria had declared war on Russia and guaranteed Illyria and Dalmatia to the French.

Danese's report[53] informed Fremantle that the person he had sent to the Bishop a few days before had returned with the letter he enclosed (presumably that dated 3/17 September). Danese made no mention of the enclosed copy of the letter from Gauthier or the all-imporatant news about Chichagov contained in it. The Bishop had nothing official from the army of Valachia because his nephew had still not returned. However, it was said that the Russian column to Dalmatia was suspended because of the alliance of Austria and France and that Cichagoff was still at Bucharest. On the arrival of the nephew, Danese would not fail to report any news and he would go to Scutari to wait for the arrival of a Montenegrin courier. Fremantle should keep a ship off Antivari or the mouth of the Bojana ready to take any news back to Lissa.

Danese also reported that peace between the Turks and the Russians was certain. The Turkish commander at Antivari had the previous day assured him that a letter from Constantinople to the Vizier (i.e. the Pasha of Scutari) had confirmed this. Also the master of a boat returning to the the the Bocca who had departed from Constantinople on 15 August, had seen the formal entry of the Russian ambassador Italinsky. Although, after the opening of the Black Sea had seen a large number of merchant ships departing for the Crimea and Bessarabia, there was no news of the Russian squadron at Sebastopoli.

The Bishop sent another letter to Danese dated Zettigne (Cetinje) 21 September (no indication whether Russian or western calendar).[54] This acknowledged a letter dated 19 September. But this letter, in Italian, repeats so much of the content of the letter dated 3/17 September translated into English, that it is possibly the same. The Bishop had also received news from various sources to confirm the peace between Russia and the Ottoman Porte and that Italinski had passed to Constantinople as ambassador of the sovereign court of Russia. Concerning the Russian army in Valachia and Moldavia that was to have united with the Serbs to pass into Dalmatia and Montenegro, it was said that it was suspended for the time being because the Austrian court had declared war on the Emperor of Russia in alliance with Napoleon Bonaparte. It was understood that Chigacov (Chichagov) might be at Bucharest, together with other Russian generals and the commanding chiefs of Serbia to discuss the current war situation. It was 30 days since the Bishop had sent his nephew to Chichagov. Some other Montenegrins had accompanied him to the river Lim. As soon as the Bishop had news he would immediately communicate it to the Rear Admiral (Fremantle) and Danese know. He complained that a Turkish commander, bribed by the French consul Bruer, was attacking Montenegro. He asked Danese to use his influence to persuade the Pasha to suppress these attacks. Despite the many similarities with the letter of 3/17 September, there is no reference to General Gauthier.

On 27 September, the same day he wrote to Admiral Pellew, Fremantle wrote to Bentinck enclosing a copy of his letter to Pellew and adding that as the Russians were still at Bucharest

---

[53] Fremantle Papers D/FR 40/10/4 but undated possibly from Antivari.
[54] National Maritime Museum Fremantle Papers FR 8

Figure 15. The battles of Napolean's Russian campaign 1812 and
Russian occupied lands to the west of the Black Sea.

there was little prospect of them acting in Dalmatia that year. Danese had been a Antivari a
few days earlier. He would be useful in giving Bentinck the earliest information and Fremantle
would keep him there. As we have seen, Johnson was to arrive on Lissa on 7 October with
instructions that Danese should report to him. Fremantle probably resented this and the rather
petty rivalry between Fremantle, Robertson and Johnson, all of who reported separately and
independently to Bentinck, together with their numerous disagreements were to continue
to bedevil life on Lissa. It was symptomatic that Colonel Robertson, the commander of the
British garrison on Lissa, felt it necessary to send his own separate report to Bentinck on 27
September that Austria had declared war on Russia and that the Russian troops at Bucharest

which were said to be on the march to the Bocca still remained there.[55] This report was received by Bentinck on 8 November.

So when did the British finally realise that Chichagov had long since withdrawn his army from the Danube and marched north to participate in the main campaign against Napoleon's invasion of Russia? It was perhaps Liston, the British ambassador in Constantinople, who had definite news of it from Italinsky. On 13-14 November Liston enclosed in letters to Bentinck copies of letters from Tchitchagoff (Chichagov) to Italinsky. Both dated 26 September (Russian calendar?) they had been sent from his headquarters near Brest in Lithuania (on the Bug river separating Poland from the Russian Empire now in Belarus) and had been received by Italinsky on 14/26 October. In the first Chichagov informed Italinsky that he had received a letter from him of 5/19 September when he was pursing the Austrian and Saxon and Polish army that had invaded Wolhinie (Volhynia the province of the Russian Empire east of the Bug now in the north-west Ukraine), which had been delivered from these allies of the French. The second letter enclosed a Russian army bulletin of 22 September/4 October stating that on 10 September the army of the Danube commanded by Admiral Tchitchagoff (Chichagov) had reached the army of General Tormassoff (Tormasov) . (The Russian Fourth army of Tormasov had covered the eastward advance of the Austrian and Saxon armies under Schwarzenburg and Reynier to the south of Napoleon and the Grande Armée). The enemy army had retired beyond the Bug without fighting and Wolhinie had been liberated. On 25 September/7 October Tchitchagoff (Chichagov) had some days previously taken over command of the (fourth) army from Tormassoff.

Having ensured that the Austrian and Saxon armies, which withdrew into Poland, could not unite their forces with Napoleon, now on his disastrous retreat from Moscow, Chichagov captured Minsk on 18 November. Napoleon had been hoping to replenish the remnant of the Grande Armée from the large stocks of supplies he had left there. Chichagov's army, advancing from the south-west, together with those of Kutuzov and Wittgenstein, respectively closing in on Napoleon from the east and the north, almost closed the trap on him at the Berezina river at the end of November. But Napoleon was saved by a thaw that prevented cossacks crossing on the ice. He was able to dupe Chichagov about the exact point at which he crossed the river by pontoon bridge. While suffering serious losses, he was able to escape and would soon abandon the small remainder of the massive army with which he had entered the Russian Empire in June. Chichagov was blamed by Tsar Alexander for having allowed Napoleon to escape, resigned his command and went to England. He later went to live in France where he died in 1849.

After Chichagov

There were to be a number of echoes of the failed Chichagov diversion in the Balkans. Some additional light was shed on it in June 1813. Liston in Constantinople wrote to Bentinck on 21 June[56] to say that he was sending to Sicily a certain M. de Nikitsch (Nikić), who had been recommended to him by Italinsky, on the understanding that Bentinck was interested in

---

[55] Portland Papers 4743
[56] Portland Papers 3150

recuiting officers from other armies, especially the Austrian army. Nikitsch had an interesting story to tell.[57]

> In 1812, when Chischakove was to go with a great part of his army from Valachy through Servia and Bohemia (Bosnia?) to Dalmatia, he had entrusted Nikitsch with an important commission to go before him to try to gain to the Russian interest some of the principal persons in French service among the six Illyrian regiments (the Croatian Grenzer or Frontier regiments) then stationed in those provinces (the Liccaner, Ottochaner, Oguliner, Sluiner and the 1st and second Banell) from Carloviz in Croatia (Karlovac) as far as the Boche di Catona (Cattaro/Kotor) Dobrovnic (Dubrovnik) and Scadra (Scutari?). On 28 April 1813 he had left Belgrade. Being an Illyrian himself, having traversed several times those provinces, and having served against the French with the said regiments for 12 years, he succeeded in meeting several officers and an important personage in a neutral village called Negusch in Montenegro at the beginning of June 1812. (Njegos was the village in Montenegro from which the family of the Vladika of Montenegro took its name). He obtained their promise that as soon as a Russian army came they would rise against the French. With this answer he had hastily returned to Bucharest where Admiral Chischacove had received him with joy and thanks. Nikitsch had received his directions in writing (still in his possession) to form in the neighbourhood of Bucharest four battalions of Foreign (?) Light Infantry of 1000 men each as an advance guard on the march to Dalmatia. He had already assembled in a short time 1800 men when about the end of July 1812 orders were received from the Emperor to evacuate the provinces of Valachai and Moldova and to march against Prince Swartzenberg towards Russian Poland. At Bresttiravi (Brest?) nr Wershau (Brest was east of Warsaw but not near), Chischacove ordered him to hand over command of his 1800 men to Major-General Orsuck (the Orok mentioned elsewhere?) and join his headquarters, where he was given fresh orders to proceed to Belgrade in service, from whence to keep a correspondence with the Illyrians in Dalmatia to persuade them in the Russian interest until at least March 1813. But at last not having heard from the Admiral who had already left the service and as Prince Cutosow (Kutuzov) soon after died, he went to Constantinople to talk to the Russian ambassador Italinski. He referred Nikitsch to Liston who in turn referred him to Bentinck. (A Nikitsch was with the Vladika's forces in the Bocca in 1814 and is presumably the same).

There was another interesting footnote to the whole episode. As we have seen, General Gauthier at Cattaro/Kotor seems to have known about the Chichagov project. In November 1812, the Pasha of Travnik in Bosnia, Ibraham Pasha, had confided to the French Consul David that four months earlier the English and the Russians, aided by Ali Pasha (the powerful pasha of southern Albania) had tried to draw the Porte into an alliance against the Emperor Napoleon. They prepared an expedition against Illyria, and were assured of revolts in their favour not only at Cattaro and Dalmatia but in Croatia proper, where they had many partisans. The Bishop of Montenegro descended at the same time to Niksich (Nikšić) where he had secret talks with several inhabitants of Cattaro who were Russian agents. It appeared that the general commanding at Cattaro, had suspicions and ordered the shooting of several

---

[57] Portland Papers 3151a

Figure 16A. Henry Bathurst, 3rd Earl Bathurst (1762–1834), engraving by Henry Meyer after Thomas Phillips' stipple engraving, 1810 (National Portrait Gallery).

Figure 16B. Christoph von Lieven (1774–1839), copy of original portrait by Sir Thomas Lawrence c. 1826 (Hermitage Museum).

individuals. The Pasha would have warned consul David but, not knowing what side would be taken by the Porte, he had been forced to only drop hints.[58]

There were other echoes of the Chichagov project on the British side. When it was clear to all that Napoleon had suffered a massive defeat in Russia, on 5 December 1812, Bentinck in Sicily wrote to Lord Bathurst at the War Office in London to propose that the possibility of a Russian diversionary attack in the Mediterranean be reconsidered and the Russians told of British readiness to agree to their earlier proposal for cooperation with a Russian corps, particularly to liberate Italy.[59] Admiral Grieg had told Bentinck that there was no shortage on the Russian side of men but of money and equipment. The Russian force would be conveyed to the Mediterranean by the Russian Black Sea fleet, which Bentinck suggested should be commanded by Grieg. Bathurst replied to Bentinck on 19 February 1813.[60] Count Lieven, the Russian ambassador in London had told him there was no possibility of reviving the project, especially following the withdrawal of Tchitchagoff's (Chichagov) army into Poland.

---

[58]   Quoted Paul Pisani: La Dalmatie de 1797 a 1815 Paris 1893 pp 404-405
[59]   WO 1/312 Bentinck to Bathurst
[60]   WO 6/57

Johnson, coordinating the network of 'confidential agents' from Lissa, wrote to the Foreign Office in London on 24 February.[61] He was sorry that the Russian government had not before then made any effort to avail itself of the very extensive influence that it possessed in the Illyrian Provinces. He hoped that in the approaching campaign, when the Russians would no longer have to contend for their existence, they would turn their thoughts to the eastern coast of the Adriatic, where a popular movement might be achieved by Russian agents without military aid. This would have a considerable effect on the politics of the Austrian court (after the debacle of the Russian campaign, it was trying to stay neutral). Johnson thought that 6,000 Russians would be sufficient to expel the French from the Bocche di Cattaro, Dalmatia, Croatia and Istria and that a force of 15,000 men would make a serious impression on the north of Italy.

The priest Brunazzi, one of Johnson and Nugent's agents then at Malta, wrote on 2 April 1813 to Lucius Concannon (the Whig politician who plied Bentinck with information) to report that there were rumours that the Russian fleet with troops would soon pass through the Dardanelles for the Meditarranean.[62] However, by now a degree of scepticism had finally set in and he feared that such rumours were without foundation.

Despite the failure of the Chichagov project, the Russian campaign of 1812 was to affect developments on the east side of the Adriatic in 1813-14. Napoleon had taken away all French troops, leaving Italians and Croatians. The latter were ready to mutiny against their French officers, deliver over their forts and garrison towns, and desert in large numbers to the British, afterwards finding service with the Austrians. Fremantle, with his squadron based at Lissa was able to capture first the Dalmatian islands, before attacking Fiume/ Rijeka and helping General Nugent to force the French out of Istria and then Trieste. Ships of his squadron also supported other Austrian forces marching down the coast to reclaim Dalmatia. Encouraged by these developments, and with limited assistance from two ships from Fremantle's squadron, the Vladika of Montenegro in October 1813 attacked the French on the coast and in the Bocca of Cattaro. However, agreements between the allies, including Britain, Austria and his patron Russia, forced him to surrender his gains to the Austrians in 1814.

Malcolm Scott Hardy
London September 2012
(illustrated 2023)

---

[61] FO 7/111 no. 1 (1813)
[62] Portland Papers 1687